www.wadsworth.com

wadsworth.com is the World Wide Web site for Wadsworth and is your direct source to dozens of online resources.

At *wadsworth.com* you can find out about supplements, demonstration software, and student resources. You can also send email to many of our authors and preview new publications and exciting new technologies.

wadsworth.com
Changing the way the world learns®

THE ROAD TO THE WHITE HOUSE, 2004

The Politics of Presidential Elections

Stephen J. Wayne
Georgetown University

THOMSON ™

WADSWORTH

Australia Canada Mexico Singapore Spain United Kingdom United States

THOMSON

WADSWORTH

Publisher: Clark Baxter
Executive Editor: David Tatom
Development Editor: Stacey Sims
Assistant Editor: Heather Hogan
Editorial Assistant: Reena Thomas
Technology Project Manager: Melinda Newfarmer
Marketing Manager: Janise Fry
Marketing Assistant: Mary Ho
Advertising Project Manager: Nathaniel Bergson-Michelson
Project Manager, Editorial Production: Ray Crawford
Print/Media Buyer: Kris Waller

Permissions Editor: Joohee Lee
Production Service: Publisher's Studio
Photo Researcher: Publisher's Studio
Copy Editor: Leslie Connor
Cover Designer: Brian Salisbury
Cover Image: © 2003 Brian Salisbury and
CampaignButtons.com
Cover Printer: Webcom Limited
Compositor: Stratford Publishing Services
Printer: Webcom Limited

Printed in Canada

1 2 3 4 5 6 7 06 05 04 03

For more information about our products, contact us at:
Thomson Learning Academic Resource Center
1-800-423-0563

For permission to use material from this text,
contact us by: **Phone:** 1800-730-2214
Fax: 1-800-730-2215
Web: http://www.thomsonrights.com

Library of Congress Control Number: 2003107458

ISBN 0-534-61425-6

Wadsworth/Thomson Learning
10 Davis Drive
Belmont, CA 94002-3098
USA

Asia
Thomson Learning
5 Shenton Way #01-01
UIC Building
Singapore 068808

Australia
Thomson Learning
102 Dodds Street
Southbank, Victoria 3205
Australia

Canada
Nelson
1120 Birchmount Road
Toronto, Ontario M1K 5G4
Canada

Europe/Middle East/Africa
Thomson Learning
High Holborn House
50/51 Bedford Row
London WC1R 4LR
United Kingdom

Latin America
Thomson Learning
Seneca, 53
Colonia Polanco
11560 Mexico D.F.
Mexico

Spain
Paraninfo
Calle/Magallanes, 25
28015 Madrid, Spain

To my mother, Muriel Wayne,
and to the memory of my grandmother, Hattie Marks,
and my father, Arthur G. Wayne.

PREFACE

We are just beginning another presidential election cycle. It follows the longest and one of the most controversial elections in U.S. history, an election marked by strident rhetoric, multiple promises, exaggerated claims, personal attacks, all replete with positive and negative political imagery, and a very, very close vote in which the candidate who received the most popular votes did not receive the most electoral votes. Did the campaign matter? Did the system work?

Your answers may depend on how satisfied you were with the process and with the outcome, and there were many who objected to both. But despite the Florida vote controversy and the way it was resolved, a new president and vice president were sworn into office on Inauguration day; they were seen as legitimate by the vast majority of the American people; and government continued to function in accordance with the Constitution and laws of the land. It was the fifty-fourth time that the American electorate has chosen its president in a peaceful manner. The electoral system worked although not perfectly.

Moreover, the campaign affected the outcome. The election of 2000 was not one that was ordained by the political environment, predetermined by conditions, or dictated by the events. If it had been, Gore would have won, at least that is what was predicted by political scientists who created empirical models based on past voting behavior, current economic and international conditions, and public approval of President Clinton's job performance. Bush's Electoral College victory suggests that the personal and policy appeals of the candidates, their parties, and nonparty groups combined with the strategies they pursued and the tactics they used had some impact on the electorate's decision.

Hopefully, many of you followed the last election closely. It was probably easier to follow than to understand. You may have read about it in newspapers, viewed campaign events, such as the national nominating conventions and the political debates, on television, heard about them on the radio, or accessed the parties' or candidates' Web sites; you may have even seen one of them in person although that is usually rarer. But regardless of what you observed, it was only a portion of the campaign, and as seen through your eyes, a subjective perception at that. Candidates, their advisers, media representatives, and other groups have their own perspectives and judgments that they wish to convey to influence our decision on election day.

There is more, however, to presidential elections than meets the eye. Campaign planners work hard to design strategies to maximize their candidate's appeal and enlarge their vote. They understand the intricacies of the process. They know how the system works, who its likely participants are, and where they should concentrate their campaign resources. They understand the requirements of finance legislation—how to comply with it, get around it, and take advantage of it. They appreciate the psychological and social motivations of voters and have a feel for which appeals are likely to be most effective and why most of the time. They are aware of party rules and the ways to build a winning coalition during the nomination period. They can sense the rhythm of conventions and know when events should be scheduled, how they should be presented, and what it will take to placate the various factions that comprise their party's electoral coalition. They know how to organize, plan, and conduct a general election campaign. They do long-range planning and run day-to-day war rooms. They know about polls and focus groups, media spin and message manipulation, issue advocacy, confrontational advertising, and grassroots activities, all aimed toward informing the electorate, generating momentum, and turning out the vote. They employ the latest technology to reach and convince the electorate of the merits of their cause, the qualifications of their candidates, and the inclusiveness of their party. They also have experts who read the mood, predict the outcome, and explain the results of the election in a way that enhances their political position and governing potential. They may not need to read this book.

On the other hand, people who want to get behind the scenes of presidential campaigns, who want to know why particular strategies are being adopted, why certain tactics are utilized (and others are not), whether these strategies and tactics are likely to achieve the desired results, and at what cost, why particular appeals are made, to whom, and with what impact, how the candidates try to influence the news media and how the news media try to cover the campaign and break through the imagery and sound bites that the candidates and their handlers present, why the election turns out the way it does, and what it augurs for the direction of public policy and the new administration's ability to govern should benefit from the information contained in this book.

OUTLINE

The Road to the White House, 2004: The Politics of Presidential Elections is a straightforward, "nuts-and-bolts" discussion of how the system is designed and works. It is primarily concerned with facts, not opinions; with practice, not theory; with implications, not speculations. It summarizes the state of the art and science of presidential electoral politics at the beginning of the twenty-first century.

The book is organized into four main parts. The first discusses the arena in which presidential elections occur. Its three chapters examine the electoral system, campaign finance, and the political environment. Chapter 1 provides a historical overview of nominations as well as elections with a special section devoted to the Florida vote controversy in 2000 and its implications for future presidential elections. Chapter 2 examines recent developments in campaign finance, particularly the explosion of revenues and expenditures, the new attempt at regulation, the McCain–Feingold bill and its legal challenges, and the likely impact of this reform on the 2003–2004 election cycle. In the third chapter, the continuities and changes in the political environment serve as the principal focus. Here too, we attempt to provide a perspective on the trends within and between the major parties and the effect that these trends have had and may continue to have on electoral outcomes.

Part II describes the distinct yet related stages of the presidential nomination: the race to win delegates during the competitive phase of primaries and caucuses; the interregnum that follows after the nominees have been effectively determined but before the national nominating conventions are held, and then finally the purpose, organization, operation, and influence of the conventions as the candidates move into the general election itself. Chapter 4 examines reforms in the delegate selection process and their impact on the nomination strategy of the candidates. Chapter 5 carries this discussion from the end of the contested phase of the nominating process through the conventions themselves, the official launch of the presidential campaign.

Part III discusses the general election campaign. In Chapter 6, the organization, strategy, and tactics of presidential campaigns are assessed in the light of the new technologies used to identify the interests of voters, design and target appeals to them, and measure their effect as the election progresses. Chapter 7 turns to media politics, how the press covers the campaign and how the candidates try to affect as well as counter that coverage through paid advertising and scripted public performances. The chapter evaluates the impact that media-driven forces can have on electoral voting behavior.

The fourth part of the book looks at the election and beyond it. Chapter 8 discusses and evaluates the presidential vote: What does it mean? Is there a mandate? How does the election affect the president's ability to govern? Chapter 9 considers problems in the electoral system and possible reforms to alleviate these problems. It examines some of the major difficulties that have affected the political system from party rules to finance issues to media coverage and to the Electoral College itself. This chapter also looks at proposals being discussed or actions recently implemented for improving the electoral system, for making it more equitable to the citizenry, more responsive to popular choice and less prone to human error and personal discretion, and more likely to guide and facilitate those in government in their policy-making responsibilities.

PURPOSE

Elections link the people with their public officials, a vital democratic role. However, that link is far from perfect. Voting is individualized, yet governing is a collective undertaking. Everyone does not participate in elections, but government makes rules for all the people. Presidential candidates regularly over promise and under deliver. They create unrealistic expectations that are impossible to achieve, certainly not by themselves in a system of shared powers and divided government. People become disillusioned, apathetic, and cynical.

How can we improve elections? How can we encourage more of the citizenry to participate? How can we persuade the most qualified to run? How can we level the electoral playing field? How can we ensure that the mood of the voters will be reflected in the results of the election and that those results will be accurately interpreted by newly elected public officials? In other words, how can we make sure that elections achieve their principal democratic goals—select the most qualified representatives, provide them with a blueprint for governing, and make sure that we hold them individually and collectively accountable for their decisions and actions in government?

Without information on how the system works, we can do none of the above. We cannot cajole the citizenry to meet their civic responsibilities and vote; we cannot recruit the best and the brightest to run; we cannot improve the people–government–public policy connection for which elections are the critical link. In the case of presidential politics, ignorance is definitely not bliss nor is the norm always or usually the ideal.

The road to the White House is long and arduous. In fact, it has become more difficult to travel than in the past. Yet, surprisingly, given all the criticism, there continue to be many travelers. Evaluating their journey is essential to rendering an intelligent judgment on election day. However, more is at stake than simply choosing the occupant of the Oval Office. The system itself is on trial in every presidential election. That is why it is so important to understand and appreciate the intricacies of the process. Only an informed citizenry can determine whether the nation is being well served by the way we go about choosing our president.

ACKNOWLEDGEMENTS

Few books are written alone, and this one was no exception. For the 2004 edition, I was fortunate to have an excellent research assistant, Will Adams. An exceptional undergraduate student at Georgetown University, Will helped me review and synthesize the recent literature on presidential elections.

I would also like to express my thanks to the political scientists who have reviewed one or more of the first six editions of this book: John Bruce, University of Mississippi; Richard L. Cole, University of Texas at Arlington; Anthony Corrado Jr., Colby College; Stephen C. Craig, University of Florida at Gainesville; James W. Davis, Washington University; Gordon Friedman, Southwest Missouri State University; Jay S. Goodman, Wheaton College; Anne Griffin, the Cooper Union; Marjorie Randon Hershey, Indiana University; Hugh L. LeBlanc, George Washington University; Kuo-Wei Lee, Pan-American University; Robert T. Nakamura, State University of New York at Albany; Richard G. Niemi, University of Rochester; Diana Owen, Georgetown University; Charles Prysby, the University of North Carolina at Greensboro; Michael Robinson, Georgetown University; Lester Seligman, University of Illinois; Earl Shaw, Northern Arizona University; John W. Sloan, University of Houston; Priscilla Southwell, University of Oregon at Eugene; William H. Steward, University of Alabama; Edward J. Weissman, Washington College; and Clyde Wilcox, Georgetown University.

I also wish to acknowledge the people at Wadsworth and Publisher's Studio, a division of Stratford Publishing Services, who helped in the editing, publishing, and marketing of this book, especially copy editor Leslie Connor and development editor Stacey Sims.

Finally, everyone makes personal sacrifices in writing a book. My wife, Cheryl Beil, and my sons, Jared and Jeremy, were no exceptions. As always, they gave me lots of encouragement and were very accommodating to my writing schedule even though they did not always agree with my political judgments, or worse yet, failed to laugh at my political humor.

Stephen J. Wayne
Georgetown University

ABOUT THE AUTHOR

Stephen J. Wayne is a Professor of Government at Georgetown University. A Washington-based expert on the American presidency, he has authored or edited nine books, several in multiple editions, and over one hundred articles, chapters, and book reviews. In addition to *The Road to the White House*, he has coauthored *Presidential Leadership* (with George Edwards) and *The Politics of American Democracy* (with G. Calvin Mackenzie and Richard L. Cole), all published by Wadsworth. His most recent books include *Is This Any Way to Run a Democratic Election?* and *The Election of the Century and What It Tells Us about the Future of American Politics* (with Clyde Wilcox).

A much-quoted source for journalists covering the White House, he frequently appears on television and radio news programs and consults for television documentaries. He has testified before Congress on presidential elections, appeared before both Democratic and Republican advisory committees on the presidential nomination process, directed a presidential transition project for the National Academy of Public Administration, and participated in the 2000 White House transition project conducted by the Presidency Research Group. Professor Wayne lectures widely throughout the United States and abroad on the contemporary presidency and presidential elections.

CONTENTS

Preface   vii
About the Author   xiii

PART I   THE ELECTORAL ARENA

1   Presidential Selection: A Historical Overview   3
Introduction   3
The Creation of the Electoral College   4
The Development of Nominating Systems   6
The Evolution of the General Election   13
The 2000 Presidential Election Controversy   17
    The Legal Challenges   17
    The Public Relations Campaign   20
The Politics of Electoral College Voting   23
Summary   25
Where on the Web?   27
Exercises   27
Selected Reading   28
Notes   29

2   Campaign Finance   32
Introduction   32
The Costs of Campaigning   33
The Sources of Support   36
Finance Legislation   38
    Box 2–1: Exploiting the Soft Money Loophole   *41*
    Box 2–2: Contribution Limits
        (before and after McCain–Feingold)   *43*
The Impact of the Law   44
    Revenue   44
    Box 2–3: The Well-Funded Candidate's Dilemma:
        To Accept or Reject Government Funds   *50*
    Box 2–4: The Money Race for the 2000 Nomination   *51*

Expenditures   53
Competition Between Parties and Their Candidates   56
Money and Electoral Success   57
Summary   58
Where on the Web?   60
Exercises   61
Selected Reading   61
Notes   62

3   The Political Environment   65
Introduction   65
Turnout   66
    The Expansion of Suffrage   68
    Other Influences on Turnout   71
    Box 3–1: Registering to Vote   *72*
    Turnout and Partisanship   76
The Partisan Basis of Politics   77
    A Model of the U.S. Voter   77
    A More Refined Theory of Voting   79
    Partisan Voting Patterns   80
    Partisan Deviations   81
The Social Basis of Politics   83
    The New Deal Realignment   83
    Evolving Political Coalitions   85
    The Future of the Parties   92
Summary   93
Where on the Web?   94
Exercises   95
Selected Reading   95
Notes   96

PART II   THE NOMINATION

4   The Race for Delegates   103
Introduction   103
Reforming the Nomination Process   104
    Democratic Rules, 1968–1980   104
    Box 4–1: The Iowa Caucus: How It Works   *107*
    Democratic Rules, 1981–Present   108
    Republican Rules   110
The Legality of Party Rules   111
The Impact of the Rules Changes   114
    Turnout   114

Representation 115
Party Organization and Leadership 116
Winners and Losers 117
Campaigning for Delegates 118
Basic Strategic Guidelines 118
Box 4–2: The Air Wars of 2000: The Nominations 128
The Non-Front-Runner Strategy:
Stepping-Stones to Prominence 136
Box 4–3: Non-Front-Runner Strategies in 2000 137
Other Non-Front-Runner Approaches: Using the
Campaign as a Pulpit 142
The Front-Runner Strategy: Amassing Delegates 143
Box 4–4: Front-Runner Strategies in 2000 144
Summary 148
Where on the Web? 149
Exercises 151
Selected Reading 151
Notes 152

**5   Spring Interregnum: Consolidating Victory
      and Posturing for the Election   159**
The Noncompetitive Phase of the Nomination Campaign 159
Image Repair 159
Repositioning and Reprioritizing the Issues 161
Healing Partisan Discord 162
The Prelude to the Conventions 162
National Nominating Conventions 164
The Tradition 164
The Official Proceedings 166
Intra- and Interparty Disputes 170
Convention Strategies and Tactics 172
*Box 5–1: Contrasts in the 2000 Republican and
Democratic Party Platforms* 173
The Mediated Convention: Theater and News 174
Box 5–2: Minor Party Conventions 178
Assessing the Convention's Impact 179
Characteristics of the Nominees 182
Summary 184
Where on the Web? 186
Exercises 186
Selected Reading 187
Notes 187

PART III   THE PRESIDENTIAL CAMPAIGN

6   Organization, Strategy, and Tactics   193
Introduction   193
Organization   197
    Running the Campaign   197
    Transitioning to Government   200
Strategic Objectives   201
    Designing a Basic Appeal   202
    Creating a Leadership Image   204
    Dealing with Incumbency   207
    Building a Winning Geographic Coalition   208
    Box 6–1: An Incumbency Balance Sheet   *209*
Tactical Considerations   212
    Reaching Voters   212
    Orchestrating the Campaign   213
    Targeting Messages   215
    Timing Appeals   216
    Turning Out Voters   216
Summary   217
Where on the Web?   219
Exercises   220
Selected Reading   220
Notes   221

7   Media Politics   225
Introduction   225
Traditional Coverage: Hard News   228
    The Bad News Syndrome   230
    The Story Line   232
    Impact of the News Media   234
Nontraditional Coverage: Soft News   235
Presidential Debates   237
    Preparation   240
    Strategy and Tactics   241
    Evaluation and Impact   242
Campaign Advertising   245
    Techniques and Timing   246
    Targeting   249
    Images and Messages   249
    Box 7–1: The Air Wars of 2000: Advertising Strategies   *253*
The Cumulative Impact of the Media   257
Summary   257
Where on the Web?   259
Exercises   260

Selected Reading   260
Notes   262

PART IV   THE ELECTION

8   Understanding Presidential Elections   269
Introduction   269
Predicting Presidential Elections   270
    Formal Models   270
    Public Opinion Polls   272
    Television Forecasts   276
Interpreting the Election   278
    Models of Voting Behavior   279
    1952–1956: The Impact of Personality   280
    1960–1972: The Increasing Importance of Issues   281
    1976–1996: The Evaluation of Performance   282
    2000: The Anticipation of Future Performance   289
Converting Electoral Choice into Public Policy   291
    The President's Imprecise Mandate   291
    Party Platforms, Campaign Pledges,
        and the New Agenda   293
    Expectations and Performance   293
    The Electoral Coalition and Governing   294
    Personality Politics and Presidential Leadership   295
Summary   298
Where on the Web?   300
Exercises   300
Selected Reading   301
Notes   302

9   Reforming the Electoral System   306
Introduction   306
Modifying Recent Changes   307
    Party Rules   307
    Finance Laws   312
    News Media Coverage   315
Enhancing Electoral Choice   317
    Turnout   317
    Electoral Reform   320
    The Electoral College   321
Summary   328
Where on the Web?   330
Exercises   331
Selected Reading   331
Notes   332

PART V   APPENDIXES

Appendix A: Results of Presidential Elections, 1900–2000   336
Appendix B: 2000 Electoral and Popular Vote Summary   338
Appendix C: 2000 Electoral Vote Distribution   340
Appendix D: Tentative Democratic Caucus and
        Primary Schedule, January–March 2004   341
Appendix E: Republican and Democratic Party
        Conventions and Nominees, 1900–2004   342

Index   **345**

PART I

THE
ELECTORAL
ARENA

PRESIDENTIAL SELECTION: A HISTORICAL OVERVIEW

1

INTRODUCTION

The road to the White House is circuitous and bumpy. It contains numerous hazards and potential dead ends. Those who choose to traverse it need considerable skill, perseverance, and luck if they are to be successful. They also need substantial amounts of time and money. For most candidates there is no such thing as a free or easy ride to the presidency.

The Framers of the Constitution worked for several months on the presidential selection system, and their plan has since undergone a number of constitutional, statutory, and precedent-setting changes. Modified by the development of parties, the expansion of suffrage, the growth of the media, and the revolution in modern communications technology, the electoral system has become more open and participatory but also more contentious, more complex, and more expensive. It has also "turned off" more people who for a variety of reasons have chosen not to participate.

This chapter is about that system: why it was created; what it was supposed to do; what compromises were incorporated in the original plan; how it operated initially; what changes subsequently affected that operation; whom these changes have benefited; and what effect all of this has had on the parties, the electorate, and American democracy.

In addressing these questions, I have organized the chapter into five sections. The first discusses the creation of the presidential election process. It explores the motives and intentions of the delegates at Philadelphia and describes the procedures for selecting the president within the context of the constitutional and political issues of that day.

The second section examines the development of nominating systems. It explores the three principal methods that have been used—partisan congressional

3

caucuses, brokered national conventions, and state primaries and caucuses. It also describes the political forces that helped to shape them and, in the case of the first two, destroyed them.

The third section discusses presidential elections. It focuses on the most controversial ones that occurred in the nineteenth century: those decided by the House of Representatives (1800 and 1824), those influenced by Congress (1876), and those unreflective of popular choice (1888). The chapter also examines elections in the twentieth century in which a relatively small number of votes could have changed the outcome (1960, 1968, and 1976). In doing so, the section highlights the strengths and weaknesses of the Electoral College.

The fourth section discussions the 2000 election controversy—the legal and political issues, the resolution of those issues by the judiciary, the changes in electoral laws that followed, and the impact of the 2000 dispute on future presidential elections.

The final section of the chapter examines the current system. It describes that system's geographic and demographic biases, whom they benefit, and whom they hurt. The section also discusses the Electoral College's major party orientation and its adverse impact on third-party candidacies.

THE CREATION OF THE ELECTORAL COLLEGE

Among the many issues facing the delegates at the Constitutional Convention of 1787 in Philadelphia, the selection of the president was one of the toughest. Seven times during the course of the convention the method for choosing the executive was altered.

The Framers' difficulty in designing electoral provisions for the president stemmed from the need to guarantee the institution's independence and, at the same time, create a technically sound, politically effective mechanism that would be consistent with a republican form of government: a representative government based on consent, but not a direct democracy in which everyone had an opportunity to participate in the formulation of public policy. They wanted an electoral system that would choose the most qualified person but not necessarily the most popular. There seemed to be no precise model to follow.

Three methods had been proposed. The Virginia Plan, a series of resolutions designed by James Madison and introduced by Governor Edmund Randolph of Virginia, provided for legislative selection. Eight states chose their governors in this fashion at the time. Having Congress choose the president would be practical and politically expedient. Moreover, members of Congress could have been expected to exercise a considered judgment. Making a reasoned, unemotional choice was important to the delegates at Philadelphia, since many of them did not consider the average citizen capable of doing so.

The difficulty with legislative selection was the threat it posed to the institution of the presidency. How could the executive's independence be preserved if the election of the president hinged on popularity with Congress and reelection on the legislature's appraisal of the president's performance in office? Only if the president were to serve a long term and not be eligible for reelection, it was thought, could the institution's independence be protected so long as Congress was the electoral body. But ineligibility also posed problems, as it provided little incentive for the president to perform well and denied the country the possibility of reelecting a person whose experience and success in office demonstrated qualifications that were superior to others.

Reflecting on these concerns, Gouverneur Morris urged the removal of the ineligibility clause on the grounds that it tended to destroy the great motive to good behavior, the hope of being rewarded by a reappointment.[1] A majority of the states agreed. Once the ineligibility clause was deleted, however, the term of office had to be shortened to prevent what the Framers feared might become unlimited tenure. With a shorter term of office and permanent reeligibility, legislative selection was not nearly as desirable, since it could make the president beholden to the legislature.

Popular election was another alternative, although one that did not generate a great deal of enthusiasm. It was twice rejected in the convention by overwhelming votes. Most of the delegates felt that a direct vote by the people was neither desirable nor feasible.[2] Lacking confidence in the public's ability to choose the best qualified candidate, many delegates also believed that the size of the country and the poor state of its communications and transportation in the eighteenth century precluded a national campaign and election. The geographic expanse was simply too large to permit proper supervision and control of the election. Sectional distrust and rivalry also contributed to the difficulty of holding a national election.

A third alternative was some type of indirect election in which popular sentiment could be expressed but would not dictate the selection. James Wilson first proposed this idea after he failed to generate support for a direct popular vote. Luther Martin, Gouverneur Morris, and Alexander Hamilton also suggested an indirect popular election through intermediaries. It was not until the debate over legislative selection divided and eventually deadlocked the delegates, however, that election by electors was seriously considered. Proposed initially as a compromise toward the end of the convention, the Electoral College design was accepted by the delegates after a short debate. Viewed as a safe, workable solution to the election dilemma, it was deemed consistent with the constitutional and political features of the new government. Popular election of the electors was not precluded, but neither was it encouraged by the compromise.

According to the proposal, presidential electors were to be chosen by the states in a manner designated by their legislatures. To ensure their independence, the electors could not simultaneously hold a federal government position. The number of electors was to equal the number of senators and representatives from each state. At a designated time the electors would vote and send the results to Congress, where they would be announced to a joint session by the president of the Senate—the vice president. Each elector had two votes since a president and vice president were to be selected separately. The only limitations on voting were that the electors could not cast both their ballots for inhabitants of their own states, and they could not designate who they wished to be president and vice president.[3]

Under the initial plan, the person who received a majority of votes cast by the Electoral College was elected president, and the one with the second highest total, vice president. In the event that no one received a majority, the House of Representatives would choose from among the five candidates with the most electoral votes, with each state delegation casting one vote. If two or more individuals were tied for second, then the Senate would select one as vice president. Both of these provisions were subsequently modified by the Twelfth Amendment to the Constitution.

The electoral system was a dual compromise. Allowing state legislatures to establish the procedures for choosing electors was a concession to the proponents of a federal system; having the House of Representatives decide if there was no Electoral College majority was designed to please those who favored a stronger national government. Designating the number of electors to be equal to a state's congressional delegation gave the larger states an advantage in the initial voting for president; balloting by states in the House, if the Electoral College was not decisive, benefited the smaller states.

The large-small state compromise was critical to the acceptance of the Electoral College plan. It was argued during the convention debates that in practice the large states would nominate the candidates for president and the small states would exercise equal influence over the final choice.[4] So great were sectional rivalries and distrust at the time, that the prospect of a majority of the college agreeing on anyone other than George Washington seemed remote.

THE DEVELOPMENT OF NOMINATING SYSTEMS

Although the Constitution prescribed a system for electing a president, it made no reference to the nomination of candidates. Political parties had not emerged prior to the Constitutional Convention. Factions existed, and the Framers of the Constitution were concerned about them, but the development of a party system was not anticipated. Rather, it was assumed that electors, whose interests were not tied to the national government, would make an independent judgment in choosing the best possible person as president.

In the first two elections the system worked as intended. George Washington was the unanimous choice of the electors. There was, however, no consensus on who the vice president should be. The eventual winner, John Adams, benefited from some informal lobbying by prominent individuals prior to the vote.[5]

A more organized effort to agree on candidates for the presidency and vice presidency was undertaken in 1792. Partisan alliances were beginning to develop in Congress. Members of the two principal groups, the Federalists and the Anti-Federalists, met separately to recommend individuals. The Federalists chose Vice President Adams; the Anti-Federalists picked Governor George Clinton of New York.

With political parties evolving during the 1790s, the selection of electors quickly became a partisan contest. In 1792 and 1796, a majority of the state legislatures chose them directly. Thus, the political group that controlled the legislature also controlled the selection of electors. Appointed for their political views, electors were expected to exercise partisan judgment. When in 1796 a Pennsylvania elector did not do so, he was accused of faithless behavior. Wrote one critic in a Philadelphia newspaper: "What, do I chuse Samuel Miles to determine for me whether John Adams or Thomas Jefferson shall be President? No! I chuse him to act, not to think."[6]

Washington's decision not to serve a third term forced Federalist and Anti-Federalist members of Congress to recommend the candidates in 1796. Meeting separately, party leaders agreed among themselves on the tickets. The Federalists urged their electors to support John Adams and Thomas Pinckney, while the Anti-Federalists (or Democratic-Republicans, as they began to be called) suggested Thomas Jefferson and Aaron Burr.

Since it was not possible to specify presidential and vice presidential choices on the ballot, Federalist electors, primarily from New England, decided to withhold votes from Pinckney (of South Carolina) to make certain that he did not receive the same number as Adams (of Massachusetts). This strategy enabled Jefferson with 68 votes to finish ahead of Pinckney with 59, but behind Adams, who had 71. Four years of partisan differences followed between a president who, though he disclaimed a political affiliation, clearly favored the Federalists in appointments, ideology, and policy, and a vice president who was the acknowledged leader of the opposition party.

Beginning in 1800, partisan caucuses, composed of members of Congress, met for the purpose of recommending their party's nominees. The Democratic-Republicans continued to choose candidates in this manner until 1824; the Federalists did so only until 1808. In the final two presidential elections in which the Federalists ran candidates, 1812 and 1816, top party leaders, meeting in secret, decided on the nominees.[7]

"King Caucus" violated the spirit of the Constitution. It effectively provided for members of Congress to pick the nominees. After the decline of the Federalists, the nominees of the Democratic-Republicans, or simply Republicans as they became known, were, in fact, assured of victory—a product of the dominance of that party.

There were competing candidates within the Republican caucus, however. In 1808, Madison prevailed over James Monroe and George Clinton. In 1816, Monroe overcame a strong challenge from William Crawford. In both cases, the electors united behind the successful nominee. In 1820, however, they did not. Disparate elements within the party selected their own candidates.

Although the caucus was the principal mode of candidate selection during the first part of the nineteenth century, it was never formally institutionalized. How, by whom, and when meetings were called varied from election to election. So did attendance. A sizable number of representatives chose not to participate at all. Some stayed away on principle; others did so because of the choices they would have to make. In 1816, less than half of the Republican members of Congress were at their party's caucus. In 1820, only 20 percent attended, and the caucus had to adjourn without formally supporting President Monroe and Vice President Daniel D. Tompkins for reelection. In 1824, almost three-fourths of the members boycotted the session.

The 1824 caucus did nominate candidates. But with representatives from only four states constituting two-thirds of those attending, the nominee, William Crawford, failed to receive unified party support. Other candidates were nominated by state legislatures and conventions, and the electoral vote was divided. Since no candidate obtained a majority, the House of Representatives had to make the final decision. John Quincy Adams was selected on the first ballot. He received the votes of thirteen of the twenty-four state delegations.

The caucus was never resumed. In the end it fell victim to the decline of one of the major parties, the decentralization of political power, and Andrew Jackson's stern opposition. The Federalist Party had collapsed as a viable political force. As the Republican Party grew from being the majority to the only party, factions developed within it, the two principal ones being the National Republicans and the Democratic Republicans. In the absence of a strong opposition there was little to hold these factions together. By 1830, they had split into two separate groups, one supporting and one opposing President Jackson.

Political leadership was changing as well. A relatively small group of individuals had dominated national politics for the first three decades following the ratification of the Constitution. Their common experience in the Revolutionary War, the Constitutional Convention, and the early government produced personal contacts, political influence, and public respect that contributed to their ability to agree on candidates and to generate public support for them.[8]

Those who followed them in office had neither the tradition nor the national orientation in which to frame their presidential selection nor the national recognition to build support across the country for their candidates. Most of this new generation of political leaders owed their prominence and political influence to states and regions and their loyalties reflected these bases of support. The growth of party organizations at the state and local level affected the nomination system. In 1820 and 1824, it evolved into a decentralized mode of selection with state legislatures, caucuses, and conventions nominating their own candidates. Support was also mobilized on regional levels.

Whereas the congressional caucus had become unrepresentative, state-based nominations suffered from precisely the opposite problem. They were too sensitive to sectional interests and produced too many candidates. Unifying diverse elements behind a national ticket proved extremely difficult, although Jackson was successful in doing so in 1828. Nonetheless, a system that was more broadly based than the old caucus and could provide a decisive and mobilizing mechanism was needed. National nominating conventions filled the void.

The first such convention was held in 1831 by the Anti-Masons. A small but relatively active third party, it had virtually no congressional representation. Unable to utilize a caucus, the party turned instead to a general meeting, which was held in a saloon in Baltimore, with 116 delegates from thirteen states attending. These delegates decided on the nominees as well as on an address to the people that contained the party's position on the dominant issues of the day.

Three months later a second convention was held in the same saloon by opponents of President Jackson. The National Republicans (or Whigs, as they later became known) also nominated candidates and agreed on a platform critical of the Jackson administration.

The following year the Democratic-Republicans (or Democrats, as they were later called) also met in Baltimore. The impetus for their convention was Jackson's desire to demonstrate popular support for his presidency as well as to ensure the selection of Martin Van Buren as his running mate. In 1836, Jackson resorted to another convention—this time to handpick Van Buren as his successor.

The Whigs did not hold a convention in 1836. Believing that they would have more success in the House of Representatives than with the nation as a whole, they ran three regional candidates, nominated by the states, who competed against Van Buren in their areas of strength. The plan, however, failed to deny Van Buren an electoral majority. He ended up with 170 votes compared with a total of 124 for the other principal contenders.

Thereafter, the Democrats and their opponents, first the Whigs and then their Republican successors, held nominating conventions to select their candidates. The early conventions were informal and rowdy by contemporary standards, but they also set the precedents for later meetings.

The delegates decided on the procedures for conducting the convention, developed policy statements (addresses to the people), and chose nominees. Rules for apportioning the number of delegates were established before the meetings were held. Generally speaking, states were accorded as many votes as their congressional representation merited, regardless of the number of actual participants. The way in which the delegates were chosen, however, was left up to the states. Local and state conventions, caucuses, or even committees chose the delegates.

Public participation was minimal. It was party leaders who designated the delegates and made the deals. In time it became clear that successful candidates owed their selection to the heads of the powerful state organizations, not to their own political prominence and organizational support. But the price they had to pay, when calculated in terms of patronage and other political payoffs, was often quite high.

Nineteenth-century conventions served a number of purposes. They provided a forum for party leaders, particularly at the state level. They constituted a mechanism by which agreements could be negotiated and support mobilized. By brokering interests, conventions helped unite the disparate elements within a party, thereby converting an organization of state parties into a national coalition for the purpose of conducting a presidential campaign.

Much of the bartering was conducted behind closed doors. Actions on the convention floor often had little to do with the wheeling and dealing that occurred in the smaller "smoke-filled" rooms. Since there was little public preconvention activity, many ballots were often necessary to reach the number that was required to win the party's nomination, usually two-thirds of the delegates.

The nominating system buttressed the position of individual state party leaders, but it did so at the expense of rank-and-file participation. The influence of the state leaders depended on their ability to deliver votes, which in turn required that the delegates not exercise independent judgment. To guarantee their loyalty, the bosses controlled their selection.

Demands for reform began to be heard at the beginning of the twentieth century. The Progressive movement, led by Robert La Follette of Wisconsin and Hiram Johnson of California, aimed to break the power of state bosses and their machines through the direct election of convention delegates or, alternatively, through the expression of a popular choice by the electorate.

Florida became the first state to provide its political parties with such an option. In 1904, the Democrats took advantage of it and held a statewide vote for convention delegates. One year later, Wisconsin enacted a law for the direct election of delegates to nominating conventions. Others followed suit. By 1912, fifteen states provided for some type of primary election. Oregon was the first to permit a preference vote for the candidates themselves.

The year 1912 was also the first in which a candidate sought to use primaries as a way to obtain the nomination. With almost 42 percent of the Republican delegates selected in primaries, former President Theodore Roosevelt challenged incumbent William Howard Taft. Roosevelt won nine primaries to Taft's one, yet lost the nomination. (See Table 1–1.) Taft's support among regular party leaders who delivered their delegations and controlled the convention was sufficient to retain the nomination. He received one-third of his support from southern delegations, although the Republican Party had won only a small percentage of the southern vote in the previous election.

Partially in reaction to the unrepresentative, "boss-dominated" convention of 1912, additional states adopted primaries. By 1916, more than half of the states held a Republican or Democratic contest. Although a majority of the delegates in that year were chosen by some type of primary, many of them were not bound to support specific candidates. As a consequence, the primary vote did not control the outcome of the conventions.

The movement toward popular participation was short-lived, however. Following World War I, the number of primaries declined. State party leaders, who saw primaries as a threat to their own influence, argued against them on three grounds: they were expensive; they did not attract many voters; and major candidates tended to avoid them. Moreover, primaries frequently encouraged factionalism, thereby weakening a party's organizational structure.

In response to this criticism the reformers, who supported primaries, could not claim that their principal goal—rank-and-file control over the selection of party nominees—had been achieved. Public involvement was disappointing. Primaries rarely attracted more than 50 percent of those who voted in the general election, and usually much less. The minority party, in particular, suffered from low turnout for an obvious reason—its candidates stood little chance of winning the general election. In some states, rank-and-file influence was further diluted by the participation of independents.

As a consequence of these factors, some states that had enacted new primary laws reverted to their former method of selection. Others made their primaries advisory rather than mandatory. Fewer convention delegates were elected in them. By 1936, only fourteen states held Democratic primaries, and twelve held Republican ones. Less than 40 percent of the delegates to each convention that year were chosen in this manner. For the next twenty years the number of primaries and the percentage of delegates hovered around this level.

Theodore Roosevelt's failure in 1912 and the decline in primaries thereafter made them at best an auxiliary route to the nomination. Although some presidential aspirants became embroiled in primaries, none who depended on them won. In 1920, a spirited contest between three Republicans (General Leonard Wood, Governor Frank Lowden of Illinois, and Senator Hiram Johnson) failed to produce a convention majority for any of these candidates and resulted in party leaders choosing Warren Harding as the standard-bearer. Similarly, in 1952, Senator Estes Kefauver, who chaired the highly publicized and televised Senate hearings on organized crime, entered thirteen of seventeen presidential primaries, won twelve of them, and became the most popular Democratic contender, but failed to win his party's nomination.

The reason Kefauver could not parlay his primary victories into a convention victory was that a majority of the delegates were not selected in this manner. Of those who were, many were chosen separately from the presidential preference vote. Kefauver did not contest these separate delegate elections. As a consequence, he obtained only 50 percent of the delegates in states where he actually won the presidential preference vote. Moreover, the fact that most of his wins occurred against little or no opposition undercut Kefauver's claim to being the most popular and electable Democrat. He had avoided primaries in four states where he feared that he might either lose or do poorly.

Not only were primaries not considered to be an essential road to the nomination, but running in too many of them was interpreted as a sign of weakness, not strength. It indicated a lack of national recognition, a failure to obtain the support of party leaders, or both. For these reasons, leading candidates tended to choose their primaries carefully, and the primaries, in turn, tended to reinforce the position of the leading candidates.

Those who entered primaries did so mainly to test their popularity rather than to win convention votes. Dwight D. Eisenhower in 1952, John F. Kennedy in 1960, and Richard M. Nixon in 1968 had to demonstrate that being a general, a Catholic, or a once-defeated presidential candidate would not be fatal to their chances. In other words, they needed to prove they could win the general election.

With the possible exception of John Kennedy's victories in West Virginia and Wisconsin, primaries were neither crucial nor decisive for winning the nomination until the 1970s. When there was a provisional consensus within the party, primaries helped confirm it; when there was not, primaries could not produce it.[9] In short, they had little to do with whether the party was unified or divided at the time of the convention.

Primary results tended to be self-fulfilling in the sense that they confirmed the front-runner's status. Between 1936 and 1968, the preconvention leader, the candidate who was ahead in the Gallup Poll before the first primary, won the nomination seventeen out of nineteen times. The only exceptions were Thomas E. Dewey in 1940, who was defeated by Wendell Willkie, and Kefauver in 1952, who lost to Adlai Stevenson. Willkie, however, had become the leader in public opinion by the time the Republican convention met. Even when leading candidates lost a primary, they had time to recoup. Dewey and Stevenson, defeated in early primaries in 1948 and 1956, respectively, went on to reestablish their credibility as front-runners by winning later primaries.

This situation in which the primaries were not the essential route to the nomination changed dramatically after 1968. Largely as a consequence of the tumultuous Democratic convention of that year, in which the party's nominees and platform were allegedly dictated by party "bosses," demands for a larger voice for rank-and-file partisans increased. In reaction to these demands, the Democratic Party began to look into the matter of delegate selection. It enacted a series of reforms designed to ensure broader representation at its convention. To avoid challenges to their delegations, a number of states that had used caucus and convention systems changed to primaries. As Table 1–1 indicates, the number of primaries began to increase as did the percentage of convention delegates chosen from them.

TABLE 1–1 🏵

NUMBER OF PRESIDENTIAL PRIMARIES AND PERCENTAGE OF CONVENTION DELEGATES FROM PRIMARY STATES, BY PARTY, 1912–2000

	Democratic†		Republican	
Year	Number of State Primaries	Percentage of Delegates from Primary States*	Number of State Primaries	Percentage of Delegates from Primary States
1912	12	32.9%	13	41.7%
1916	20	53.5	20	58.9
1920	16	44.6	20	57.8
1924	14	35.5	17	45.3
1928	17	42.2	16	44.9
1932	16	40.0	14	37.7
1936	14	36.5	12	37.5
1940	13	35.8	13	38.8
1944	14	36.7	13	38.7
1948	14	36.3	12	36.0
1952	15	38.7	13	39.0
1956	19	42.7	19	44.8
1960	16	38.3	15	38.6
1964	17	45.7	17	45.6
1968	17	37.5	16	34.3
1972	23	60.5	22	52.7
1976	29*	72.6	28*	67.9
1980	31*	74.7	35*	74.3
1984	26	62.9	30	68.2
1988	34	66.6	35	76.9
1992	39	78.8	38	80.4
1996	34	62.6	43	90.0
2000	40	85.7	43	93.1

*Does not include Vermont, which holds nonbinding presidential preference votes but chooses delegates in state caucuses and conventions.

†Includes party leaders and elected officials chosen from primary states.

Sources: 1912–1964, F. Christopher Arterton, "Campaign Organizations Face the Mass Media in the 1976 Presidential Nomination Process" (paper delivered at the Annual Meeting of the American Political Science Association, Washington, D.C., September 1–4, 1977); 1968–1976, Austin Ranney, *Participation in American Presidential Nominations, 1976* (Washington, D.C.: American Enterprise Institute, 1977), table 1, 6; reprinted with permission of the American Enterprise Institute for Public Policy Research, Washington, D.C. The figures for 1980 were compiled by Austin Ranney from materials distributed by the Democratic National Committee and the Republican National Committee; figures for elections since 1980 were compiled by the author from data supplied by the Democratic and Republican National Committees and the Federal Election Commission.

New finance laws, which provided for government subsidies for preconvention campaigning, and increased media coverage, particularly by television, also added to the incentive to enter primaries. By 1972, primaries had become decisive. In that year, Senator Edmund Muskie, the leading Democratic contender at the beginning of the process, was forced to withdraw after doing poorly in the early contests. In 1976, President Gerald Ford came close to being the first incumbent president since Chester A. Arthur in 1884 to be formally denied his party's nomination because of a primary challenge by Ronald Reagan. In 1980, President Jimmy Carter was also challenged for renomination by Senator Edward Kennedy, as was George H. W. Bush by Pat Buchanan in 1992. Bill Clinton was not challenged in 1996, but he had to raise money and wage a major campaign to ensure that a credible candidate would not oppose him—a strategy George W. Bush pursued prior to the 2004 Republican nominating convention.

Since the 1970s, primaries have revolutionized the presidential nomination process. They have been used to build popularity rather than simply reflect it. Challengers can no longer hope to succeed without entering them; incumbents can no longer ignore them.

The impact of primaries has been significant, affecting the strategies and tactics of the candidates, the composition and behavior of the convention delegates, and the decision-making process at the national conventions. These nomination contests have shifted power within the parties. They have enlarged the selection zone of potential nominees. They have also made governing more difficult. Each of these developments will be discussed in subsequent chapters.

THE EVOLUTION OF THE GENERAL ELECTION

The general election has changed as well. The Electoral College no longer operates in the manner in which it was designed. It now has a partisan coloration. There is greater public participation, but it is still not direct. Although the system bears a resemblance to its past form, it has become more subject to democratic influences. However, it continues to contain electoral biases.

The electoral system for president and vice president was one of the few innovative features of the Constitution. It had no immediate precedent, although it bore some relationship to the way the state of Maryland selected its senators. In essence, it was invented by the Framers, not synthesized from British and American experience, and it is one aspect of the constitutional system that has rarely worked as intended.

Initially, the method by which the states chose their electors varied. Some provided for direct election in a statewide vote. Others had the legislatures do the choosing. Two states used a combination of popular and legislative selection.

As political parties emerged at the beginning of the nineteenth century, state legislatures maneuvered the selection process to benefit the party in power. This maneuvering resulted in the selection of more cohesive groups of electors who shared similar partisan views. Gradually, the trend evolved into a winner-take-all system, with most electors chosen on a statewide basis by popular vote. South Carolina was the last state to move to popular selection, doing so only after the Civil War.

The development of the party system changed the character of the Electoral College. Only in the first two elections, when Washington was the unanimous choice, did the electors exercise a nonpartisan and presumably independent judgment. Within ten years from the time the federal government began to operate, electors quickly became the captives of their party and were expected to vote for its candidates. The outcome of the election of 1800 vividly illustrates this new pattern of partisan voting.

The Federalist Party supported President John Adams of Massachusetts and Charles C. Pinckney of South Carolina. The Democratic-Republicans, who had emerged to oppose the Federalists' policies, backed Thomas Jefferson of Virginia and Aaron Burr of New York. The Democratic-Republican candidates won, but, unexpectedly, Jefferson and Burr received the same number of votes. All electors who had cast ballots for Jefferson also cast them for Burr. Since it was not possible in those days to differentiate the candidates for the presidency and vice presidency on the ballot, the results had to be considered a tie, though Jefferson was clearly his party's choice for president. Under the terms of the Constitution, the House of Representatives, voting by state, had to choose the winner.

On February 11, 1801, after the results of the Electoral College vote were announced by the vice president, who happened to be Jefferson, a Federalist-controlled House convened to resolve the dilemma. Since the winners of the 1800 election did not take office until March 4, 1801, representatives from a "lame-duck" Congress would have to choose the next president.[10] A majority of Federalists supported Burr, whom they regarded as the more pragmatic politician, a person with whom they could deal. Jefferson, on the other hand, was perceived as a dangerous, uncompromising radical by many Federalists. Alexander Hamilton, however, was outspoken in his opposition to Burr, a political rival from New York, whom Hamilton regarded as "the most unfit man in the United States for the office of President."[11]

On the first ballot taken on February 11, Burr received a majority of the total votes, but Jefferson won the support of more state delegations.[12] Eight states voted for Jefferson, six backed Burr, and two were evenly divided. This left Jefferson one short of the needed majority. The House took nineteen ballots on its first day of deliberations, and a total of thirty-six before it finally elected Jefferson. Had Burr promised to be a Federalist president, it is conceivable that he could have won.

The first amendment to reform voting procedures in the Electoral College was enacted by the new Congress, controlled by Jefferson's party, in 1803. It was accepted by three-fourths of the states in 1804. This amendment to the Constitution, the twelfth, provided for separate voting for president and vice president. It also refined the selection procedures in the event that the president or vice president did not receive a majority of the electoral vote. The House of Representatives, still voting by state, was to choose from among the three presidential candidates with the most electoral votes, and the Senate, voting by individual, was to choose from the top two vice presidential candidates. If the House could not make a decision by March 4, the amendment provided for the new vice president to assume the presidency until such time as the House could render a decision.

The next nondecisive presidential vote did not occur until 1824. That year, four people received electoral votes for president: Andrew Jackson (99 votes), John

Quincy Adams (84), William Crawford (41), and Henry Clay (37). According to the Twelfth Amendment, the House of Representatives had to decide from among the top three, since none had a majority. Eliminated from the contest was Henry Clay, who happened to be Speaker of the House. Clay threw his support to Adams, who won. It was alleged that he did so in exchange for appointment as secretary of state, a charge that Clay vigorously denied. After Adams became president, however, he nominated Clay for secretary of state, a position Clay readily accepted.[13]

Jackson was the winner of the popular vote in 1824. In eighteen of the twenty-four states that chose electors by popular vote that year, he received 192,933 votes compared with 115,696 for Adams, 47,136 for Clay, and 46,979 for Crawford. Adams of Massachusetts, however, had the backing of more state delegations. He enjoyed the support of the six New England states, and with Clay's help, the representatives of six others backed his candidacy. The votes of thirteen states, however, were needed for a majority. New York seemed to be the pivotal state and Stephen Van Rensselaer, a Revolutionary War general, the swing representative. On the morning of the vote, Speaker Clay and Representative Daniel Webster tried to persuade Van Rensselaer to vote for Adams. It was said that they were unsuccessful.[14] When the voting began, Van Rensselaer bowed his head as if in prayer. On the floor he saw a piece of paper with "Adams" written on it. Interpreting this as a sign from the Almighty, he dropped the paper in the box. New York went for Adams by one vote, providing him with the barest majority.[15]

Jackson, outraged at the turn of events, urged the abolition of the Electoral College. His claim of a popular mandate, however, was open to question. The most populous state at the time, New York, did not permit its electorate to participate in the selection of electors. Rather, the New York legislature made the decision. Moreover, in three of the states in which Jackson won the electoral vote but lost in the House of Representatives, he had fewer popular votes than Adams.[16]

Opposition to the system mounted, however, and a gradual democratization of the process occurred. More states began to choose their electors directly by popular vote. In 1800, ten of the fifteen used legislative selection. By 1832, only South Carolina retained this practice.

The trend was also toward statewide election of an entire slate of electors. States that had chosen their electors within legislative districts converted to a winner-take-all system in order to maximize their voting power in the Electoral College. This change, in turn, created the possibility that there could be a disparity between the popular and electoral vote. A candidate could be elected by winning the popular vote in the big states but losing most of the small states or vice versa.

The next disputed election did not occur until 1876. In that election Democrat Samuel J. Tilden received the most votes. He had 250,000 more popular votes and 19 more electoral votes than his Republican rival, Rutherford B. Hayes. Nonetheless, Tilden fell one vote short of a majority in the Electoral College. Twenty electoral votes were in dispute. Dual election returns were received from Florida (four votes), Louisiana (eight votes), and South Carolina (seven votes). Charges of fraud and voting irregularities were made by both parties. The Republicans, who controlled the three state legislatures, contended that Democrats had forcibly prevented newly freed slaves from voting. The Democrats, on the other hand, alleged that many nonresidents and nonregistered people had participated. The other disputed electoral vote occurred in the state of Oregon. One Republican elector was challenged on the grounds that he held another federal position (postmaster) at the time he was chosen and thus was ineligible to be an elector.

Three days before the Electoral College vote was to be officially counted, Congress established a commission to examine and try to resolve the dispute. The electoral commission was to consist of fifteen members: ten from Congress (five Republicans and five Democrats) and five from the Supreme Court. Four of the Supreme Court justices were designated by the act (two Republicans and two Democrats), and they were to choose a fifth justice. David Davis, a political independent, was expected to be selected, but on the day the commission was created, Davis was appointed by the Illinois legislature to the U.S. Senate. The Supreme Court justices then picked Joseph Bradley, an independent Republican. Bradley sided with his party on every issue. By a strictly partisan vote, the commission validated the credentials of all the Republican electors, thereby giving Hayes a one vote margin of victory in the Electoral College.[17]

Before the election of 2000, the only other one in which the winner of the popular vote was beaten in an undisputed Electoral College vote occurred in 1888. Democrat Grover Cleveland had a plurality of 95,096 popular votes, but only 168 electoral votes compared with 233 for Republican Benjamin Harrison. Cleveland's losses in Indiana by about 3,000 votes and New York by about 15,000 led to his defeat.

Although all other leaders in the popular vote have won a majority of electoral votes, shifts of just a few thousand popular votes in a few states could have altered the results of other elections. In 1860, a shift of 25,000 in New York from Abraham Lincoln to Stephen A. Douglas would have denied Lincoln a majority in the Electoral College. A change of less than 30,000 in three states in 1892 would have given Harrison another victory over Cleveland. In 1916, Charles Evans Hughes needed only 3,807 more votes in California to have beaten Woodrow Wilson. Similarly, Thomas E. Dewey could have denied Harry S Truman a majority in the Electoral College with 12,487 more California votes in 1948. A change of less than 9,000 in Illinois and Missouri in 1960 would have meant that John F. Kennedy lacked an Electoral College majority. In 1968, a shift of only 55,000 votes from Richard M. Nixon to Hubert H. Humphrey in three states (New Jersey, Missouri, and New Hampshire) would have thrown the election into the House—a House controlled by Democrats. In 1976, a shift of only 3,687 in Hawaii and 5,559 in Ohio would have cost Jimmy Carter the election.[18]

Not only could the results of these elections have been affected by very small voter shifts in a few states, but in 1948, 1960, 1968, and 1992, there was the added possibility that the Electoral College itself would not be able to choose a winner. In each of these elections, third-party candidates or independent electoral slates threatened to secure enough votes to prevent either of the major candidates from obtaining a majority. In 1948, Henry Wallace (Progressive Party) and Strom Thurmond (States' Rights Party) received almost 5 percent of the total popular vote, and Thurmond won 39 electoral votes. In 1960, fourteen unpledged electors were chosen in Alabama and Mississippi.[19] In 1968, Governor George Wallace of Alabama, running on the American Independent Party ticket, received almost 10 million popular votes, 13.5 percent of the total, and 46 electoral votes. In 1992, independent H. Ross Perot received 19.7 million popular votes (18.9 percent of the total vote) but none in the Electoral College.[20] In 1996, he received 8.1 million votes (8.4 percent of the total), but again no electoral votes. Ralph Nader received less than 3 percent of the vote in 2000. Nonetheless, it is clear that close competition between the major parties, combined with a strong third-party movement, provides the Electoral College with its most difficult test.

THE 2000 PRESIDENTIAL ELECTION CONTROVERSY

In the 2000 election, the first condition—tight party competition—was present and, for a time, it appeared that the second one—a strong third-party campaign—might be as well. With partisanship driving the vote and dividing the electorate, even a relatively small impact by a third-party candidate such as Ralph Nader of the Green Party could have affected the popular vote in several key states. This potential encouraged the Gore campaign to target Nader voters in most of the close states but not in Florida.

Contributing to the closeness of the 2000 election was the concentration of the campaign in five (Illinois, Michigan, Ohio, Pennsylvania, and Wisconsin) of the eight large states. The Democrats' success in winning four of these states along with New York and California ensured a sizable vote for Vice President Al Gore. But with the exception of the Northeast and Pacific Coast regions, the remainder of the country tilted toward Texas Governor George W. Bush with the outcome in Florida in doubt. Not only did the Florida situation create a potential discrepancy between the popular and electoral vote, but until it was decided, neither candidate had an Electoral College majority. Thus, the presidential campaign continued into a postelection phase, a contest that was waged in the courts and the public arena and took five weeks to resolve.

The objectives of the Bush and Gore campaigns during the postelection period were the same: to win the Florida vote; to enhance their own stature and claim of victory in the eyes of the public; and to position themselves as favorably as possible to take over the reins of government.

The postelection campaign was expensive. It forced both sides to go back to their major donors for more money. Bush raised an additional $13.8 million and Gore, $3.7. These funds helped pay for the legal fees, travel costs, office expenses, polling and consulting charges, and other expenditures incurred in the fight for Florida's twenty-five electoral votes. Both parties consulted hundreds of lawyers, assembled thousands of partisans and bused them throughout the state, and investigated the many claims of those who alleged that they were denied the right to vote, incurred harassment while voting, or were confused by voting procedures and the ballots that were used.

The Legal Challenges

Although there were myriad legal issues in the Florida election, four stood out: ballot confusion, ballot validation, ballot tabulation, and the official certification of the results. The confusion stemmed from a "butterfly ballot" used in Palm

Beach County where many retirees live. Designed by a Democratic campaign official, the ballot was intended to help senior citizens read the names of the candidates more clearly by using larger type. To fit all the names on a single punch card, however, two columns had to be used with the punch holes for voting, or "chads" as they are called, between them. Although Democrats Al Gore and Joe Lieberman were listed second on the left-hand column, their chad was positioned third, after the chad of the candidates on the right-hand column, Pat Buchanan and Ezola Foster of the Reform Party. Some voters, who claimed that they intended to vote for the Democratic candidates, punched out the second rather than the third chad, which registered as a vote for Buchanan. Others, in confusion, pushed out both the second and third chads, automatically voiding their ballots.[21]

Aggrieved Democrats in the county immediately filed a lawsuit to contest the election and demand a new vote. A Florida state court, however, rejected their request, effectively terminating the revote option.

A second issue concerned ballots that were not properly included in the machine count. Many counties in Florida still used the punch-card system of voting in which chads, a small perforated box on the card, must be removed with a specially designed instrument. The holes in the card are then tabulated by a machine. However, if a chad is not completely removed, the vote may not be counted. The Gore campaign alleged that thousands of presidential votes in three Democratic counties—Miami-Dade, Broward, and Palm Beach—were not counted because part or all of a chad was still attached to the ballot. In other words, voters had not completely punched through the card. Democrats appealed to county officials for a hand count of these ballots.

One county, Palm Beach, began such a count; another, Miami-Dade, initiated a sample count to see whether a hand count was merited; the third, Broward, initially chose not to do so. Gore's representatives put pressure on the reluctant counties to proceed with a hand count of these uncounted ballots while Bush's attorneys went to federal court to stop it, arguing that a selective hand count in some counties was unfair to people in other counties.

THE PALM BEACH BALLOT

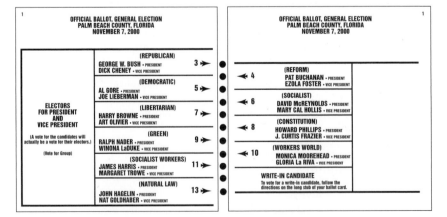

Source: WPBF Eyewitness News 25, West Palm Beach, FL.

Before the courts had rendered a judgment, however, Florida's secretary of state, a Republican appointee, certified the original county vote as the official one to which only absentee ballots, postmarked no later than election day and received by the counties within one week of the election, could be added. The secretary of state's certification prompted Gore's legal team to go to state court to force the secretary to accept hand-counted votes and an amended vote total submitted after the certification.

A Florida circuit court ruled that the secretary had discretion to accept or reject additional vote counts submitted by counties as long as she did not exercise that discretion arbitrarily. The secretary then asked the counties to justify why they wished to amend their original submission with an additional hand count of some votes. After they did so, however, she rejected their arguments, thereby forcing Gore's attorneys to take the entire matter to the Florida Supreme Court.

In an extraordinary session, televised across the country, lawyers for both sides debated the hand count and vote deadline issues within the context of state and federal law and the U.S. Constitution. The Gore side claimed that the only way to ensure a "full, fair, and accurate" vote that represented the will of the Florida electorate would be to count the disputed ballots by hand. But Bush's legal counsel contended that a hand count was blatantly unfair to those who had voted in accordance with the rules and procedures of the state. Besides, they contended, extending the deadline for certified results violates an 1887 federal law that requires states to choose their electors by laws which are enacted *prior* to election day.

The Florida Supreme Court, consisting of eight judges, all but one of whom were appointed by Democratic governors, sided with Gore and proceeded to give the counties an additional six days to submit a revised vote that included hand-counted ballots. Bush's lawyers appealed the Florida Supreme Court's decision to the U.S. Supreme Court.

What followed was a frantic hand count in two counties while a third, Miami-Dade, decided not to go ahead with one, in part because officials believed that they could not do so within the time frame established by the court.[22]

Meanwhile in another part of the state, Democrats filed suit to exclude all absentee ballots from certain counties because Republicans had been given an opportunity to add required voter registration numbers to the forms, omitted erroneously by a glitch in the software program that printed the request forms, in order to obtain absentee ballots. Democrats had not been given a chance to do so. However, a circuit judge ruled against the Democrats' claim.

On Monday, December 4, nearly a month after the presidential election, the U.S. Supreme Court vacated the Florida Supreme Court's verdict that had extended the deadline for hand-counted ballots in the three Florida counties on the grounds that its legal basis for this decision was unclear. The Court remanded the case back to the Florida Supreme Court for clarification and judgment.

Later in the day, a Florida state court judge dismissed Gore's claims for an additional hand count of thousands of ballots from Palm Beach and Miami-Dade counties that had registered no presidential preference as well as the hand-counted ballots that had been submitted after the court-imposed deadline.[23] The judge also refused to overturn the certification of Florida's electoral vote for Bush. In a last-ditch effort to salvage a Florida victory, Gore appealed this state court judgment to the Florida Supreme Court.

Thus, the state supreme court was faced with two issues: One concerned its decision and the legal basis on which it was predicated for extending the state certification deadline for those counties that chose to submit an amended vote based on disputed hand-counted ballots; the other was Gore's appeal to overturn the lower court's decision that additional hand counts and time to certify results were not merited. The Supreme Court of Florida again sided with Gore, ordering an immediate recount of ballots that had not been included in the machine tabulation in *all* Florida counties. Bush's lawyers immediately appealed that decision to the U.S. Supreme Court.

The final legal maneuvering ended in the U.S. Supreme Court. After agreeing to hear the appeal, the Court stopped the recount of the disputed ballots, pending its judgment on the matter. On December 11, 2000, one day before Florida law required the designation of its electors, the Court heard oral arguments in *Bush v. Gore*. Its decision, announced the next evening, reversed the Florida Supreme Court's judgment that ordered the hand count to be resumed. The Court stated that the absence of a single standard to be used throughout the state by election officials violated the Fourteenth Amendment, which requires states to provide equal protection under the laws. A majority of the U.S. Supreme Court went on to conclude that there was not sufficient time, given the state legislature's intent to designate Florida's electors by December 12, to establish such a standard. Hence the certified vote that had Bush leading by 537, was final.

Four justices dissented from the finding that time had run out on the Florida Supreme Court. Two of these justices believed that the deadline for the designation of electors specified by U.S. law, the first Monday following the second Wednesday in December, the 18th in 2000, took precedence over the state legislature's date of December 12th and thus provided sufficient time for the state supreme court to establish a single statewide standard for recounting the votes. The two other dissenters felt that the Florida Supreme Court had acted properly, that the vote count was legal, and that it should not have been halted by the U.S. Supreme Court.

Gore was naturally disappointed with the Supreme Court's decision but had no viable options. All of his legal remedies had been exhausted. On December 13, 2000, he conceded the election. Bush had won Florida by 537 votes out of over 6 million cast. Florida's twenty-five electoral votes gave him a bare majority of Electoral College. Bush won 271 electoral votes, 4 more than Gore, despite the fact that Gore won the popular vote by almost 540,000.

The Public Relations Campaign

During the period in which attorneys for the candidates were engaged in their legal battle, campaign spokespeople were engaged in a public relations campaign for the hearts and minds of the American people. James Baker III, former White House chief of staff and treasury secretary for President Reagan and secretary of state for President George H. W. Bush, was the principal spokesman for Bush while Warren Christopher, secretary of state during the first term of the Clinton administration, handled public relations for Gore.

Throughout the recount, the Bush campaign contended that the Florida vote had been properly tabulated and retabulated, that their candidate had won the initial count and the recount, and that the only way that he could lose the election was if the Democrats "stole" it from him in Florida. They also argued that the extended controversy in Florida constituted a crisis that threatened to undermine support for the electoral system and constitutional government in America.

Democrats naturally saw and explained the situation differently. They defended the principle that every vote should be counted, urged patience, and disputed the notion that the country was mired in a constitutional crisis, noting that electors did not have to be designated until December 18, 2000.

Both candidates' public relations efforts seem to have their desired effect. For Bush, his campaign successfully reinforced the impression that he was ahead and would be the likely winner. It also diverted attention from the results of the popular vote in which he trailed the vice president. For Gore, the public relations campaign bought him time, legitimized his challenge, and maintained partisan support for his candidacy. Most Americans subscribed to the principle that counting all the votes was necessary and proper. Nor did Americans feel that the system was in crisis although opinion turned against Gore as the controversy dragged on. Table 1–2 indicates the shift in public opinion.

TABLE 1–2 🏆

PUBLIC OPINION DURING THE FLORIDA VOTE CONTROVERSY

Question	Percentage	
Approve of the Candidates' Handling of the Situation	**Bush**	**Gore**
November 11–12	53	52
November 19	55	49
November 26–27	54	42
December 2–4	57	39
Favorable Opinion of Each of the Candidates		
November 13–15	53	53
December 2–4	56	46
Gore Should Concede Now	**Yes**	**No**
November 19	46	54
November 26–27	56	46
December 2–4	58	42
December 10	53	47

Source: Gallup Poll, "Public Opinion on Key Issues in the Florida Recount Situation," December 2000, <http://www.gallup.com. Reprinted by permission.

One of the reasons for the public's growing impatience was the media frenzy that surrounded the controversy. In the first week following the election, the television evening news shows devoted 183 stories to the Florida vote, more than to the Clinton–Lewinsky scandal during its first week and more than to Princess Diana and John F. Kennedy Jr. in the first week after their tragic deaths.[24]

Not only was the issue given extensive coverage on the regular news programs, it was also given considerable live coverage. The oral arguments before the Florida Supreme Court were televised as were the arguments before the state circuit court; the arguments before the U.S. Supreme Court were heard on radio immediately after the Court's session. The Florida verdicts were broadcast as were several short public announcements by Gore and Bush. Even the movement of the ballots from Miami-Dade and Palm Beach counties to Tallahassee were televised by a camera crew in a helicopter that hovered over the trucks transporting the ballots.

And the public did pay attention. A national survey taken for the Joan Shorenstein Center at Harvard University in early December found that most Americans said they were paying reasonably close attention to developments in Florida. However, the survey also revealed that levels of interest were declining over the course of the controversy, as were levels of satisfaction in the electoral process. In fact, two out of three people found the situation "depressing."[25]

Despite the strong emotions, largely along partisan lines, that the controversy engendered, electoral system survived the challenge. Bush's victory was generally accepted by the American people. According to a Gallup poll conducted in December 2000, almost half the population believed that he won the election fair and square compared to 18 percent who thought he had stolen it and 32 percent who said that he won it on a technicality.[26] Even in light of the Florida controversy, a majority of people believed the electoral system to be fair, although in December 2000, they also believed it needed a major or complete overhaul. One year later, people voiced more support for the equity of the system and less desire to overhaul it.[27] After his first few weeks in office, President Bush received a positive job approval rating from 57 percent of the population. In short, public opinion snapped back quickly.

Florida changed its elections law. The state legislature enacted electoral reforms in the aftermath of the election to prevent a repetition of the problems that beset and embarrassed the state in 2000. The new law provided more training for election workers, more accurate registration keeping, and provisional voting for those who claimed they were registered but whose names did not appear on voting lists. The state allocated money for counties to replace their antiquated punch-card machines with more accurate scanning equipment and with computerized voting. National electoral reforms, along the lines of the Florida law, were also enacted by Congress in 2002.

A lawsuit brought by the NAACP and other civil rights groups against state and local officials was also settled. Without admitting to any allegations of wrongdoing, the state of Florida agreed to revisit its stringent registration criteria, make registration easier by distributing and collecting forms at various state offices, and appointing an official to monitor the implementation of the National Voter Registration Act.

Nor, in retrospect, did it appear that courts had reversed the judgment of the people of Florida. A recount of the contested ballots in the counties in which Gore had challenged the vote still produced a Bush victory. Even in the more extensive statewide recount of the presidential undervote, the ballots in which no presidential vote was recorded, that Florida Supreme Court had ordered, but the U.S. Supreme Court had terminated, Bush would probably have won according to the results of the press consortium, which reexamined the actual ballots on which there was dispute. On the other hand, and ironically, had there been a recount of all the ballots in which there was an undervote or overvote for president, the comprehensive recount that the Bush campaign demanded if a state recount had to be conducted, Gore might have won. In any case, the vote was very, very close.[28]

THE POLITICS OF ELECTORAL COLLEGE VOTING

The election of 2000 was conditioned by the Electoral College. The strategies the candidates pursued, the resources they utilized, and the major efforts their campaigns conducted were calculated on the basis of Electoral College politics, not the popular vote.

The Electoral College is not neutral. No system of election can be. The way votes are aggregated does make a difference. It benefits some of the electorate and adversely affects others. The Electoral College usually works to the advantage of the candidate who wins the most popular votes. More often than not, it tends to exaggerate that candidate's margin of victory. Bill Clinton received only 43 percent of the popular vote in 1992 but 69 percent of the electoral vote; in 1996, he received 49 percent of the popular vote, 54.6 percent of the two-party vote, and 70.4 percent of the electoral vote. Similarly in 1968, Richard Nixon won only 43.4 percent of the popular vote but 56 percent of the electoral vote. In 1980, Ronald Reagan received 51 percent of the popular vote but a whopping 91 percent of the electoral vote.

Why does the Electoral College usually enhance the margin of the popular vote winner? The reason has to do with the winner-take-all system of voting that has developed in most states. In almost every instance the presidential and vice presidential candidates who receive a plurality of the popular vote within the state get all its electoral votes. This translates into a larger percentage of the Electoral College vote than it would with a direct popular vote.[29] According to one study of presidential elections from 1924 to 1992, the plurality winner who received more than 53.5 percent of the two-party vote received over 75 percent of the electoral vote.[30]

The Electoral College contains a number of built-in biases. One of them has already been mentioned—it tends to enhance the margin of victory of the candidate with the largest popular vote. In addition to benefiting the candidate with the most votes, it increases the influence of the largest states, not only because of the number of electoral votes they cast but because the votes are almost always cast in a bloc.[31] Moreover, the advantage that the citizens of the largest states receive increases in proportion to their states' population. This large-state advantage is why candidates spend a larger share of their campaign time and resources in these states, even if their chances of winning are relatively modest.

By giving an edge to the larger and more competitive states, the Electoral College also works to benefit groups that are geographically concentrated within those states and have cohesive voting patterns. Those who live in urban areas have a particular advantage. Jewish and Hispanic voters and certain immigrant populations fall into this category. Rural voters do not. In general, African Americans are disadvantaged by the Electoral College because of their high concentration in small- and medium-sized southern states.[32]

There is also an offsetting gain for the very smallest states which receive a minimum of three electoral votes regardless of their size. This increases the voting power of sparsely populated states such as Wyoming, Nevada, and Alaska. For example, if Wyoming's 2000 voting-age population of approximately 353,000 were divided by its three electoral votes, there would be one elector for every 117,666 people. Dividing California's population of 24,222,000 by its fifty-four electoral votes yields one elector for every 448,555 people.[33] Medium-sized states are comparatively disadvantaged.[34]

Additionally, the Electoral College works to benefit the two major parties.[35] The reason it does so is that the winner-take-all system of Electoral College voting by states when combined with the need for a majority of the total electoral vote makes it difficult for third parties to accumulate enough votes to win an election.

Which of the major parties is advantaged by the Electoral College has been much debated. Before Bill Clinton's victories in 1992 and 1996, the conventional wisdom held that the Republicans had an advantage. They could increasingly depend on support from the smaller Mountain states, which exercised influence disproportionate to their population because of the two electors they received for their senate representation.[36] The solid South is considered another bastion of Republican strength. Combined, the Mountain and southern states give the Republicans a larger and more dependable block of votes than the Democrats received from the few states that consistently voted for their party.

The problem the Republicans faced is that about half of the larger states (such as New York, Michigan, Pennsylvania, and California) seem to lean to the Democrats and only one, Texas, leans Republican. When the winner-take-all votes of the states are considered, these larger states exercise disproportionate influence. Bill Clinton won six of the big eight in 1992, seven of eight in 1996, losing only Texas, and Gore won five in 2000. Victories in these states are all but essential for Democrats to overcome the advantages Republicans have in the South, and in the Rocky Mountain region and other states in the West.

Regardless of which of the major parties the Electoral College benefits, it definitely disadvantages third-party candidates. To have any effect, these minor party candidates must have support that is geographically concentrated, as Strom Thurmond's was in 1948 and George Wallace's in 1968, rather than more broadly distributed across the country, as Henry Wallace's was in 1948, H. Ross Perot's in 1992 and 1996, and Ralph Nader's in 2000.

Given the limitations on third parties, their most realistic electoral objectives would seem to be to defeat one of the major contenders rather than to elect their own candidate. In 1912, Theodore Roosevelt's Bull Moose campaign split the Republican Party, thereby aiding the Democratic Party candidate, Woodrow Wilson. More recently, Ralph Nader's vote, though small, hurt Gore more than Bush and cost him a victory in Florida. In other elections, third parties may have dipped into the major two-party vote but do not appear to have changed the outcome of elections.

SUMMARY

The quest for the presidency has been and continues to be influenced by the system designed in Philadelphia in 1787. The objectives of that system were to protect the independence of the institution, to ensure the selection of a well-qualified candidate, and to do so in a way that was politically expedient. It was intended to be consistent with the tenets of a republican form of government.

Although many of the objectives are still the same, the system has changed significantly over the years. Of all the factors that have influenced these changes, none has been more important than the advent of political parties. This development created an additional first step in the process, the nomination, which has influenced the selection and behavior of electors ever since.

The nomination process is necessary to the parties, whose principal interest is to get their candidates elected. At first, members of Congress, meeting in partisan caucuses, decided on the nominees. On the basis of common friendships and shared perspectives, they reached a consensus and then used their influence to mobilize support for it. In effect, the system provided for legislative selection of the president in violation of the letter and spirit of the Constitution.

The caucus method broke down with the weakening of the parties, the demise of the Federalists, and the factionalization of the Republicans. It was never restored. In its place developed a more decentralized mode of selection reflective of the increasing sectional composition of the parties.

The new nomination process, controlled by state leaders, operated within the framework of a brokered national convention. There was little rank-and-file participation—the wheeling and dealing were done for the party's electorate, not by them. Demands for greater public involvement eventually opened the system, thereby reducing the influence of state leaders and decreasing the dependence of presidential candidates on them. Power eventually shifted from the political leaders to the candidates themselves, with the people making the final judgment.

Similar trends, rooted in the development of parties and the expansion of suffrage, affected the way in which the electors were selected and how they voted. Instead of being chosen on the basis of their qualifications, electors were selected on the basis of their politics; instead of being elected as individuals, they were elected as part of a slate of electors; instead of exercising independent judgment, the electors became partisan agents who were morally and politically obligated to support their party's choice. The predictable soon happened: bloc voting by electors in states.

The desire of the populace for greater participation also had an effect. It accelerated the movement to choose electors directly by the people, which resulted in an increased likelihood of the electoral vote's reflecting, even exaggerating, the popular vote. Prior to the 2000 election, there were only three times in U.S. history that the plurality winner was not elected—1824, 1876, and 1888; however, the shift of a very small number of votes in a few states could have altered the results of other elections, most recently in 1960, 1968, 1976, and, of course, 2000. This situation has raised doubts about the Electoral College system, doubts that were put to a severe test in 2000.

Many of the problems that emerged in 2000 were not new. Voter intimidation, inaccurate registration lists, machine malfunctions, and tabulation disputes have characterized elections in the past, occasionally becoming issues as in 1960, but rarely affecting the outcome of the presidential election. The closeness of the national vote combined with Florida's relatively large number of electors magnified these problems in 2000 by focusing attention on the popular vote of one state, which would determine the outcome of the national election.

Partisan politics shaped the legal challenges and fueled the public debate. The principal issues revolved around who voted and who could not do so, how the ballots were designed, distributed, and votes cast on them, and how those votes were tabulated and that tabulation validated. The constitutional calendar forced these decisions into a tight time frame, which the U.S. Supreme Court concluded on December 12, 2000, with its judgment in *Bush v. Gore.*

The resolution of the issue affirmed the constitutional framework within which the Electoral College operates. It also reinforced the distinctiveness of the presidential election within an increasingly democratic political system. The aggregation of the popular vote by states, not the sum of the popular vote itself, once again determined the winner. That determination, dictated by the politics of the Electoral College, is not lost on those who organize, strategize, and conduct presidential campaigns.

The Electoral College favors the larger and the more competitive states and thereby forces the bulk of the campaigning into them. Within those states, it encourages candidates to target those groups that are better organized, more geographically concentrated, and more cohesive in their voting behavior. Their vote is maximized by the winner's taking all the state's electoral votes and the state's having a larger share of the total Electoral College.

In summary, the electoral system works, but it does so imperfectly. It permits a partisan choice but recently has not contributed to the strength of the party inside or outside the government. It facilitates participation in the nomination process but has not raised the level of public involvement in general elections. The winning candidate often obtains only a plurality of the voters, and in 2000, not even a plurality. Considering that barely half of the voting-age population cast ballots, a newly elected president receives the support of only about one out of four adults, hardly the mandate we might expect or desire in a democracy nor one that is usually sufficient for governing effectively.

WHERE ON THE WEB?

General Sites

- **C-SPAN: Road to the White House 2004**
  http://www.cspan.org
  Contains up-to-date information about the campaign.
- **Web White & Blue**
  http://www.webwhiteblue.org
  Site sponsored by the Markle Foundation that hosts an online debate among candidates and the public.
- **Yahoo**
  http://www.yahoo.com
  A comprehensive link for campaign news and information.

The Electoral System

- **Federal Election Commission**
  http://www.fec.gov
  Easily accessible data on election turnout, voting, and money.
- **National Archives and Records Administration;**
  Office of the Federal Register
  http://www.archives.gov/federal_register/electoral_college
  You can access federal laws and presidential documents on this site as well as statistics on past presidential elections and information on the Electoral College.
- **The White House**
  http://www.whitehouse.gov
  Provides information on the activities of the president and vice president: what they say, who they meet, and their positions on current issues.

The Florida Vote Controversy

- **The Supreme Court**
  http://www.supremecourtus.gov
  Summarizes the petitions, arguments, and opinions in the Florida election dispute of 2000.
- **NORC-Florida Ballots Project**
  http://www.norc.org
  Provides information about the news organization project to recount all the disputed votes in Florida after the election.

EXERCISES

1. Get up-to-speed on the Electoral College by accessing and reviewing "A Procedural Guide to the Electoral College" at the National Archives site, <http://www.archives.gov>. On this site, go to the Federal Register, and access U.S. Electoral College; then answer the question, to what extent do the procedures really matter?

2. Contrast the 1876 and 2000 electoral vote controversies. First read about the 1876 crisis by accessing *HarpWeek* at <http://elections.harpweek.com/controversy>. This site notes the parallels between the two disputed elections as well as the plan that was designed in 1876 to settle that dispute. Next go to a source that contains a wealth of information about the Florida debacle such as Yahoo, <http://yahoo.com>, and search for the 2000 presidential election. Find articles on the Florida election controversy. Compare the legal/partisan issues in the two cases, the plans to resolve them, and the parties' and public's reaction to these plans. Do either of these controversies call into question the Electoral College system?

SELECTED READING

Abbot, David W., and James P. Levine. *Wrong Winner: The Coming Debacle in the Electoral College.* New York: Praeger, 1991.

Berns, Walter, ed. *After the People Vote: A Guide to the Electoral College,* rev. ed. Washington, D.C.: American Enterprise Institute, 1992.

———. "Third Party Candidates Face a High Hurdle in the Electoral College." *American Enterprise* (January/February 1996): 48–49.

Best, Judith. *The Choice of the People? Debating the Electoral College.* Lanham, Md.: Rowman & Littlefield, 1996.

Bickel, Alexander M. *Reform and Continuity: The Electoral College, the Convention, and the Party System.* New York: Harper & Row, 1971.

Brunell, Thomas, and Bernard Grofman, "The 1992 and 1996 Presidential Elections: Whatever Happened to the Republican Electoral College Lock?" *Presidential Studies Quarterly* (Winter 1997): 134–138.

Destler, I. M. "The Myth of the Electoral College Lock." *PS* (September 1996): 189–193.

Glennon, Michael J. *When No Majority Rules: The Electoral College and Presidential Succession.* Washington D.C.: Congressional Quarterly, 1993.

Hardaway, Robert M. *The Electoral College and the Constitution: The Case for Preserving Federalism.* Westport, Conn.: Praeger, 1994.

Longley, Lawrence D., and James D. Dana Jr. "The Biases of the Electoral College in the 1990s." *Polity* 25 (Fall 1992): 123–145.

———, and Neal R. Peirce. *The Electoral College Primer.* New Haven, Conn.: Yale University Press, 1996.

Rabinowitz, George, and Stuart Elaine MacDonald, "The Power of the States in U.S. Presidential Elections." *American Political Science Review* 80 (March 1986): 65–87.

Roseboom, Eugene H. *A History of Presidential Elections.* New York: Macmillan, 1957.

Schumaker, Paul D., and Burdett A. Loomis, eds. *Choosing a President.* New York: Chatham House, 2002.

Smith, Eric R. A. N., and Peverill Squire. "Direct Election of the President and the Power of the States." *Western Political Quarterly* 40 (March 1987): 29–44.

United States Senate, Committee on the Judiciary. *The Electoral College and Direct Election.* Hearings, 95th Cong., 1st sess. Washington, D.C.: Government Printing Office, 1977.

————. *Direct Popular Election of the President and Vice President of the United States.* Hearings, 95th Cong., 1st sess. Washington, D.C.: Government Printing Office, 1979.

NOTES

1. Gouverneur Morris, *Records of the Federal Convention,* ed. Max Farrand (New Haven, Conn.: Yale University Press, 1921), 2, 33.
2. The first proposal for direct election was introduced in a very timid fashion by James Wilson, delegate from Pennsylvania. James Madison's *Journal* describes Wilson's presentation as follows: "Mr. Wilson said he was almost unwilling to declare the mode which he wished to take place, being apprehensive that it might appear chimerical. He would say however at least that in theory he was for an election by the people; Experience, particularly in N. York & Massts, shewed that an election of the first magistrate by the people at large, was both convenient & successful mode." Farrand, *Records of the Federal Convention,* vol. I, 68.
3. So great was the sectional rivalry, so parochial the country, so limited the number of people with national reputations, that it was feared electors would tend to vote primarily for those from their own states. To prevent the same states, particularly the largest ones, from exercising undue influence in the selection of both the president and vice president, this provision was included. It remains in effect today.
4. George Mason declared, "Nineteen times out of twenty, the President would be chosen by the Senate." Farrand, *Records of the Federal Convention,* vol. II, 500. The original proposal of the Committee on Unfinished Business was that the Senate should select the president. The delegates substituted the House of Representatives, fearing that the Senate was too powerful with its appointment and treaty-making powers. The principle of equal state representation was retained. Choosing the president is the only occasion on which the House votes by state.
5. Thomas R. Marshall, *Presidential Nominations in a Reform Age* (New York: Praeger, 1981), 19.
6. Quoted in Neal R. Peirce and Lawrence D. Longley, *The People's President* (New Haven, Conn.: Yale University Press, 1981), 36.
7. Marshall, *Presidential Nominations,* 20.
8. Ibid., 21.
9. Louis Maisel and Gerald J. Lieberman, "The Impact of Electoral Rules on Primary Elections: The Democratic Presidential Primaries in 1976," in *The Impact of the Electoral Process,* ed. Louis Maisel and Joseph Cooper (Beverly Hills, Calif.: Sage, 1977), 68.
10. Until the passage of the Twentieth Amendment, which made January 3 the date when members of Congress took their oaths of office and convened, it was the second session of the preelection Congress that convened after the election. This made it a lame-duck session.
11. Quoted in Lucius Wilmerding, *The Electoral College* (New Brunswick, N.J.: Rutgers University Press, 1953), 32.
12. There were 106 members of the House (58 Federalists and 48 Republicans). On the first ballot, the vote of those present was for Burr, 53-51.

13. In those days being secretary of state was considered a stepping-stone to the presidency. With the exception of Washington and John Adams, all the people who became president prior to Andrew Jackson had first held this position.

14. Peirce and Longley, *People's President*, 51.

15. Marquis James, *The Life of Andrew Jackson* (Indianapolis: Bobbs-Merrill, 1938), 439.

16. He captured the majority of electoral votes in two of these states because the electors were chosen on a district rather than statewide basis. William R. Keech, "Background Paper," in *Winner Take All: Report of the Twentieth Century Fund Task Force on Reform of the Presidential Election Process* (New York: Holmes & Meier, 1978), 50.

17. The act that created the commission specified that its decision would be final unless overturned by both houses of Congress. The House of Representatives, controlled by the Democrats, opposed every one of the commission's findings. The Republican Senate, however, concurred. A Democratic filibuster in the Senate was averted by Hayes's promise of concessions to the South, including the withdrawal of federal troops. Tilden could have challenged the findings in court but chose not to do so.

18. Richard M. Scammon and Alice V. McGillivray, *America Votes 12* (Washington, D.C.: Congressional Quarterly, 1977), 15.

19. In Alabama, slates of electors ran against one another without the names of the presidential candidates appearing on the ballot. The Democratic slate included six unpledged electors and five loyalists. All were elected. The unpledged electors voted for Senator Harry Byrd of Virginia, while the loyalists stayed with the Kennedy–Johnson ticket. In Mississippi, all eight Democratic electors voted for Byrd.

20. He came in second in two states in 1992, Maine and Utah. In 1996, Perot did not come in second in any state.

21. The actual vote tabulation in this county provided some evidence of the confusion. The Buchanan vote was larger in Palm Beach than in any other Florida county. Palm Beach has a large elderly Jewish population unlikely to have supported Buchanan. Moreover, Palm Beach had a larger percentage of ballots in which no presidential vote was recorded than all but two of the sixty-seven counties in the state.

22. At the time of the court-imposed deadline, only one county, Broward, had submitted a recount that moved Gore to within 537 votes of Bush. Palm Beach County was unable to get its votes in by the 5:00 PM deadline. That county submitted its revised tabulation several hours later, too late to be included in the revised state vote count. Still trailing his Republican opponent, Gore went back to state court to seek a court order forcing an immediate hand count in Miami-Dade, but a Florida appeals court refused to do so as did the state supreme court. These refusals prompted Gore to return to state court to ask for a court order to count the disputed ballots in Miami-Dade and include the revised vote totals from Palm Beach that had been completed after the deadline.

23. The judge held that Gore's attorneys had not provided statistical evidence to demonstrate the *probability*, not a mere *possibility*, that the results of the Florida election would be different if a hand count were to occur and be included in the vote totals.

24. Center for Media and Public Affairs, "Media Feeding Frenzy in Florida," press release, November 22, 2000.

25. Joan Shorenstein Center on the Press, Politics, and Public Policy, Harvard University, "As Election Contest Drags on, Americans' Dissatisfaction Grows," press release, December 7, 2000, <http://www.vanishingvoter.org>.

26. David W. Moore, "One Year after Election, Controversy over Winner Appears Less Serious," Gallup News Service, press release, November 6, 2001, <http://www.gallup.com>.

27. Ibid.

28. Dan Keating and Dan Balz, "Florida Recounts Would Have Favored Bush," *Washington Post,* November 12, 2001, <http://www.washingtonpost.com/wp-dyn/articles/A12623-2001nov11.html>.

29. Thomas Brunell and Bernard Grofman, "The 1992 and 1996 Presidential Elections: Whatever Happened to the Republican Electoral College Lock?" *Presidential Studies Quarterly* (Winter 1997): 134–138.

30. I. M. Destler, "The Myth of the Electoral Lock," *PS* (September 1996): 491.

31. Theoretically, two states, Maine and Nebraska, will not always vote as a bloc because they do not select all their electors on an at-large basis. Two are chosen at large and the remaining ones are elected in each of the states' congressional districts. Since these states have enacted their electoral laws, however, they have cast all their electoral votes for the same candidate.

32. Lawrence D. Longley and James D. Dana Jr., "The Biases of the Electoral College in the 1990s," *Polity* 25 (Fall 1992): 140–145.

33. Federal Election Commission, "FEC Announces 2000 Presidential Spending Limits," press release, March 1, 2000, 2–3.

34. Longley and Dana, "The Biases of the Electoral College in the 1990s," 134. There are two other, less obvious, biases in the Electoral College. The distribution of electoral votes is calculated on the basis of the census, which occurs every ten years. Thus, the college does not mirror population shifts within this period. Nor does it take into account the number of people who actually cast ballots. It is a state's population, not its turnout, that determines the number of electoral votes it receives, over and above the automatic three.

35. James C. Garand and T. Wayne Parent, "Representation, Swing, and Bias in U.S. Presidential Elections, 1872–1988," *American Journal of Political Science* 35 (November 1991): 1024, 1029.

36. John E. Berthoud, "The Electoral Lock Thesis: The Weighting Bias Component," *PS* (June 1997): 189–193.

2 | CAMPAIGN FINANCE

INTRODUCTION

Running for president is very expensive. In the 1999–2000 election cycle, more than $3 billion was spent on federal elections. Of that amount, a little over $600 million was expended by or on the presidential campaigns. The parties spent or distributed over $1.1 billion, with interest groups and congressional races accounting for the remainder.[1]

The magnitude of these expenditures poses serious problems for presidential candidates, who must raise considerable sums during the preconvention struggle, closely monitor their expenses, make important allocation decisions, and conform to the intricacies of finance laws during both the nomination and general election campaigns, as well as answer to party leaders who must also solicit, distribute, and spend millions on behalf of their candidates for national office. Moreover, such large expenditures raise important issues for a democratic selection process. This chapter explores some of these problems and those issues.

The chapter is organized into five sections. The first details the costs of presidential campaigns, paying particular attention to the increase in expenditures since 1960. The next section looks briefly at the contributors, the size of their gifts, and the implications of large donations for a democratic election. What happens when the individual's right to give conflicts with the majority's desire to set limits and have its elected representatives level the playing field? Who prevails? Congressional attempts to limit contributions, control spending, and subsidize elections are discussed in the third section. The fourth section examines the impact of campaign finance laws on revenues and expenditures in presidential campaigns and on the party system. In the final section, the relationship between campaign spending and electoral success is explored. Can money buy elections? Have the big spenders been the big winners?

THE COSTS OF CAMPAIGNING

Candidates have always spent money in their quest for the presidency, but it was not until they began to campaign personally across the country that these costs rose sharply. In 1860, Abraham Lincoln spent an estimated $100,000. By the turn of the century, those costs had escalated. William McKinley reputedly raised and spent between $6 and $7 million in his 1896 campaign for the presidency compared to William Jennings Bryan's paltry $650,000.

With the advent of the electronic campaign following World War II, campaign costs soared once again. In 1960, John Kennedy and Richard Nixon each spent a hundred times the amount Lincoln spent one hundred years earlier. In the twelve years following the 1960 general election, expenditures increased from about $20 million to over $90 million, an increase that far outstripped the inflation rate during that period. Table 2–1 lists the costs of the major party candidates in presidential elections from 1860 to 1972, the last general election in which campaign spending by major party candidates was unrestricted.

Prenomination costs have risen even more rapidly than those in the general election (see Table 2–2). Until the 1960s, large expenditures were the exception, not the rule, for gaining the party's nomination. General Leonard Wood spent an estimated $2 million in an unsuccessful quest to head the Republican ticket in 1920. The contest between General Dwight D. Eisenhower and Senator Robert A. Taft in 1952 cost about $5 million, a total that was not exceeded until 1964, when Nelson Rockefeller and Barry Goldwater together spent approximately twice that amount.

Since 1968, preconvention expenditures have generally exceeded those in the general election. The increasing numbers of primaries, caucuses, and candidates, combined with the willingness of several recent hopefuls to forego federal matching grants and the expenditure limits that go with these funds, have been largely responsible for the rise. In the 1950s, the preconvention contests were optional; since the 1970s, they have been mandatory. Even incumbent presidents may have to enter them, and they must spend money even when they are not challenged. In 1984, the Reagan campaign committee spent almost $28 million during the nomination period, much of it on voter registration drives for the general election; in 1992, George H. W. Bush spent over $27 million in defeating Pat Buchanan, a conservative newspaper columnist who had not previously sought public office. In 1996, Bill Clinton spent almost $35 million running unopposed for the Democratic nomination. The record for contributions and expenditures was set four years later by George W. Bush who raised $94.5 million and spent $89.1 million in his successful quest for the Republican presidential.[2]

Why is it so expensive to run for president today? It costs money to raise money, something candidates have to do during the precandidacy phase, during the phase when they are officially seeking their party's nomination, and increasingly,

TABLE 2–1 🏆

COSTS OF PRESIDENTIAL GENERAL ELECTIONS, MAJOR PARTY CANDIDATES, 1860–1972

Year	Democrats		Republicans	
1860	Stephen Douglas	$50,000	Abraham Lincoln*	$100,000
1864	George McClellan	50,000	Abraham Lincoln*	125,000
1868	Horatio Seymour	75,000	Ulysses Grant*	150,000
1872	Horace Greeley	50,000	Ulysses Grant*	250,000
1876	Samuel Tilden	900,000	Rutherford Hayes*	950,000
1880	Winfield Hancock	335,000	James Garfield*	1,100,000
1884	Grover Cleveland*	1,400,000	James Blaine	1,300,000
1888	Grover Cleveland	855,000	Benjamin Harrison*	1,350,000
1892	Grover Cleveland*	2,350,000	Benjamin Harrison	1,700,000
1896	William Jennings Bryan	675,000	William McKinley*	3,350,000
1900	William Jennings Bryan	425,000	William McKinley*	3,000,000
1904	Alton Parker	700,000	Theodore Roosevelt*	2,096,000
1908	William Jennings Bryan	629,341	William Taft*	1,655,518
1912	Woodrow Wilson*	1,134,848	William Taft	1,071,549
1916	Woodrow Wilson*	2,284,950	Charles Evans Hughes	2,441,565
1920	James Cox	1,470,371	Warren Harding*	5,417,501
1924	John Davis	1,108,836	Calvin Coolidge*	4,020,478
1928	Alfred Smith	5,342,350	Herbert Hoover*	6,256,111
1932	Franklin Roosevelt*	2,245,975	Herbert Hoover	2,900,052
1936	Franklin Roosevelt*	5,194,751	Alfred Landon	8,892,972
1940	Franklin Roosevelt*	2,783,654	Wendell Willkie	3,451,310
1944	Franklin Roosevelt*	2,169,077	Thomas Dewey	2,828,652
1948	Harry Truman*	2,736,334	Thomas Dewey	2,127,296
1952	Adlai Stevenson	5,032,926	Dwight Eisenhower*	6,608,623
1956	Adlai Stevenson	5,106,651	Dwight Eisenhower*	7,778,702
1960	John Kennedy*	9,797,000	Richard Nixon	10,128,000
1964	Lyndon Johnson*	8,757,000	Barry Goldwater	16,026,000
1968†	Hubert Humphrey	11,594,000	Richard Nixon*	25,042,000
1972	George McGovern	30,000,000	Richard Nixon*	61,400,000

* Indicates winner.

† George Wallace spent an estimated $7 million as the candidate of the American Independent Party in 1968.

Source: Data based on *Financing Politics: Money, Elections, and Political Reform,* 3e, by Herbert E. Alexander. Copyright © 1984 by Congressional Quarterly, Inc.

TABLE 2–2 🏵

COSTS OF PRESIDENTIAL NOMINATIONS, 1964–2000 (IN MILLIONS OF DOLLARS)

Year	Democrats	Republicans
1964	(uncontested)	$10.0
1968	$25.0	20.0
1972	33.1	*
1976	40.7	26.1
1980	41.7	86.1
1984	107.7	28.0
1988	94.0	114.6
1992	66.0[†]	51.0
1996	46.1	187.0
2000	95.9	232.7

* During a primary in which Richard M. Nixon's renomination was virtually assured, Representative John M. Ashbrook spent $740,000 and Representative Paul N. McCloskey spent $550,000 in challenging Nixon.

[†] Estimates based on Alexander and Corrado, *Financing the 1992 Elections*, Tables 2–1 and 2–4.

Sources: 1964–1972, Herbert E. Alexander, *Financing Politics* (Washington, D.C.: Congressional Quarterly, 1976), 45–47; 1976–1984, Federal Election Commission, "Reports on Financial Activity, 1987–88," *Presidential Pre-Nomination Campaigns* (August 1989), Table A–7, 10; Herbert E. Alexander, "Financing the Presidential Elections" (paper presented at the Institute for Political Studies in Tokyo, Japan, September 8–10, 1989), 4, 10; Herbert E. Alexander and Anthony Corrado, *Financing the 1992 Elections* (Armonk, N.Y.: Sharpe, 1995); Federal Election Commission, "Presidential Campaign Disbursements" (inception through July 31, 2000). 1964–1972 based on data from *Financing Politics: Money, Elections, and Political Reform*, 3e, by Herbert E. Alexander, 45–47. Copyright © 1984 by Congressional Quarterly, Inc. 1992 data based on Tables 2–1 and 2–4 in *Financing the 1992 Election* by Herbert E. Alexander and Anthony Corrado. Copyright © 1995 by M. E. Sharpe, Inc. Reprinted with permission of the publishers.

during the presidential election as well. Moreover, candidates are now forced to campaign simultaneously in several states for several months. To do so, they need to use the electronic media, radio, and television. That too is costly.

In contrast, when electioneering was conducted within a highly partisan press environment before the Civil War, there were few expenses other than for the occasional biography and campaign pamphlet printed by the party and sold to the public at less than cost. With the advent of more active public campaigning toward the middle of the nineteenth century, candidate organizations turned to buttons, billboards, banners, and pictures to symbolize and illustrate their campaigns. By the beginning of the twentieth century, the cost of this type of advertising in each election exceeded $150,000, a lot of money then but a minuscule amount by contemporary standards.[3]

In 1924, radio was employed for the first time in presidential campaigns. The Republicans spent approximately $120,000 that year, whereas the Democrats spent only $40,000.[4] Four years later, however, the two parties together spent more than $1 million. Radio expenses continued to equal or exceed a million dollars per election for the next twenty years.[5]

Television emerged as a vehicle for presidential campaigning in 1952. Both national party conventions were broadcast on television as well as radio. Although there were only 19 million television sets in the United States at that time, almost one-third of the Americans were regular television viewers.

The number of households with television sets rose dramatically over the next four years. By 1956, an estimated 71 percent had television, and by 1968 the figure was close to 95 percent; today it exceeds 99 percent, with most homes having two or more sets. Cable and satellite subscribers have increased to more than two out of three households.

The first commercials for presidential candidates appeared in 1952. They became regular fare thereafter, contributing substantially to campaign costs. Film biographies, interview shows, political rallies, town meetings, and election eve telethons have all been seen with increasing frequency.

In 1948, no money was spent on television by either party's candidate. Twenty years later, $13 million was expended for television advertising, approximately one-fourth of the total cost of the campaign. By 2000, television expenses for the presidential race alone exceeded $205 million and $578 million when the congressional elections were included.[6]

The use of other modern technology, polling and focus groups, computerized mailings, and robot telephoning has also contributed to the explosion in costs. Take fund-raising for example. The need for private funds combined with the declining proportion of givers (only about 6 percent of the population) has forced candidates to devote considerable time, effort, and funds to fund-raising. An additional 20 percent, over and above what federally subsidized candidates are permitted to spend in the quest for their party's presidential nomination, is allocated for fund-raising. In 2000 alone, the major parties spent $70 million raising almost $500 million in so-called soft money (see pages 53–55).[7]

Three major issues arise from the problems of large expenditures. One pertains to the donors. Who pays, how much can they give, and what do they get for their money? A second relates to the costs. Are they too high, and can they be controlled without impinging on First Amendment freedoms? The third concerns the impact of spending on the election itself. To what extent does it improve a candidate's chances of winning? The next section turns to the first of these questions—private sources of financial support and attempts to regulate them.

THE SOURCES OF SUPPORT

Throughout most of U. S. electoral history, parties and candidates have depended on large contributions. In the midst of the industrial boom at the end of the nineteenth century, the Republicans were able to count on the support of the Astors, Harrimans, and Vanderbilts; while the Democrats looked to financier August Belmont (American representative of the Rothschild banking interests) and inventor-industrialist Cyrus McCormick. Corporations, banks, and life insurance companies soon became prime targets of party fund-raisers. The most notorious and probably most adroit fund-raiser of this period was Mark Hanna. A leading official of the Republican Party, Hanna owed most of his influence to his ability to obtain substantial political contributions. He set quotas, personally assessing the amount that businesses and corporations should give. In 1896, and again in 1900, he was able to obtain contributions of $250,000 from Standard Oil. Theodore Roosevelt personally ordered the return of some of the Standard Oil money in 1904 but accepted large gifts from magnates E. H. Harriman and Henry C. Frick. Roosevelt's trust-busting activities during his presidency led Frick to remark, "We bought the son of a bitch and then he did not stay bought."[8]

Sizable private gifts remained the principal source of party and candidate support until the mid-1970s. In 1972, Richard Nixon and George McGovern raised an estimated $27 million from fewer than two hundred individual contributors.[9] In general, the Republicans benefited more than the Democrats from wealthy contributors, known in the campaign vernacular as "fat cats." Only in 1964 was a Democrat, incumbent president Lyndon B. Johnson who enjoyed a large lead in the preelection polls, able to raise more money from large donors than his Republican opponent, Barry Goldwater, although Bill Clinton came close to doing so in 1996.

The reluctance of regular Republican contributors to support the Goldwater candidacy forced his organization to appeal to thousands of potential supporters through direct mail. The success of this effort, raising $5.8 million from approximately 651,000 people, showed the potential of a popular appeal for funds and shattered what had been an unwritten "rule" of politics that money could not be raised through the mail. In 1968, Alabama Governor George Wallace, running as a third-party candidate, solicited the bulk of his funds in this fashion as have other lesser-known candidates since then.

Despite the use of mass mailings and party telethons to broaden the base of political contributors in the 1960s, dependence on large donors continued. In 1964, more than $2 million was raised in contributions of $10,000 or more. Eight years later, approximately $51 million was collected in gifts of this size or larger. Some gifts were in the million-dollar range.

The magnitude of these contributions, combined with the heavy-handed tactics of the Nixon fund-raisers in 1971–72, brought into sharp focus the difficulty of maintaining a democratic selection process that was dependent on private funding.[10] Reliance on large contributors who did not wish to be identified, the inequality of funding between parties and candidates, and the high cost of campaigning, especially in the mass media, all raised serious issues. Were there assumptions implicit in giving and receiving? Could elected officials be responsive to individual benefactors and to the general public at the same time? Put another way, did the need to obtain large contributors and keep them "happy" affect decision making in a manner that was inconsistent with the tenets of a democratic society that all people have equal influence on the selection of and access to public officials? Did the high cost of campaigning, in and of itself, eliminate otherwise qualified candidates from running? Were certain political parties, interest groups, or individuals consistently advantaged or disadvantaged by the distribution of funding? Had the presidency become an office that only the wealthy could afford, or that only those with wealthy supporters could seek?

FINANCE LEGISLATION

Reacting to these issues, Congress in the 1970s enacted far-reaching legislation designed to reduce dependence on major donors who contribute large amounts of money, discourage illegal contributions, broaden the base of public support, and control escalating costs at the presidential level. Additionally, the Democratic Congress that passed these laws wanted to equalize the funds available to the Republican and Democratic nominees. Finally, the legislation was designed to buttress the two-party system, making it more difficult for minor candidates to challenge the major parties' nominees for elective office successfully.

One law, the Federal Election Campaign Act of 1971 (FECA), set ceilings on the amount of money presidential and vice presidential candidates and their families could contribute to their own campaigns.[11] It allowed unions and corporations, which had been prohibited from contributing, to form political action committees (PACs), consisting of their members, employees, and stockholders, to solicit voluntary contributions to be given to candidates or parties or to fund the group's election activities. The FECA also established procedures for public disclosure of all contributions over a certain amount.

A second statute, the Revenue Act of 1971, created tax credits and deductions to encourage private contributions. It also provided the basis for public funding by creating a presidential election campaign fund. Financed by an income tax checkoff provision, the fund initially allowed a taxpayer to designate one dollar of federal income taxes to a special presidential election account.

These laws began a period of federal government regulation of national elections. The history of that regulation is a history of good intentions built on political compromise but marred by unintended consequences of the legislation and its implementation, caused by candidates and parties circumventing the letter and spirit of the law to gain electoral advantage.

Partisan compromises in the enactment of campaign finance legislation were evident from the outset. Although the original funding provision was enacted in 1971, it did not go into effect until the 1976 presidential election. Most Republicans, including President Nixon, had opposed the policy of government financial support and regulation. In addition to conflicting with their general ideological position that the national government's role in the conduct of elections be limited, it offset their party's traditional fund-raising advantage. President Nixon was persuaded to sign the bill, however, after Democrats agreed to delay the effective start of the bill until after his likely reelection.[12]

The 1972 election was marked by heavy-handed fund-raising tactics. The Nixon campaign in that election cycle raised more than any other previous campaign had for a presidential election. In addition to aggressive solicitation, the expenditures of the Nixon reelection effort also became an issue, albeit after the election. Investigative reporting by the *Washington Post* and hearings conducted by a Senate committee revealed that the Committee to Reelect the President, referred to by Nixon's opponents as CREEP, had spent some of its funds on "dirty tricks" and other unethical and illegal activities, such as the break-in at the Democratic National Committee's headquarters at the Watergate office building. These revelations aroused public ire and created the incentive for a Democratic Congress to enact new and even more stringent legislation.

The FECA was amended to include public disclosure provisions, contribution ceilings for individuals and groups, spending limits for the campaigns, federal subsidies for major party candidates in the nomination process, and complete funding for them in the general election. The law also restricted the amount candidates could contribute to their own campaign and the amount that others could spend independently on their behalf. Finally, it established a six-person commission, the Federal Election Commission (FEC), to implement and enforce the law.

The 1974 amendments were highly controversial. Critics immediately charged a federal giveaway, a raid on the treasury. Opponents of the legislation also argued that the limits on contributions and spending violated the constitutionally guaranteed right to freedom of speech, that the funding provisions unfairly discriminated against third-party and independent candidates, and that Congress' appointment of some of the commissioners violated the separation of powers.

In the landmark decision of *Buckley v. Valeo* (424 U.S. 1, 1976), the Supreme Court upheld the right of Congress to regulate campaign expenditures but negated the overall limits on spending by individuals and nonparty groups and the appointment by Congress of four of the six election commissioners. The majority opinion contended that by placing restrictions on the amount of money a person or organization could spend during a campaign, the law directly and substantially restrained freedom of speech, a freedom protected by the First Amendment to the Constitution. The Supreme Court did allow limits on contributions to candidates' campaigns, however, and limits on expenditures of those candidates who accepted public funds but not those who refused these funds. In doing so, the justices acknowledged that large, often secret, contributions and rapidly increasingly expenditures did pose problems for a democracy, problems that Congress could address.

The Court's decision required that the election law be amended once again. It took Congress several months to do so. In the spring of 1976, during the presidential primaries of that year, amendments were enacted that continued public funding of the presidential nomination and election campaigns, based on a figure of $10 million in 1974 to be adjusted for inflation, but did so on a voluntary basis. Candidates did not have to accept government funds, but if they did, they were limited in how much they and others could contribute to their own campaigns and how much those campaigns could spend. The Federal Election Commission was reconstituted with all six members to be nominated by the president and appointed subject to the advice and consent of the Senate. The law required that three commissioners be Democrats and three be Republicans to ensure that the Commission would be fair to both major parties.

In 1979, additional amendments to the FECA were passed. Designed to reduce the reporting requirements of the law, these amendments raised the minimum contribution and expenditure that had to be filed from $100 to $200. To encourage voluntary activities and higher voter turnout, they also permitted party committees to raise and spend unlimited amounts of money on party-building activities such as on registration and getting out the vote.[13]

Known as the *soft money* provision, this amendment created a gigantic loophole in the law. It permitted, even encouraged, the major parties to solicit large contributions and distribute the money to their state and local affiliates as they saw fit. It was not until 1992 that the FEC imposed reporting requirements on this soft money.

The amendments to the FECA also increased the base grant for nominating conventions of the major parties to $3 million in 1979 and $4 million in 1984.

The next amendment to the law was enacted in 1993. The fund used to subsidize candidates for their party's presidential nomination and provide general election grants had been shrinking. The failure to tie the amount of money taxpayers could designate for the fund to inflation, the decline in the percentage of taxpayers making such a designation, and the increasing number of candidates vying for party nominations all contributed to the shortfall that was expected to only get worse in the years ahead. To rectify the problem, Congress increased the income tax checkoff from $1 to $3, a little less than the cost-of-living adjustment since the provision originally went into effect. However, the portion of taxpayers designating a payment to the fund had fallen significantly from its high of 28.7 percent in 1980 to about 12 percent today.

A new problem of a very different magnitude emerged in 1996—the exploitation of the soft money loophole to circumvent the law's intended contribution and expenditure limits. This exploitation resulted from a very creative interpretation of the 1979 amendments by the parties and, subsequently, by the FEC and the courts. Box 2–1 describes the beginnings of the soft money debacle and the Democratic fund-raising controversy that accompanied it.

Favorable FEC rulings and judicial interpretations provided the parties with a legal basis for their actions, and in the process, effectively scuttled the contribution and spending limits on the presidential candidates. Table 2–3 documents the exponential increase in soft money contributions and expenses during the 1990s and the 2000 presidential election.

Although congressional hearings into the Democratic fund-raising scandal were conducted by the Republican-controlled Congress, no new laws were passed to rectify the problems that had developed. As a consequence, residual anger over the campaign finance situation directed toward politicians and their parties, both Democrat and Republican, remained. The issue resurfaced during the 2000

BOX 2–1 🌿

EXPLOITING THE SOFT MONEY LOOPHOLE

In 1995, President Clinton and his advisers began planning for his reelection campaign. The strategy was to position Clinton as a centrist in the eyes of the electorate by airing a series of advertisements that touted his record and favorably contrasted it with that of the congressional Republicans. The ad campaign was costly. Two million dollars was spent in the first three months alone during the summer of 1995.

Such a large expenditure of funds raised concerns within the Clinton camp. Would there be sufficient money in the campaign to handle a challenge for the Democratic nomination if one developed and still respond to a strong Republican opponent in the general election?

The president and his principal adviser, Dick Morris, wanted to continue the advertising; the president's White House aides were less enthusiastic given the high price tag and the financial risks involved. The dilemma, how to continue the ads without draining the campaign's coffers, was resolved in September 1995 by Harold Ickes, deputy White House chief of staff, principal political coordinator, and a critic of Clinton's early advertising expenditures. Since the commercials were policy-oriented and did not specifically and directly urge the president's reelection, Ickes argued that the Democratic Party could pay for the ads with soft money which the president would help raise. Lawyers for the party agreed.

What followed was a frantic, no-holds-barred, fund-raising effort. The Democrats raised and spent more than they ever had. But in doing so, the party did not take the time to screen the contributions to make sure that they were legal, completely voluntary, and given by respectable donors who were American citizens or legal residents and who would not directly benefit from policy decisions of the administration. The failure to screen donors embarrassed the party and forced it to return some of the money after the news media reported that contributions had been received from foreign nationals and people with criminal backgrounds.

The president and the vice president actively encouraged and participated in these fund-raising efforts. The largest donors, those in the $50,000 to $100,000+ category, were treated to small dinners with the president at expensive Washington hotels, sleepovers in the Lincoln bedroom in the White House, state dinners with world leaders, rounds of golf with Clinton, and even trips on Air Force One. Somewhat smaller contributors were rewarded with dinners with the vice president, VIP treatment at Democratic Party functions such as its 1996 nominating convention, meetings with cabinet officials, and coffee hours with the president in the White House. Corporate executives were invited to join the commerce secretary on official U.S. trade missions abroad.

Naturally, Republicans were outraged by these activities, particularly the use of public office for partisan purposes. Their party officials and elected leadership protested, and congressional investigations followed, but to no avail. In the end, the Republicans resorted to the same tactics as the Democrats, using their control of Congress as leverage to raise their own soft money. They eventually netted more of it than did the Democrats.

Pandora's box had been opened.

TABLE 2–3 🌿

THE SOFT MONEY EXPLOSION (IN MILLIONS), 1992–2000

	Democrats		Republicans	
Year	Revenue	Expenditure	Revenue	Expenditure
1992	____	36.3 (19%)*	____	49.8 (16%)
1996	123.9	121.8 (37)	138.2	149.7 (26)
2000	245.2	244.9 (47)	249.9	252.8 (35)

*Indicates percentages of total campaign expenditures for the party from soft money.

Source: Federal Election Commission, "FEC Reports Increase in Party Fundraising for 2000," May 15, 2001.

nomination campaign largely as a consequence of John McCain's and Bill Bradley's attempts to highlight the finance issue as evidence of the special interest politics in America. Although McCain's bid for the Republican nomination and Bradley's for the Democratic failed, the campaign finance issue put both Bush and Gore on the defensive and led to cries for reform. In April 2001, the Senate enacted legislation, known as the McCain–Feingold bill, to close the soft money loophole which presidential candidates of the major parties had used to circumvent the law and to restrict the use of the principal instrument to which soft money had been applied, issue advocacy advertising. Nine months later the House of Representatives followed suit and in March 2002, the Bipartisan Campaign Reform Act was passed.

The new law raised individual and overall contribution limits to candidates and parties, banned soft money solicitation and distribution by the national parties, and restricted the use of issue advocacy ads in which candidates were named to periods that exceeded thirty days before a primary and sixty days before the general election. Box 2–2 lists the new contribution limits.

Opponents of the law immediately took their case to court. Such disparate groups as the National Rifle Association, the American Civil Liberties Union, and the Christian Coalition argued that the ban on issue advocacy advertising in which candidates were mentioned by name thirty days or less before the primary and sixty days or less before the general election violated the First Amendment's protection of freedom of speech and freedom of the press. The Republican National Committee claimed that the prohibition on soft money violated the state parties' right to raise money to organize and mobilize voters in all elections in which state representatives were selected. In contrast, groups representing poorer Americans argued that the increase in amount of money that could be contributed by individuals violated their rights under the Fifth Amendment's equal protection clause.

On the other side, supporting the law, were the bill's sponsors, the FEC, Common Cause and other public interest groups, and twenty-one state attorneys general who saw no violation of states' rights in the new federal legislation.

There also were disputes about how the law should be implemented. The FEC rejected a series of tough new regulations that would have prevented national

BOX 2–2 ☙

Contribution Limits (Before and After McCain–Feingold)

	To any candidate or candidate committee (per election*)	To any national party committee (per year)	To any PAC, state/local party, or other political committee (per year)	Aggregate total
Individual can give:†	*Old law:* $1,000	$20,000	$5,000	$25,000 per year
	New law: $2,000, subject to the aggregate limit‡	$25,000 per party committee, subject to the aggregate limit	°$10,000 to each state or local party committee °$5,000 to each PAC or other political committee, subject to the aggregate limit	°$95,000 per two-year election cycle as follows: °$37,500 per cycle to candidates; and °$57,500 per cycle to all national party committees and PACs ($20,000 to $57,500 per cycle to all national party committees, and a maximum $37,500 per cycle to PACs)
Multicandidate committee can give:§	*Old law:* $5,000	$15,000	$5,000	No limit
	New law: Same	Same	Same	Same
Other political committee can give:	*Old law:* $1,000	$20,000	$5,000	No Limit
	New law: Same	Same	Same	Same

* Primary and general elections count as separate elections.

† Individual contribution limits under the new law will be indexed for inflation.

‡ Individual contribution limits under the new law are higher to candidates facing wealthy opponents financing their own election.

§ Multicandidate committees are those with more than fifty contributors, that have been registered for at least six months, and (with the exception of state party committees) have made contributions to five or more federal candidates.

Source: The Center for Responsive Politics, <http://www.opensecrets.org/basics/law/index.asp>.

parties, federal candidates, and states from circumventing the letter and spirit of the law. The FEC's new rules permit state parties to solicit and spend soft money on activities, including mass media advertising, that can indirectly impact federal elections such as on voter identification, registration, and get-out-the-vote drives. Leadership PACS (see p. 47) are still allowed to raise large sums as are nonprofit groups, so-called 527s, which are exempt from federal taxation. The 527s have become the organizations of choice by groups that in the past had solicited significant amounts of soft money for the national parties. As long as these organizations are not affiliated with the political parties, they can raise and spend unlimited amounts on issue advocacy. And federal candidates can still appear at state fundraising events as long as they do not directly ask for contributions.

A special three-judge federal panel established to determine the constitutionality of the law delivered a mixed judgment in May 2003, setting the stage for a Supreme Court review of the law prior to the 2004 election. By a 2 to 1 majority, the panel upheld and even broadened the issue advocacy provision of the law. But it also ruled that the national parties could not be prohibited from raising soft money although they could be limited in how they spent it. The court, however, stayed the enforcement of its decision until the Supreme Court considered the case upon appeal.

THE IMPACT OF THE LAW

Campaign finance legislation has had a significant impact on presidential elections. It has affected the base of contributors, the modes of solicitation, and the objects of spending. It has changed the role of the government, modifying the relationship between the party and its nominees, and influencing the strategies and tactics of the campaign.

Revenue

Individual Contributors. One of the most important objectives of the law was to reduce the influence that a small number of major contributors had on the presidential nomination and election. To some extent it has succeeded, particularly during the nomination phase of the process. No longer can candidates depend on a few wealthy friends to finance their quest for their party's nomination. The limit on individual donors ($1,000 per candidate, per election until 2002, $2,000 per candidate, per election thereafter), the $250 ceiling on matching grants, and the eligibility requirements for federal funds have made the solicitation of a large number of contributors absolutely essential, more so now than in the past.

Not only are campaigns increasingly expensive but the purchasing power of today's dollar is also less than one-third of what it was in 1976. Candidates thus need many more donors than they did when the law first went into effect. They also have become increasingly dependent on contributors who give the maximum amount. In 2000, George W. Bush received about three-fourths of his funds from donors who "maxed out."[14] Similarly in the race for the 2004 Democratic nomination, Democratic candidates reported that they received more than half of their initial contributions, during the first quarter of the 2003–2004 election cycle, from donors who gave $1,000 and more than one-third from those who gave the maximum of $2,000.[15]

The emphasis placed on large donors was not accidental. Candidate fundraisers approached their principal sources—law firms, investment banking firms, labor union leaders, and business executives—with the hope that they could obtain "bundled" donations. In some cases, the pressure to give was too intense. Senator John Edwards had to return $10,000 to a law firm when a law clerk indicated to a newspaper reporter that her $2,000 contribution would be reimbursed by one of the partners of the firm.[16]

In addition to gifts from individuals, which are the largest single source of revenues, candidates have found other ways to supplement their campaign funds. They can provide some of their own money. There is no restriction on the amount of their personal funds that can be spent in the years prior to the election, until their candidacy is formally established. At the point of candidacy, a $50,000 personal contribution limit is imposed if a candidate accepts federal funds. There is no personal limit for the candidate who does not accept federal funds. Thus, in 1992, H. Ross Perot was able to spend over $63 million of his own money on his campaign in lieu of accepting government funds. Although he chose to accept federal funds in 1996, and thus was limited to $50,000, he spent more than $8 million of his money to secure the Reform Party nomination, fund its nominating conventions, and get the party on the ballot in all fifty states for the general election. The single largest personal contributor in presidential elections has been Steve Forbes, who spent close to $38 million of his own fortune in 1996 and more than $48 million in 2000 on his unsuccessful attempts to win the Republican nomination.

Borrowing money from financial institutions is also allowed. The law permits candidates to obtain loans (if they can), provided that the terms of payment are clear and that the money is lent in accordance with regular business practices. Most major party candidates borrow money. They have to do so. The increasing number of early primaries and caucuses have forced them to get as much up-front money as soon as possible.[17]

Funds raised but not spent by candidates in their campaigns for other offices, such as for the Senate, House of Representatives, or a state governorship, can be used in their quest for the presidential nomination. John McCain transferred $2 million from his Senate account to fund the initial stages of his 2000 campaign for the Republican nomination. Democratic hopefuls did the same for the 2004 nominations. Both Kerry and Gephardt were able to transfer $2.5 million from their congressional campaign war chests to finance the initial stage of their 2004 primary campaigns.

Although cash contributions are restricted, voluntary goods and services are not. Artists and musicians, in particular, can generate considerable revenue for candidates by offering their time and talent. Concerts, and to a lesser extent art

TABLE 2–4

Prenomination Revenues of Major Party Candidates in 2000 (through July 31, 2000)

Candidate	Federal Matching Funds	Individual Contributions Minus Refunds	PAC Contributions Minus Refunds	Adjusted Other Revenues	Campaign Total
Democratic					
Bradley	$12,462,045	$29,270,589	$0	$409,931	$42,142,565
Gore	$15,317,872	$33,871,206	$0	$ 13,667	$49,202,745
LaRouche	$1,184,372	$3,319,038	$590	$ 1,658	$4,505,658
Total Democrats	$28,964,289	$66,460,833	$590	$425,256	$95,850,968
Republicans					
Alexander	$0	$2,301,747	$80,383	$703,501	$3,085,631
Bauer	$4,632,803	$7,553,317	$6,000	-$55,572	$12,136,548
Bush	$0	$91,331,951	$1,960,060	$1,174,330	$94,466,341
Dole	$0	$5,001,635	$118,292	$7,905	$5,127,832
Forbes	$0	$5,752,150	$0	$42,392,826	$48,144,976
Hatch	$0	$2,124,707	$173,016	$255,000	$2,552,723
Kasich	$0	$1,702,668	$77,224	$1,411,191	$3,191,083
Keyes	$3,325,340	$7,663,253	$10,100	$1,059	$10,999,752
McCain	$14,467,788	$28,143,613	$405,599	$2,030,937	$45,047,937
Quayle	$2,087,748	$4,083,201	$43,200	$103,546	$6,317,695
Smith	$0	$1,522,128	$17,070	$75,000	$1,614,198
Total Republican	$24,513,679	$157,180,370	$2,890,944	$48,099,723	$232,684,716
Others					
Buchanan	$3,852,247	$6,651,221	$1,000	31,967	$10,536,435
Hagelin	$314,135	755,319	$0	$110,526	$1,179,980
Nader	$100,000	$1,319,434	$0	$44,133	$1,463,567
Browne	$0	$1,217,198	$0	$31,000	$1,248,198
Total Others	$4,266,382	$9,943,172	$1,000	$217,626	$14,428,180
Grand Total	$57,744,350	$233,584,375	$2,892,543	$48,742,605	$342,963,864

Source: Federal Election Commission, September 2000.

sales, have become excellent sources of revenue. Thousand dollar-a-plate dinners have become a particularly popular way to bring in large amounts of money early in the nomination process. Incumbents who run for reelection have tried to use their fund-raising prowess to raise considerable sums for themselves and their parties in this manner.

Nonparty Groups and Other Organizations. Although election law prohibits corporations and labor unions from making direct contributions to political campaigns, it does allow their employees, stockholders, or members to form PACs and fund them through voluntary contributions. These groups can directly affect the presidential selection process in four ways: by endorsing a candidate, by giving up to $5,000 to a single candidate, by spending an unlimited amount of money independently for or against a candidate, and by communicating to their members and then using their organization to turn out voters.

Surprisingly, direct donations to the presidential candidates are their least important source of revenue. Candidates receive only a small portion of their contributions from PACs, if they accept those contributions at all. With the differential between individual and group contributions declining in 2004, this portion can be expected to decline even further. George W. Bush banked the most money from PACs, but it constituted only 2 percent of the total amount he received in 2000. Neither Bill Bradley nor Al Gore accepted PAC donations in that campaign.

Leadership PACs. PACs have even proven to be so useful in the precandidacy stage that candidates now regularly create their own leadership PACs to fund organizational activities, build support, and defray travel and other expenses in the years preceding the presidential election. In addition, money is often given to other candidates for their campaigns in the midterm elections. This money is intended to generate reciprocal support for the presidential nominee later on.[18]

Leadership PACs have also become an important mechanism for identifying and tapping potential donors, not once but continually until they have given the maximum amount permitted by law. The advent of this type of PAC has effectively elongated the presidential selection process by encouraging candidates to create their own PAC and involving them in campaign activities in the year or two before the election cycle begins.[19] All of the major Democratic contenders in 2004 had their own leadership PACs in the years prior to the 2003–2004 nomination cycle.

In addition to leadership PACs, candidates have also established advocacy PACs in states that do not limit the size of contributions. Money raised by these PACs cannot be used in federal campaigns, but it can be spent on issue advocacy, polling to gauge public reaction to this advocacy, as well as expenses which are incurred in the promotion of its views.

Matching Funds and Government Grants. In addition to individuals and non-party groups, a third source of money is the government itself. Presidential candidates can receive government matching grants for the nomination process and outright support for the general election. In 2000, these federal subsidies and grants amounted to over $61 million. Figure 2–1 shows matching fund grants since 1976. In starting up their campaigns, lesser-known candidates are especially dependent on this type of funding.

Here's how matching grants work. Eligible federal candidates who receive individual contributions up to $250 in the year of or in the year before the election can match those contributions by an equal amount from the federal election fund, not to exceed $250, in the calendar year of the election. To be eligible, candidates must raise $5,000 in twenty states in contributions of $250 or less, a total of $100,000.

FIGURE 2–1

MATCHING GRANTS, 1976–2000
(IN MILLIONS OF DOLLARS)

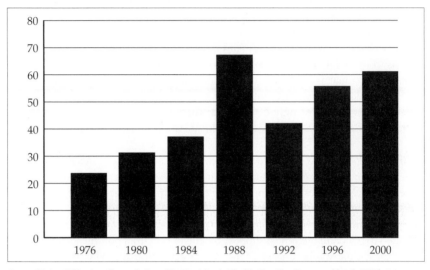

Source: Federal Election Commission, *The Presidential Public Funding Program* (April 1993), 9; updated with data supplied by the Federal Election Commission through September 30, 2000.

Remaining eligible for matching funds is somewhat harder than qualifying to receive them because of the 10 percent rule, a requirement that candidates receive at least 10 percent of the vote in two consecutive primaries in which they are entered. If they are entered in more than one primary on a given day, they need to win 10 percent in only one of them. Failing to receive 10 percent negates their eligibility for federal funds until such time as they receive at least 20 percent of the vote in a subsequent primary.[20] This rule helps front-runners and hurts lesser known candidates. Twice during the 1984 campaign Democrat Jesse Jackson lost his eligibility for matching funds, only to regain it later. Consequently, to ensure their continued eligibility, marginal candidates have tended to avoid nonessential contests.[21]

Minor party candidates are also able to receive matching funds if they seek their party's nomination. Lenora Fulani, New Alliance Party, and John Hagelin, Natural Law Party, qualified in 1992 and Hagelin qualified again in 1996 and 2000, as did Pat Buchanan (Reform Party) and Ralph Nader (Green Party), but the amount they received was minimal compared to candidates for major party nominations. Nonetheless, the eligibility of minor party candidates has led to the criticism that this provision encourages people to run who have no chance of winning, wasting taxpayers' money in the process.

Although the matching fund provision provides opportunities for candidates who begin with less funding, it has not substantially reduced the financial advantage that nationally recognized candidates have. Moreover, it encourages all candidates to begin their fund-raising well before the election in order to qualify as soon as possible. Finally, it places limits on campaign expenditures (see pages 53–55), which puts federally subsidized candidates at a distinct disadvantage when competing against privately funded candidates. McCain was approaching this limit when the 2000 nominations were effectively decided. Had he chosen to stay in the race and compete in the later primaries, he would have quickly reached the maximum amount that he could have spent under the law.

Since the matching funds are not indexed to inflation as contributions have become in the new Bipartisan Campaign Reform Act (2002), matching funds will represent a decreasing proportion of the total revenues. Thus not only will they become less important, but increasingly, accepting government money may be viewed as a liability rather than an asset. Unless the law is changed, better-known candidates who have the potential to raise money will have an increasing incentive *not* to accept matching funds because of the expenditure limits they impose, a consequence that undermines the very purpose of the legislation.

Convention and Election Grants. Federal funding also extends to the major parties for their national nominating conventions. The convention grant in 2000 was $13,512,000; in 2004 it is expected to be about $14,600,000. The Reform Party received $2.5 million, an amount based on its percent of the vote in the last election. Parties may also seek convention funding from the cities and states in which the event occurs as well as goods and services from the private sector. These supplements can be substantial. In 2000, the Parties received $161 million with about $56 million from private sources, mostly companies. In 2004, the private sector is expected to contribute even more.[22]

Once the major party candidates have been officially chosen, they too are eligible for a direct grant for the presidential candidates. In 2000, $67.6 million was given to the Republican and Democratic candidates; in 2004, it will be in the range of $73.0 million. The actual dollar figure is calculated in the election year by the FEC on the basis of the rate of inflation.

To be eligible for federal funds, major party candidates must agree to limit their campaign expenditures in the general election to the amount of the grant. To comply with the law, they cannot accept private contributions except those designated for accounting, legal fees, and compliance costs. Although the total amount that they can raise for these expenditures is not limited by law, individual gifts to this fund are subject to the individual contribution limit of $2,000. In the 2000 presidential election, each major party candidate received about $15 million to their general election legal, accounting, and compliance (GELAC) accounts.

Minor party candidates, who may receive private contributions, are also eligible for federal funds in amounts equal to the proportion of the vote they receive, provided it is at least 5 percent of the total. Had Perot accepted federal funds in 1992, he would have received $25.96 million, 47 percent of the amount the major party candidates were given; however, he would have received it after the election was over. Automatically eligible for federal funds in 1996 because of the size of the vote he received in 1992, Perot got $29 million; in 2000, the Reform Party nominee, Pat Buchanan, was eligible for $12.6 million from the campaign fund, but the small vote he received makes the Reform Party ineligible for federal funds in 2004. Nor did Green Party candidate Ralph Nader receive sufficient votes to qualify his party for funding in 2004.

When Perot decided not to accept federal funds in 1992, he was exempted from the $50,000 limit on personal contributions. His campaign was also exempted from the overall spending limits to which the major party candidates were subject. Perot's campaign expenditures totaled $68.4 million compared to $55.2 for Clinton and Bush (plus their legal and accounting expenses which are not subject to this limit). Because he chose to accept federal funds in 1996, Perot could not use more than $50,000 of his own money, but he could raise additional funds to bring his total amount up to the level of the two major party candidates. His campaign, however, conducted only a modest fund-raising effort.

George W. Bush's prodigious fund-raising in 2000 and at the beginning of 2003 raised speculation and generated an internal debate (see Box 2–3) whether he should accept federal matching funds or a federal election grant in 2004; most candidates do not have such an option. The time and effort required to meet, much less exceed, the amount of the federal grant (at a maximum contribution of $2,000 per person) encourages all but the wealthiest, or perhaps a popular incumbent president with proven fund-raising skills, to accept the government funding.

In the seven presidential elections since the law went into effect, Democratic primary and presidential candidates have received a total of $638 million and their Republican counterparts have received about $659 million. In contrast, only $50 million have gone to minor party or independent candidates.

BOX 2–3

THE WELL-FUNDED CANDIDATES'S DILEMMA: TO ACCEPT OR REJECT GOVERNMENT FUNDS

Although matching funds and election grants provide significant financial resources for those seeking the presidency, they also come with strings attached. Thus, and increasingly so, candidates who have large amounts of money or have the potential to raise it under the existing law need to consider the pros and cons of accepting federal funds.

Pro
- Accepting federal funds creates the impression that a candidate is willing to play by the same rules as everyone else.
- Accepting federal funds downplays the perception that money "buys" elections; that the wealthy candidates are always advantaged; for the Republicans, it also works against the Democratic stereotype of them as the party of the rich.
- Accepting federal funds reduces the time and effort that candidates need to devote to fund-raising activities, an original intent of the FECA, and increases the time they have for discussing the issues and interacting with voters.

- Accepting federal funds leaves more money available to other candidates within the party; the presidential candidate does not drain the party's coffers.
- Accepting federal funds, in light of an expected shortfall in 2004, leaves less money available to the other candidates, particularly Democrats who are competing for their party's nomination and any potential Republican challenger, thereby advantaging a popular incumbent president seeking re-election.

Con

- For front-runners, accepting federal funds decreases their initial financial advantage and the flexibility that their superior war chest affords.
- Accepting federal funds imposes spending limits.
- Accepting federal funds leaves little money for campaigning after the nomination has been effectively won but before the conventions, a handicap that can no longer be compensated with soft money.
- Accepting federal funds for the general election equalizes spending and thereby undercuts the potential advantage that popular incumbents have in raising large sums of money.

If you were advising George W. Bush, what would you suggest he do about accepting matching funds during the nomination and federal grants during the general election? What would your advice be to the Democratic front-runner?

BOX 2–4 🏛️

THE MONEY RACE FOR THE 2000 NOMINATION

The money race for the 2000 presidential election began two years before the nomination when George W. Bush and Al Gore mapped their initial strategies and began to assemble their fund-raising teams. Both patterned their plans on Bill Clinton's highly successful reelection fund-raising operation in 1996. Their goals were similar to Clinton's: demonstrate their strength within the party, reduce the money available for other challengers, and have sufficient funds to react to any contingency that might occur.

THE REPUBLICAN CONTEST WITH BUSH AS THE LEADER

George W. Bush's fund-raising strategy was straightforward. In late 1998 and early 1999, he invited prominent Republicans to Austin, Texas, for informal discussions over lunch. Those who expressed support for Bush's candidacy were invited to join a team of "pioneers," a group of individuals who each promised to raise $100,000 once Bush gave the word that he probably would be a candidate. When an exploratory Bush for President Committee was established in the spring of 1999, the pioneers went to work. In just twenty-eight days, they raised a whopping $7.6 million.[23] This torrential fund-raising pace continued throughout the year of 1999, with the campaign netting almost $70 million in revenues—the most ever raised by a single presidential candidate.[24]

The size of Bush's war chest helped his campaign in several ways. It was interpreted by the press as a sign of his candidacy's strength. Not only was Bush acknowledged as the Republican front-runner, but his success in fund-raising also indicated that he was way ahead of the pack. As a consequence, Bush received more press coverage and gained greater recognition of his front-runner status, which in turn, generated more contributions.

In addition, the money enabled Bush to establish a relatively large organization of political consultants and campaign operatives, set up field operations in thirty-four states, gain political endorsements and the organizational support of other Republicans, and engage in extensive advertising. Having a large war chest also afforded Bush more flexibility in designing his campaign strategy than any other Republican candidate, with the possible exception of millionaire Steve Forbes. Only he and Forbes could afford to launch multistate efforts; the rest of the field had to concentrate almost entirely on the early contests.

Finally, Bush's large financial lead discouraged other presidential hopefuls from continuing when they found themselves unable to raise anywhere near the amount Bush had. In short, Bush's money served to thin out the Republican field faster than the primaries and caucuses. It clearly established the significance of the pocketbook vote.

Only Steve Forbes could match Bush's war chest. As long as Forbes continued in the race, he spent lavishly, at or above Bush's level, a total of over $42 million. But Forbes's money could not overcome his image as unelectable. His campaign was mercifully short-lived.

John McCain was not in as dire financial straits as the other Republican candidates. Although he had not raised much more money than they had, he was helped by his decision not to contest Iowa and by the $2 million he was able to transfer from previous Senate campaigns to his presidential effort. This money got him through the pre–New Hampshire period. Once McCain was able to demonstrate his electability by winning big in New Hampshire, he got a large fund-raising bump. Enough money flowed to his campaign to enable him to compete with Bush in the next round of primaries, but never on a completely even keel. McCain had much less to spend on the big state primaries in New York, California, and Ohio on Super Tuesday and practically no funds to spend on the other contests that day or after, had he continued. Money was not the only reason McCain lost, but it contributed to his quick exit after the first Tuesday in March.

THE DEMOCRATIC CONTEST WITH GORE AND BRADLEY TIED

Al Gore was not able to achieve the kind of money advantage that Bill Clinton enjoyed and that he, as Clinton's heir apparent, was expected to have. His campaign did raise almost $9 million in the first quarter of 1999, but donations declined thereafter. The press quickly interpreted this decline as a lack of enthusiasm for Gore as well as the product of a poorly run fund-raising effort. In October 1999, Gore shook up his sagging campaign, changed top personnel, moved them to Nashville, and began to spend more time "stroking" large donors.[25] His efforts paid off. He eventually raised the maximum amount permitted by law. But he got no advantage from this success. Trailing Bush in the polls, having less money to spend than Bradley, appearing increasingly vulnerable to his Democratic challenger and presumptive Republican opponent, Gore's financial difficulties became a media metaphor for a disappointing campaign. In the eyes of the press, and to some extent the public, Gore was in the process of losing more than the money race.

Fund-raising was an important component of Bradley's strategy. His plan was to challenge Gore's inevitable renomination by first illustrating his popularity and viability with dollars. Using his contacts from professional basketball, the Wall Street investment community, and Silicon Valley, he matched Gore's bankroll, even exceeding it in the fourth quarter of 1999. Because Bradley did not have an organization of the size and experience of Gore's, he did not incur the same administrative expenses. He ended 1999 with more money in his campaign account than did Gore. His financial success was perceived by the news media as an indication of his strength and Gore's weakness. But Bradley was not able to take advantage of this perception. His financial resources were insufficient to overcome his own limitations as a candidate: his personal reserve and standoffish manner, his idealistic policy goals and the vague proposals he offered for achieving them, and his inability to relate to core Democratic constituencies. In the end it was these limitations, not a lack of money, that doomed his candidacy.

Expenditures

The additional sources of revenue are necessary because campaign costs keep rising with more candidates seeking their party's nomination and with greater use of advanced communications technology and mass media to reach the electorate and the grassroots organizations necessary to turn them out to vote. Moreover, in most elections these increases have exceeded the rate of inflation.

The crunch in expenditures represents the greatest problem for candidates at the initial stages of the nomination process. The need to gain recognition, get a boost, or maintain a lead has prompted candidates of both parties to spend much of their money early, well before the first contest is held, and to focus their attention on the states that have the first caucuses and primaries.

As states with small populations, Iowa and New Hampshire have low spending limits. The desire to be free of these limits led three Republican aspirants, John Connally (1980), Steve Forbes (1996 and 2000), and George W. Bush (2000), to reject matching funds. Because of the need for high early spending, most campaigns have accepted government funds and then use their ingenuity to circumvent the state spending limits. In doing so, they have employed a variety of "legal" tactics and some not-so-legal ones. It has become common practice for campaign workers to commute to the early small states from neighboring ones, thus allowing the campaign to allocate only a portion of its expenses to the state in which the early primary will be held. Another legal technique is to use national phone banks to canvas voters within these states. Television ads, particularly those directed at New Hampshire, are aired on Boston television, where 85 percent of the cost can be applied to the Massachusetts limit.[26]

Other questionable tactics include encouraging friendly groups to design and air their own commercials, set up telephone banks, and mount other grassroots activities in support of the campaign. PACs are allowed to communicate with their members but not under the direction or indirect auspices of a candidate's official campaign or party organization. Yet they can have an impact on the campaign. Republicans for Clean Air spent $2.5 million to help George W. Bush. The AFL-CIO ran $21 million of issue ads from January 1999 to August 31, 2000, to help Democrats in general and Al Gore in particular.[27]

In addition to the expenditure ceilings in states based on voting-age population, there is an overall prenomination spending limit. In 2000, it was $33.8 million plus 20 percent for fund-raising and 15 percent for compliance with the FEC's reporting requirements, a total of approximately $46 million; in 2004, it will be about $49 million. (See Table 2–5.)

As the campaign progresses candidates do bump up against the total spending ceiling, but since the contests have been effectively settled fairly early in the calendar year, the overall limits have not been as much of a problem as the individual state limits in Iowa and New Hampshire. As noted previously, the overall limits would have been a problem for McCain, however, had he stayed in the race after March 7, and they quickly would have become one for Gore and Bradley as well had the Democratic contest continued. They were also a problem for Dole in

TABLE 2–5 🏛

Presidential Spending Limits and COLAS for the Democratic and Republican Parties, 1976–2004 (in millions)

	1974	1976	1980	1984	1988	1992	1996	2000	2004*
Primary election limit†	$10	$10.9	$14.7	$20.2	$23.1	$27.6	$31.0	$33.8	$36.5
General election limit‡	$20	$21.8	$29.4	$40.4	$46.1	$55.2	$61.8	$67.6	$73.0
Party convention limit§	$2	$2.2	$4.4	$8.1	$9.2	$11.0	$12.4	$13.5	$14.6
Party general election limit		$3.2	$4.6	$6.9	$8.3	$10.3	$11.6	$13.7	$14.8

*2004 figures are estimated.

†Primary candidates receiving matching funds must comply with two types of spending limits: a national limit (listed in this table) and a separate limit for each state. The state limit is $200,000 or 16¢ multiplied by the state's voting-age population, whichever is greater. (Both amounts are adjusted for increases in the cost of living.) The maximum amount of primary matching funds a candidate may receive is half of the national spending limit. In addition, candidates may spend up to 20 percent of their primary election limit on fund-raising.

‡Legal and accounting expenses to comply with the law are exempt from this limit. These funds may be raised through private contributions.

§This limit has been raised twice by legislation: once in 1979 and once in 1984.

Source: Federal Election Commission, *Annual Report, 1984* (June 1, 1985), 8–9, updated by the author with data supplied by the Federal Election Commission. For 2000, see Federal Election Commission, "Monthly Record," April 2000, 10.

1996, but only after he had effectively secured the Republican nomination. Dole had spent within $1.5 million of the maximum amount prior to his nomination by the Republicans by the end of March. He thus had little money left with which to campaign between April and the August 11th start of the Republican national convention. In contrast, his opponent, Bill Clinton, had between $16 and $20 million that he had to spend prior to the Democratic convention in late August. Knowledge of Dole's problem was a major reason why George W. Bush decided not to accept government funds in the 2000 nomination process and why he may not do so again in 2004.

With the concentration of primaries and caucuses on the same days at the beginning of the nomination process, the only way for candidates to reach voters in a number of states during the same time period is through the mass media. Television advertising, in particular, is one of the most expensive forms of communication. Its use increases the costs of running for the major contenders, who need to raise large sums of money well *before* the first primary or caucus is held.

Independent expenditures have also played a role in the nomination and general election processes. In 1980, $13.7 million was reported to the FEC as being spent independently on the presidential campaign. Between 1984 and 1996, independent spending declined substantially, but in 2000 it increased although the exact amount is difficult to calculate. If internal costs by independent groups to communicate with their members are added to the groups' outright expenses such as advertising, polling, and campaign staff, the total rises to between $13.5 and $22.5 million.[28]

The line between independent expenditures, internal communications, and campaign-related organizational activities has blurred in recent elections, raising questions about illegal collusion among the parties, candidates, and like-minded groups, groups whose advocacy benefits one side over the other. In 1996, the FEC charged that the Christian Coalition violated the law by coordinating its nonpartisan advocacy advertising with the Republican Party and its candidates, but a federal court dismissed the charges. The Republicans made similar accusations against organized labor in 1996 when union dues financed a $35 million campaign in seventy-five key congressional districts primarily for Democratic candidates.

There have been numerous other allegations about illegal campaign finance activities. Republicans claimed that a Democratic Party fund-raiser in a Buddhist temple in Los Angeles in which Vice President Gore participated violated the law because of that religious institution's nonpartisan status as a tax exempt organization precluded its use for a partisan fund-raiser. Questions were also raised about the $5,000 contributions from monks who had taken a vow of poverty and thus probably did not have much, if any, personal wealth. None of the monks were prosecuted, however, and the Democrats returned the money, but the accusation plagued Gore throughout his 2000 presidential campaign.[29]

Competition between Parties and Their Candidates

The FECA created competition within and between the major parties and their nominees. This competition was not the intent of the law, but it has been a consequence of it. By providing funds directly to individuals who seek major party nominations, the law facilitates candidacies and candidate organizations within the national parties, thereby initially fractionalizing those parties. The organization of the successful candidate is not dismantled after the nomination; it is expanded and in some elections competes with the regular party organization. On the other hand, the fund-raising efforts of the national party have strengthened its influence over the election of federal candidates as did the party's solicitation and distribution of soft money through the 2002 election.

AP/Wide World Photos

Questionable Fund-Raising Activity   In April 1996, Vice President Al Gore appeared at a ceremony and fund-raiser at a Buddhist temple allegedly in Los Angeles where illegal contributions were made to the Democratic Party. Gore claimed that he did not know the event was a fund-raiser; the party was forced to return the money.

MONEY AND ELECTORAL SUCCESS

The relationship between money and electoral success has spurred considerable debate in recent years and generated much anger by those who believe unequal resources undermine the democratic character of the U.S. electoral process. Is the conventional wisdom correct? Do those with more money have an advantage? Do they usually win?

The simple answer is usually yes, but the longer answer is more complicated. First, who has or gets the money? Second, what difference does the money make in the election?

Two types of candidates tend to have disproportionate resources at their disposal: those who are personally wealthy and those who are well-known public figures. Money can buy recognition as it did for Steve Forbes in 1996; it gave him a chance that he otherwise would not have had. But obviously, it cannot, in and of itself, buy a victory. Similarly, front-runners, such as Robert Dole in 1996, George Bush in 1988, and his son George W. Bush in 2000, can raise more money because they are perceived as likely to win the nomination and that money in turn contributes to their likelihood for success. Although it increases the odds, especially for winning their party's nomination, it does not make that nomination inevitable.

The task is harder and more difficult for non-front-runners. They have to establish their viability as candidates. The best way and perhaps the only way to accomplish this is to do surprisingly well early and thereby gain media coverage in time to use that coverage to raise additional funds as John McCain did in 2000. However, the need to do well early creates another money problem—having sufficient funds to spend in the first round of caucuses and primaries. Even if they are successful as McCain was, they may still face an uphill financial battle with a wounded but wealthier front-runner, particularly if that front-runner has not accepted federal funds. Yet non-front-runners have few other options. The failure to do better than expected and/or to gain the media coverage necessary to "change" public expectations will likely doom them financially, which makes their defeat almost inevitable.[30]

The second money issue pertains to the difference money makes in the vote. Have candidates with the largest bankrolls generally been victorious? In the general elections at the presidential level, the answer seems to be yes, but it is difficult to determine precisely the extent to which money contributed to victory or simply flowed to the likely winner.

Between 1860 and 1972, the winner outspent the loser twenty-one out of twenty-nine times. Republican candidates have spent more than their Democratic opponents in twenty-five out of twenty-nine elections during this period. The four times they did not, the Democrats won. The trend has continued even when independent expenditures, partisan communications, and soft money are considered. In the 1980s, considerably more was spent on behalf of Republican nominees than for their Democratic opponents. In the 1990s, the Democrats benefited from substantial expenditures by organized labor to mobilize their members, but their total spending was still less than the Republicans. George W. Bush was the financial as well as electoral victor in 2000.

What do all these trends suggest? The pattern of greater spending and electoral victories indicates that money contributes to success, but potential success also attracts money. Having more funds is an advantage, but it does not guarantee victory. The fact that heavily favored incumbent Richard Nixon outspent rival George McGovern more than 2 to 1 in 1972 does not explain McGovern's huge defeat, although it probably portended it. On the other hand, Hubert Humphrey's much narrower defeat by Nixon four years earlier was partially influenced by Humphrey's having spent less than $12 million, compared with more than $25 million spent by Nixon. The closer the election, the more the disparity in funds can make a difference.

Theoretically, campaign spending should have a greater impact on the nomination process than on the general election and at the beginning of the process rather than at the end. According to political scientists Michael Robinson, Clyde Wilcox, and Paul Marshall, money matters most when the candidates are least known to the voters, when they do not receive a lot of news coverage, and when paid advertising, which of course is expensive, can bring recognition and enhance images.[31]

As the nomination process progresses, as candidates become more easily recognized by the public, the expenditure of funds is not as critical to electoral success. What money buys is recognition, organizational support, and a turn-out-the-vote operation. It certainly does not guarantee success, as Phil Gramm and Steve Forbes found out in 1996 and Forbes and Bill Bradley discovered in 2000. Once the nomination is decided, however, money can still be a factor, especially if there are several months until the national nominating conventions.

Is the expenditure of funds by candidates an important consideration in the general election? Most candidates believe it to be. The 2000 election was characterized by extensive fund-raising by both major parties with the aid and support of their presidential nominees. But whether spending more money on more advertising or additional grassroots activities made a difference is difficult to say.[32]

SUMMARY

Campaign finance became an important aspect of presidential elections by the end of the nineteenth and the beginning of the twentieth centuries. In recent years, however, it has become even more important as costs have escalated. Expanded use of high technology and multiple channels of communication to reach the voters has been primarily responsible for the increase.

With few exceptions, candidates of both major parties turned to large contributors, the so-called fat cats, for financial support in the early and mid-twentieth century. Their dependence on a relatively small number of large donors, combined with spiraling costs, created serious problems for the democratic selection process. The 1972 presidential election, with its high expenditures, "dirty tricks," and illegal campaign contributions, vividly illustrated some of these problems and generated public and congressional support for rectifying them.

In the 1970s, Congress enacted and amended the Federal Election Campaign Act to bring donors into the open and to prevent their exercising undue influence on elected officials. By placing limits on contributions, controlling expenditures, and subsidizing the election, Congress hoped to make the selection process less costly and more equitable. It also established the Federal Election Commission to monitor activities, oversee compliance, and prosecute offenders.

But the legislation was only partially successful. It increased the importance of having a large base of contributors during the preconvention period but did not eliminate the impact of large donors on the parties' and candidates' efforts in the general election. It limited the expenditures of individual campaigns in both the nomination process and general election but has not reduced the amount of money spent on presidential elections. It produced greater equity by its limits on contributions and expenditures and by its federal subsidies but has not achieved equity among candidates or between parties in either phase of the electoral process. It provided greater opportunities for those candidates who lack national recognition, but it has not lessened the advantages that national recognition can bring to those who seek their party's nomination. It has benefited major party candidates in the general election but also has fractionalized their parties during the nomination. It has weakened the party leaders' control over the nomination process and over the conduct of the general election campaign, but it has also enhanced the strategic value of the national parties' fund-raising, particularly when they solicited and distributed soft money. It has encouraged the formation and involvement of nonparty groups, but it has also increased the importance of state and local party organizations on the campaigns of their candidates for national office.

Finally, the law has contributed to knowledge about the conduct of campaigns, placing contributions and expenditures on the public record. Although it has forced campaigns to engage in additional bookkeeping and reporting procedures, it has generated a wealth of data about campaign finance—who gives what to whom—and made those data easily available to the press, electorate, and other political candidates. The reporting and publicizing of campaign contributions and expenditures has generated more media scrutiny, more public awareness, greater activity by citizen watchdog groups, and in the cases of possible violations, congressional investigations and FEC sanctions.

The inequities created by the law, many of them unintended consequences of the 1979 amendments to the FECA that permitted unlimited donations for party building, issue advocacy, and get-out-the-vote activities, led Congress to enact reforms in 2002. The Bipartisan Campaign Reform Act banned soft money solicitation and distribution by the national parties, prohibited candidates from being named directly in issue ads thirty days or less before a primary and sixty days or less before the general election, and raised the individual contribution limits.

The new law, which took effect after the 2002 midterm election, was immediately challenged by those who objected to the newly imposed government restrictions. Judicial briefs were filed by a variety of groups seeking to overturn parts of it. Interest groups such as the National Rifle Association, the Christian Coalition, and the American Civil Liberties Union saw the restrictions placed on issue advocacy as violating the constitutional protections of the First Amendment. The Republican National Committee, another partner to the suit, objected to the constraints that restricted electoral activities of state and local parties which might indirectly benefit national candidates from the states. A coalition of groups representing nonwealthy Americans argued that the increase in contribution limits denied those who lacked the money to contribute equal protection under the law as required by the Fifth Amendment to the Constitution. The FEC also got caught in the cross fire when it issued rules for implementing the new law.

Meanwhile, the national parties and nonparty groups busied themselves in devising creative ways to legally circumvent the new financial rules. The adage, where there is a will, there is a way, continued to dominate thinking about campaign finance and incentivized the hunt for sufficient money to fund the next election.

WHERE ON THE WEB?

- **Brennan Center for Justice**
  http://www.brennancenter.org
  Conducted a major study on the costs of political advertising in the 2000 election. Sponsors a campaign finance report project.
- **Brookings Institution Campaign Reform Initiative**
  http://brookings.org
  Provides an online source book of key documents and scholarly research on campaign finance reform updated by its authors.
- **The Campaign Finance Institute**
  http://www.cfinst.org
  A nonprofit institute that collects and analyses current information on campaign finance and reviews the impact of reform legislation.
- **Center for Public Integrity**
  www.publicintegrity.org
  Evaluates public service, government accountability, and various ethical issues on democratic governance. Has been concerned with campaign finance reform.
- **Center for Responsive Politics**
  http://www.opensecrets.org
  A nonpartisan, public interest group that is concerned with the conduct of federal elections, particularly how money is raised and spent. Publishes alerts, press releases, and major studies on campaign finance.
- **Common Cause**
  http://www.commoncause.org
  Another public interest group that is concerned with large and unreported contributions and expenditures and has continually urged campaign finance reform.
- **Democracy 21**
  http://www.democracy21.org
  Another public interest group interested in campaign finance reform.

- **Federal Election Commission**
  http://www.fec.gov
  The first stop for any study of campaign finance, the FEC collects and dissemi-
  nates data on contributions to and expenditures of candidates seeking federal
  office as well as for parties and PACs.
- **Public Campaign**
  http://www.publicampaign.org
  A public interest organization devoted to campaign reform to reduce role of
  special interest money and large contributors in American politics.

EXERCISES

1. During the preelection period, see if you can identify the leadership PACs and
   other groups that potential candidates have used to prepare for their 2004
   nomination campaign. You can find these groups on the Web site of the Center for Responsive Politics. Note how well these groups raised money, from
   whom, and to what effect.
2. Compile a running summary of revenue and expenditures as filed with the
   FEC <http://www.fec.gov>, by candidates who have officially declared themselves for their party's 2004 presidential nomination. Does the differential in
   their war chests explain their respective campaign activities and /or their position in the public opinion polls?
3. Note the proposals for campaign finance reform that became law in 2002. Follow their legal challenges in the courts by indicating which arguments seem
   most and least compelling to the judges who have heard the cases. How do you
   expect the legal issues to be eventually resolved?

SELECTED READING

Corrado, Anthony. "Financing the 2000 Elections." In *The Elections of 2000,*
    edited by Gerald M. Pomper, 92–124. New York: Chatham House, 2001.
Corrado, Anthony, Thomas E. Mann, Daniel Ortiz, and Trevor Potter. *The New
    Campaign Finance Sourcebook.* Washington, D.C.: Brookings Institution, 2002.
Damore, David F. "A Dynamic Model of Candidate Fund-Raising: The Case of
    Presidential Nominating Campaigns." *Political Research Quarterly* (June
    1997): 343–364.
Gais, Thomas. *Improper Influence: Campaign Finance Law, Political Interest Groups
    and the Problem of Equity.* Ann Arbor: University of Michigan Press, 1996.
Haynes, Audrey A., Paul-Henri Gurian, and Stephen Nichols. "The Role of
    Candidate Spending in Presidential Nomination Campaigns." *Journal of
    Politics* (February 1997): 213–235.
Magleby, David B., ed. *Financing the 2000 Elections.* Washington, D.C.: Brook-
    ings Institution, 2002.
Sorauf, Frank J. *Money in American Elections.* Glenview, Ill.: Scott Foresman,
    1988.

Stephenson-Horne, Marilee. "The Road to Hell: Unintended Consequences of Unwise Federal Campaign Finance Reforms." *Northern Kentucky Law Review* 17 (Spring 1990): 547–570.

Wayne, Stephen J. "The 2000 Presidential Election: Traveling the Hard and Soft Roads to the White House," In *The Interest Group Connection: Electioneering, Lobbying, and Policymaking,* 2nd. ed., edited by Paul S. Herrnson, Ronald Shaiko, and Clyde Wilcox. New York: Chatham House, 2003.

NOTES

1. Candice J. Nelson, "Spending in the 2000 Elections," in *Financing the 2000 Election,* ed. David B. Magleby (Washington, D.C.: Brookings Institution, 2002), 24; see also Larry Makison, et al., *The Big Picture: The Money Behind the 2000 Elections* (Washington, D.C.: Center for Responsive Politics, 2001), and Anthony Corrado, "Financing the 2000 Elections," in *The Election of 2000,* ed. Gerald M. Pomper (New York: Chatham House, 2001), 92–124.
2. Federal Election Commission, "Revenues and Disbursements of the 1999–2000 Presidential Campaign," <http://www.fec.gov/finance_reports.html>.
3. Herbert E. Alexander, "Making Sense about Dollars in the 1980 Presidential Campaigns," in *Money and Politics in the United States,* ed. Michael J. Malbin (Washington, D.C.: American Enterprise Institute/Chatham House, 1984), 24.
4. Edward W. Chester, *Radio, Television, and American Politics* (New York: Sheed & Ward, 1969), 21.
5. Herbert E. Alexander, *Financing Politics: Money, Elections, and Political Reform,* 3rd ed. (Washington, D.C.: Congressional Quarterly, 1984), 11–12.
6. Craig B. Holman and Luke P. McLoughlin, *Buying Time 2000: Television Advertising in the 2000 Federal Elections* (New York: Brennan Center for Justice, 2001), 39–40.
7. Ibid., 68.
8. Quoted in Jasper B. Shannon, *Money and Politics* (New York: Random House, 1959), 35.
9. Herbert E. Alexander and Brian Haggerty, *Financing the 1984 Election* (Lexington, Mass.: Lexington Books, 1987), 148.
10. In 1972, the chief fund-raiser for the Nixon campaign, Maurice Stans, and Richard Nixon's private attorney, Herbert Kalmbach, collected contributions, some of them illegal, on behalf of the president. They exerted strong pressure on corporate executives, despite the prohibition on corporate giving. Secret contributions totaling millions of dollars were received, and three special secured funds were established to give the White House and the Committee to Reelect the President (known as CREEP) maximum discretion in campaign expenditures. It was from these funds that the "dirty tricks" of the 1972 campaign and the Watergate burglary were financed.
11. The 1971 act also limited the amount that could be spent on media advertising, but that limit was eliminated in 1974.
12. There was also a short but critical delay in the effective date for the disclosure provision of the other 1971 campaign finance act. Signed by the president on February 14, 1972, it was scheduled to take effect in sixty days. This delay precipitated a frantic attempt by both parties to tap major donors who wished to remain anonymous. During this period, the Republicans collected an estimated $20 million, much of it pledged beforehand, and some of it in forms that could not even be traced.
13. The original provision did not even require that the contributions be reported to the FEC. In 1992, the Commission ruled that all donations of $200 or more had to be

reported as well as the total amount of money that the national parties allocated to the states. The costs of raising this money also had to be submitted to the FEC.

14. In contrast, most of McCain's contributors gave $199 or less.

15. Daniel Lathrop, "The Money Race: After First Quarter, Kerry Leads," Center for Public Integrity, *The Buying of the President—2004,* April 24, 2003, <http://www. publicintegrity.org/dtaweb/bop2004>.

16. Ibid.

17. Those who do not do well and are forced out early are often saddled with sizable debts. Frequently, for the sake of party unity and to obtain the backing of their opponents, party nominees promise to try to help raise money to pay off their rivals' debts.

18. One of the earliest and most successful of these leadership PACs was Citizens for the Republic. Started in 1977, this organization had within a year raised $2.5 million and spent $1.9 million on operations. Most of this money was used for fund-raising, travel, and other expenses of the PAC's principal speaker, Ronald Reagan. In the process of raising money, the organization developed a list of more than 300,000 contributors. This list was purchased for a nominal fee by the Reagan campaign committee. The Reagan PAC became the prototype for other presidential candidates.

19. It costs more to engage in prospective fund-raising, going to people who have not contributed for donations, than to go back to those who have. Sometimes, in fact, the costs of prospective fund-raising can exceed the dollar return. This is one of the reasons that potential candidates wish to shift these costs to a leadership PAC rather than have them come out of the campaign fund-raising budget and thus detract from the total amount that can be spent prior to the convention. Having a mailing list in hand also helps obtain money for the critical start-up costs of the campaign.

20. The FEC sought to impose still another eligibility rule—how matching funds had been spent in the past. The commission denied matching funds to Lyndon LaRouche in 1992 on the grounds that his campaign had misused such funds in a previous election. LaRouche, who had been convicted and jailed for engaging in fraudulent fund-raising practices, appealed the FEC's decision and won. On July 2, 1993, the U.S. Court of Appeals ruled that the law did not give the FEC authority to prejudge how a candidate would use his government funds—that was up to the voters. LaRouche received over $1.2 million in matching funds in 2000.

21. Candidates can also notify the FEC that they wish to exclude certain primaries from the 10 percent rule and not campaign in those states even though their names may appear on the ballot.

22. Campaign Finance Institute, "New Campaign Finance Institute Analysis Charts Leap in Private Financing of Political Conventions," June 2, 2003, 2.

23. Don Van Natta Jr., "Early Rush of Contributions Opened Floodgates for Bush," *New York Times,* January 31, 2000, A20. Don Van Natta Jr., "Bush Is Hardly a Passive Fund-Raiser," *New York Times,* May 16, 2000, A20. In 2004, a $200,000 category was established and a title of Ranger for those who achieved. Richard A. Oppel Jr. "Bush's Heaviest Hitters to be Called Rangers," *New York Times,* May 24, 2003.

24. Four hundred people took the pioneer pledge; 226 raised or exceeded $100,000. Susan Glasser, "Bush Raised $69 Million, Spent $37 Million in '99," *Washington Post,* February 1, 2000, A4. Susan Glasser, "George W. Bush's Dash for Cash," *Washington Post,* weekly edition, April 1999, 10.

25. John M. Broder and Katharine Q. Seelye, "Gore Campaign Responds to Money Crunch," *New York Times,* November 20, 1999, A9.

26. Beginning with the 1992 nomination process, the FEC took these practices into account by liberalizing its cost allocation policy. It permitted candidates to allocate expenses if they pertained to media, mailings, telephoning, polling, and overhead. Moreover, the commission allowed up to 50 percent of the expenses to be considered fund-raising and thus entirely exempt from the state spending limits.

27. Erika Falk, "Issue Advocacy Advertising through the Presidential Primary 1999–2000 Election Cycle," Annenberg Public Policy Center, University of Pennsylvania, September 20, 2000.

28. John C. Green and Nathan S. Bigelow, "The 2000 Presidential Nominations: The Costs of Innovation," in *Financing the 2000 Election,* ed. David B. Magleby, 57 (Washington, D.C.: Brookings Institution, 2002), 49–78.

29. Beaulieu of America, a large carpet manufacturer, was not as fortunate as the Buddhist monks. Accused of funneling $36,000 in illegal contributions to Lamar Alexander's 1996 campaign, the company entered into a plea-bargaining agreement with the government in which it agreed to pay a $1 million fine and civil penalties to be determined by the FEC. Kevin Sack, "Campaign Finance Case Costs a Carpet Company $1 Million," *New York Times,* December 2, 1998, A23.

30. David F. Damore, "A Dynamic Model of Candidate Fundraising: The Case of Presidential Nominating Campaigns," *Political Research Quarterly* (June 1997): 343–364.

31. Michael Robinson, Clyde Wilcox, and Paul Marshall, "The Presidency: Not for Sale," *Public Opinion* II (March/April 1989): 51.

32. In an examination of campaign advertising spending by George H. W. Bush in 1988, a group of political scientists found an inverse relationship between advertising costs and public support for the candidates. They write, "When Bush spent more in one week than he had in the previous week, the size of his lead actually grew smaller." Audrey A. Haynes, Paul-Henri Gurian, and Stephen Nichols, "The Role of Candidate Spending in Presidential Nomination Campaigns," *Journal of Politics* (February 1997): 213–225.

THE POLITICAL ENVIRONMENT

INTRODUCTION

The nature of the electorate influences the content, images, and strategies of the campaign and affects the outcome of the election—an obvious conclusion to be sure, but one that is not always appreciated. Campaigns are not conducted in ignorance of the voters. Rather, they are calculated to appeal to the needs and desires, attitudes and opinions, and associations and interactions of the electorate.

Voters do not come to the election with completely open minds. They come with preexisting views. They do not see and hear the campaign in isolation. They observe it and absorb it as part of their daily lives. In other words, their attitudes and associations affect their perceptions and influence their behavior. Preexisting views make it important for students of presidential elections to examine the formation of political attitudes and the patterns of social interaction.

Who votes and who does not? Why do people vote for certain candidates and not others? Do campaign appeals affect voting behavior? Are the responses of the electorate predictable? Political scientists have been interested in these questions for some time. Politicians have been interested in them for even longer.

A great deal of social science research and political savvy have gone into finding the answers. Spurred by the development of sophisticated survey techniques and methods of data analysis, political scientists, sociologists, and social psychologists have uncovered a wealth of information on how the public reacts and the electorate behaves during a campaign. They have examined correlations between demographic characteristics and voter turnout. They have explored psychological motivations, social influences, and political pressures that contribute to voting behavior. This chapter examines some of their findings.

It is organized into three sections. The first discusses who votes. Describing the expansion of suffrage in the nineteenth and twentieth centuries, the section then turns to recent trends. Turnout is influenced by partisan, economic, and social factors. It is also affected by laws that govern elections and by circumstances of the vote itself, such as interest in the election, the closeness of the contest, the effectiveness of the campaign, and even the weather on election day. The impact of these variables on the decision of whether to cast a ballot at all is the principal focus of this section.

The second and third sections of the chapter study influences on the vote. First, the partisan basis of politics is examined. How have political attitudes changed over the years and how do they affect the ways people evaluate the campaign and shape their actual voting decisions? Models of voting behavior are presented and then used to help explain contemporary voting patterns.

Next, the social basis of politics is analyzed. Dividing the electorate into distinct and overlapping demographic, socioeconomic, and religious groupings, this section deals with the relationship of these groupings to voting behavior. It places primary emphasis on the formation of party coalitions during the 1930s and their evolution through the 1990s into the twenty-first century.

The final part of this chapter looks to the future. What is happening to the electoral coalitions of the two major parties? Are they going through a period of realignment, dealignment, or reentrenchment? Are voters becoming more independent in their allegiances and their voting decisions? Recent research provides some answers to these questions.

TURNOUT

Who votes? In one sense, this is a simple question to resolve. Official election returns indicate the number of voters and the states, even the precincts, in which the votes were cast. By easy calculation, the percentage of those eligible who actually voted can be determined. In 1992, 55.2 percent of the voting-age population cast ballots in the presidential election; in 1996, 49.0 percent voted; in 2000, 51.3 percent did.[1] (See Table 3–1 for turnout in other presidential elections.)

For campaign strategists and political analysts, however, more information than simple percentages of the proportion of the population that voted is needed. In planning a campaign, it is necessary to design and target appeals to attract specific groups of voters. In assessing the results, it is also essential to understand how particular segments of the electorate responded. By evaluating turnout on the basis of demographic characteristics and partisan attitudes, strategists and analysts alike obtain the information they need to make sophisticated judgments.

Voting turnout has varied widely over the years. In the first national election, only about 11 percent of the potentially eligible population participated. The presidential vote was even smaller, since most of the electors were designated by the state legislatures and not chosen directly by the people.

In the early period from the end of the eighteenth century until 1824, voters constituted only about 20 to 25 percent of those who were eligible to vote in most states. Without parties or a tradition of participation in politics, the public deferred to the more politically prominent members of the society.[2]

Turnout increased in the 1820s, however, spurred by a political reform movement. Known as Jacksonian Democracy, this movement advocated greater public participation in the electoral process. By the 1830s, 50 to 60 percent of the eligible electorate voted. With the rise of competitive, mass-based parties in the 1840s and their campaigns appealing to voters, turnout increased to 80 percent and

TABLE 3–1

SUFFRAGE AND TURNOUT

Year	Total Adult Population (including aliens)*	Total Presidential Vote	Percentage of Adult Population Voting
1824	3,964,000	363,017	9.0
1840	7,381,000	2,412,698	33.0
1860	14,676,000	4,692,710	32.0
1880	25,012,000	9,219,467	37.0
1900	40,753,000	13,974,188	35.0
1920	60,581,000	26,768,613	44.0
1932	75,768,000	39,732,000	52.4
1940	84,728,000	49,900,000	58.9
1952	99,929,000	61,551,000	61.6
1960	109,672,000	68,838,000	62.8
1964	114,090,000	70,645,000	61.9
1968	120,285,000	73,212,000	60.9
1972	140,777,000	77,719,000	55.5
1976	152,308,000	81,556,000	53.5
1980	164,595,000	86,515,000	52.6
1984	174,447,000	92,653,000	53.1
1988	182,600,000	91,602,291	50.2
1992	189,044,000	104,426,659	55.2
1996	196,507,000	96,277,564	49.0
2000	205,815,000	105,586,284	51.3

*Restrictions based on sex, age, race, religion, and property ownership prevented a significant portion of the adult population from voting in the nineteenth and early twentieth centuries. Of those who were eligible, however, the percentage casting ballots was often quite high, particularly during the last half of the nineteenth century.

Sources: Population figures for 1824 to 1920 are based on estimates and early census figures that appear in Neal R. Peirce, *The People's President* (New York: Simon & Schuster, 1968), 206; copyright renewed © 1979 by Neal R. Peirce. Reprinted by permission of Yale University Press. Population figures from 1932 to 1984 are from the U.S. Department of Commerce, Bureau of the Census, *Statistical Abstract of the United States* (Washington, D.C.: Government Printing Office, 1987), 250. Figures from 1988 to the present were compiled from official election returns supplied by the Federal Election Commission.

remained within the 70 to 80 percent range for the next fifty years in all regions except the South.[3] There, the rise of one-party politics following the Civil War, the disfranchisement of African Americans after the withdrawal of federal troops, and the introduction of various impediments to voting such as poll taxes, literacy tests, and "private" primaries in which only whites could participate, plus the imposition of more restrictive residence requirements, all substantially reduced the proportion of adults who voted.

Although the size of the electorate continued to grow, the percentage of those eligible who actually voted did not. Populated by thousands of immigrants, who initially spoke little English, the size of the eligible electorate increased but the proportion of those voting decreased. Similarly, the enfranchisement of women in 1920 had much the same effect. In 1924, only 44 percent of the electorate cast ballots. Within a period of thirty years, turnout had declined almost 40 percent.[4]

Although voter turnout grew moderately during Franklin Roosevelt's presidency and the post–World War II era, it began to decline again following the 1960 presidential election, an election in which 64 percent voted. With the exception of 1992, the trend has been mostly downward. In the 1996 presidential election, fewer than half of those eligible voted; in 2000 barely more than half did. In nonpresidential elections the proportion of eligible voters participating is even lower, in the range of 40 percent or less for midterm congressional elections.

Among the 50 states, there is also considerable variation in turnout. Some of it has to do with the ease of registration. States that permit election day registration (such as Minnesota and Wisconsin) or do not require it at all (North Dakota) tend to have higher turnouts. The level of electoral competition within states is also a factor, as is the amount of campaigning, advertising, and grassroots activity by the candidates and parties. The battleground states in 2000 had a modest increase in turnout while those in other states remained steady or even decreased.[5]

What has caused the decline in voter turnout since 1960? Why do so many people not vote? Does low turnout indicate voter satisfaction or alienation? Does it contribute to stability or create conditions for instability within the democratic political system? What party and which programs benefit and which groups suffer when so many people do not vote? These questions are addressed in an examination of turnout and its implications for the political system.

The Expansion of Suffrage

The Constitution empowers the state legislatures to determine the time, place, and manner of holding elections for national office. Although it also gives Congress the authority to alter such regulations, Congress did not do so until the Civil War. Thus, the states were free to restrict suffrage, and most did. In some states, property ownership was a requirement for exercising the franchise; in others, a particular religious belief was necessary. In most, it was essential to be white, male, and over twenty-one.[6]

By the 1830s, most states had eliminated property and religious restrictions, thereby extending suffrage to approximately 80 percent of the adult white male population.[7] The Fifteenth Amendment, ratified in 1870, removed race and color as qualifications for voting. In theory, it enabled all nonwhite males to vote. In practice, it enfranchised those in the North and border states but not those in the South, where a series of restrictive voting laws combined with social pressure to prevent African Americans from voting in large numbers for another hundred years. In every southern state, a majority of eligible African Americans were not registered to vote until the mid- to late 1960s.[8]

Following the Civil War, both the number of eligible voters and the percentage of actual voters increased. More competition between the parties contributed to this higher level of participation, as did the absence of registration procedures and the use of secret ballots in some states.

In the twentieth century, the passage of the four constitutional amendments expanded the voting-age population still further. In 1920, women received the right to vote at the national level (Nineteenth Amendment) although some states and territories had granted women suffrage earlier.[9] In 1961, the District of Columbia was granted three electoral votes, thereby extending the franchise to its residents in presidential elections (Twenty-third Amendment); in 1964, the collection of a poll tax was prohibited in national elections (Twenty-fourth Amendment); in 1971, suffrage was extended to all citizens eighteen years of age and older (Twenty-sixth Amendment).

Moreover, the Supreme Court and Congress began to eliminate the legal and institutional barriers to voting. In 1944, the Court outlawed the white primary.[10] In the mid-1960s, Congress, by its passage of the Civil Rights Act (1964) and the Voting Rights Act (1965), banned literacy tests in federal elections for all citizens who had at least a sixth-grade education in a U.S. school. Where less than 50 percent of the population was registered to vote, federal officials were sent to facilitate registration. No longer was drawn-out and costly litigation necessary to ensure the right to vote. Amendments to the Voting Rights Act have also reduced the residence requirement for presidential elections to a maximum of thirty days.

The expansion of suffrage has produced more voters. It has enlarged the electorate, but initially that enlargement also contributed to the smaller percentage of that electorate who voted. The reason for the smaller percentage is that newly enfranchised voters cast ballots less regularly than those who have previously enjoyed the right to vote.

It takes time to develop the practice of voting. For example, although women first voted on a national scale in 1920, the proportion of women who voted was less than the proportion of men who cast ballots for another sixty years. By 1980, however, the rate at which women and men turned out to vote was approximately the same. Since 1988, women have been slightly more likely to vote than men—between 2 and 3 percent more likely.[11]

Concern has been voiced about the relatively low turnout of voters in the United States compared with other democratic countries. As Table 3–2 demonstrates, voting turnout is much higher in most European democracies than in the United States. If the percentage of those registered who actually vote is the basis for comparison, the United States fares better, but it still trails numerous other democratic countries.[12]

Unlike many other countries, the United States does not impose penalties on those who fail to register and vote; nor does it have a national system for automatic registration as do many other democracies. Election day is a workday in the United States whereas in most other countries, it occurs on Sunday or on a national holiday.

In 1993, Congress responded to the registration problem by enacting legislation that requires states to allow people to register by mail or at the time they obtain or renew their driver's license.[13] The motor-voter bill, as it is called, also states that registration materials should be available at certain agencies that provide social services such as welfare offices and those that serve the disabled. The law took effect in 1995 and voter registration has increased since then. By 2000, about 72.6 percent of the voting-age population was registered to vote with 38 percent of the new registrants completing their forms at motor vehicle bureaus.[14] (See Box 3–1, "Registering to Vote," page 72.)

Two groups, the youngest eligible voters and the poorest, were expected to increase their electoral participation the most as a result of this law. Although eighteen- to twenty-four-year-olds have traditionally had the lowest registration rates (only about 40 percent), they have much higher driving rates (85 percent have driver's licenses). By making registration available at the same time and place where people get or renew their licenses, it was thought that the law could double the number of registered voters in the lowest age cohort. Similarly, by making registration available at centers for public assistance, the legislation could also help increase the proportion of poorer people who register to vote, and initially it did.[15]

Had the proportion of younger voters and poorer voters increased substantially, the Democrats would probably be helped more than the Republicans, at least that was what some Republican governors feared who tried to delay the implementation of the motor-voter bill in their states. But voting turnout has only marginally increased since the enactment of the legislation. Although over 22 million new registrants have been added since the law was enacted, millions more have been deleted from the voting lists or declared inactive and will subsequently be deleted if they fail to vote in the next federal election. Besides, registering to vote and voting are two different actions. Thus the proportion of the population who are registered exceeds the proportion of the population who votes.

Even if the obstacles of registering are surmounted, other obstacles to voting remain. Finding the correct location, getting to the polls, figuring out how to cast a vote can be difficult for beginners, for those who have limited English language skills, and for people with various mental and physical handicaps. Since election day is a workday for most people, and a school day for some, obtaining time to vote may also be a problem, or if not, at least a good excuse for not voting.

Table 3–3 indicates levels of turnout in federal elections since the law became effective. With turnout averaging around 50 percent in presidential elections and 40 percent or less for midterm elections, the easing of registration has obviously not, in and of itself, accomplished its desired goal, although it may have moderated the trend of declining turnout in the United States a little.[16]

Legal barriers to voting remain. The Florida vote controversy in 2000 points to some of them: errors in registration rolls, confusion in making and casting ballots, even alleged intimidation and arbitrary decisions by election officials.

Another impediment to extended suffrage has been the growth of the prison population in the United States. People convicted of a felony or dishonorably discharged from the military lose their right to vote in many states. Only three states allow people who are currently incarcerated to vote. These restrictions impact disproportionately on African American males, disenfranchising about 1.4 million out of 10.4 million in the population.[17]

Other Influences on Turnout

There are also psychological, social, and political influences on who comes out to vote. Interest in the election, concern over the outcome, feelings of civic responsibility, and sense of political efficacy (the belief that one's vote really counts) are factors that influence voting.[18]

TABLE 3–2

INTERNATIONAL VOTER TURNOUT (IN PERCENTAGES)

Country	Year	Type of Election	Turnout of Registered Voters
Argentina	1995	Presidential	80.9
Australia	1998	Legislative	95.2
Belgium	1999	Parliamentary	90.5
Brazil	1998	Presidential	78.5
Canada	1997	General	67.0
Greece	1996	Parliamentary	76.3
India	1998	Parliamentary	62.0
Israel	1999	Parliamentary	78.7
Japan	1995	Parliamentary	44.5
Mexico	2000	Presidential	60.0
Poland	1995	Presidential	64.7/68.2*
Russia	2000	Presidential	67.8
Turkey	1995	Parliamentary	87.1
United States	2000	Presidential	51.3† (67.5% of registered voters)
	2002	Legislative	39.0†

* Two rounds.

† VAP = Voting-age population.

Source: Federal Election Commission, Office of Election Administration, May 2, 2003, <http://www.fec.gov>.

BOX 3–1 🏛️

REGISTERING TO VOTE

It is easy to register to vote. There are several ways to do so.

1. Contact your state's chief election official. In most states, it is the secretary of state; in some, it is the head of the Board of Elections; in a few, it may be the lieutenant governor.

   Simply request a registration form, complete it, and return it to the address indicated. If you are uncertain whom to contact, call the Federal Election Commission (FEC) on its toll-free number (800) 424-9530 to find out. The FEC also has a Web site, <http://www.fec.gov>, from which you can access the national registration form, download it, and print it on standard paper. Most but not all states will accept downloaded copies of this form or photocopies of it as registration applications. The FEC Web site notes the exceptions.

2. Go to your nearest department of motor vehicles, military recruitment, or public assistance office to obtain a copy of the registration form. Complete it and give it to the appropriate person at the office at which you have obtained the form.

3. Access the Web site of an organization called Rock-the-Vote at <http://www.rockthevote.org>. You will be asked to complete some basic information. The group will then transmit this information to a central clearinghouse, which will print it on an application card and mail it to you in about two weeks along with the address of the office in your state to which it should be mailed. If you register in this way, the group will also send you a reminder to vote a few days before the election.

Naturally, people who feel more strongly about the election are more likely to get involved. Those with more intense partisan feelings are more likely to have this interest, more likely to participate in the campaign, and more likely to vote on election day. Voters are also more likely than nonvoters to believe that their participation in elections makes a difference. For many, voting becomes a civic responsibility, the result of a personal conviction, even a habit. The more people have done it in the past, the more likely they will do it in the future. Table 3–3 provides empirical support for the proposition that the newly eligible vote with less regularity than those who have previously exercised their franchise. Voting turnout increases with age up to about seventy-five years old.

What are the reasons that young people vote less often? They are more mobile and have fewer economic interests and looser political ties to the community in which they live. Moreover, many young people have not yet developed the habit of voting or, in some cases, even of identifying with a political party. Nor do partisan appeals to younger voters seem to have the same resonance as appeals to those who have developed stakes within their communities.

Breaking the habit of nonvoting may be difficult. Peer group pressure is low because so many in this younger age group have not voted or even registered to

TABLE 3–3 ✦

TURNOUT 1980–2000 (NUMBERS IN THOUSANDS; CIVILIAN NONINSTITUTIONAL POPULATION WHO REPORTED THAT THEY VOTED)

Region, Race, Hispanic Origin, Gender, and Age	Presidential Elections of					
	2000	1996	1992	1988	1984	1980
United States						
Total voting age (millions)	202,600	193,651	185,684	178,098	169,963	157,085
Percent voted	54.7	54.2	61.3	57.4	59.9	59.2
White	60.4	56.0	63.6	59.1	61.4	60.9
Black	54.1	50.6	54.0	51.5	55.8	50.5
Hispanic origin*	27.5	26.7	28.9	28.8	32.6	29.9
Male	53.1	52.8	60.2	56.4	59.0	59.1
Female	56.2	55.5	62.3	58.3	60.8	59.4
18 to 24 years	32.3	32.4	42.8	36.2	40.8	39.9
25 to 44 years	49.8	49.2	58.3	54.0	58.4	58.7
45 to 65 years	64.1	64.4	70.0	67.9	69.8	69.3
65 years and over	69.9	67.0	70.1	68.8	67.7	65.1
Northeast, Midwest, and West						
Total, voting age	130,774	125,571	122,025	117,373	112,376	106,524
Percent voted	53.2	55.3	62.5	58.9	61.6	61.0
White	58.2	57.4	64.9	60.4	63.0	62.4
Black	53.2	51.4	53.8	55.6	58.9	52.8
South						
Total voting age	71,835	68,080	63,659	60,725	57,587	50,561
Percent voted	53.5	52.2	59.0	54.5	56.8	55.6
White	58.2	53.4	60.8	56.4	58.1	57.4
Black	54.2	50.0	54.3	48.0	53.2	48.2

*Hispanics may be of any race.

Source: Current Population Reports, Series P20, Nos. 143, 192, 253, 322, 370, 405, 440, 466, and the November 1996 Current Population Survey. Taken from "Voting and Registration in the Election of November 1996," by Lynne M. Casper and Loretta E. Bass, U.S. Census Bureau; Current Population Survey, Series P 20-542, February 27, 2002, <http://www.census.gov>.

vote. Thus it is the older generation with whom young people interact as they move into voting age that influences who votes. Parents, teachers, community, and religious leaders provide critical information and model civic behavior that affects the initial decision of whether to vote. The act of voting, however, makes subsequent positive voting decisions easier. Over time, voting becomes a habit, a ritual that is dutifully followed every election day.[19]

As people age, they become more regular voters, up until the period in which poor health may prevent them from voting. With advances in medicine, however, this age has increased with political activity continuing into the senior years. It is not until the age of seventy-five, that voting turnout begins to decline. However, the increasing proportion of the electorate in the youngest and very oldest age groups has contributed to a lower percentage of voter turnout, as have other factors, such as the weakening of partisan attitudes.

Other demographic characteristics related to turnout are education, income, and occupational status. As people become more educated, as they move up the socioeconomic ladder, as their jobs gain in status, they are more likely to vote. Education is the most important of these variables. It has a larger impact than any other single social characteristic.[20] As Table 3–3 demonstrates, the higher the level of education, the greater the percentage voting.

The reason education is so important is that it provides the skills for processing and evaluating information; for perceiving differences among the parties, candidates, and issues; and for relating these differences to personal values and behavior. Education also affects personal success. It increases a person's stake in the system, interest in the election, and concern over the outcome. Since the lesson that voting is a civic responsibility is usually learned in the classroom, schooling may also contribute to a more highly developed sense of responsibility about voting. Finally, education provides the knowledge and confidence to overcome voting hurdles—to register on time, to file absentee ballots properly, and to mark the ballot or use the voting machine or punch-hole ballot correctly on election day.[21]

Given the relationship of education to turnout, why should the rate of turnout have declined since 1960 when the general level of education in the United States has increased? One explanation for this trend has been the larger number of younger voters who entered the electorate, the so-called Generation Xers, and their weak tie to others within the community. As people get old, marry, and join groups, their link to the community grows stronger. They have more at stake, and as a consequence, are more likely to vote.[22] A second explanation has to do with the increase of resident aliens in the population who cannot vote, and a third, the number of people who are incarcerated and are temporarily or permanently prohibited from voting.

There are other factors. The weakening of partisan attitudes, the growth of political cynicism and apathy among the electorate, particularly among those in the lower socioeconomic groups, and until recently, the declining sense of political efficacy that people can make a difference in what the government does or does not do have all contributed. Before examining each of these factors, however, it is important to understand that the decline in turnout occurred despite increasing education levels, certainly not because of them. Professors Paul R. Abramson, John H. Aldrich, and David W. Rohde estimate that turnout would have declined two and one-half times as much had education levels not increased.[23]

For the last three decades of the twentieth century, the strength of partisan loyalties declined, while the proportion of the electorate identifying themselves as independent grew. Since party allegiances are a motivation for voting, the weakening of partisan attitudes contributed to the decrease in turnout as has the growth of self-identified independents. As a group, independents are 12 percent less likely to vote than are strong partisans.[24]

Moreover, the personal contact that parties have with their partisans has declined. In the last election, only 36 percent of the electorate reported that they were contacted by a political party. Personal contact is important. Those people who have been contacted personally are more likely to vote than those who have not been.[25]

As the parties have become more personalized and factionalized and as campaigns become more candidate centered, voting decisions have become more confusing to more voters. The difficulty people have in deciding whose election would be most beneficial to them has contributed to nonvoting, particularly among those with less education, who tend to have less information and less highly developed analytical skills.

Since the 1960s, people have also become more disillusioned about the political system and, correspondingly, less confident that their vote matters, or that they can change the way government works or public officials behave. This lower sense of efficacy has also depressed the vote. Abramson and his colleagues argue that about two-thirds of the decline in turnout since 1960 can be attributed primarily to the combined effects of weaker partisan affiliation and feelings of less political effectiveness with the latter being twice as important.[26] Trust in government, however, does not appear to be as important a factor as political efficacy.[27]

A class bias also exists in voting that is connected to negative feelings people have about their own ability to influence events and the trust they place in political leaders. The decline in turnout has been greatest among those in the lowest socioeconomic groups, thereby enlarging the participation gap between the haves and have-nots. This gap has produced an electorate that is less representative of the population as a whole, an electorate that is better educated and has higher incomes than the general public. To the extent that government responds to the electorate rather than to the general population, its policies take on a "have" rather than a "have not" coloration.

This class bias in voting produces a tragic irony in American politics. Those who are most disadvantaged, who have the least education, and who need to change conditions the most, actually participate the least. Those who are the most advantaged, who benefit from existing conditions and presumably from the public policy that contributes to those conditions, vote most often. These trends in voting behavior work to reflect, even to perpetuate, the status quo.

Generational and racial divisions accentuate the problem. Younger people and racial minorities are disproportionately found in the lower socioeconomic strata. There is a difference in turnout between white and African Americans, with whites voting at higher levels than African Americans although the difference declined slightly in 2000.

Demographic characteristics may suggest patterns in turnout, who votes and why, but these characteristics are also affected by the electoral environment. In 1992, for example, turnout increased by 5 percent. If the demographic factors were fairly constant then what explains the increase? The recession of 1991–1992 may have energized some of those adversely affected by it; Perot's candidacy appealed to independents who are generally less interested in politics and less likely to vote; and new media formats reached and informed new voters. Singularly and together, these factors momentarily reversed the downward cycle in the proportion of the electorate that voted in that election.

The prosperity of the 1990s reduced the economic dissatisfaction level by 1996. Nor did Perot have the same appeal as he had four years earlier. The electorate was more content; turnout declined.

Turnout stayed relatively low in 2000 despite the competitiveness of the two major party candidates throughout the campaign. Economic prosperity and world peace muted divisive national issues. Although the third-party candidates may have brought out additional voters, these candidates did not receive a sizable portion of the total vote, thereby only marginally increasing turnout. Despite effective advertising and grassroots campaigns by party and nonparty groups, despite the people's more positive attitudes toward government and their own civic responsibilities, despite the closeness of the election, it was the major party candidates, themselves, who failed to arouse the electorate, according to two political scientists who examined the turnout effects in 2000, Steven Finkel and Paul Freedman.[28]

In short, campaigns and electoral environments matter. They affect who comes out to vote. Compared to 1992, people in 1996 and 2000 were less interested and excited about the election. As a consequence, turnout declined.

Turnout and Partisanship

Turnout has partisan implications as well. Since the Democratic Party draws more of its electoral support from those in the lower socioeconomic groups, those with less formal education, and those with fewer professional opportunities, lower turnout tends to hurt that party more than the GOP. In 1992 and 1996, however, it did not. The increase in turnout was greater among Democrats than Republicans, thereby eliminating the partisan advantage the Republicans usually have from turning out a larger proportion of their partisans to vote.

Republicans have also benefited from their party's greater financial resources, which have enabled them to mount more effective campaigns to identify and register new voters. They have had the resources to employ an individualized, targeted system to get out their vote, whereas the Democrats, with help from organized labor and African American and Hispanic organizations, have generally utilized a strategy that directs mass appeals to these key Democratic blocs of voters. In 2000, the Democrats were successful in mobilizing a large vote from several of their core constituencies, African Americans and labor unions. They were much less successful in the 2002 midterm elections as the Republicans mounted an effective seventy-two-hour get-out-the-vote drive among their key supporters. That drive was viewed as a critical factor in helping Republicans regain control of the Senate.

The lesson, turnout matters in close elections, has not been lost on the Democrats. Vowing to compete more effectively with the Republicans at the grassroots level, the Democrats have amassed a database of 158 million voters from which they hope to solicit donations, target specific messages, and turn out voters in the next election.[29]

Despite the turnout differential and demographic differences that exist between voters and nonvoters, some evidence suggests that results of most presidential elections would not have been any different had more people voted, though the election of 2000 might have been an exception. Nonvoters surveyed after recent elections indicated that they preferred the winner by approximately the same percentage as the national averages in these elections. One reason that nonvoters follow the dominant mood of the electorate is that they tend to be influenced by shorter-term factors that affect the outcome of the election, perhaps even more so than voters whose partisan allegiances can more readily resist these short-term forces.

To understand the impact of partisanship on turnout we turn to the partisan basis of politics.

THE PARTISAN BASIS OF POLITICS

Why do people vote as they do? Considerable research has been conducted to answer this question. Initially, much of it was done under the direction of the Center for Political Studies at the University of Michigan. Beginning in 1952, the center conducted nationwide surveys during presidential elections.[30] To identify the major influences on voting behavior, a random sample of the electorate was interviewed before and after each election. Respondents were asked a series of questions designed to reveal their attitudes toward the parties, candidates, and issues. On the basis of their answers to these questions, researchers have amassed a wealth of data to explain the voting behavior of the U.S. electorate.

A Model of the U.S. Voter

One of the earliest and most influential theories of voting behavior based on the Michigan survey data was presented in a book entitled *The American Voter* (1960).[31] The model on which the theory is based assumes that individuals are influenced by their partisan attitudes and social relationships in addition to the political environment in which an election occurs. In fact, these attitudes and those relationships condition the impact of that environment on individual voting behavior.

According to the theory, people develop attitudes early in life, largely as a consequence of interacting with their families, particularly their parents. These attitudes, in turn, tend to be reinforced by neighborhood, school, and religious associations. The reasons they tend to be reinforced lie in the psychological and social patterns of behavior. Psychologically, it is more pleasing to have beliefs and attitudes supported than challenged. Socially, it is more comfortable and safer to associate with "nice," like-minded people—those with similar cultural, educational, and religious experiences—than with others. This desire to increase one's "comfort level" in social relationships explains why the environment for most people tends to be supportive much of the time.[32]

Attitudes mature and harden over the years. The older people become, the less amenable they are to change. They are more set in their ways. Consequently, their behavior is more predictable. Political attitudes are no exception to this general pattern of attitude formation and maintenance. They too are developed early in life, are reinforced by association, grow in intensity, and become more predictable with time.

Of all the factors that contribute to the development of a political attitude, an identification with a political party is the most important. It affects how people see campaigns, how they evaluate candidates, and how they vote on election day. Party identification operates as a conceptual framework, a lens through which the campaign is understood and evaluated. It provides cues for interpreting the issues, for judging the candidates, and for deciding whether and if so, how to vote. The stronger these attitudes, the more compelling the cues; conversely, the weaker the attitudes, the less likely they will affect perceptions during the campaign and influence voting on election day.[33]

When identification with a party is weak or nonexistent, other factors, such as the personalities of the candidates and their issue positions, are correspondingly more important. In contrast to party identification, which is a long-term stabilizing factor but one that can be changed over time, candidate and issue orientations are shorter term, more variable factors, often shifting from election to election.

As elections have become more candidate centered, so too is partisanship more influenced by the image of the party's nominee. It is a two-way relationship. Party helps shape the image of the candidate, and candidates affect the image of the party. Moreover, the impact of candidates on partisan images can extend beyond the election itself.[34]

Candidate images turn on performance and policy dimensions. People form general impressions about candidates on the basis of what they know about the candidates' personal experiences, their leadership capabilities, and their character. For an incumbent president seeking reelection, accomplishments in office provide much of the criteria for evaluating how well the president has done. Other characteristics, such as trustworthiness, integrity, empathy, and candor, are also important. How important they are depends on the nature of the times. Following a presidency besmirched by scandal, such as Nixon's and Clinton's, integrity, credibility, and character assume more importance than at other times. For the challenger, it is the potential for office as demonstrated by experience, knowledge, confidence, and assertiveness, plus a host of personal qualities that help determine qualifications for a leadership position such as president.[35]

Candidates' stands on the issues, however, seem less critical than do their partisanship and performance in office. The principal explanation for downgrading the importance of issues has been the low level of information and awareness that much of the electorate possesses. To be important, issues must be salient. They must attract attention—they must hit home. Without personal impact, they are unlikely to be primary motivating factors in voting. In addition, the candidates must take sufficiently different positions on the issues for voters to decide which of those positions is the one they find most acceptable. To the extent that issue positions are not known or distinguishable between the principal candidates, their respective personal images become a stronger influence on the vote.

Ironically, that portion of the electorate who can be more easily persuaded, weak partisans and independents, tend to have the least information.[36] Conversely, the most committed tend to be the most informed. They use their information to support their partisanship.

The relationship between degree of partisanship and amount of information has significant implications for a democratic society. The traditional view of a democracy holds that information and awareness are necessary to make an intelligent judgment on election day. However, the finding that those who have the most information are also the most committed, and that those who lack this commitment also lack the incentive to get more information, has upset some of the assumptions about the motivation for acquiring information and using it to vote intelligently.

A More Refined Theory of Voting

The model of voting behavior first presented in 1960 has engendered considerable controversy. Critics have charged that the theory presumes that most of the electorate is uninformed and vote habitually rather than rationally. One well-known political scientist, the late V.O. Key, even wrote a book dedicated to "the perverse and unorthodox argument . . . that voters are not fools."[37] Key studied the behavior of three groups of voters between 1936 and 1960: switchers, stand-patters, and new voters. He found those who switched their votes to be interested in and influenced by their own evaluation of policy, personality, and performance. In this sense, Key believed that they exercised an intelligent judgment when voting.

Key's conclusion that most voters were not automatons and that most of their voting decisions were not solely or even primarily the product of their psychological dispositions and social pressures is accepted today by most students of electoral behavior. Even though voters may have limited information, they use it to arrive at reasoned political judgments. They take into account their present situation, their beliefs about government, and their assessments of how the country is doing under its current leadership and will do in the future. In the words of political scientist, Samuel Popkin:

> They consider not only economic issues but family, residential, and consumer issues as well. They think not only of their immediate needs, but also of their needs for insurance against future problems; not only about private good but also about collective goods.[38]

How do they do this? What criteria do they use in making judgments?

Morris Fiorina, in his provocative study *Retrospective Voting in American National Elections* (1981), tries to answer these questions. Utilizing a rational choice model adopted from economics, Fiorina argues that voting decisions are calculations people make on the basis of their accumulated political experience. They make these calculations by assessing the past performance of the parties and their elected officials in light of the promises they made and political events that have occurred. Fiorina calls this a retrospective evaluation.[39]

Retrospective evaluations are not only important for influencing voting in a given election, they are also important for shaping partisan attitudes, which Fiorina defines as "a running tally of retrospective evaluations of party promises and performance."[40] In other words, the running tally is a summary judgment of how well the parties and their leaders have done and are doing.

As a political attitude, partisanship is fairly stable. It can change but usually does not do so quickly. Nonetheless, changes in partisan attitudes have taken place over the last several decades, and these changes have had an impact on voting behavior.

Partisan Voting Patterns

The initial model of voter behavior was based on research conducted in the 1950s. Since that time, the U.S. electorate has experienced a divisive, unsuccessful war in Southeast Asia; a cohesive, successful one in the Persian Gulf; an end to the Cold War; a terrorist attack and domestic and international responses to it; a major scandal (Watergate) that led to the resignation of a president and the impeachment and acquittal of another president; other scandals involving public officials, from cabinet secretaries to members of Congress, in their private behavior and in the exercise of their public responsibilities; large-scale social movements for extending equal rights and opportunities to women, racial and ethnic minorities, and those with same-sex orientations; and periods of economic recession, inflation, and prosperity. Naturally, these events and the reaction of government officials to them have had an impact on the partisan attitudes of the electorate.

Three major trends stand out. First, over the last half of the twentieth century, there has been a reduction in the percentage of the voting-age population who identify with a party and, concurrently, an increase in the percentage of self-proclaimed independents. That increase occurred primarily in the 1970s, with the Democratic Party the big loser. Second, there has been a decline in the strength of partisan identities. Third, there has been a shift in partisan loyalties, with the Democratic Party losing and the Republican Party gaining adherents. Each of these changes has important long- and short-term implications for electoral politics in America.

Table 3–4 lists the percentage of party identifiers and independents. As the table indicates, during a forty-eight-year period from 1952 to 2000, there has been a 15 percent decline in people who identify with a political party and a 17 percent increase in the number of self-proclaimed independents. Most of this shift occurred between 1964 and 1980. The table also suggests that the decline was principally in the strong partisan category during the 1970s.

Although partisanship has weakened, with some strong partisans becoming weaker partisans and weak partisans considering themselves independents, how independently voters actually behave on election day is another matter. Truly independent voting has increased far less rapidly than has independent identification by the electorate. In other words, a sizable portion claim that they are independent but continue to vote for candidates of the same party. These voters appear in Table 3–4 as independent but leaning in a partisan direction.[41]

The decline in partisanship and the growth of independents have produced, at least in theory, a more volatile and manipulable electorate. With weaker partisan allegiances and more independent identifiers, campaigns, candidates, and issues can become more important influences on the vote.

Partisan Deviations

There has been an increase in split-ticket voting in the period from the late 1960s through the 1970s and into the 1980s.[42] The defections come primarily from weak partisans.

Defections from partisan voting patterns have tended to help the Republicans more than the Democrats. Without votes from Democratic defectors, the GOP could not have won a majority of the presidential elections between 1952 and 2000. Much of the help, however, has been short term. Although the Republicans have won eight elections at the presidential level beginning with their victory in 1952, they still do not command the loyalty of even a plurality of the electorate. In 1992 and in 1996, defections among Republicans were actually higher than among Democrats; in 2000, they were not.

The gap between self-identified Republicans and Democrats has narrowed, however. In 1952, the Democrats enjoyed a 20-percent advantage in party identification. Twenty years later that advantage had declined to 18 percent. The 1980s witnessed an even greater reduction in the partisan differential. By 1984, the parties were at rough parity with one another, and they have remained so since then although the Democrats still hold a slight advantage in party identifiers but less when turnout is taken into account.

Partisan ties have also become weaker, which in turn has produced more candidate-oriented voting and, to a lesser extent, more issue-oriented voting, especially at the presidential level. Why have these trends developed?

The reactions to Vietnam and Watergate and to the credibility gaps and political abuses of the so-called imperial presidents generated feelings of mistrust and hostility that were directed at politicians and their parties. Those who became eligible to vote, particularly during and after the 1970s were less willing to identify with a political party.

A second reason for the decline in partisan allegiances has been the lowering of the voting age to eighteen. Over the last thirty years, the percentage of the electorate twenty-four years of age and under has nearly doubled. Since party identification tends to develop and harden over time, the influx of younger voters has contributed to the weakening of partisan loyalties and growth of independents. This trend may change as the electorate ages.

A third factor has to do with contemporary modes of campaigning. In the past, political parties provided the organizations, planned campaigns, and made

TABLE 3-4

PARTY IDENTIFICATION, 1952–2000* (IN PERCENTAGES†)

Party Identification	1952	1956	1960	1964	1968	1972	1976	1980	1984	1988	1992	1996	2000
DEMOCRAT	47	44	45	52	45	41	40	41	37	36	35	38	34
Strong	22	21	20	27	20	15	15	18	17	18	17	18	19
Weak	25	23	25	25	25	26	25	23	20	18	18	20	15
INDEPENDENTS§	23	23	23	23	30	35	37	34	34	36	39	34	40
Leaning Democrat	10	6	6	9	10	11	12	11	11	12	14	14	15
Nonpartisan	6	9	10	8	11	13	15	13	11	11	12	8	12
Leaning Republican	7	8	7	6	9	11	10	10	12	13	13	12	13
REPUBLICAN	27	29	30	25	25	23	23	23	27	28	26	29	25
Strong	14	14	14	14	15	13	14	14	15	14	15	13	12
Weak	13	15	16	11	10	10	9	9	12	14	11	16	12
APOLITICALS													
"Don't know"/other	4	4	3	1	1	1	1	2	2	2	1	1	1

* The survey question was "Generally speaking, do you usually think of yourself as a Republican, a Democrat, an Independent, or what?" If Republican or Democrat, "Would you call yourself a strong (R) (D) or a not very strong (R) (D)?" If Independent, "Do you think of yourself as closer to the Republican or Democratic Party?"

† Percentages may not equal 100 due to rounding.

§ The people who fall into this category are those who declare themselves to be Independent, but in follow-up questions indicate that they may lean in a partisan direction.

Sources: National Election Studies (NES), Inter-University Consortium for Political and Social Research, Center for Political Studies, University of Michigan, 1952–2000.

partisan appeals. In doing so, they trumpeted their own cause. Today, candidates' organizations direct their own campaigns. In doing so, they focus attention on the candidates' personal attributes and policy agenda rather than the party's.

Nonetheless, it is premature to write an obituary for partisanship and its impact on the electorate. The proportion of the population who continues to identify with a party remains significant and that identification either directly or indirectly influences people's voting behavior.[43] There continues to be a strong relationship between perceived partisanship and presidential voting. In 2000, 86 percent of self-identified Democrats voted for Gore and 91 percent of people who considered themselves Republicans voted for Bush. Finally, partisan allegiances have stabilized and influences on the vote have increased in recent elections.

To summarize, it is not as strong an influence on how people evaluate candidates or issues, and ultimately on how they vote, as it once was, but it is still a major factor. Correspondingly, short-term factors, such as the candidates, issues, and economic and social environment, are more important. The combination of these campaign-specific factors with partisan attitudes helps explain election outcomes.

But that is not all. When individuals develop attitudes and opinions, they are also influenced by the associations they have with others and by the groups with which they are affiliated. These social influences can affect voting behavior, at least that was the theory first postulated by Paul F. Lazarsfeld, Bernard R. Berelson, and others who examined the sociology of electoral politics almost fifty years ago in their groundbreaking studies, *The People's Choice* and *Voting*.[44]

Although more attention has been devoted to the psychological influences on voting behavior since the publication of *The American Voter* in 1960, a recent study by Paul Allen Beck and others lends support to the theory that the social context in which elections occur matters. The authors of that study found that intermediaries between the candidates and voters (individuals, media, and groups) provided information that contributed to voters' decisions whether to vote, and if so, for whom. The intermediaries had most effect on those voters who were less tied to parties, and for the most part, less informed and interested in electoral politics. Coming into contact with others who had political information and were interested brought the election home to some who might otherwise have avoided it.[45] In the next section we turn to these intermediaries and their influences on voting behavior. Specifically, we look at the groups that are part of the major parties' electoral coalitions and the support they provide in presidential elections.

THE SOCIAL BASIS OF POLITICS

The New Deal Realignment

Political coalitions form during periods of partisan realignment. The last time a classic realignment occurred was in the 1930s. Largely as a consequence of the Great Depression, the Democrats emerged as the dominant party.[46] Their coalition, held together by a common economic belief that the government should play a more active role in dealing with the nation's economic problems, supported Franklin Roosevelt's New Deal program. Those who saw government involvement as a threat to the free enterprise system opposed much of Roosevelt's domestic legislation. They remained Republican in attitude and voting behavior.

The Democrats became the majority party during this period by expanding their base. Since the Civil War, the Democrats had enjoyed support in the South. White Protestants living in rural areas dominated the southern electorate; African Americans were largely excluded from it. Only in the election of 1928, when Al Smith, the Catholic governor of New York, ran as the Democratic candidate, was there a sizable southern popular and electoral vote for a Republican candidate at the presidential level. Being a Catholic and an opponent of prohibition made Smith unacceptable to many white Protestant fundamentalists who lived in the South.

As a group, Catholics also voted Democratic before the 1930s. Living primarily in the urban centers of the North, they became increasingly important to the Democrats as their numbers grew in the population. Poor economic and social conditions, combined with the immigrant status of many Catholics, made them dependent on big-city bosses, who were able to deliver a sizable Democratic vote. In 1928, for the first time, a majority of the cities in the country voted Democratic. Catholic support for Smith and the Democratic Party figured prominently in this vote.

The harsh economic realities of the Great Depression enabled Roosevelt to expand Democratic support in urban areas still further, especially among those in the lower socioeconomic strata. Outside the South, Roosevelt's political coalition was differentiated along class lines. It attracted people with less education and income and those with lower-status jobs. Organized labor, in particular, threw its support to Roosevelt. Union members became a core group in the Democratic Party's electoral coalition.

In addition to establishing a broad-based, blue-collar, working-class coalition, Roosevelt also lured specific racial and ethnic groups, such as African Americans and Jewish Americans, from their Republican roots. African Americans, who lived outside of the South, voted Democratic primarily for economic reasons, and Jewish Americans supported Roosevelt's liberal domestic programs and his anti-Nazi foreign policy. Neither of these groups provided the Democratic Party of the 1930s with a large number of votes, but their loyalty to it and long-term impact on it have been considerable.

In contrast, during the same period the Republican Party shrank. Not only were Republicans unable to attract new groups to their coalition, they were unable to prevent the defection of some supporters whose economic situation affected their partisan loyalties and influenced their vote. Although the Republicans did retain the backing of many business and professional people, they lost the support of much of the white Protestant working class. Republican strength remained concentrated in the Northeast, particularly in the rural areas.

Evolving Political Coalitions

The coalition that formed during the New Deal held together, for the most part, until the 1960s. During this period, African Americans and Jewish Americans increased their identification with and support of the Democratic Party and its candidates. Catholics tended to remain Democratic, although they fluctuated more in their voting behavior at the presidential level. Nonsouthern white Protestants continued to support the Republicans.

Some changes did take place, however, mainly along socioeconomic lines. Domestic prosperity contributed to the growth of a larger middle class. Had such a class identified with the Republicans for economic reasons, the Democratic majority would have been threatened. This identification did not occur, however. Those who gained in economic and social status did not, as a general rule, discard their partisan loyalties. The Democrats were able to hold on to the allegiance of a majority of this group and improve their position with the professional and managerial classes, which had grown substantially during this period. The Republicans continued to maintain their advantage with those in the upper socioeconomic strata. The economic improvement in the country had the effect of blurring class distinctions that were evident during the 1930s and 1940s.[47]

Partisan attitudes, however, were shifting in the South. White southerners, particularly those who first voted after 1940, began to desert their party at the presidential level, largely over civil rights issues. In 1948, Harry Truman won 52 percent of the southern vote, compared with Roosevelt's 69 percent four years earlier. Although Adlai Stevenson and John Kennedy carried the South by reduced margins, the southern white Protestant vote for president went Republican for the first time in 1960.

Major shifts in the national electorate began to be evident in the mid-1960s and continued through the 1990s. (See Table 3–5.) The continued defection of southern white Protestants to Republican candidates, not only at the presidential level but at the other levels as well, has been the most significant and enduring of these changes.

Since 1952, the decline in the partisan loyalty of southern whites has been substantial. Then, 85 percent of them identified with the Democratic Party; forty years later, that proportion had shrunk to less than 40 percent with the ratio of Democrats to Republicans in the South declining from approximately six to one to less than two to one.[48] Moreover, in the 1994 midterm elections, Republican congressional candidates won a majority of the southern vote, the first time that has happened since Reconstruction.[49] In subsequent elections, the Republicans maintained their southern majority in the House. The South was also the region of the country that voted most heavily for Robert Dole and George W. Bush.

Despite Republican gains in the South, it is still not as solidly Republican today as it was solidly Democratic from 1876 through 1944. According to political scientists Earl and Merle Black, Franklin Delano Roosevelt averaged 78 percent of the southern vote during his four presidential elections compared with 57 percent for Republican presidential candidates from 1972 to 1988.[50]

Beginning in 1988, southern whites have been less apt to vote for the Democratic presidential candidate than have whites in any other region of the country. Arkansas Democrat, Bill Clinton, managed to split the southern vote with Robert Dole in 1996, with each receiving approximately 46 percent, but Tennessean Al Gore received only 36 percent. Had it not been for the growth of the African American electorate in the South and its overwhelming support for Democratic candidates, the defection of the southern states from the Democratic camp would have been even more dramatic.

Another potentially important shift has been occurring among new voters, particularly younger ones. During the 1980s, a plurality of this group turned to the Republican Party after being more Democratic than their elders since the 1950s. In 1984, eighteen- to twenty-nine-year-olds supported Ronald Reagan in his reelection bid just as strongly as did those over thirty. (See Table 3–5.) Their support of George Bush in 1988 was even greater. In 1992, however, the vote of younger Americans more closely reflected national voting trends, and in 1996, they provided Bill Clinton with more support than any other age cohort in the population. In 2000, voters under thirty leaned slightly toward Bush.

While Democrats have lost the allegiance of southern whites at the presidential level and have lost support from southern voters generally, they also saw electoral support dwindle from several of their key coalitions. Organized labor is a good example. In six of the eight presidential elections between 1952 and 1976, this group favored the Democratic candidate by an average of nearly 30 percentage points. In the 1980s, the results were closer although the Democrats still enjoyed an advantage. Labor support for the Democrats increased in recent presidential elections. Clinton received 55 percent of the vote from people who lived in union households in 1992 and 59 percent in 1996, while Gore also got 58 percent in 2000. However, as a group, organized labor has declined as a proportion of the total population. Members of union households made up 25 percent of the electorate in 1952; today they constitute only about 13 percent.[51] Although the proportion of the total vote the Democrats receive from labor has declined, the party's support among middle-class voters has increased.

Catholic allegiance to the Democratic Party has also weakened, declining from its high of 78 percent in 1960 to a low of 39 percent in 1984. Since then, Democratic candidates have recovered some of these losses. Clinton won 53 percent of the Catholic vote in 1996; Gore won 50 percent in 2000. They were both helped by the considerable support they received from the Hispanic community. In general, Catholics as a group now seem more susceptible to candidate-centered and issue-specific appeals than they were when their partisan identification had a stronger impact on them.[52]

Jewish voters have evidenced a much smaller decrease in their Democratic partisan sympathies and voting behavior, although as a group Jews have declined as a proportion of the population. They have remained loyal to the Democratic Party; approximately two-thirds of this group identify with the Democratic Party, and three-fourths have voted for its presidential candidates since 1928. The only election since World War II in which a majority of Jews did not vote Democratic occurred in 1980 when only 47 percent cast ballots for President Carter. Independent candidate John Anderson was the principal beneficiary of this defection, winning 14 percent of the Jewish vote. As a group, Jewish Americans returned to their traditional voting patterns after that election. Contributing to their support for the Democratic candidates has been the party's liberal position on social issues and, in 2000, the nomination of the first Jewish vice presidential candidate, Democrat Joseph Lieberman.

The Democratic electoral coalition has also retained and even increased its support among other key groups, notably African Americans and Hispanics. Today, more than 75 percent of African Americans consider themselves Democrats, with less than 10 percent considering themselves Republicans compared to the late 1950s when almost 25 percent considered themselves Republican.[53] While other groups have weakened their loyalty to the Democrats, African Americans have increased theirs; in fact, the smaller the Democratic vote, the larger the African American proportion of it. In 1996, one out of six Clinton voters was African American; and in 2000, one out of five of Gore's votes came from an African American voter.

But there has been a flip side to this African American support. Democratic positions on social issues, particularly civil rights, that appeal to African Americans have alienated some white working-class voters whose support for the Democrats has declined over the last three decades.[54]

Hispanic voters have also become an important component of the Democrats' electoral coalition, particularly as that group expands within the population. With the exception of Cuban Americans concentrated in south Florida, a majority of Hispanic voters identify with the Democratic Party, and two-thirds of them tend to vote for its candidates on a regular basis. Clinton received the support of almost three out of four Hispanic voters in 1996, and Gore, almost two out of three in 2000.

Since 1980, there have been discernible differences in the partisan identities and electoral voting patterns of men and women. This differential has produced a "gender gap," with women more likely to identify with and vote Democratic and men more likely to prefer the Republican Party and its candidates.[55] The gap had been in the range of 4 to 8 percent until 1996, when it rose to 11 percent and remained at about that level in 2000. It is larger among whites than nonwhites, larger among those in the higher socioeconomic brackets than in lower groups, and larger among those with more formal education than less.[56] It is also greater among those who are unmarried than those who are married and those without children than those with them.[57]

In the light of these shifts, how can the composition of the major political parties be described today? The Democrats have become a diverse party in which ethnic and racial minorities and, increasingly, women constitute core constituencies. They still receive overwhelming support from those with the lowest incomes and those who live in the cities. However, the relatively small size of the latter two groups within the electorate today make them less important than they were in the past. The same can be said for organized labor which continues to vote Democratic but now accounts for a smaller percentage of the total electorate. Southern whites have exited in the largest proportions, but the Democrats have picked up

TABLE 3–5 🐾

VOTE BY GROUPS IN PRESIDENTIAL ELECTIONS, 1968–2000 (IN PERCENTAGES)

	1968			1972		1976			1980		
	Humphrey	Nixon	Wallace	McGovern	Nixon	Carter	Ford	McCarthy	Carter	Reagan	Anderson
NATIONAL	43.0	43.4	13.6	38.0	62.0	50.0	48.0	1.0	41.0	51.0	7.0
Sex											
Men	41	43	16	37	63	53	45	1	38	53	7
Women	45	43	12	38	62	48	51	—	44	49	6
Race											
White	38	47	15	32	68	46	52	1	36	56	7
Nonwhite	85	12	3	87	13	85	15	—	86	10	2
Education†											
College	37	54	9	37	63	42	55	2	35	53	10
High School	42	43	15	34	66	54	46	—	43	51	5
Grade School	52	33	15	49	51	58	41	1	54	42	3
Occupation											
Prof. and Business	34	56	10	31	69	42	56	1	33	55	10
White Collar	41	47	12	36	64	50	48	2	40	51	9
Manual	50	35	15	43	57	58	41	1	48	48	5

Age

Under 30	47	38	15	52	48	53	45	1	47	41	11
30–49 years	44	41	15	67	33	48	49	2	38	52	8
50 years and older	41	47	12	64	36	52	48	—	41	54	4

Religion

Protestants	35	49	16	70	30	46	53	—	39	54	6
Catholics	59	33	8	52	48	57	41	1	46	47	6

Politics

Republicans	9	86	5	95	5	9	91	—	8	86	5
Democrats	74	12	14	33	67	82	18	—	69	26	4
Independents	31	44	25	69	31	38	57	4	29	55	14

Region

East	50	43	7	58	42	51	47	1	43	47	9
Midwest	44	47	9	60	40	48	50	1	41	51	7
South	31	36	33	71	29	54	45	—	44	52	3
West	44	49	7	59	41	46	51	1	35	54	9

Labor Union

Union families	56	29	15	54	46	63	36	1	50	43	5

(continued)

TABLE 3–5 ❦ *(continued)*

VOTE BY GROUPS IN PRESIDENTIAL ELECTIONS, 1968–2000 (IN PERCENTAGES)

	1984		1988		1992			1996			2000*		
	Mondale	Reagan	Dukakis	Bush	Clinton	Bush	Perot	Clinton	Dole	Perot	Gore	Bush	Nader
NATIONAL	41.0	59.0	46.0	54.0	43.2	37.8	19.0	50.0	41.0	9.0	48.0	48.0	3.0
Sex													
Men	36	64	44	56	41	37	22	45	44	11	42	51	4
Women	45	55	48	52	46	38	16	54	39	7	49	43	3
Race													
White	34	66	41	59	39	41	20	46	45	9	39	59	4
Nonwhite	87	13	82	18	77	11	12	82	12	6	81	9	5
Education†													
College	39	61	42	58	43	40	17	47	45	8	46	48	4
High School	43	57	46	54	40	38	22	52	34	14	41	51	5
Grade School	51	49	55	45	56	28	16	58	27	15	48	42	4
Age													
Under 30	40	60	37	63	40	37	23	54	30	16	43	46	8
30–49 years	40	60	45	55	42	37	21	49	41	10	43	51	3
50 years and older	41	59	49	51	46	39	15	50	45	5	48	43	3

Religion													
Protestants	39	61	42	58	41	41	18	44	50	6	—	—	9
Catholics	39	61	51	49	47	35	18	55	35	10	—	—	9
Politics													
Republicans	4	96	7	93	7	77	16	10	85	5	7	91	9
Democrats	79	21	85	15	82	8	10	90	6	4	85	10	9
Independents	33	67	43	57	39	30	31	48	33	19	37	42	3
Region													
East	46	54	51	49	47	35	18	60	31	9	52	38	6
Midwest	42	58	47	53	44	34	22	46	45	9	43	47	4
South	37	63	40	60	38	45	17	44	46	10	36	56	3
West	40	60	46	54	45	35	20	51	43	6	43	47	6
Labor Union													
Union families	52	48	63	37	—	—	—	—	—	—	58	31	6

*Gallup data in 2000 underestimated Gore's vote in most demographic categories (see Table 8–3, pages 286–287).

†In 2000, categories comprised College, Some college, and No college.

Notes: National figures are based on actual election outcomes, repercentaged to exclude minor third-party candidates. Demographic data are based on Gallup poll final preelection surveys, repercentaged to exclude "no opinions"; for 2000, data are based on Gallup six-day average, October 31–November 5, 2000, except Region.

Source: Gallup Organization, "Vote By Groups," <http://www.gallup.com/poll/trends>, November 6, 2000; "Final Preelection Poll," November 7, 2000. Reprinted by permission.

support in the Northeast and the Pacific coast. Additionally, those voters who came of age during the Roosevelt presidency remain the party's most loyal age group but their children and grandchildren do not share the same strong Democratic allegiances.

Although the Democrats' New Deal coalition has eroded, the groups within that coalition, with the exception of southern whites, have not become Republican. They have simply provided less support for the Democrats. Although the Republican Party has gained adherents, it has not done so by virtue of a major exodus of groups from one party to the other, except in the South.

As a party, the Republicans have become more white, more middle class, more suburban, and more male. They have gained support in the South and Southwest, the so-called Sunbelt. Additionally, Republicans have gained adherents from white evangelical Christian groups that had supported the Democratic Party and voted for its candidates through 1976. By the end of the 1980s, a plurality of this group thought of themselves as Republican, with 80 percent voting for George Bush in 1988 and a similar percentage for his son in 2000. In 1992 and 1996, the Republican evangelic vote declined slightly. White evangelicals now constitute a core bloc within the Republican Party's electoral coalition almost as important to the GOP as African Americans are to the Democrats.[58]

The shift of white evangelical Christians, who constitute approximately one-fourth of the population, to the Republican Party has offset some of the reduction in that party's support from mainline Protestants, particularly those with liberal social views. The presidential votes of members of the latter group declined in the 1990s, as did their identification with the Republican Party. In general, regular churchgoers within both evangelical and mainline Protestant groups are more Republican in their party identification and voting behavior than those who do not attend church regularly. Nonchurchgoers, those who think of themselves as secular and rarely attend religious services, have become the least Republican group of all.[59] The contemporary Republican Party thus consists of racial and religious majorities, those in the higher socioeconomic brackets, and those in the professional and managerial ranks.

What conclusions can we draw about the social basis of politics today? It is clear that the old party coalitions have evolved and, in the Democrats' case, weakened. Today, voters exercise a more independent judgment on election day, a judgment that is likely to be influenced by factors that condition the environment in which the election occurs and by the campaign itself.

THE FUTURE OF THE PARTIES

Will there be a new partisan realignment? Will the GOP emerge as the new majority? The answer is still unclear, but three basic trends stand out.

1. The gap between the major party identifiers has narrowed, and when turnout is considered, may have been eliminated entirely.

2. The attachments people feel toward political parties have weakened over the years although partisan loyalties have held relatively constant since the late 1980s. Split-ticket voting, which had been rising, has also stabilized today.

3. There has been some partisan realignment. White southerners have switched their allegiances to the GOP while northeasterners have become less Republican. Group coalitions within the parties have also shifted. On balance, these changes have benefited the Republicans, but not to the extent of making them a plurality, much less majority party.

The major parties continue to be highly competitive at the national level. Within the states, however, the crafting of legislative districts to create as many safe seats as possible for the parties has reduced that competitiveness, particularly in elections for members of the House of Representatives. Today, the major parties remain at rough parity with one another, the presidential election one that either party can win.

SUMMARY

The electorate is not neutral. People do not come to campaigns with completely open minds. Rather, their preexisting attitudes and accumulated experiences color their perceptions and affect their judgments, much as stimuli from the campaign affect those attitudes and experiences.

Of the political beliefs people possess, partisanship has the strongest impact on voting. It provides a perspective for evaluating the campaign and for deciding whether and how to vote. It is also a motive for being informed, for getting involved, and for turning out to vote.

Since 1960, there has been a decline in the proportion of the population who voted. This decline can be partially attributed to the weakening of party ties, to the increasing proportion of younger voters, and to the cynicism and apathy of the population as a whole.

Partisan attitudes have also eroded, particularly in the period from 1964 to the end of the 1980s. The percentage of people identifying with a party has declined. One consequence has been the increasing importance of short-term factors on voting. A second related one has been more split-ticket ballots. The relative parity of the major parties today has resulted in national elections that either party can win. It has produced a presidential vote that has less carryover to congressional and state elections. Presidential coattails have not been evident since 1980.

Group ties to the parties have also loosened. Partisan coalitions have shifted. The Democratic Party, which became dominant during the New Deal period, has lost the support of a majority of southern whites in presidential and congressional elections and has suffered defections from other groups such as non-Hispanic Catholics and Protestant fundamentalists. That some of these groups have also declined as a proportion of the population or have lower-than-average turnout has further aggravated the Democrats' problem. Racial minorities, such as African Americans and Hispanics, however, have retained their loyalty to the Democrats as have Jewish Americans. Women have become much more supportive of Democratic candidates and men more supportive of Republicans. Those with secular views have become more Democratic and those with sectarian views more Republican.

The Republicans have benefited from the fraying of the Democrats' partisan majority. The Republicans have gained in the South, benefited from the increased social and economic conservatism of a growing middle and upper-middle class, and made strides among younger voters. Although they won eight of the thirteen presidential elections beginning with the election of 1952, thus far they have not been able to expand their electoral coalition into a partisan plurality much less majority.

These changes within the political environment have important implications for presidential politics. The weakening of partisan attitudes and the splintering of the New Deal coalitions have augured in a new era in presidential electoral politics, one that is highly competitive. Partisan parity has increased the importance of short-term factors including political campaigns on election outcomes.

WHERE ON THE WEB?

- **Democracy Network**
  http://www.dnet.org
  A public interest site sponsored by the education fund of the League of Women Voters on which you can find out candidate positions on the issues as well as connect to grassroots groups on a variety of salient issues.
- **Democratic National Committee**
  http://www.democrats.org
  Information on Democratic Party history, rules, convention, and campaigns. Links to Democratic youth and state party affiliates.
- **Green Party**
  http://www.greenpartyus.org
  Information on the Green Party, its rules, convention, and candidates.
- **League of Women Voters**
  http://www.lwv.org
  Information on candidates, their positions, and how to register and vote.
- **Reform Party**
  http://www.reformparty.org
  Information on the Reform Party, its rules, conventions, and candidates.
- **Republican National Committee**
  http://www.rnc.org
  Information on Republican Party history, rules, convention, and campaigns. Links to Republican youth and state party affiliates.
- **Rock-the-Vote**
  http://www.rockthevote.org
  An organization whose goal is to encourage young people to register and vote. Enables you to fill out a registration form online, as well as obtain an absentee ballot.

• **Project Vote Smart**
http://www.vote-smart.org
An organization that provides a wealth of information on candidates and their
issue positions and evaluates their performance in office.

EXERCISES

1. If you are a U.S. citizen, eighteen years of age or older, and haven't already done
so, register to vote by accessing the FEC at <http://www.fec.gov> and down-
loading the national voter registration form, completing it, and sending it to
your state, or access Rock-the-Vote at <http://www.rockthevote.org> and provide that organization with information to begin the registration process.
2. Indicate all the services that the major parties are providing their candidates in
the general election by accessing their sites and going through their menu of
services. Which of these services do you think will be most helpful to the presidential candidates?
3. Go to the FEC Web site <http://www.fec.gov> to determine the states with
the highest and lowest turnout of voters in 2000. Group these states on the
basis of their turnout rates and then compare their registration requirements
(also obtainable at the FEC site) to see if differences in these requirements
help explain the turnout differential. In addition to registration requirements,
what other factors might explain the differences in turnout?
4. Describe the composition of the major parties' electoral coalitions. On the
basis of your description, locate interest groups that represent these types of
supporters. Access their sites and note what they have done to mobilize their
members and sympathizers in the presidential campaign.

SELECTED READING

Abramson, Paul R., John H. Aldrich, and David W. Rohde. *Change and Continu-
ity in the 2000 Elections.* Washington, D.C.: Congressional Quarterly, 2002.
Black, Earl, and Merle Black. *The Vital South: How Presidents Are Elected.* Cam-
bridge, Mass.: Harvard University Press, 1992.
Box-Steffensmeier, Janet M., and Renee M. Smith. "The Dynamics of Aggregate
Partisanship." *American Political Science Review* (September 1996): 567–580.
Burnham, Walter D. "The Turnout Problem." In *Elections American Style,* edited
by A. James Reichley, 97–133. Washington, D.C.: Brookings Institution,
1987.
Campbell, Angus, Philip E. Converse, Warren E. Miller, and Donald E. Stokes.
The American Voter. New York: Wiley, 1960.
Keith, Bruce E., David B. Magleby, Candice Nelson, and Elizabeth Orr. *The
Myth of the Independent Voter.* Berkeley: University of California Press, 1992.
Ladd, Everett Carll, Jr., with Charles D. Hadley. *Transformations of the American
Party System.* New York: Norton, 1978.
Leege, David, and Lyman A. Kellstedt. *Rediscovering the Religious Factor in Amer-
ican Politics.* New York: M. E. Sharpe, 1993.

Lyons, William, and Robert Alexander. "A Tale of Two Electorates: Generational Replacement and the Decline of Voting in Presidential Elections." *Journal of Politics* 62 (November 2000): 1014–1034.

Miller, Warren E. "Party Identification, Realignment, and Party Voting: Back to the Basics," *American Political Science Review* 85 (June 1991): 557–570.

Nardulli, Peter F., Jon K. Dalager, and Donald E. Greco, "Voter Turnout in U.S. Presidential Elections: A Historical Overview and Some Speculation." *PS* (September 1996): 480–490.

Nie, Norman H., Sidney Verba, and John R. Petrocik. *The Changing American Voter.* Cambridge, Mass.: Harvard University Press, 1976.

Patterson, Thomas E. *The Vanishing Voter.* New York: Knopf, 2002.

Piven, Frances Fox, and Richard A. Cloward. *Why Americans Don't Vote.* New York: Pantheon, 1988.

Popkin, Samuel L. *The Reasoning Voter: Communication and Persuasion in Presidential Campaigns.* Chicago: University of Chicago Press, 1991.

Putnam, Robert D. *Bowling Alone: The Collapse and Revival of American Community.* New York: Simon & Schuster, 2000.

Rapoport, Ronald B. "Partisanship Change in a Candidate-Centered Era." *Journal of Politics* (February 1997): 185–199.

Stanley, Harold W., and Richard G. Niemi. "Party Coalitions in Transition: Partisanship and Group Support, 1952–1996," in *Reelection 1996: How Americans Voted,* edited by Herbert F. Weisberg and Janet M. Box-Steffensmeier, 162–180. New York: Chatham House, 1999.

Tate, Katherine. "Black Political Participation in the 1984 and 1988 Presidential Elections." *American Political Science Review* 85 (December 1991): 1159–1176.

Teixeira, Ruy A. *The Disappearing American Voter.* Washington, D.C.: Brookings Institution, 1992.

Wattenberg, Martin P. *The Decline of American Political Parties: 1952–1996.* Cambridge, Mass.: Harvard University Press, 1998.

Wolfinger, Raymond E., and Steven J. Rosenstone. *Who Votes?* New Haven, Conn.: Yale University Press, 1980.

NOTES

1. Calculating turnout on the basis of voting-age population results in a lower percent for a country such as the United States that has high immigration rates, and as a result, many resident aliens living within its borders. Resident aliens are not citizens and cannot vote. See Samuel L. Popkin and Michael McDonald, "Turnout's Not as Bad as You Think," *Washington Post,* November 5, 2000, B1, 2.

2. Ronald P. Formisane, "Deferential-Participant Politics: The Early Republic's Political Culture, 1789," *American Political Science Review* 68 (June 1974): 473–487.

3. Walter Dean Burnham, "The Turnout Problem," in *Elections American Style,* ed. A. James Reichley (Washington, D.C.: Brookings Institution, 1987), 112–116.

4. Peter F. Nardulli, Jon K. Dalager, and Donald E. Greco, "Voter Turnout in U.S. Presidential Elections: An Historical View and Some Speculation," *PS* (September 1996): 480.

5. Steven Finkel and Paul Freedman, "The Half-Hearted Rise: Voter Turnout in the 2000 Election" (paper presented at the Conference on Assessing the Vitality of Electoral Democracy in the U.S: The 2000 Election, Columbus, Ohio, March 8–9, 2002), 9.

6. Although some states initially permitted all landowners to vote, including women, by 1807 every one of them limited voting to men. Michael X. Delli Carpini and Ester R. Fuchs, "The Year of the Woman: Candidates, Voters, and the 1992 Election," *Political Science Quarterly* 108 (Spring 1993): 30.

7. Ibid.

8. Earl Black and Merle Black, *The Vital South: How Presidents Are Elected* (Cambridge, Mass.: Harvard University Press, 1992), 217.

9. The territory of Wyoming was the first to grant women the vote in 1867.

10. In the case of *Smith v. Allwright* (321 U.S. 649, 1944), the Supreme Court declared the white primary unconstitutional. In its opinion the Court rejected the argument that parties were private associations and thus could restrict participation in their selection processes.

11. In 1992, women were about 2.1 percent more likely to vote than men; in 1996, they were 2.7 more likely and in 2000, 3.1 more likely according to the Census Bureau's Current Population Survey. U.S. Census, "Current Population Reports," P20-453; P20-466.

12. David P. Glass, Peverill Squire, and Raymond E. Wolfinger, "Voter Turnout: An International Comparison," *Public Opinion* 5 (December/January 1984): 49–55.

13. Approximately half the states had motor-voter laws of their own prior to the enactment of federal legislation.

14. Federal Election Commission, "The Impact of the National Voter Registration Act on Federal Elections, 1999–2000," 2000, <http://www.fec.gov>.

15. "Record Numbers Register Under 'Motor Voter' Law," *Washington Post,* March 27, 1996, A16; A20; "Million 'Motor Voters,'" *New York Times,* October 16, 1996, A15.

16. Steven J. Rosenstone and John Mark Hansen, *Mobilization, Participation, and Democracy in America* (New York: Macmillan, 1993), 214–215.

17. In addition, thirty-two states prohibit those on parole from voting and twenty-nine prohibit those on probation. Fox Butterfield, "Many Black Males Barred from Voting," *New York Times,* January 30, 1997, A12; Michael A. Fletcher, "Voting Rights for Felons Win Support," *Washington Post,* February 22, 1999, A1, 6.

18. Angus Campbell, Philip E. Converse, Warren E. Miller, and Donald E. Stokes, *The American Voter* (New York: Wiley, 1960), 102.

19. For a very interesting article on the life cycle and voting see Eric Plutzer, "Becoming a Habitual Voter: Inertia, Resources, and Growth in Young Adulthood," *American Political Science Review* 96 (March 2002): 41–56.

20. Raymond E. Wolfinger and Steven J. Rosenstone, *Who Votes?* (New Haven, Conn.: Yale University Press, 1980), 13–26.

21. Ibid., 18–20, 35–36.

22. Ruy Teixeira describes "social connectedness" as the "interpersonal, community, and general social ties [that] provide a substantial proportion of an individual's motivation to vote." *The Disappearing American Voter* (Washington, D.C.: Brookings Institution, 1992), 36. See also Paul R. Abramson, John H. Aldrich, and David W. Rohde, *Change and Continuity in 1992* (Washington, D.C.: Congressional Quarterly, 2004), 115.

23. Paul R. Abramson, John H. Aldrich, and David W. Rohde, *Change and Continuity in the 2000 Elections* (Washington, D.C.: Congressional Quarterly, 2002), 85.

24. Finkel and Freedman, "The Half-Hearted Rise," 20.

25. Abramson, Aldrich, and Rohde, *Continuity and Change in 2000,* 90.

26. Ibid., 88.
27. Marc J. Hetherington, "The Effect of Political Trust on the Presidential Vote, 1968–1996," *American Political Science Review* 93 (1999): 311–326.
28. Finkel and Freedman, "The Half-Hearted Rise," 26.
29. Dan Balz, "Democrats Pin 2004 Hopes on Turnout Project," *Washington Post*, February 20, 2003, A11.
30. Actually, a small interview–reinterview survey was conducted in 1948, but the results were never published. In contrast to the emphasis on political attitudes of the large-scale interview projects in the 1950s, the project in 1948 had a sociological orientation.
31. Campbell, Converse, Miller, and Stokes, *The American Voter*, 102.
32. Ibid., 146–152.
33. Ibid., 133–136. Party identification is determined by the following question: "Generally speaking, do you usually think of yourself as a Republican, Democrat, an Independent, or what?" To discern the strength of the identification, a second question is asked (if Republican or Democrat): "Would you call yourself a strong (R) (D) or a not very strong (R) (D)?"; or (if Independent): "Do you think of yourself as closer to the Republican or Democratic Party?" In examining the concept of party identification, Michigan analysts have stressed two dimensions: direction and strength. Others, however, have criticized the Michigan model for overemphasizing party and underemphasizing other factors, such as social class, political ideology, and issue positions. For a thoughtful critique, see Jerrold G. Rusk, "The Michigan Election Studies: A Critical Evaluation" (paper presented at the annual meeting of the American Political Science Association, New York, September 3–6, 1981).
34. Janet M. Box-Steffensmeier and Renee M. Smith, "The Dynamic of Aggregate Partisanship," *American Political Science Review* (September 1996): 567–580; Ronald B. Rapoport, "Partisanship Change in a Candidate-Centered Era," *Journal of Politics* (February 1997): 185–199.
35. For a more extensive discussion of desirable presidential images, see Chapter 6 of this book and Benjamin I. Page, *Choices and Echoes in Presidential Elections* (Chicago: University of Chicago Press, 1978), 232–265.
36. Campbell, Converse, Miller, and Stokes, *The American Voter*, 143, 547. Independents who lean in a partisan direction tend to be better informed than those who do not. These independent leaners have many of the characteristics of party identifiers including loyalty to the party's candidates. They do not, however, identify themselves as Republicans or Democrats.
37. V. O. Key Jr., *The Responsible Electorate* (Cambridge, Mass.: Harvard University Press, 1966), 7.
38. Samuel L. Popkin, *The Reasoning Voter* (Chicago: University of Chicago Press, 1991), 43.
39. Morris P. Fiorina, *Retrospective Voting in American National Elections* (New Haven: Conn.: Yale University Press, 1981), 65–83.
40. Ibid., 84.
41. For an analysis of independents and their voting patterns, see Bruce E. Keith, David B. Magleby, Candice Nelson, and Elizabeth Orr, *The Myth of the Independent Voter* (Berkeley: University of California Press, 1992).
42. Arthur H. Miller and Martin P. Wattenberg, "Policy and Performance Voting in the 1980 Election" (paper presented at the annual meeting of the American Political Science Association, New York, September 3–6, 1981). See also Barry C. Burden and David C. Kimball, *Why Americans Split Their Tickets: Campaigns, Competition and Divided Government* (Ann Arbor: University of Michigan Press, 2002).
43. Warren E. Miller, "Party Identification, Realignment, and Party Voting: Back to the Basics," *American Political Science Review* 85 (June 1991): 559.

44. Paul F. Lazarsfeld, Bernard R. Berelson, and Hazel Gaudet. *The People's Choice: How the Voter Makes Up His Mind in a Presidential Campaign* (New York: Columbia University Press, 1948); Bernard R. Berelson, Paul F. Lazarsfeld, and William N. McPhee, *Voting: A Study of Opinion Formation in a Presidential Campaign* (Chicago: University of Chicago Press, 1954).

45. Paul Allen Beck, Russell J. Dalton, Steven Greene, and Robert Huckfeldt, "The Social Calculus of Voting: Interpersonal, Media, and Organizational Influences on Presidential Choices," *American Political Science Review* 96 (2002): 67–69.

46. This description of the New Deal realignment is based primarily on the discussion in Everett Carll Ladd Jr., with Charles D. Hadley, *Transformations of the American Party System* (New York: Norton, 1975), 31–87.

47. Ibid., 93–104.

48. Black and Black, *The Vital South,* 27.

49. Thomas B. Edsall, "Huge Gains in South Fueled GOP Vote in '94," *Washington Post,* June 27, 1995, A8.

50. Ibid.

51. Abramson, Aldrich, and Rohde, *Continuity and Change in 2000,* 112.

52. Lyman A. Kellstedt, John C. Green, James L. Guth, and Corwin E. Schmidt, "Religious Voting Blocs in the 1992 Election: Year of the Evangelical?" *Sociology of Religion* 55 (1994): 307–326; Robert B. Fowler and Allen D. Hertzke, *Religion and Politics in America: Faith, Culture, and Strategic Choice* (Boulder, Colo.: Westview Press, 1995).

53. Everett Carll Ladd, "The 1992 Vote for President Clinton: Another Brittle Mandate?" *Political Science Quarterly* 108 (Spring 1993): 4. For a discussion of turnout among African Americans in 1984 and 1988, see Katherine Tate, "Black Political Participation in the 1984 and 1988 Presidential Elections," *American Political Science Review* 85 (December 1991): 1159–1176.

54. For an extended discussion of the impact of race on the Democratic Party, see Robert Huckfeldt and Carol Weitzel Kohfeld, *Race and the Decline of Class in American Politics* (Urbana: University of Illinois Press, 1989).

55. There is also a gender gap within the parties. In an analysis of voting behavior in presidential primaries from 1980 to 2000, Professor Barbara Norrander found women more likely to consider themselves partisans than men. The differences were greater among Democratic voters than Republicans. Barbara Norrander, "The Intraparty Gender Gap: Differences between Male and Female Voters in the 1980–2000 Presidential Primaries," *PS: Political Science and Politics* 36 (April 2003): 181–186.

56. Abramson, Aldrich, and Rohde, *Change and Continuity in 2000,* 100–102.

57. Partisan voting trends are also evident on the basis of sexual orientation. According to the VNS exit polls in 2000, 70 percent of those who indicated that they were gay or lesbian voted for Gore.

58. The conservative policy orientation of this group has also colored the Republicans' position on some important and divisive social issues. For an excellent discussion of the religious right and its impact on the 1992 election see Kellstedt, Green, Guth, and Schmidt, "Religious Voting Blocs in the 1992 Election."

59. Ibid.

PART II

THE
NOMINATION

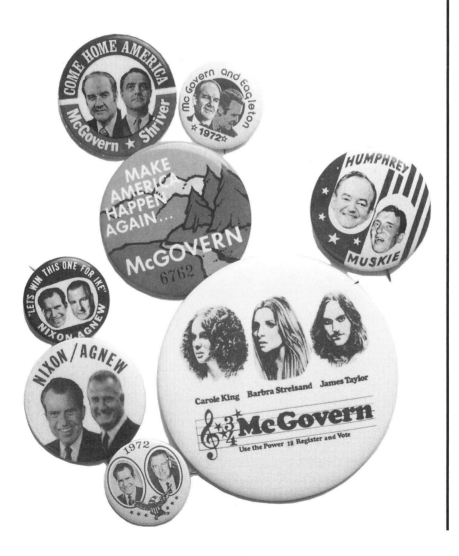

THE RACE FOR DELEGATES

4

INTRODUCTION

Presidential nominees are selected by the delegates to their party's national convention. The way those delegates are chosen, however, influences the choice of nominees. It also affects the influence of the state and its party leadership.

Procedures for delegate selection are determined by state law. Today, these procedures also have to conform to the general guidelines and rules established by the national parties. Prior to the 1970s, they did not. Under the old system, statutes passed by the state legislature reflected the needs and desires of the political leaders who controlled each state. Naturally, these laws were designed to buttress that leadership and extend its clout.

Although primaries were held, many of them were advisory; the actual selection of the delegates was left to caucuses, conventions, or committees, which were more easily controlled by party officials. Favorite son candidates, tapped by the leadership, prevented meaningful contests in many states There were also impediments to potential delegates getting on the ballot: high fees, lengthy petitions, and early filing dates. Winner-take-all provisions gave a great advantage to organization candidates, as did rules requiring delegates to vote as a unit.

Popular participation in the selection of convention delegates is a relatively recent phenomenon in the history of national nominating conventions. It was the Democrats who took the lead in encouraging their partisans to become involved in the nomination process by adopting a series of reforms that affected the period during which delegates could be selected, the procedures for choosing them, and ultimately their behavior at the convention. Although these Democratic Party rules limited the states' discretion, they did not result in uniform primaries and caucuses. Considerable variation still exists in how delegates are chosen, how the vote is apportioned, and who participates in the selection.

This chapter explores these rules and their consequences for the nomination process. It is organized into four sections. The first details the changes in party rules. The second considers the legal challenges to these rules and the Supreme Court's decisions on such challenges. The third section examines the impact of the rules changes on the parties and their electorates, and the fourth discusses how the rules have affected the candidates and how those candidates have responded with strategies designed for today's participatory nomination politics.

REFORMING THE NOMINATION PROCESS

Historically, states set their own rules for nominating candidates with relatively little guidance from the national party. Some rules discouraged popular involvement; others encouraged it but made no effort to translate the public's opinion of the candidates into delegate support for them. In very few states was the delegation as a whole representative, demographically or ideologically, of the party's electorate within that state.

Democratic Party reforms have attempted to change this situation. The party had two principal objectives in altering its rules to promote more internal democracy. Democrats wanted to encourage greater rank-and-file participation and to select delegates who were more representative of the party's supporters. The problem has been how to achieve these goals and still win elections.

The Democratic Party has gone through two stages in reforming its delegate selection procedures. During the first, 1968–1980, it adopted a highly structured set of national rules aimed at achieving its two principal aims: greater participation and more equitable representation. It imposed these rules on the states. Since that time the party has modified these rules to improve the chances of its nominees in the general election. Unlike the Democrats, the Republican Party has mandated very few national rules on its state parties. Republican state parties, however, have been affected by Democratic reforms, which have been implemented by the enactment of new election laws by the states.

Democratic Rules, 1968–1980

The catalyst for the rules changes was the tumultuous Democratic convention of 1968, a convention in which Senator Hubert Humphrey won the nomination without actively campaigning in the party's primaries. Yet the primaries of that year were very important. They had become the vehicle by which Democrats could protest the Johnson administration's conduct of the war in Vietnam.

Senator Eugene McCarthy, the first of the antiwar candidates, had challenged Lyndon Johnson in the New Hampshire primary. To the surprise of many political observers, McCarthy received 42.4 percent of the vote, almost as much as the president, who got 49.5 percent.[1] Four days after McCarthy's unexpectedly strong showing, Senator Robert Kennedy, brother of the late president and a political rival of Johnson, declared his candidacy for the nation's highest office.

With protests against the war mounting and divisions within the Democratic Party intensifying, Johnson bowed out, declaring that he did not want the country's involvement in Southeast Asia to become a divisive political issue.

Johnson's withdrawal cleared the way for Hubert Humphrey, the vice president, to run. Humphrey, however, waited almost a month to announce his intentions. His late entrance into the Democratic nomination process intentionally precluded a primary effort since filing deadlines had expired in most of the states. Like Johnson, Humphrey did not want to become the focal point of antiwar opposition. Nor did he have a grassroots organization to match McCarthy's and Kennedy's. What he did have was the support of most national and state Democratic leaders, including the president.

The last big-state primary in 1968 was California's. In it, Kennedy scored a significant win, but during the celebration that followed, he was assassinated. His death left McCarthy as the principal antiestablishment, antiwar candidate, but he was far short of a convention majority. Despite the last-minute entrance of Senator George McGovern, who hoped to rally Kennedy delegates to his candidacy, Humphrey easily won the nomination. To make matters worse for those who opposed Humphrey and the administration's war efforts, an amendment to the party platform calling for an unconditional end to the bombing of North Vietnam was defeated. McCarthy and Kennedy delegates felt victimized by the nomination process and the resulting Humphrey victory. They were angry. They demanded reform and eventually got it. A divided convention approved the establishment of a party committee to reexamine the rules for delegate selection.

Compounding the divisions within the convention were demonstrations outside the hall. Thousands of youthful protesters, calling for an end to the war, congregated in the streets of Chicago. To maintain order, the police, under direction from Mayor Richard Daley, used strong-arm tactics to disperse the crowds. Clashes between police and protesters followed. Television news crews filmed these confrontations, and the networks showed them during their convention coverage. The spectacle of police beating demonstrators further inflamed emotions and led to calls for party reform, not only from those who attended the convention but from those who watched it on television.

After the election, a commission, chaired initially by Senator George McGovern, was appointed to study procedures for electing and seating convention delegates and to propose ways of improving them. The commission recommended that delegate selection be a *fair reflection* of Democratic sentiment within the state and implicitly, less closely tied to the wishes of state party leaders. Rules to make it easier for individuals to run as delegates, to limit the size of the districts from which they could be chosen, and to require that the number of delegates elected be proportional to the popular vote that they, or the candidates to whom they were pledged, received were approved by the party. A requirement that delegates be chosen no earlier than the calendar year of the election was also approved.

Additionally, Democrats tried to prevent independents and, especially, partisans of other parties, from participating in the selection of Democratic delegates. The difficulty, however, was to determine who was a Democrat, since some states did not require or even permit registration by party. When implementing this rule, the national party adopted a very liberal interpretation of Democratic affiliation. People identifying themselves as Democrats at the time of voting, or those requesting Democratic ballots, were considered to be Democrats for the purpose of participating in the primaries. This process of identification effectively permitted crossover voting, allowing Republicans or independents to cross over and vote in the Democratic primaries in some states. The only primaries that the Democratic rules effectively prohibited were *open primaries,* those in which voters are given the ballots of both major parties, discard one, and vote the other.

In addition to translating public preferences into delegate selection, another major objective of the reforms was to equalize representation on the delegations themselves. Three groups in particular—African Americans, women, and youth—had protested their underrepresentation on party councils and at the conventions. Their representatives and others who were sympathetic to their plight pressed hard for more power and better representation for women and minorities. The reform commission reacted to these protests by proposing a rule requiring that all states represent these particular groups in reasonable relationship to their presence in the state population. Failure to do so was viewed as *prima facie* evidence of discrimination. In point of fact, the party had established quotas.

Considerable opposition developed to the application of this rule during the 1972 nomination process, and it was subsequently modified to require that states implement affirmative action plans for those groups that had been subject to past discrimination.[2] The Democrats went one step further with respect to women. Beginning with its 1980 nominating convention, the party required that each state delegation be equally divided between the sexes.

Still another goal of the reforms, to involve more Democrats in the selection process, was achieved not only by the fair reflection rule but by making primaries the preferred method of delegate selection. To avoid a challenge to the composition of their delegation, states switched to primaries in which delegates were elected directly by the people.[3]

Caucuses in which party regulars selected the delegates were still permitted, but they, too, were redesigned to encourage greater rank-and-file participation. (See Box 4–1, "The Iowa Caucus: How It Works.") No longer could state party leaders vote a large number of proxies for the delegates of their choice. Caucuses had to be publicly announced with adequate time given for campaigning. Moreover, they had to be conducted in stages, and three-fourths of the delegates had to be chosen in districts no larger than those for members of Congress.

Other consequences, not nearly as beneficial to the goal of increased participation, were a lengthening of the process, escalation of its costs, candidate fatigue, public boredom, and increased partisan division. Since the contests at the beginning of the quest for the nomination received the most attention from the news media, candidates, and public alike, states began moving their primaries forward, "front-loading" the schedule and forcing candidates to start their campaigns in the year prior to the election, another trend that has continued and accelerated in recent elections.

Selecting convention delegates in primaries and caucuses made it more difficult for elected officials and party leaders automatically to attend the nominating

---

BOX 4–1 ❧

THE IOWA CAUCUS: HOW IT WORKS

STAGES

Step 1. Caucuses are held in 2,166 precincts to choose more than 1,500 delegates to 99 county conventions.

Step 2. Approximately one month later, conventions are held in counties to choose 3,000 delegates to the five congressional district conventions.

Step 3. Conventions are held in congressional districts to elect district-level delegates to national party conventions. The same delegates also attend the state convention.

Step 4. State conventions elect at-large delegates to national party convention. Democrats also select their state party and elected official delegates.

PROCEDURES FOR THE FIRST-ROUND PRECINCT CAUCUSES

Democrats: Only registered Democrats who live in the precinct and can vote may participate. Attendees are asked to join preference groups for candidates. A group must consist of at least 15 percent of those present to be viable. Nonviable groups are dissolved, and those who were members of them may join other viable groups. Much lobbying occurs at this stage of the meeting. Delegates are allocated to candidates strictly on the basis of each group's proportion to the caucus as a whole.

Republicans: Attendees, who must be eligible to vote but do not have to be registered as Republicans, cast a presidential preference vote by secret ballot, which is tabulated on a statewide basis. Delegates to the county convention are then selected by whatever method the caucus chooses, either by direct election (winner-take-all) or proportionally on the basis of a straw vote.

---

conventions. As a consequence, their attendance declined. The absence of these leaders generated and extended cleavages between the nominees and their electoral coalitions on one hand and the party's organization and its leadership on the other. These cleavages created serious problems, adversely affecting the chances of the party's nominees in the general election, and in 1976, in governing the country. During the presidential campaign, the divisiveness impaired a unified organizational effort, tarnished the images of party candidates, and increased partisan defections. After the election, it made establishing an agenda and building a majority coalition more difficult.

In short, the early party reforms produced unintended consequences. These consequences—the proliferation of primaries, the lengthening of the process, the divisiveness within the party, the poor representation of elected leaders, and, most importantly, the failure to win elections and govern successfully—prompted the Democrats to reexamine and modify their rules for delegate selection beginning in the 1980s.

Democratic Rules, 1981–Present

The changes that have been made fall into three categories: those that affect the time frame and procedures of the selection process, those that affect the representation of public officials and party leaders, and those that govern the behavior of delegates at the convention itself.

The objective of the original reforms, to encourage participation by rank-and-file party supporters and to reflect their sentiment in the allocation of delegates, was impeded by three problems:

1. The states that held their primaries and caucuses early seemed to exercise disproportionate influence on the selection of the party's nominee. This situation created an incentive for other states to front-load the process, for candidates to expend most of their resources at the beginning of the campaign or as soon as they got them, and for participants to turn out more regularly in March than in May.

2. A relatively small percentage of the vote in a state, known as a *threshold*, was needed for candidates to be awarded delegates. This small percentage encouraged multiple candidacies, factionalizing the party and providing an incentive for those without national experience, reputation, and even party ties to run. By obtaining the votes of as little as 15 percent of those who participated in a primary or caucus, relatively unknown candidates could win delegates, gain public recognition, and use this recognition to build a constituency and become a national figure.

3. The various proportional voting formulas initially accepted by the party did not always reflect the popular vote. And even when they did, the impact on the party was not always advantageous. For the national party, proportional voting extended the nomination process, disadvantaging it and its nominees in the general election. For the state parties, proportional voting diffused power and reduced the collective influence of party officials. For the candidates, proportional voting sometimes discouraged them from investing resources in districts that were highly competitive and from which they could gain only minimal advantage and encouraged them to concentrate on less competitive districts in which they enjoyed the most support. This concentration of resources adversely affected turnout.

To modify the first of these problems, the party imposed a "window" during which primaries and caucuses could be held. Initially, the official period extended from the second Tuesday in March to the second Tuesday in June. Beginning in 1992, it was moved one week earlier to the first Tuesday in March; in 2004 it was moved a month earlier to the first Tuesday in February.

What to do with those states, such as Iowa and New Hampshire, whose laws require that they choose their delegates before others, has been a perennial issue.[4]

Believing that it could not conduct its own selection process in these states, the national party decided that the best it could do was establish the window and grant these states an exception.

Front-loading remains more of a problem than ever. In 1996, almost two-thirds of all the convention delegates were selected within a forty-four-day period beginning mid-February and continuing through March 26, 1996. In 2000, two-thirds of the delegates for both parties had been chosen by the end of the second Tuesday in March. In 2004, it will be even more front-loaded. (See Appendix D for the tentative dates of the 2004 primaries and caucuses.)

Not only is front-loading inequitable, increasing the influence of the states that hold their contests early and decreasing that of those which go later, but it also reduces the period in which candidates can meet personally with voters and forces them to campaign and raise money earlier and earlier. Front-loading advantages candidates who begin with national recognition, are able to amass sizable war chests, gain organizational support within the party apparatus, and have telegenic skills for multimedia campaigning.

Another change has involved modifications to the so-called fair reflection rule. One modification affected the minimum percentage of the vote necessary to be eligible for delegates; the other pertained to the methods by which the primary vote is allocated. After some experimenting with the minimum vote necessary to receive delegates, the Democrats settled on a 15 percent threshold.[5] They also require that delegates be chosen strictly on the basis of the proportion of the vote they receive in the primaries.

Another reform was the addition of party leader and elected official delegates (PLEOs), known as *superdelegates.* Unhappy with the decreasing number of its party leaders and elected officials who attended the convention as delegates in the 1970s, the party wished to ensure that its leadership participated in conventions that selected its nominees. The absence of this leadership, particularly national elected officials, was thought to have contributed to the lack of support that the nominees received during the campaign and after the election. Jimmy Carter's difficulties in dealing with Congress were cited as evidence of the need for closer cooperation between congressional party leaders and their presidential standard-bearer.

To facilitate closer ties, the Democrats established a new category of *add-on* delegates to be composed of PLEOs. One group of these add-on delegates, chosen from designated party leaders (including all members of its national committee) and from those who held high elected positions in government (including all Democratic governors and members of Congress plus a number of other national, state, and local officials), were to be unpledged. It was thought that this group of distinguished Democrats might be in a position to hold the balance of power if the primaries produced a mixed verdict and the convention remained divided, a situation that has not occurred since the rules were changed.

Additionally, the party also provided for the selection of pledged add-on delegates equal to 15 percent of the state's base delegation. Although these super-delegates have not been in a position to broker a divided convention, they have had an impact on the delegate selection process, an impact that reinforces the front-runner's advantage. Naturally this advantage has incurred criticism from non-front-runners who desire the selection process to be open and not dominated by national legislators and party officials.[6] Approximately 18 percent of the delegates in 2004 are expected to be superdelegates.

Finally, the Democrats have reversed a rule adopted in 1980 that delegates who are publicly committed must vote for the candidate to whom they are pledged. Democratic delegates today can vote their consciences, although when they are initially selected as pledged delegates, they must sign an advanced pledge of presidential preference to ensure that they are supporters of the candidates who have slated them to run as their delegates. Under the circumstances, it is unlikely that many delegates will change their minds at the convention, unless their candidate encourages them to do so.

Republican Rules

The Republicans have not changed their rules after each recent national convention as the Democrats have. Nor can they do so. It is the Republican convention itself that approves the rules for choosing delegates for the next Republican convention. Under normal circumstances, these rules cannot be altered by the Republican National Committee or by special commissions the party creates.

Republicans, however, have been affected by the Democratic rules changes in several ways. Since state legislatures enact laws governing party nominations, and since the Democrats controlled many of these legislatures in the 1970s and 1980s when primary laws were changed to conform to the new Democratic rules, some of the reforms were literally forced on the Republicans by the states. Moreover, the Republicans have also made changes of their own to eliminate discrimination and prevent a small group from controlling the nomination process.

Unlike the Democrats, the Republicans have not mandated national guidelines for their state parties. Although they do not have a window period during which all primaries and caucuses must be held, their nominations process is still heavily front-loaded, too much so from the perspective of the party's national committee. Prior to the 2000 nomination, the party tried to encourage states to hold their nomination contests later in the cycle by offering them additional convention delegates if they did so.[7] There were few takers, however, prompting the national committee to appoint an advisory commission once again to study the process.

Chaired by former senator and party chairman Bill Brock, the commission recommended the implementation of a population-based nominating system in which states would be placed in one of four groups, based on size, rather than geography. The states in each group would hold their primary or the first stage of their caucus selection on the same day. The group containing the least-populated states would go first and the one with the largest states last. The dates on which the four groups would hold their contests would be spaced approximately one month apart, beginning on the first Tuesday in March.[8]

Opposition to the plan quickly developed from the large states fearful that the nominee would be effectively determined before they had a chance to vote.

Concerns were also expressed about the added costs to the candidates if they had to compete for four months, much less the wear and tear they would encounter.[9] Not wanting any issue to divide the 2000 convention and interfere with his launch for the presidency, George W. Bush vetoed the idea, thereby killing it for at least the short term.

Whereas the Democrats prescribe a minimum threshold to receive delegate support, the Republicans do not. Their threshold varies from state to state. Whereas the Democrats impose proportional voting, the Republicans do not. They permit winner-take-all voting within districts or within the state. Such a voting system greatly advantages front-runners, who can win the large states. In 1988, George H. W. Bush won 59 percent of the popular vote in states holding some type of winner-take-all voting on Super Tuesday but won 97 percent of the delegates, giving him an almost insurmountable lead over his principal opponent that year, Robert Dole. In 1996, Dole, the Republican front-runner, was similarly advantaged and built a huge delegate lead in the winner-take-all states. As part of its recommendations to improve the delegate selection process, the party's advisory commission on nomination reform proposed that all delegates be allotted to candidates on a proportional basis, but the rules committee of the 2000 convention did not approve this change as well.

Finally the Republicans do not have special categories of delegates for party leaders and elected officials, although their state and national leaders have traditionally attended Republican conventions in greater proportion than their Democratic counterparts. Nor do the Republicans require that 50 percent of each state delegation be women. Since the 1980s, the proportion of women at Republican conventions has ranged from a low of 29 percent to a high of 44.

A summary of delegate selection rules for the 2004 nomination appears in Table 4–1.

THE LEGALITY OF PARTY RULES

As previously mentioned, party reforms, to be effective, must be enacted into law. Most states have complied with the new rules. A few have not, sometimes resulting in confrontation between these states and the national party. When New Hampshire and Iowa refused to move the dates of their respective primary and caucuses into the Democrats' window period in 1984, the national party backed down. But previously, when Illinois chose its 1972 delegates in a manner that conflicted with new Democratic rules, the party sought to impose its rules on the state.

In addition to the political controversy that was engendered, the conflict between the Democratic National Committee and Illinois also presented an important legal question: which body—the national party or the state—has the higher authority? In its landmark decision, *Cousins v. Wigoda* (419 U.S. 477, 1975), the Supreme Court sided with the national party. The Court stated that political parties were private organizations with rights of association protected by the Constitution. Moreover, choosing presidential candidates was a national experience that states could not abridge unless there were compelling constitutional

TABLE 4–1 🌿

DELEGATE SELECTION RULES

	Democrats	Republicans
Rank-and-file participation	Open to all voters who wish to participate as Democrats.	No national rule.*
Apportionment of delegates within states	75 percent of base delegation elected at congressional district level or lower; 25 percent elected at large on a proportional basis.	No national rule; may be chosen at large.
Party leaders and elected officials	Current members and former chairs of the national committee, all Democratic members of Congress, former House Speakers and minority leaders and Senate party leaders, current and past presidents and vice presidents, all Democratic governors.	None.
Composition of delegations	Equal gender division; no discrimination; affirmative action plan required with goals and timetables for specified groups (African Americans, Native Americans, and Asian/Pacific Americans).	No gender rule but each state is asked to try to achieve equal gender representation; "Positive action" to achieve broadest possible participation required.
Time frame	First Tuesday in February to second Tuesday in June. Exceptions: Iowa, New Hampshire, and Maine.	No national rule.
Allocation of delegates	By proportional vote. Only in primaries or caucuses.	May be selected in primaries, caucuses, or by state committee on basis of a proportional vote or by direct election within congressional districts or on an at-large basis.
Threshold	15 percent.	No national rule.
Delegation voting	May vote their conscience.	No national rule.
Enforcement	Automatic reduction in state delegation size for violation of time frames, allocation, or threshold rules.	Each state party to enforce its own rules; certain types of disputes may be appealed to the national party.

* Republican national rules prescribe that selection procedures be in accordance with the laws of the state.

reasons to do so. Although states could establish their own primary laws, the party could determine the criteria for representation at its national convention.

Crossover voting in open primaries prompted still another court test between the rights of parties to prescribe rules for delegate selection and the rights of states to establish their own election law. Democratic rules prohibit open primaries. Four states had conducted this type of election in 1976. Three voluntarily changed their law; a fourth, Wisconsin, did not. It permitted voters, who participated in the primary, to request the ballot of either party. The national party's Compliance Review Commission ordered the state party to design an alternative process. It refused. The case went to court. Citing the precedent of *Cousins v. Wigoda,* the Supreme Court held in the case of *Democratic Party of the U.S. v. Wisconsin ex. rel. La Follette* (450 U.S. 107, 1981) that a state had no right to interfere with the party's delegate selection process unless it demonstrated a compelling reason to do so. It ruled that Wisconsin had not demonstrated such a reason; hence, the Democratic Party could refuse to seat delegates who were selected in a manner that violated its rules.[10]

In the case of *California Democratic Party v. Jones* (99-401, 2000), the Supreme Court reiterated its judgment by invalidating California's "blanket" primary system, which voters had approved in a 1996 ballot initiative. The new procedure required that state officials provide a uniform ballot in which voters, regardless of their partisan affiliation, could vote for any candidate of any party for any elected position. Naturally, the parties were upset by the possibility that their nominees could be determined by people who did not consider themselves partisans of their party. Four California state parties, including the Democrats and Republicans, went to court to challenge the constitutionality of the initiative, claiming that it violated their First Amendment right to freedom of association. The Supreme Court agreed. Its majority opinion held that the blanket primary system represented "a clear and present danger" to the parties and was therefore unconstitutional.

Although these Court decisions have given the political parties the legal authority to design and enforce their own rules, the practicality of doing so is another matter. Other than going to court if a state refuses to change its election law, a party, particularly a national party, has only two viable options: require the state party to conduct its own delegate selection process in conformity to national rules and penalize it if it does not do so, or grant the state party an exemption so that it can abide by the law of the state. In 1984, the Wisconsin Democratic Party was forced by the national Democratic Party to adopt a caucus mode of selection since the Republican-controlled legislature refused to change the state's open primary system. Turnout declined in the Wisconsin caucus. Subsequently, the Democrats have given Wisconsin and Montana, another state with a tradition of open primaries, exemptions to the closed primary rule.

The rule for allocating delegates to the states has also generated legal controversy, but in this case, within the Republican Party. The formula that the Republicans use contains a bonus for states that voted Republican in the previous presidential election.[11] Opponents of this rule contend that it discriminates against the large states because bonuses are allocated regardless of size. Moreover, they argue that the large states are apt to be more competitive and thus less likely to receive a bonus. Particularly hard hit are states in the Northeast and on the Pacific Coast which have gone Democratic in recent elections. The Ripon Society, a moderate Republican organization, has twice challenged the constitutionality of this apportionment rule, but it has not been successful.

The Democratic apportionment formula, which results in larger conventions than the Republicans, has also been subject to some controversy, but not in recent nominations.[12]

THE IMPACT OF THE RULES CHANGES

The new rules adopted by the parties have produced some of their desired effects. They have opened up the nomination process by allowing more people to participate. They have increased minority representation at the conventions. But they have also decreased the influence of state and national party leaders over the selection of delegates, ultimately weakened the power of party leaders in the presidential electoral process, and have exacerbated divisions within the parties.

Turnout

One objective of the reforms was to involve more of the party's rank and file in the delegate selection process. This goal has been partially achieved. In 1968, before the reforms, only 12 million people participated in primaries, approximately 11 percent of the voting-age population (VAP). In 1972, the first nomination contest after changes were made, that number rose to 22 million. In 1988, it peaked. With two contested nominations, turnout increased to 35.1 million, approximately 21 percent of the VAP. It remained relatively high in 1992, dipped in 1996, and rose again in 2000. Approximately 36 million people voted in the 2000 primaries, about 15 percent of the VAP.[13] Of those who participated, 20.7 million voted in forty-three Republican primaries, the most ever for the GOP, compared to only 14.7 million for the Democrats.[14]

The level of participation also varies. It has always been greater in primaries than caucuses. In Iowa, which traditionally holds the first caucus, only about 4 percent of the VAP participated, despite extensive media coverage.

Turnout tends to be greater in states that hold their contests earlier than in those that hold them later in the process and greater in those in which there is more competition than in states in which there is less. New Hampshire generally has a high turnout; in 2000, 54 percent of the state's eligible population voted in the Republican primary.[15] South Carolina and Michigan also had unusually high Republican turnout because of the attention given to the Bush–McCain contest. Approximately 19 percent of the VAP voted in both states' Republican primaries.

Not only does turnout vary among states, it also varies among population groups within them. The better-educated, higher-income, older members of society vote more often than do younger, less-educated, and poorer people. In general, the lower the turnout, the greater the demographic differences between voters and non-voters. Although this pattern of participation has persisted in recent elections, the success of the Jackson campaigns in 1984 and 1988 in attracting minority voters and, to a much lesser extent, the campaign of Pat Robertson in 1998, which appealed to white, evangelical Protestants, muted some of the differences that had existed between primary voters and their party's electorate in these elections.

There have also been claims that primary voters tend to be more ideologically extreme in their political beliefs than the average party voter, with Democrats being more liberal and Republicans more conservative than their party as a whole. Strong empirical evidence has not been found to support this contention although studies have shown southern Democrats who participate in their party's primary tend to be more moderate than the southern electorate as a whole.[16] For most of the country, primary voters do not appear to be more ideologically extreme than people who vote in the general election, but convention delegates who represent them do.[17]

Representation

A principal goal of the reforms was to make the national nominating convention more representative of those who identified with the party. Before 1972, the delegates were predominantly white, male, and well educated. Mostly professionals whose income and social status placed them considerably above the national mean, they were expected to pay their own way to the convention. Large financial contributors, as well as elected officeholders and party officials, were frequently in attendance.

In 1972, the demographic profile of convention delegates began to change. The proportion of women rose substantially. Youth and minority participation, especially in Democratic conventions, also increased. Since 1976, when the Democrats changed from a quota system to an affirmative action commitment, the representation of minorities has remained fairly constant. The percentage of women has increased, largely as a consequence of the Democratic requirement that half its delegates be women. But attendance by those under age thirty, a group that has been removed from the specified minorities list, has declined.

Despite the changes in composition, the income and educational levels of the delegates have remained well above the national average. Most of the delegates have much more formal education than do their party's rank and file.

It is more difficult to determine the extent to which ideological and issue perceptions of recent delegates differed from those of their predecessors and from the electorate as a whole. In general, convention delegates tend to be more conscious of issues than their party's rank and file. The issue stands of the delegates tend to confirm the ideological cleavage among them. Republican and Democratic delegates consistently take more conservative and liberal positions, respectively, on a range of policy matters. If these positions were plotted on an ideological continuum, they would appear to be more consistent (or ideologically pure) than the partisan electorate they represent and much more consistent (or pure) than the general public.

The delegate selection process seems to have contributed to the purity of these ideological beliefs by encouraging activists, who have less of a tie to the party and more of a tie to a candidate and that candidate's ideological and issue positions, to get involved and run for delegate. To the extent that this trend has resulted in the election of more issue purists and fewer partisan pragmatists, compromise in government has become more difficult. One objective of the creation of superdelegates by the Democrats was to reverse the trend of party fragmentation.

In summary, despite the reforms, there continue to be differences between the ideological and demographic characteristics of convention delegates and those of their party members and of the electorate as a whole. Convention delegates reflect some demographic characteristics of their party's rank and file more accurately than in the past, but they are not necessarily more ideologically representative. In fact, delegates have tended to exaggerate the differences between the beliefs and attitudes of Republicans and Democrats. Whether this trend makes contemporary conventions more or less representative is difficult to say. One thing is clear: It is difficult to achieve representation, reward activism, maintain an open process, unite the party, and win elections, all at the same time.

Party Organization and Leadership

Although increasing turnout and improving representation have been two desired effects of the reforms, weakening the state party structures and their leadership has not. Yet this development seems to have been an initial consequence of the increasing number of primaries. By promoting internal democracy, the primaries helped devitalize party organizations already weakened by new modes of campaigning and party leadership already weakened by the loss of patronage opportunities and the growth of social services by state and local governments. Although the growth of caucuses and primaries has enhanced participation in the general election by enlarging the pool of people who are more likely to become active, stay involved, and vote, it has also contributed to struggles for control of the party organization and ultimately produced more divisions within it.[18] Moreover, the rules changes have encouraged the proliferation of candidates, which in turn has led to the creation of separate electoral organizations that can rival the regular party organization.

The power of elected party leaders has also been weakened. No longer able to control their state's delegation, party officials now have to compete with the supporters of the successful candidate for influence over the campaign. State party organizations and state party leaders, however, continue to exercise influence. The soft money they were given by the national parties or solicited on their own provided them with more opportunities to influence the election. The increasing importance of providing funds and organizational support for the presidential candidates has also benefited these state party officials.

The nominees are affected as well. Political scientists have argued that the more divisive the nomination process, the more likely that it will adversely affect the successful nominee's chances in the general election.[19] Other factors such as the quality of the candidates and the particular environment in which the election occurs also affect the final general election results.[20]

Nonetheless, a divisive nomination process is rarely an asset; it is usually perceived as a liability. Undergoing rigorous and critical examination by one's partisan opponents can damage a nominee's image at the beginning of the general election campaign. Candidates who avoid a challenge for the nomination do not have to contend with this problem. However, it often is the potential vulnerability of a candidate that encourages others to seek the nomination in the first place. Challenges and perceived vulnerability go hand-in-hand.

Winners and Losers

Rules changes are never neutral. They usually benefit one group at the expense of another. Similarly, they tend to help certain candidates and hurt others. That is why candidates have tried to influence the rules and why the rules themselves have been changed so frequently. Candidate organizations and interest groups have put continuous pressure on the Democratic Party to amend the rules to increase their own clout in the selection process.

Clearly, the prohibition of discrimination, the requirement for affirmative action, and the rule requiring an equal number of men and women in state delegations have improved representation for women and minorities, and coincidentally, reduced the proportion of white male delegates. For candidates seeking their party's nomination, this change has necessitated that slates of delegates supporting a candidate be demographically balanced to ensure that a multitude of groups are included.

The openness of the process and the greater participation by the party's rank and file have encouraged those who have not been party regulars to become involved and have created opportunities for outsiders to seek their party's nomination. Businessman Steve Forbes (1996 and 2000), ministers Jesse Jackson (1984) and Pat Robertson (1988), columnist Pat Buchanan (1992, 1996, and 2000), and former Senator Paul Tsongas (1992), and to some extent even governors Michael Dukakis (1988) and Bill Clinton (1992), as well as former Senator Bill Bradley and Senator John McCain (both in 2000) have literally come out of political nowhere to run for their party's nomination.

On the other hand, the more the process concentrates the number and location of primaries at the beginning of the delegate selection process, the more those who have access to the largest amounts of money and the most political endorsements, particularly from governors who control their state party organizations, are likely to benefit.

All of this has affected the candidates' quest for the nomination and their ability to govern if elected. It has made campaigning more arduous and governing more difficult. It has created incentives for candidates to promise more than they can deliver. Thus, the quest for the nomination and what it takes to win may ultimately weaken a newly elected president by hyping performance expectations and then generating discontent when these expectations cannot be realized.

CAMPAIGNING FOR DELEGATES

Rules changes, finance laws, and television coverage have affected the strategies and tactics of the candidates. Prior to the 1960s, entering primaries was optional for leading candidates and necessary only for those who did not enjoy party support or national recognition. Today, entering primaries is essential for everyone, even an incumbent president. No longer can a front-runner safely sit on the sidelines and wait for the call. The winds of a draft may be hard to resist but, more often than not, it is the candidate who is manning the bellows.

In the past, candidates carefully chose the primaries they entered and concentrated their efforts where they thought they would run best. Today, they have much less discretion, particularly at the beginning of the process, when gaining press coverage is essential. Before 1972, it was considered wise to wait for an opportune moment in the spring of the presidential election year before announcing one's candidacy. Today, planning for a nomination run starts years in advance.

Basic Strategic Guidelines

Plan Far Ahead. Creating an organization, devising a strategy, and raising the amount of money necessary to conduct a national campaign all take time. These needs prompted George McGovern to announce his candidacy for the 1972 presidential nomination in January 1971, almost a year and a half before the Democratic convention, and Jimmy Carter to begin his quest in 1974, two years before the 1976 Democratic convention. Similarly, President Clinton began planning his reelection campaign following the Democrat's defeat in the 1994 midterm elections although he never formally announced his candidacy in order to convey the impression that his actions and decisions during this period were motivated solely by the needs of his office, not his candidacy. (See Boxes 4–3 and 4–4 for a description of the nomination strategies of the principal candidates in 2000, on pages 137 and 144.)

Candidates for their party's nomination in 2000 began forming their prenomination organizations in 1998 prior to the midterm elections. Al Gore established Leadership '98 ostensibly to raise money for other Democrats but also to lay the groundwork for his presidential campaign in 2000. Similarly, Republican presidential hopeful George W. Bush began to plan his campaign in 1998 and formed an exploratory committee in the spring of 1999. He and other GOP aspirants made numerous trips to Iowa and New Hampshire in the two years before the 2000 race officially got under way.

The Democratic campaign for its 2004 nomination has followed a similar pattern. Governor Howard Dean of Vermont was the first to form an advisory committee in the fall of 2002. He was followed by Senator John Kerry of Massachusetts. Pressure was exerted on Al Gore to decide whether he would run again. In December 2002, he said he would not. Other Democratic aspirants, Representative Richard Gephardt, and Senators Tom Daschle, John Edwards, Bob Graham, and Joseph Lieberman, all of whom had established leadership

PACs, also began exploring the possibility of running, setting up their campaign committees and raising money in the winter of 2002.

Two years to test the waters is now almost standard practice. In addition to visiting the early states, would-be nominees hire a political team, create donor lists, start fund-raising, and appeal to state and federal party officials for support. Both Gephardt and Kerry used their 2002 congressional campaigns and their leadership PACs to build direct-mail donor databases for their anticipated presidential quests in 2004.[21]

Concentrate Efforts in the Early Contests. Doing well in the initial caucuses and primaries and qualifying for matching funds are the principal aims of most candidates today. The early contests are particularly important for lesser-known aspirants, less for the number of delegates they can win than for the amount of publicity they can generate and the people they can meet.

Personal contact is particularly important in this period. It informs and motivates potential supporters. It may produce contributors and volunteers down the road. The small states provide these "living-room" opportunities that are lost in multistate media campaigns.

By tradition the first official selection of delegates occurs in Iowa. Jimmy Carter in 1976, George Bush in 1980, and Gary Hart in 1984 got great boosts from their unexpectedly good showings in this state. Conversely, Ronald Reagan in 1980, John Glenn in 1984, and George Bush in 1988, and Robert Dole in 1996, were hurt by their disappointing performances. In 2000, Iowa simply confirmed the front-runner's status that George W. Bush and Al Gore each enjoyed over their rivals.

Doing well in Iowa can enhance the fortunes of a lesser-known candidate. A good example was Gary Hart's performance in 1984. He received only 16.5 percent of the Democratic vote, compared with front-runner Walter Mondale's 48.9 percent. But Mondale's victory was expected; Hart's second-place finish was not. As a consequence, Hart shared the media spotlight with Mondale but profited from more laudatory coverage.

Similarly, Pat Robertson's surprising second-place finish ahead of Vice President George Bush in 1988 in Iowa and Pat Buchanan's strong challenge to Dole in 1996 generated favorable media coverage for them. Their gains were at the expense of front-runners Bush and Dole.[22]

The Iowa caucus has been more important for lesser-known candidates than those with national reputations. The victories of Carter (1976), Bush (1980), and Hart (1984) gave these candidates opportunities to establish their credentials, opportunities which they might not have had in a big state primary. Although a defeat or poor showing by a front-runner such as happened to Reagan, Bush, and Dole in 1980, 1988, and 1996, respectively, may diminish their luster, it does not necessarily terminate their candidacy. Front-runners have other opportunities made possible by their larger war chests, greater organizational support, and the political capital with which they start their quest for the nomination. For lesser-known candidates, it is a different story. A loss or poor showing in Iowa may be the beginning of the end.[23]

"WILL SOMEBODY PLEASE SEND ME BACK TO SQUARE ONE?"

Source: Herblock, *Washington Post*, November 1, 1988, A18.

The importance of the Iowa caucus has diminished in recent presidential campaigns because of the front-loading of the nomination process. With New Hampshire nine to ten days later and an increasing number of primaries occurring in February and early March, there is simply not enough time to parlay success in Iowa into raising more money. Yet candidates continue to spend more time and money, not less, in this first caucus contest.

Iowa "winners" face another problem. Expectations of their future performance increase and media coverage tends to become more negative. Professor Craig Allen Smith describes the Iowa caucus as a "Venus fly-trap for presidential candidates," a description he embellishes in the following manner:

> Dramatic logic lures them to the sticky leaves of the precinct caucuses where, prodded by journalists and Iowans, they pour more and more of their time, money, people, and strategic options into the gaping mouth of the plant until, at the very moment of victory, it snaps shut on their ability to win subsequent contests. Iowa provides no significant delegates, its New Hampshire momentum is soon reversed, its Super Tuesday momentum is transient, and the resources it devours are rarely recovered.[24]

After Iowa, attention turns to New Hampshire, traditionally the first state to hold a primary in which the entire electorate participates.[25] Candidates who do surprisingly well in this primary have benefited enormously. Eugene McCarthy in 1968, George McGovern in 1972, Jimmy Carter in 1976, Gary Hart in 1984, Bill Clinton in 1992, Pat Buchanan in 1996, and John McCain in 2000 all gained visibility and credibility from their New Hampshire performances, although none had a majority of the vote and only Carter and McCain had pluralities. Bill Clinton actually came in second with 25 percent of the vote in 1992, 8 percent less than former Massachusetts, and New Hampshire neighbor, Senator Paul Tsongas. Clinton's relatively strong showing, however, in the light of allegations of marital infidelity and draft dodging made his performance more impressive in the eyes of the news media than Tsongas's expected win. Tsongas was not considered to be a viable candidate; Clinton was. Similarly, John McCain's impressive victory in 2000 over front-runner George W. Bush by 18 percent elevated him overnight from just another candidate to serious contender.

Like Iowa, New Hampshire also receives extensive media attention. Together with Iowa, it usually accounts for the bulk of prenomination television coverage on the national news. (See Figure 4–1.) Is it any wonder that candidates spend so much time, money, and effort in these early contests?

For non-front-runners there are few options other than to contest these initial contests. Unless they can demonstrate their voter appeal, they are not likely to gain the financial and organizational support, much less the press coverage, necessary to mount a serious challenge to the front-runner.

Al Gore and John McCain tried a variation of this strategy, Gore in 1988 and McCain in 2000. Both skipped the Iowa caucus and concentrated on other early primaries where they believed they would run stronger; Gore focused on the southern regional primaries while McCain concentrated first in New Hampshire, then in his home state of Arizona, and subsequently South Carolina and Michigan.

McCain gained a short-term advantage from this strategy, largely on the basis of his victories in New Hampshire and Michigan, but Gore did not.

Although the early contests are extremely important, particularly for those who lack a national following, the odds of doing well are not great. A failure to stand out frequently forces candidates to drop out, usually because they are unable to raise sufficient money to continue and see the handwriting on the wall. Steve Forbes left the 2000 Republican contest on February 10 after he received only 15 percent of the vote in New Hampshire and 20 percent in Delaware, two states in which his campaign had targeted and spent considerable resources.

On the other hand, doing surprisingly well in these early contests is no guarantee of success. Pat Buchanan won New Hampshire in 1996, but little after that.

FIGURE 4–1 🌿

NEWS COVERAGE OF THE PRESIDENTIAL NOMINATIONS, 1988–2000

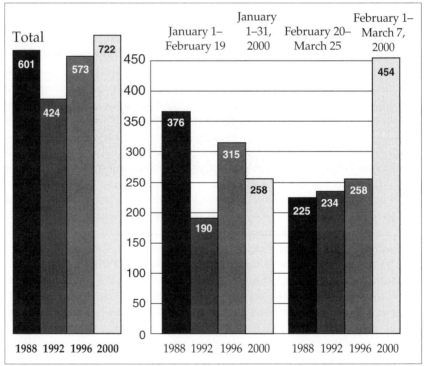

Note: Based on number of election stories on the ABC, CBS, and NBC evening news programs.

Source: "The Parties Pick Their Candidates," *Media Monitor* VI (March 1992): 2; "The Bad News Campaign," *Media Monitor* X (March/April 1996): 1–3; "Campaign 2000—The Primaries," *Media Monitor* XIV (March/April 2000): 1–3. *Media Monitor* is published by the Center for Media and Public Affairs, a nonpartisan and nonprofit research organization. Reprinted with permission of the Center for Media and Public Affairs.

McCain's surprisingly large victory over George Bush in 2000 extended his campaign for five more weeks before Bush's successes in New York, California, and Ohio effectively forced McCain to terminate his efforts.

For front-runners, the needs and opportunities are different. The early caucuses and primaries present a situation in which their resources can be used to eliminate or preclude competition, demonstrate electability, perhaps even invulnerability, and build a delegate lead. Winning confirms the front-runner's status, losing jeopardizes it. While recovery is possible, as Ronald Reagan demonstrated in 1980, Walter Mondale in 1984, George H. W. Bush in 1988, Bob Dole in 1996, and George W. Bush in 2000, an early loss can raise questions about a front-runner's viability, questions that may linger into the general election.

Raise and Spend Big Bucks Early. Having a solid financial base at the outset of the nomination process provides a significant strategic advantage. It allows a presidential campaign to plan ahead, to decide where to establish its field organizations and how much media advertising to buy, as well as where and on which groups to focus that advertising. It is no coincidence that those candidates who raise and spend the most money tend to win their party's nomination.[26]

The impact of early money is particularly significant for candidates who do not begin the quest for their party's nomination with a national reputation, candidates such as Michael Dukakis in 1988, Bill Clinton in 1992, and John Edwards in 2004. The ability to raise relatively large amounts of money early, particularly in comparison with one's rivals, gives a candidate an edge in gaining media recognition, building organizational support, raising even more money, and discouraging potential rivals from entering the race. In fact, the amount of money raised is frequently viewed by the press as a harbinger of future success or failure in the primaries. That Senator John Edwards of North Carolina outraised all the other Democratic contenders in the first reporting period of the 2003–2004 election cycle garnered significant media attention as did Edwards's return of some of the money which may have been contributed illegally.[27]

Democrats Michael Dukakis (1988), Bill Clinton (1992), Al Gore (2000), and Republicans George Bush (1988), Robert Dole (1996), and George W. Bush (2000) used their superior fund-raising to build and staff large organizations in the early primary and caucus states, develop and target their media to key groups, and focus their personal efforts on campaigning, whereas most of their principal opponents lacked the resources to do so competitively.

Early money is considered important for several reasons. It buys recognition for those who need it. Steve Forbes bought that recognition in 1996 with the expenditure of more than $42 million, much of it his own money. But public recognition also brings increased scrutiny by the news media and increased criticism by the other candidates.

Early money also buys legitimacy. The press evaluates the credibility of candidates in part on the basis of how much money they can raise and how willing people are to contribute. Candidates who cannot raise much money are not usually taken seriously by the news media and by other potential contributors, even if they are well known, as was Elizabeth Dole in 2000. Six of the twelve Republican candidates for the 2000 nomination were forced to terminate their quest for their party's nomination three months *before* the first caucus and primary. All cited financial reasons for their withdrawal. On the other hand, Bill Bradley's campaign was given a boost in the eyes of the news media when he was able to match Al Gore's fund-raising during 1999 and the beginning of 2000, even though Bradley had not demonstrated any vote-getting ability.

Another important reason for having early money is that it gives a candidate the opportunity to hire an expert staff and develop a deep field organization in the early primary states. In the event of an early mishap, such an organization can come to the rescue as it did in South Carolina for George W. Bush after his defeat in New Hampshire. Having up-front money also provides flexibility in designing a strategy. In short, money can be used to build support, win delegates, generate momentum, and deliver an early knockout of one's opponents. Lacking such resources candidates have little choice but to compete in Iowa, New Hampshire, and other early contests in which most of their competitors are also running, thereby decreasing their odds of winning. Front-loading also forces the candidates to spend more money earlier and earlier. As noted previously, McCain reached his maximum in early March. Had he not dropped out after Super Tuesday, he would not have been able to spend much more money. Gore and Bradley spent about 75 percent of their total legal limit by the first Tuesday in March. One can only imagine the type of campaign they could have waged with so little money left for the next four months.

George W. Bush lost a lot of his initial fund-raising advantage by spending almost all the money he raised during the competitive phase of the Republican nomination process. Although he ended that phase of the process with less money available than his Democratic rival, Al Gore, because Bush did not accept federal funds, he could raise additional sums, and he did; Gore could not. One reason that Bush chose not to take federal funds is that he did not want to be in the position Dole was in 1996, the acknowledged winner with little money to spend from mid-March until the Republican convention in July.

Two principal consequences follow from the need for early money: the financial campaign in the years before the nomination has assumed greater importance than in the past, and non-front-runners are disadvantaged even more than they were previously unless they are independently wealthy. The odds against a little-known outsider using Iowa, New Hampshire, and the other early states to obtain the resources necessary to compete seriously for the nomination have increased in recent years.

Gain Media Attention. Candidates cannot win if they are not known. Gaining recognition is most important at the beginning of the nomination process when the electorate starts to pay some attention to the contests that loom ahead.

Since lesser-known aspirants are not as likely to have large war chests, unless they are independently wealthy or have substantial sums left over from previous campaigns, they need free media. Their problem is that coverage and public recognition go hand-in-hand. Better-known candidates get more coverage because they are better known and more likely to do well. It is not news when a long shot loses; it is news when a front-runner does. On the other hand, when a long shot does well in raising money, gaining endorsements, drawing crowds, winning straw votes and especially delegates, the press follows the story of the "conquering hero."

Take the Bradley–Gore and McCain–Bush challenges for example. In 1999, Al Gore and George W. Bush were the big television news, measured in terms of coverage they received. Bush was the focus of eighty-six stories on the evening news compared to fifty-six for all his Republican competitors combined. Similarly, Gore was the subject of seventy-three stories while his opponent, Bill Bradley, was featured in forty.[28]

Coverage became more balanced as the caucuses and primaries approached. From January 1 to January 31, 2000, the day of the New Hampshire primary, McCain and Bradley received almost as much attention on the evening news as did Gore and Bush. From New Hampshire until the nomination was effectively decided, they continued to attract similar amounts.[29] (See Figure 4–2.)

FIGURE 4–2

TELEVISION COVERAGE OF THE CANDIDATES IN THE 2000 CAMPAIGN

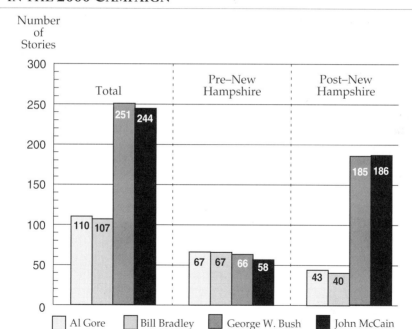

Note: Based on the number of stories on the ABC, CBS, and NBC evening news. More than one candidate may be featured in a story.

Source: "Campaign 2000—The Primaries," *Media Monitor* XIV (March/April 2000): 2. *Media Monitor* is published by the Center for Media and Public Affairs, a nonpartisan and nonprofit research organization. Reprinted with permission of the Center for Media and Public Affairs.

What can non-front-runners do to gain more coverage? They stage events, fax a stream of seemingly endless press releases to most local media outlets, leak controversial information about their opponents, and create opportunities and encourage invitations to appear on talk/entertainment programs on radio and television. Here's how Pat Buchanan's 1996 campaign manager described a typical day in Iowa before that state held the first nominating caucus:

> Gregg [Mueller, the press secretary] and Pat would get up at about five in the morning, get some coffee, get in the minivan, and go from one TV station to the other, in the local market, wherever they had morning shows and they would do a live segment on every morning television show.
>
> Then they'd come back to the hotel, read through the newspapers and at 10 A.M. we'd go out and do our theme event for the day—drive whatever our message was, get out a press release, which we faxed out everywhere and let that, hopefully, resonate into the newspapers.
>
> At noon, we'd go back to the television stations, if they would have us, or else we'd drive into a new market . . . all the time that they would be driving the van, Greg would have Pat on the cell phone doing radio interviews . . . Buchanan would literally go from one station to the other to the other, go back to the hotel, maybe take a nap in the afternoon, then you go out at 5 P.M. and you do the evening TV stations. If you literally saturated the local TV market, you try to get to the next one. You try to maximize the amount of time you could get on TV in a state while you were there.[30]

Participating in debates against their political opponents has become increasingly important for most candidates. In 2000, there were thirteen debates among the Republican contenders and eight among the Democrats, focusing on issues of concern to the party's core: taxes, foreign policy, and social issues for the Republicans and health care, education, race relations, and campaign finance reform for the Democrats.[31]

Although debates among party candidates spark local interest and educate the partisan electorate, they rarely receive national media attention. The first televised debate among the Democratic contenders for the 2004 nomination occurred on May 3, 2003, more than fourteen months before the Democratic nominating convention. It was carried on only one major network but not on most of its local affiliates. Is it any wonder that prenomination debates do not have much national impact unless, of course, one of the candidates makes a major faux pas or claim that is deemed newsworthy?

In general, there was a decline in the amount of time given to news coverage of the 2000 nomination process on the commercial television broadcast networks, even though the number of candidate stories actually increased. (See Figure 4–1.) There has been an even steeper decline in the number of people who regularly watch these shows, which helps explain why public interest in the presidential selection process has also declined.[32]

Beginning in November 1999, the Joan Shorenstein Center on the Press, Politics, and Public Policy at Harvard University conducted weekly polls measuring public interest. Researchers designed a Voter Interest Index based on whether people are following the campaign closely and whether they have thought, talked, or seen a news story about it the previous day. Figure 4–3 plots that index over the course of the 2000 nomination cycle, showing that interest was highest during the competitive phase of the nomination, particularly in those states that held primaries during this period, and after that in the summer when both parties held their national nominating conventions.[33]

With campaign news sources more dispersed, candidates must pay close attention to what viewers are watching. Increasingly, they must design and present their own messages via paid advertising. Free media is not sufficient nor is favorable coverage. John McCain and Bill Bradley both received a higher percentage of positive spin than their front-running opponents—Bradley, prior to New Hampshire, and McCain after New Hampshire.[34]

FIGURE 4–3

VOTER INVOLVEMENT INDEX, NOVEMBER 1999– AUGUST 2000

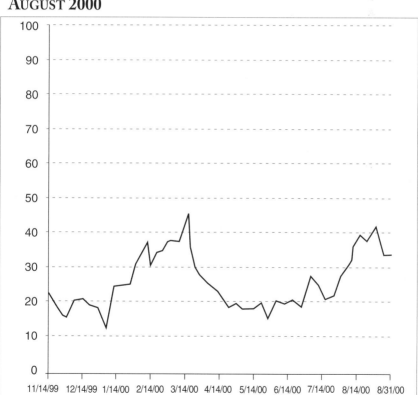

Note: Index is calculated by averaging the responses to four questions—whether people say they are currently paying close attention to the campaign, whether they are thinking about the campaign, talking about it, and following it in the news.

Source: Joan Shorenstein Center on the Press, Politics, and Public Policy, Harvard University, Vanishing Voter Project.

Advertisements remain one of the most effective ways to communicate with voters. Studies have shown that people tend to retain more information from candidate commercials than they do from the broadcast networks' evening news.[35] As a result, campaigns continue to spend the bulk of their revenues on political advertisements.

BOX 4–2 〽️

THE AIR WARS OF 2000: THE NOMINATIONS

A critical component of the nomination campaign was conducted electronically, over the airways, on cable, via satellite, and over the Internet. Most of the campaigns spent well over half their funds on designing, targeting, and presenting their messages in the form of advertisements. The election of 2000 was no exception. Record amounts were spent on political commercials by the candidates, parties, and issue advocacy groups.[36]

The first round of political advertising for the 2000 nomination took place in the campaign preseason during 1999. The bulk of the early advertising was directed toward the first contests in Iowa and New Hampshire. Initial commercials are usually positive and largely biographical, with an emphasis on broad-based goals rather than detailed policy proposals. They are designed to introduce candidates to the voters as extremely well qualified, positive, popular people who will do well if elected.

The radio and television campaigns, which were conducted primarily over local media and cable, began in June 1999 when Steve Forbes reintroduced himself to the Republican electorate as a social conservative, a proponent of a flat income tax, and a political and Washington outsider who would curb the appetite of the big government, big spending politicians.

Other Republican hopefuls soon followed Forbes onto the airways. They presented ads that trumpeted their credentials, public record, and policy goals. Some, like Dan Quayle, Orrin Hatch, and Elizabeth Dole, stressed their experience in government as well as their conservative credentials. Others, like Gary Bauer and Robert Smith, stated their strong convictions on social and national security policy, respectively.

Front-runner George W. Bush presented himself as a considerate and upbeat person, an outsider who could moderate the divisive partisanship that has characterized Washington politics during the Clinton–Gingrich era. Promising to return decency, integrity, and moral virtue to the Oval Office, Bush emphasized the positive. "I'm going to run a campaign that is hopeful and optimistic and very positive," he said. His ads, which pictured him as a highly successful governor who cut taxes, reduced spending, improved public education, and cut welfare rolls in Texas, ended with a reaffirmation of the image Bush wished to present to the American people: "George W. Bush. A compassionate conservative. A fresh start for America."[37]

John McCain's ads stressed his military experience in Vietnam and his crusade against special interest politics as illustrated by the following excerpt from one of his frequently aired commercials:

Announcer: He was a young Navy pilot who volunteered for duty in Vietnam and was shot down over Hanoi. Lieutenant Commander John McCain, dragged off by an angry mob. When found to be the son and grandson of admirals, was offered early release; he refused. McCain's commitment to country and fellow prisoners brought him repeated beatings and five and a half years in prison. . . . Navy officer, congressman, senator, taking on the establishment. And defying special interests. And never forgetting those heroes with whom he served. Today John McCain is ready to lead America into the new century. His mission: to fundamentally reform government. More experience and more courage than anyone. Ready to be president and leader of the free world.[38]

McCain campaigned as a reformer and as a Reagan Republican. "Here's some straight talk," he said in one of his ads, "I'm a Reagan Republican. I'll tear up the 44,000-page tax code that benefits special interests; stop the outrageous waste and pork barrel spending. . . . Give me your vote, and we'll give you back your government."[39]

On the Democratic side, Gore initially emphasized his role as an experienced vice president who would promote and protect traditional Democratic Party values. When his campaign foundered in the fall of 1999, his ads presented him in more human terms, working summers on the farm in Tennessee in his youth, exposing crime as a young investigative reporter, and serving his country in the Army in Vietnam as well as during his many years of public service.

Bill Bradley painted himself as a humble, low-key person, motivated by his desire to serve his country and make it a better place for more people, and qualified to do so by his success as a Rhodes scholar, Olympic gold medalist, professional basketball player, and U.S. senator. Bradley's commercials emphasized his goals of universal health care, racial equality, and unparalleled educational opportunities but did not contain many details of how he would achieve these objectives.

As the primaries and caucuses neared and the campaign heated up, so did the advertisements. They became more confrontational, although not to the extent that they had been in previous nomination cycles. Residual press and public negativity toward attack advertising slowed the introduction of negative ads in the 2000 campaign, but such ads began to appear in greater frequency before the New Hampshire primary, and they continued to be aired until the nomination process was effectively decided.[40]

Bush and McCain were particularly critical of each other in their television spots. Bush's ads referred to McCain's temper and questioned his loyalty to Republican policy, such as his opposition to across-the-board tax cuts. McCain's votes against appropriations for mass transportation, home heating oil subsidies, and breast cancer research were cited as evidence of his insensitivity to problems outside his state.[41]

McCain responded by angrily accusing Bush of distorting his record, of "talking like Clinton," and of being just another politician who could not be trusted. Bush "hit the roof" when McCain's ad made the Clinton comparison. Here are excerpts from two of their ads.

THE McCAIN AND BUSH NEGATIVE ADVERTISEMENTS

McCain

Picture: Senator McCain in blue suit and red tie.
Audio: McCain talking:

I guess it was bound to happen. Governor Bush's campaign is getting desperate, with a negative ad about me. The fact is, I'll use the surplus money to fix Social Security, cut your taxes, and pay down the debt. His ad twists the truth like

Clinton. We're all pretty tired of that. As president, I'll be conservative and always tell you the truth. No matter what.

Bush

Picture: Banners with McCain picture interspersed.
Audio: Announcer talking:

It's disappointing. Friday, John McCain promised to stop running a negative campaign. Then Sunday he attacked Governor Bush on national television with false charges on campaign finance. . . .

Governor Bush supports comprehensive reform that would outlaw foreign, corporate, and union money to political parties. Senator McCain? Five times he voted to use your taxes to pay for political campaigns. Governor Bush will devote the surplus to priorities: a strong military, education, Social Security, and tax cuts.[42]

Bush's complaints about McCain's negativity combined with the impact of his ads questioning McCain's positions on a range of conservative issues placed the senator on the defensive. Believing that his own ads undercut the positive image he was trying to project as a straight-talking political reformer, McCain pulled his confrontational ads before the South Carolina primary with much public fanfare, replacing them with positive ones that lauded his accomplishments, qualifications, and agenda and defensive ads that denied Bush's accusations.

Bush and the outside groups that supported his candidacy, however, continued to air commercials that attacked McCain. Ads that were sharply critical of the senator's statements on abortion were aired in that state as well as in Michigan and Virginia. These ads were reinforced by telephone campaigns that questioned McCain's Republican credentials on a range of social issues. Even more controversial than the calls was the $2.5 million worth of ads in New York, California, and Ohio that savaged McCain's environmental record. Sponsored by Republicans for Clean Air, a PAC financed by Texas millionaire Sam Wyly, a close friend and financial supporter of George W. Bush, the ads claimed that McCain voted against solar and renewable energy while Bush improved air quality in Texas by clamping down on coal-burning electric power plants.[43]

By contrast, the Democratic confrontational ads were less inflammatory on the surface, but no less critical in content. Bradley chided Gore for his inconsistency over the years on abortion, gun control, and tobacco, suggesting that Gore adopted and then changed his position for political purposes. In reiterating his Democratic credentials, Gore in turn accused Bradley of quitting the Senate when his party lost control rather than staying to fight for what he believed, voting for Ronald Reagan's budget, and supporting private school vouchers, another Republican policy position. He was particularly critical of Bradley's health care and prescription drug proposals.[44]

When Gore's ads seemed to be having an impact, lowering Bradley's standing in the polls, Bradley hit back. He defended his record, criticized Gore, and aired testimonials from such well-known sports stars as Michael Jordan and public officials as Senator Daniel Patrick Moynihan (D-N.Y.) and Bob Kerrey (D-Nebr.) supporting his character and candidacy.

The ad wars of the 2000 nomination process took their intended toll. Bush's ads seem to convince Republicans that he was a good human being and safe on their issues, while McCain was temperamental, unpredictable, and had his own issue agenda, which was different than the party's. Gore's commercials raised questions about Bradley's loyalty to the party and his command of the issues, while they trumpeted Gore's qualifications as an experienced vice president, a Democratic partisan, and appropriate heir to the Clinton–Gore presidency.

Develop a Deep and Wide Organization. The concentration of primaries and caucuses also requires that candidates create a deep and wide organization, one that can attend to the multiple facets of the campaign and do so in many states simultaneously. But achieving this objective has become increasingly difficult with the front-loading of the primaries, even for well-financed candidates. As a consequence the deep organization rarely extends beyond the early states, and in those states it must also be supplemented by group activity, such as with the pro-life and Christian Coalition groups that helped Pat Buchanan in 1996 and George W. Bush in 2000, and organized labor and teacher's groups that aided Al Gore, particularly in Iowa and New Hampshire. All the candidates who survive these contests must supplement their organizations with volunteers who may be encouraged by their victories or by the organizations of state parties if those parties can be persuaded to support them.

George Bush benefited enormously from the backing and organizational support of state parties in New Hampshire, South Carolina, and Illinois in 1988, as did his son in the early contests in Iowa, South Carolina, and Virginia in 2000. Similarly, Bill Clinton owed his first primary victory in Georgia in 1992 to the active campaign of Governor Zell Miller and his party organization.

The major task of any organization is to mobilize voters and build electoral coalitions among core partisan groups.[45] Media coverage alone does not suffice. Having an organization in the field is deemed especially important in caucus states in order to get supporters and sympathizers to the precinct meetings, which are less well-known than the voting places where people cast their primary ballots and also vote in the general election. In both caucuses and primaries, telephone banks must be established, door-to-door canvassing undertaken, and appropriate material mailed or hand delivered. It is also necessary to create the impression of broad public support and generate excitement. These activities involve a large grassroots effort.

Eugene McCarthy, George McGovern, and to a lesser extent Bill Bradley recruited thousands of college students to ring doorbells, distribute literature, and get supporters out to vote in 1968, 1972, and 2000. Jimmy Carter had his "Peanut Brigade," a group of Georgians who followed him from state to state in 1976. Jesse Jackson effectively used African American churches to recruit volunteers and raise money for his presidential campaigns in 1984 and 1988 while Pat Robertson depended on the 3 million people who signed petitions urging him to run for president. In contrast, Pat Buchanan had his greatest success in caucus states in 1992 and 1996 where his passionate and committed supporters could control local meetings and state conventions. In fact, the only states in those elections in which Buchanan received a majority of the delegates were caucus states.

Monitor Public Opinion. With intentions clear, money in hand, media events organized, and an organization in place, it is necessary to ascertain public sentiment, appeal to it, and try to manipulate it. To achieve these goals, state polls and focus groups are considered essential. However, they did not become part and parcel of the nomination process until the middle of the twentieth century.

Republican Thomas E. Dewey was the first to have private polling data available to him when he tried unsuccessfully to obtain the Republican nomination in 1940. John F. Kennedy was the first candidate to engage a pollster in his quest for the nomination. Preconvention surveys conducted by Louis Harris in 1960 indicated that Hubert Humphrey, Kennedy's principal rival, was potentially vulnerable in West Virginia and Wisconsin. On the basis of this information, the Kennedy campaign decided to concentrate time, effort, and money in these predominantly Protestant states. Victories in both helped demonstrate Kennedy's broad appeal, thereby improving his chances for the nomination.

Today, all major presidential candidates commission their own polls. These private surveys are important for several reasons. They provide information about the beliefs and attitudes of voters, their perceptions of the candidates, and the kinds of appeals that are apt to be most effective, as well as which ones seem to be working. Bill Clinton used polls to great advantage in 1992 to develop and target an economic appeal and to respond to allegations about his personal character. He used them even more intensely to reposition himself and launch his reelection bid following the Democrats' debacle in the 1994 midterm elections. The entire Clinton advertising campaign in 1995 and 1996 was developed and monitored through careful and constant White House polling.

Focus groups have become increasingly important. They are used to gauge the public's reaction to words and phrases as well as to evaluate the potential impact of candidate appeals on voters. Almost all campaign advertising is pretested by such groups to gauge the likely public reaction. Adjustments may then be made before the ad is aired, if it is aired. A negative reaction by the focus group may kill the ad entirely. Dick Morris, the political strategist behind Clinton's reelection campaign, described how he and his aides crafted the president's media advertising on the basis of focus group reactions:

> We prepared several different rough versions of the ads, called animatics, which [pollster] Mark Penn would arrange to test at fifteen shopping malls around the nation. After the Republicans began to attack us in their own ads, Penn tested the opposition ad and our reply at the same time to measure their relative impact. Penn's staffers would set themselves up in a mall and invite shoppers one by one to fill out a short questionnaire about Clinton, Dole, and their own political views. Then they would show the voters the ad we wanted to test. Afterward the shopper would fill in the same questionnaire and Penn would measure any changes in opinion. . . .
>
> Based on the mall tests, we decided which ad to run and whether to combine it with elements from ads that did not do as well. We worked for hours to make the ad fit thirty seconds. Then we'd send the script to Doug Sosnik, the White House political director, who gave it to the president for his OK.[46]

The Bush and Gore campaigns engaged in similar efforts in 2000. (See Box 4–2 on pages 128–131.)

Telephone polling can also be a guise for getting out the vote, for pushing a vote, or even for suppressing one. In 1992, Bush supporters in New Hampshire countered Pat Buchanan's criticism with a telephone campaign directed at women who were read statements that Buchanan had made about their fitness to have a career. The choice of the statement was designed to produce a negative effect. Similarly, in 2000, supporters of McCain and Bush raised questions about their opponents' religious tolerance to get out their own religious supporters.[47]

Poll results can also be used to build momentum, increase morale, and affect media coverage. The amount of coverage is important because the more coverage candidates have, particularly during the early months, the more volunteers they can attract and the more money they can raise.

The benefits of appearing to be popular and electable suggest why candidates have also used their private polls for promotional purposes. A good example was Nelson Rockefeller, who tied his quest for the Republican nomination in 1968 to poll data. Since he did not enter the primaries, Rockefeller's aim was to convince Republican delegates that he, not Richard Nixon, would be the strongest candidate. Private surveys, conducted for Rockefeller in nine large states, five important congressional districts, and the nation as a whole one month before the Republican convention, indicated that he would do better against potential Democratic candidates than Richard Nixon. Unfortunately for Rockefeller, the final Gallup preconvention poll, fielded two days after former President Dwight Eisenhower endorsed Nixon, did not support these findings. The Gallup results undercut the credibility of Rockefeller's polls as well as of another national poll that had Rockefeller in the lead and thus effectively ended his chances for the nomination.

Another use of private polls is to raise money. Contributors are more motivated to give to candidates who stand a reasonable chance of winning. Thus, the release of poll data to potential donors and even to the news media is often designed to demonstrate a candidate's electability.

Although polls directly affect a candidate's strategy, tactics, and fund-raising, their impact on the general public is less direct and much less pronounced. Despite the fear of many politicians, there are few empirical data to suggest that polls generate a bandwagon effect, a momentum for a candidate that causes people to jump on board. There is, however, some evidence of a relationship between a candidate's standing in the polls, success in the primaries, and winning the nomination. What is unclear is whether the public opinion leaders win because they are more popular or whether they are more popular initially because they are better known and ultimately because they look like winners.

Design and Target a Distinctive Appeal. The information obtained from polls and focus groups is used to create and sharpen leadership images and to target these images to sympathetic voters. In designing an appeal, candidates must first establish their credentials, then articulate a general approach, and finally discuss specific policy problems and solutions. For lesser-known candidates, the initial emphasis must be on themselves and their relevant experience.

With a few notable exceptions—Vice President Al Gore and Governor George W. Bush—most of the candidates in the 2000 presidential campaign were not well-known to the general public at the outset of the nomination process. In September 1999, as candidates began to organize their campaigns and vie for attention, only Gore and Bush were recognized by more than 15 percent of the voters as candidates.[48] For the rest, name recognition and image creation became their first and essential task.

The increasing front-loading of the primaries and caucuses added to the plight of these lesser-known aspirants. At a time when only a small portion of the people were paying close attention to news about the campaign, most of these non-front-running candidates who were not independently wealthy had to gain recognition in order to obtain sufficient money, media, and volunteers to run a viable campaign. Half of the Republican aspirants were unable to do so and thus were forced to drop out *before* the election year even began.

As the Republican race narrowed to a two-person contest, the policy emphases of the principal candidates became clearer. Bush, who had begun his campaign as a main street Republican, one who could unify the various factions within his party, became more conservative, emphasizing his plan to cut taxes and his support of the social policy positions of the Christian Coalition. In contrast, McCain emphasized his independence, his reform agenda with campaign finance at its center, and his credentials as a Reagan Republican.

On the Democratic side, the policy differences were narrower. Al Gore pointed to his experience as vice president in a successful administration. Desiring to share credit for the administration's accomplishments, Gore indicated some of his contributions, such as his leading role in advocating and overseeing the administration's policies designed to build an information superhighway. However, an off-the-cuff remark on television, "I took the initiative in creating the Internet," embarrassed him, illustrated his propensity to exaggerate his own importance, and effectively prevented him from raising the technology issue, much less getting credit for the administration's initiative in this area.[49] Bill Bradley spoke about the need for reform in health care, improving race relations, and ending child poverty. He presented himself as a nontraditional candidate who was motivated to do what was right, not what was politically correct.

In 2004, Howard Dean criticized U.S. policy toward Iraq while the other principal Democratic candidates defended it. Within the domestic arena, first Gephardt, and then Dean and Kerry introduced comprehensive health plans; Graham, pointing to his experience as chair of the Senate Intelligence Committee, charged the Bush administration with underemphasizing and underfunding homeland security at the expense of its foriegn and military policy initiatives while Lieberman stressed his more moderate policy stands on domestic issues.[50]

In general, the candidates' issue positions and image projections do reach voters. The Annenberg Public Policy Center at the University of Pennsylvania, which studied these policy agendas and image projections in 2000, found that overall, "people gained greater awareness and knowledge of the candidates and their positions as the primary season progressed. Knowledge gains were higher in states with primaries in which the candidates actively campaigned than in states without candidate activity."[51] The state exit polls also indicated that the candidates "hit" their targets.

Annenberg researchers also examined the impact of political endorsements and campaign attacks on the electorate. They concluded that endorsements and attacks can inform voters and influence their behavior on election day. Not only were people aware of candidate endorsements by prominent officials in their states, but these endorsements carried weight and were a factor affecting their vote. Similarly, attacks, particularly those that became items in the news, also had an effect. Criticism of McCain for voting against breast cancer research and of Bradley for his overly ambitious and expensive health care plan were cited as examples by the study.[52]

In short, what candidates say and do matters. Candidate appeals and attacks inform and influence the electorate. They may not be the only factors that affect an election's outcome, but they do make a difference.

In addition to the advertising, a staple of contemporary presidential campaigns, other methods are also used to reach voters. These include video news releases produced by the candidates, satellite interviews with local news media, and targeted telephone calls, specifically the use of a toll-free number, to raise money and gain volunteers.

One of the distinctive aspects of nomination campaigns since the beginning of the 1990s has been the propensity of candidates to circumvent the national media. They have done so in a variety of ways. The Clinton campaign in 1992, for example, distributed between 25,000 and 30,000 videotapes about the candidate to New Hampshire Democrats.[53] Video news releases were also given to local media by several of the candidate organizations. Some of the local stations even used them on their news shows without revealing the source.[54]

Satellite technology has also been used extensively. In 1992, nearly half of the local news media conducted interviews with the candidates compared with only 20 percent four years earlier.[55] Since 1992, candidates have taken advantage of free television on national talk-entertainment shows as well as news shows.

The Internet has also become another vehicle, and an increasingly important one, through which policy positions are stated and argued, and financial appeals are made. John McCain collected over $7 million in donations using his Web site, most of it after his surprisingly strong showing in New Hampshire.[56] Soliciting volunteers, communicating with supporters, and making information available to the press and other interested parties are some of the other ways in which candidates have used their Web sites as a campaign tool.

The Internet has generated problems as well. Squatters have used the names of actual and potential candidates to register Web addresses and then demanded large sums from the campaigns to give them up. Parody sites and linkages have mushroomed on the Net. Unsubstantiated rumors can be circulated so widely and rapidly that they become news. Security has also become a problem as Web sites become targets of political opponents and hackers who wish to damage candidates by invading their sites.

To summarize, timing, finance, organization, and communications affect the quest for delegates. They help shape the candidates' strategies and tactics for the nomination. Generally speaking, there have been two successful contemporary prototypical strategies, one for lesser-known aspirants, the other for front-runners. Jimmy Carter used the first of these strategies successfully in his quest for the nomination in 1976. In his run four years later, Carter adopted the second strategy. Since that time, most of the principal contenders have employed one of these strategies or a variation of them in their attempts to win their party's nomination.

The Non-Front-Runner Strategy: Stepping-Stones to Prominence

Non-front-runners lack the resources for victory: money, media, and organization. Their objective must be to obtain them and to do so as quickly as possible. The only way to do this is to run hard and fast at the outset, entering the early contests, doing well, gaining media attention, demonstrating electability, generating momentum, and eventually building a delegate base.

Jimmy Carter pursued such a strategy in 1976; it has since become the non-front-runner model. Hamilton Jordan, Carter's campaign manager, who designed the basic game plan two years before the election, described the early preconvention strategy:

> The prospect of a crowded field coupled with the new proportional representation rule does not permit much flexibility in the early primaries. No serious candidate will have the luxury of picking or choosing among the early primaries. To pursue such a strategy would cost that candidate delegate votes and increase the possibility of being lost in the crowd. I think that we have to assume that everybody will be running in the first five or six primaries.
>
> A crowded field enhances the possibility of several inconclusive primaries with four or five candidates separated by only a few percentage points. Such a muddled picture will not continue for long as the press will begin to make "winners" of some and "losers" of others. The intense press coverage which naturally focuses on the early primaries plus the decent time intervals which separate the March and mid-April primaries dictate a serious effort in all of the first five primaries. Our "public" strategy would probably be that Florida was the first and real test of the Carter campaign and that New Hampshire would just be a warm-up. In fact, a strong, surprise showing in New Hampshire should be our goal which would have tremendous impact on successive primaries.[57]

The goal was achieved. Dubbed the person to beat after his victories in the Iowa caucus and New Hampshire primary, Carter, with his defeat of George Wallace in Florida, overcame a disappointing fourth place in Massachusetts a week earlier and became the acknowledged front-runner. The Carter effort in 1976 became the strategic plan for George H. W. Bush in 1980, Gary Hart in 1984, and John McCain in 2000.

Doing well in the early caucuses and primaries is important but no longer has the payoff it had for Carter. The front-loading of the selection process has reduced the "bump" that Iowa and New Hampshire can give to a victorious non-front-runner. Yet, such candidates have few other options to increase their name recognition and at the same time demonstrate their viability as serious candidates for their party's nomination. And a win in the early caucuses and primaries, no matter how slight, confounds the odds, surprises the news media, embarrasses the front-runner, and energizes the non-front-runner's candidacy. (See Box 4–3, "Non-Front-Runner Strategies in 2000.") Media coverage expands; fund-raising is made easier; volunteers join the organization; endorsements become more likely; and momentum can be generated, at least in the short run.[58]

BOX 4–3 📖

NON-FRONT-RUNNER STRATEGIES IN 2000

MCCAIN'S "STRAIGHT-TALK" CHALLENGE

A hero, a renegade, very much his own person, but one who had little public recognition, political support, and financial backing, McCain's challenge to George W. Bush turned out to be one of the big surprises and the biggest news story of the 2000 nominations.

McCain started slowly. He had a small staff, little money, and responsibilities that kept him in the Senate for much of the 1999 preseason. Moreover, he lacked the credentials of successful Republican nominees in the past. He was not considered a party loyalist; he had not previously run a national campaign; he had few political endorsements, few major financial backers, and no discernible grassroots support. What he did have, however, was a leadership image from his service in Vietnam, a fighter, who as a Senator railed against special interests, pork barrel legislation, the tobacco industry, and soft money. McCain exuded confidence and conviction, two traits that were to take him far in his campaign.

Although he did not begin his presidential quest until December 1999, well after most of his Republican rivals, McCain had no choice but to target the early primaries as stepping-stones to the nomination. However, he did make one strategic decision that worked to his advantage—not to contest the first caucus in Iowa. This decision enabled him to conserve his resources and avoid an in-the-pack finish. As attention shifted to New Hampshire, he was the only Republican who had not lost to George W. Bush. This fact alone earned him notoriety.

McCain's campaign organization was smaller and more informal than George W. Bush's.[59] Unlike Bush who followed his handlers' advice religiously, McCain was very much his own campaign manager. He called the shots. Hating to read set speeches, he liked to engage in free-floating, unscripted discussions of his priorities. The image he presented was that of a straight shooter, an antipolitician, who like Jimmy Carter, pledged, "I will always tell you the truth."[60] Reputed to be temperamental and prone to angry outbursts by his opponents, McCain acknowledged his emotions and claimed that they reflected the strength of his convictions and his penchant for straight talk.

The Senator's appeal to patriotism, public service, and political reform resonated well with Republicans in New Hampshire, as well as with independent voters and

Democrats around the country. Core Republicans, however, were not as moved by his rhetoric. Most strong Republican loyalists still thought in terms of the language, themes, and policies that President Reagan and his disciples championed: a smaller and less intrusive national government, tax cuts, and conservative social values. None of these were at the top of McCain's principal issues.

During his campaign, Senator McCain had excellent relations with the press. In fact, he was a media favorite. The access he gave to reporters, the no-nonsense image he conveyed, and the competition he generated within the Republican campaign resulted in expansive coverage of his campaign and a more favorable press than Bush received from the New Hampshire primary until Super Tuesday.[61]

McCain's game plan was to do well in New Hampshire, gain media attention, become George W. Bush's principal challenger, and then use the recognition he would receive from a victory in the first primary to raise money, gain volunteers, and produce momentum for the next contest. The plan worked splendidly for a while. McCain won 48 percent of the New Hampshire vote compared to Bush's 30 percent and Forbes's 13 percent. His unexpectedly large victory put Bush on the defensive, hastened the departure of other candidates (Gary Bauer after New Hampshire and Steve Forbes after Delaware), and upped the ante for the next contest in South Carolina. His impressive win also gave him a big financial boost. McCain raised an additional $2 million in the days following the New Hampshire primary, much of it from appeals on his Web site.[62]

After an intervening caucus in Delaware in which only Forbes and Bush competed and that received scant press coverage, McCain turned his attention to South Carolina. With the state's Republican establishment supporting Bush, with religious conservatives comprising a major bloc of voters, with pro-tobacco groups active in the state, McCain faced big odds. Complicating his effort were negative advertising campaigns waged by his opponents—George W. Bush, antiabortion and pro-tobacco groups, the religious right, and even supporters of flying the Confederate flag over the state capitol.

The campaigns against McCain were largely confrontational and personal. They focused on the senator's position on the issues, his congressional voting record, his loyalty to the Republican Party, even rumors about his private life. These negative campaigns operated at the grassroots level. Millions of voters were contacted by phone and mail. The Bush campaign alone reached an estimated 1 million people in the final two days before the vote.[63]

Initially, McCain countered with negative ads of his own against Bush. However, when the press made negativity an issue, McCain abruptly pulled his attack ads and pledged not to go negative again. But his pledge seemed to have little impact on the outcome. Bush won handily, gaining an overwhelming proportion of the Christian Coalition vote.

The contest then moved to more friendly territory for McCain, his home state of Arizona and Michigan, a state in which religious conservatives were not as strong. McCain was also helped in Michigan by the law that permitted independents and Democrats to cross over and vote in the Republican primary and by the fact that no Democratic primaries were scheduled to be held until the first Tuesday in March. Although the establishment Republicans in Arizona and Michigan endorsed Bush, the Bush campaign spent considerable sums on media advertising in both states ($2 million in Arizona alone), and conservative antiabortion and antitax groups actively opposed his candidacy, McCain was able to overcome this opposition by appealing to independent and Democratic voters.[64] He won both contests.

At this point, McCain looked viable. His campaign was raising money. He was appealing to a cross-section of voters. In fact, hypothetical polls against the likely Democratic candidate, Al Gore, actually showed McCain running stronger than George W. Bush. This fact provided support for McCain's claim that he, not George W. Bush, was Al Gore's worst nightmare.

The next three contests, the Washington and Virginia primaries and caucus election in North Dakota, proved disappointing to McCain and essentially undercut the boost that he received from his earlier wins. In none of these states was he able to overcome Bush's lead among Republicans, the only voters who could participate. Nor did his positive advertising achieve nearly the impact that Bush's negative advertising did. And looking ahead to Super Tuesday, Bush's large war chest put him in a much stronger position to compete in the twelve primaries and two first-round caucuses that were to be held that day.

Behind in the polls and unable to match Bush's money and organization, McCain took a tactical gamble. Speaking in an area of Virginia known for its religious fundamentalism, McCain denounced two of the state's most prominent fundamentalist ministers, Jerry Falwell and Pat Robertson, calling them "agents of intolerance" and "forces of evil."[65] His remarks, which he was later forced to modify, served to unite the Christian Coalition against him and brought out an unusually large vote from this group, but did not appear to help McCain with more moderate Republican voters.[66] The gamble had backfired.

With his campaign on the rocks, McCain ran as best he could on Super Tuesday. Although he won four out of the five New England primaries, he lost everywhere else, including the delegate-rich states of California, Ohio, and New York. In each of these big states, the Republican establishment combined with outside groups to mobilize a sizable pro-Bush, anti-McCain vote. With his opponent's delegate lead all but insurmountable, McCain announced he would reevaluate his campaign. The race was over.

Though he lost, McCain gained stature from his defeat. He had attracted independent and Democratic voters. In every state in which he competed, McCain received a much higher percentage of the votes of self-declared independents than did Bush. He also got more Democratic support in states in which crossover voting was permitted. Among Republicans, he was weaker. In general, the more conservative the voter the less likely that person would cast a ballot for McCain. But his biggest weakness was among the religious right. This group voted overwhelmingly for George W. Bush.

Nonetheless, McCain's issue of campaign finance reform, his diatribe against special interest politics, even his proposals to pay down the national debt rather than give tax relief to all voters, resonated with the American electorate. He had become a force in Republican Party politics.

Bradley's Nontraditional Challenge

Bill Bradley's challenge was unexpected; his campaign, unconventional; and his candidacy, quixotic. Desiring to put government and public policy on a more moral and egalitarian foundation, Bradley espoused a variety of goals that seemed to place him to the ideological left of Gore and into the liberal, big government wing of his party.

Bradley presented himself as a candidate who disdained politics as usual, a man of deep convictions. His image as an antipolitician appealed to those who had grown increasingly cynical about the motives, decisions, and actions of people who made a career of electoral politics. His earnestness, genuineness, and self-effacing manner contrasted sharply with Gore's Washington insider image.

Bradley's campaign style was unique as well. He jealously guarded his privacy, refusing to discuss even his own religious beliefs. He was also reluctant initially to criticize his opponent or engage in the give-and-take that characterizes contemporary politics. Bradley emphasized the positive, how much better America could become if more people benefited from the country's prosperity.

At first, the press and public found Bradley's image refreshing, his fund-raising ability surprising, and his rise in the polls startling. Who would have expected this candidate to mount such an effective challenge to an incumbent vice president? As long as Bradley's image as a citizen-politician, a person with whom the average American could identify and trust, remained the story of his campaign, he did well.

Bradley's problem, however, was that he could not move beyond this image. In fact, that image initially immobilized him. When his Democratic credentials were attacked and his policies critically evaluated in face-to-face debates with Gore and by Gore's political advertising, Bradley took the high road. Rather than attacking Gore, he defended himself and his policies. His defensive posture, however, made him appear passive and timid in comparison to the aggressiveness of his opponent.

Being a nice guy also limited Bradley's ability to exploit Gore's vulnerabilities: the vice president's tendency to exaggerate, his involvement in the Democratic Party's campaign finance scandal, and his defense of the president in the Monica Lewinsky affair. By the time Bradley began to question Gore's veracity and judgment, it was too late.

The first caucus and primary were very important for Bradley. As a challenger, he had to demonstrate that he could win. Putting a lot of effort into the Iowa caucus, Bradley spent seventy-five days in the state in 1999, much more than Gore, and he was there for most of the month preceding the caucus on January 24, 2000. Bradley also spent the maximum legal amount of $2.2 million, more than half of which went into television advertising. Four hundred, mostly young, campaign volunteers combed the state for potential supporters, but Bradley's organization could not match organized labor's and the Iowa State Education Association, which turned out a large caucus vote for Gore.[67]

Despite his effort, Bradley failed to generate much excitement and support in the state. Hurt by his health care plan, which Iowa Democrats perceived as too costly, by his vote against flood relief for Iowa in 1993, and by a low turnout, the senator only received a little more than one-third of the vote, a disappointing showing for the time and resources he put into the state.

Bradley's Iowa loss weakened his New Hampshire campaign. Not only did it call into question his status as a serious challenger to Gore, but it cut into his organizing effort because he had to move his grassroots operation from New Hampshire to Iowa. By the time he and his operatives returned to the Granite State, Bradley's lead had all but vanished, and he lacked sufficient time to turn things around. Again, he had to battle the AFL-CIO in addition to Gore's campaign regulars. Labor organizers contacted every union household not once but seven times to bring out the pro-labor, pro-Gore vote.[68]

Although the New Hampshire election was closer than in Iowa, Bradley still lost. Other than a popularity contest in the state of Washington, there was no other Democratic contest scheduled until the first Tuesday in March when twelve primaries and two, initial-round caucuses were to be held. With the news media turning their attention to the Republican contests occurring in the interim, Bradley lost visibility. Although he kept campaigning, he did not pick up steam. His staff was becoming increasingly frustrated. Polls showed him losing ground to Gore.[69] The die was cast. On

Super Tuesday, March 7, Bradley was defeated in all the contests he entered. He officially ended his candidacy two days later.

Bradley lost for several reasons. His diffident manner, ephemeral style, and unassuming personality raised questions of image—whether this decent person could be a strong, decisive, and effective leader. He just didn't connect with core Democratic voters.[70] He also did not respond quickly enough and with sufficient vigor to Gore's charges in their face-to-face debates and to television advertisements in which his policy stands and Senate votes were criticized. When Bradley finally began to question his opponent's integrity, credibility, and more conservative policies, he became just another politician in the eyes of many Democrats. His uniqueness had faded.

Nor could Bradley's organization compete with Gore's. The senator's young volunteers were no match for the seasoned and skilled professionals of organized labor and the Democratic Party who helped Gore. Bradley operated as his own campaign director, but his loner style made it difficult for his campaign staff to plan far ahead. Usually, one to four events were held per day, with many of them occurring after the evening newscasts.[71] Bradley also kept reporters at a distance, even traveling separately from them.[72]

The Democratic challenger was also hurt by Republican John McCain's candidacy, particularly McCain's appeal to independent voters and weak Democrats. Although both he and McCain championed similar causes, it was McCain, not Bradley, who was seen as the leader on them.

Bradley had another problem that McCain did not. He had to contend with a Democratic electorate that was more complacent, more approving of the Clinton–Gore administration, and much less upset with its scandals than were the people to whom McCain appealed. McCain's voters were more angry, and they showed it by turning out to vote. Bradley's supporters were not, and they turned out in smaller numbers.

Although people saw Bradley as distant, they also perceived him as a man of convictions and a person with new ideas. For those Democrats who were cynical about the political process, upset with the moral and ethical shortcomings of the Clinton administration, or critical of its moderate, incremental policies, Bradley's candidacy was refreshing. For most core Democrats, however, it was not. He did not win the vote of self-declared Democrats in any of the states in which he competed against Gore. Bradley did better among independent voters, although not as well as McCain. Ideology did not seem to be the factor it was for the Republicans, but the absence of labor support clearly was. Bradley lost the vote of union households by a margin of two or three to one.

Unlike McCain, Bradley ceased to be a force in his party or even in the 2000 campaign.

On the other hand, early losses for non-front-runners doom their candidacy, forcing them to withdraw, usually on the pretext of having insufficient funds to continue.[73] There is no prize for coming in second, except perhaps a prime-time convention speech. News media often speculate that candidates who demonstrate some popular appeal would make good vice presidential candidates, but the fact of the matter is that successful nominees rarely choose their opponents to run with them. The only recent exception to this rule was Reagan's selection of George H. W. Bush—not his first choice—in 1980.

Other Non-Front-Runner Approaches: Using the Campaign as a Pulpit

Jesse Jackson was not a typical non-front-runner in 1984 and 1988, and, to some extent, neither were Pat Robertson (1988), Jerry Brown (1992), Pat Buchanan (1992, 1996, and 2000), Gary Bauer and Alan Keyes (2000), and Carol Moseley Braun, Dennis Kucinich, and Al Sharpton (2004). Jackson and Brown did not employ the prototypical challenger strategy although the rest did.

Most of these candidates could not afford large paid organizations or extensive paid media. Robertson, a television evangelic minister, relied on his congregants supplemented by a paid field organization. Others did what they could. They all used free media to gain recognition and stay in the news. Early nomination debates were a must. But they had little realistic chance of winning. Why then did they campaign for their party's nomination?

They each had several overlapping objectives: to use the campaign as a pulpit for presenting their ideas and as a vehicle for mobilizing their constituencies to promote the interests of those who were not well represented in the party and its hierarchy, to be considered as members of that hierarchy with considerable political power, and to influence the party and its platform. Bay Buchanan, Pat's sister and campaign manager, described why her brother ran in 1992:

> There were a number of reasons why we were going to run, the least of which is that we wanted to win. . . . First, we felt very strongly that the President was the heir to the Reagan legacy, that he had taken the country in a certain direction, and it was assumed it was the direction the conservatives would have taken. Pat thought that we needed a spokesperson to represent conservatives, to say this *isn't* the direction we think is in the best interest of conservatives. . . . Second was eminent domain. David Duke, who had been made a national figure, was speaking about some of those issues that we thought were ours legitimately. He was being made the ultimate spokesperson for conservatives, a development which was going to do incredible damage to the conservative movement. . . . The third was to actually move the President, force him to keep to the issues that we felt were right and proper for the Reagan legacy.[74]

To achieve their objectives, each of these candidates needed above all else to campaign. They also needed to demonstrate their political strength by winning elections if they were to remain active candidates. Jackson and Brown continued their campaigns right up to the Democratic convention although it was obvious that they would not be their party's nominee; Robertson and Buchanan dropped out, but not before gaining notoriety for their policy positions. Facing other socially conservative candidates, Buchanan decided to withdraw from the Republican contest in 2000 and run for the Reform Party's nomination, and with it, $12.6 million in federal funds as well as ballot access in a majority of the states.

Others have also used the campaign to focus attention on themselves and their ideas. Ellen McCormick ran as an antiabortion candidate for the Democratic nomination in 1976. Lyndon LaRouche has used the Democratic primaries since 1980 as a pretext for expounding his philosophy and gaining additional publicity. George McGovern entered the 1984 nomination sweepstakes, Gary Hart reentered in 1988, and Dan Quayle in 2000 in large part to participate in the public forum generated by the campaign and to try to resuscitate their damaged political images and reputations.[75]

With television a primary vehicle for conducting a national nomination campaign, and with candidates having distinctive perspectives and appeals attracting public attention, it is likely that the preconvention process will continue to be used for podium purposes.

The Front-Runner Strategy: Amassing Delegates

For front-runners the task is different. They do not need to gain recognition or establish their credentials. They do need to maintain their credibility and electability and extend their constituencies. Their strategy is simple and straightforward—acquire as many delegates as quickly as possible, build an insurmountable lead, and do not allow an early loss to discourage supporters.

The principal advantages front-runners have occur at the beginning of the process. A key element of their strategy must be to maximize these advantages. They need to make use of the benefits of a superior organization, financial base, media coverage, political endorsements, and volunteer efforts to overwhelm their opposition. The front-loading of the primaries provides added impetus to strike a knockout blow in the early rounds, when the lesser-known opponents are least able to compete with them. Scott Reed, Robert Dole's 1996 campaign manager, describes how this scheduling advantages the front-runner:

> [I]f we were well funded and well organized, we'd be able to take advantage of the condensed period. We also recognized that even if we did stumble early in New Hampshire or Iowa—and we recognized in early January that we might—it would be very difficult for somebody else to capitalize with the next six, seven, or eight primaries happening so quickly. We were the only campaign that had gone out and registered actual delegates to run in all the other states; the other campaigns had missed a few states here and there.[76]

Walter Mondale pursued this front-runner strategy in 1984, George H. W. Bush did so in 1988 and again in 1992, and Robert Dole in 1996. Michael Dukakis and Bill Clinton used variations of this approach in 1988 and 1992. They all spent heavily up front, had large paid staffs, and sought (and received) political endorsements. These resources produced early payoffs—delegate leads that encouraged most of their opponents to drop out and gave them as front-runners a hedge against any future losses against the candidates who remained.

Front-runners Al Gore and George W. Bush adopted similar strategies in their respective quests for their party's nomination in 2000. Both raised large sums of money, obtained political endorsements from most of their party's elected elite, ran as the presumptive nominee, and won. George W. Bush's image as the popular, unifying candidate was damaged more by John McCain's challenge than was Al Gore's by Bradley's.

For candidates who are unchallenged, the nomination strategy is obviously different. They can use their resources to launch their presidential campaign as Reagan did in 1984, Clinton in 1996, and Bush in 2004. The key here is to have the resources at the beginning of the nomination cycle to discourage challengers and have the flexibility to reply to critics. (See Box 4–4, "Front-Runner Strategies in 2000.")

George W. Bush's political advisers began planning his reelection campaign in the spring of 2003. The stated goal was to raise $200 million even though they did not anticipate a serious challenge to the president for the Republican nomination. The money was to be used to create an organization, establish an ongoing research agenda, conduct surveys and focus groups, and develop and air campaign advertisements prior to the Republican national nominating convention, scheduled for the last week in August 2004. Bush's advisers wanted funds on hand to respond to Democratic criticism of the president during that party's nominating contests as well as to lay the thematic foundation upon which the president's reelection campaign would rest. Such a strategy would reserve all of Bush's federal funds, about $73 million, for the short, ten-week campaign that would follow a triumphant send-off by the Republican convention and be launched close to the third anniversary of 9/11 so that the president's national security successes and his administration's ongoing antiterrorism activities could be stressed. A key element in the buildup to the reelection campaign was presenting Bush as president, not presidential candidate, using the perquisites of the office to highlight his domestic agenda and policy successes, and showcasing him as world leader. Presidential events were planned for all states deemed crucial for the 2004 election.[77]

BOX 4–4 🌿

FRONT-RUNNER STRATEGIES IN 2000

GEORGE W. BUSH: THE CONSENSUS CANDIDATE

Bush's large war chest and extensive endorsements from elected Republican leaders allowed him to pursue a typical front-runner strategy. The campaign was to be run everywhere in order to demonstrate the candidate's broad popular appeal to a diverse set of constituents from the traditional social and economic conservatives to more moderate Republicans and independent voters. Running as a compassionate conservative, Bush tried to project the image of a consensus builder, a popular governor, an outsider and reformer capable of broadening the Republican's electoral coalition and softening the party's hard-nosed conservatism. In fostering such an image, Bush took pains to distinguish himself from official Washington, his policy orientation from that of the congressional Republicans, and his moral principles, character, and personal behavior from the scandal-plagued Clinton–Gore administration.

His was a highly scripted, play-it-safe, avoid-mistakes-at-all-costs, campaign run by a close-knit group of political strategists who had helped him in his gubernatorial elections and policy advisers who had served his father during the elder Bush's years in office.[78] Bush avoided divisive issues, refused to take a position on flying the Confederate flag over the statehouse in South Carolina, equivocated when asked whether he would appoint openly gay people to his administration, and would neither embrace nor repudiate the social policy positions of the Christian right.[79]

The candidate's speeches were carefully crafted with themes and language that resonated with his audiences. In his standard stump speech, he talked about "responsibility, compassion, and love." Words such as *dreams, heart, love,* and especially *children* were sprinkled liberally throughout his prepared remarks.[80] Bush contrasted his personal ethics with Clinton's in a line that brought roars of approval from his Republican audiences: "Should I be fortunate enough to become your president, when I put my hand on the Bible, I will swear to not only uphold the laws of the land, I will swear to uphold the honor and the dignity of the office to which I have been elected, so help me God."[81] To his Christian fundamentalist supporters, he talked about his own sinful past, his day of reckoning when he stopped drinking and faced his marital responsibilities, the support he received from his renewed faith in the teachings and ministry of Jesus Christ whom Bush acknowledged to have had the greatest philosophical influence on his life.

Bush's speeches were reinforced by symbols. The candidate campaigned in Latino, African American, and Asian neighborhoods to illustrate his broad-based appeal; he appeared with Catholic clergy and at church events to counter an undercurrent that he was anti-Catholic;[82] he wore a pink ribbon in his lapel to express his concern about breast cancer at the same time his political advertising was accusing his principal opponent, John McCain, of voting against funds for cancer research.[83]

Little was left to chance. The Bush campaign even went so far as to design mock ads attacking his positions, show them to focus groups to discern their candidate's perceived vulnerabilities, and then present response ads to gauge people's overall reaction to them.[84] The Clinton campaign had used the same technique in 1992 and 1996 with great success.

Throughout the competitive phase of the nomination process, the press were kept at a distance. Spokesperson Karen Hughes protected Bush and staunchly defended him. Initially, all the sessions that he held with reporters were "off the record," so that he could not be quoted directly. Misstatements could be corrected.[85] Once the nomination had been effectively secured, the Bush campaign relaxed the off-the-record rule and made the candidate more accessible to the press.

Avoiding mistakes meant sticking to the script, repeating lines that had proven emotional impact. The contrast between the well-prepared and pretested remarks and his off-the-cuff comments were sometimes startling in their syntax and content.[86] But Bush's tendency to stay by his script also presented a problem: It reinforced the point political pundits, late-night comics, and his opponents in the Republican contest were suggesting—that he was not well informed, did not have many original ideas, was a programmed candidate, a product of his handlers, and lacked the gravitas to be president. Published reports of his mediocre school record and his failed business ventures buttressed this view.

Although Bush did loosen up as his campaign progressed, it was events, not accusations, that forced changes in the strategic plan. John McCain's rise in the public opinion polls and his impressive victory in New Hampshire, combined with the threat he posed to Bush in the next contest in South Carolina, a conservative state that had seemed safe for Bush, drove the Bush campaign to emphasize its core constituency of religious conservatives.

Bush accepted an invitation to address students and faculty at Bob Jones University, a fundamentalist Christian school which at the time did not permit interracial dating and, in fact, had accepted only Caucasians until the federal government mandated integration of its student body. The visit to Bob Jones, the backing from evangelical ministers Pat Robertson and Jerry Falwell, and the mobilization of Christian Coalition voters helped firm up Bush's support in South Carolina as did the extensive advertising campaign that was launched against Senator John McCain. Bush won the hotly contested primary election, but in the process tarnished his image as a centrist and a reformer.

The tarnish, in turn, was reinforced by Bush's conservative message in the Michigan and Virginia primaries and the support he received from antiabortion and antitax groups. Although he won most of the primaries held on the first Tuesday in March, thereby ensuring himself the Republican nomination, Bush's lead in the polls over Democratic rival Al Gore had all but dissipated, his policy priorities and positions had become associated with those of the conservative wing of his party, and his positive, people-oriented image had been marred by the negativism of his campaign. The good news for Bush was that he had won the nomination; the bad news was that his candidacy had been weakened in the process. His appeal, narrowed to core Republicans, the religious right, had to be broadened to win the general election.

AL GORE: RUNNING FROM THE VICE PRESIDENCY

Contemporary vice presidents have an advantage when seeking their party's nomination. Not only are they well known, well connected, and usually well versed on policy matters, but they have also been cast in a political role that has them doing favors for their party's candidates and its elected officials. Their quest for the presidential nomination amounts to payback time.

Vice President Al Gore had the additional advantage of serving during a period of economic prosperity and social tranquility at home and U.S. dominance abroad. Heir apparent to the Clinton presidency, he had the president's enthusiastic endorsement as well as the support of Democratic leaders and rank-and-file partisans. The only negatives were his stereotype as stiff, dull, and uninspiring; his position as number two, a follower not a leader; his penchant for verbal bloopers; and his involvement in a scandal-plagued administration.

Most of the other leading Democratic contenders had opted not to challenge Gore. Only Bill Bradley, who had been out of office and the public eye for three years, did so. Gore thought so little of Bradley's challenge initially that he chose to ignore him and campaign as if he were already running against George W. Bush. Gore did not want to make Bradley's candidacy credible by taking it seriously. Besides he was trailing Bush by double digits in the polls throughout most of 1999.

But Gore's strategy backfired. Bradley succeeded in raising money, increasing his name recognition, and building public support. He gained media coverage, was perceived as an increasingly viable candidate, and moved up in the polls at the same time that Gore and his campaign were getting a bad rap from the press for running an inept campaign. Even Bill Clinton had publicly criticized Gore's efforts.[87]

With his bloated campaign organization in disarray, his initial strategy unsuccessful, his image as a politician mired in the politics of Washington and the scandals of the Clinton administration, Gore shook up his campaign's personnel, structure, strategy, and tactics. In May 1999, he announced that a former, high-ranking Democratic congressman, Tony Coehlo, would oversee his presidential effort.[88] Known as a tough, inside-the-beltway politician, Coehlo proceeded to reinvent the campaign, the candidate, and the message. Gore also made a more concerted effort to obtain the endorsements of Democratic Party leaders and elected officials most of whom would be attending the Democratic convention as superdelegates. Additionally, the campaign directed its sights on securing support from the four pillars of the Democratic Party's electoral coalition: organized labor, African Americans, Latinos, and women.

The third change was both symbolic and real. Gore moved the campaign headquarters from K Street in Washington, D.C., where many of the most powerful special interest groups had their offices, to a home base in Nashville, Tennessee. The move was intended to diminish the perceived influence of Washington insiders as well as cut the size and expenses of the staff and eliminate its top-heavy collection of pollsters, image makers, and Democratic campaign consultants who had flocked to Gore as his campaign got under way.[89]

Finally, strategic and tactical adjustments were put into place. The vice president displayed a more human side. Formal speeches were replaced by town meetings in which the candidate would interact with the audience, answering their questions and lingering to chat with them. The candidate shed his coat and tie and rolled up his sleeves to appear more down-to-earth and more approachable. His message became more personal as well.

The focus of the vice president's campaign shifted as well. Bradley not Bush became the object of criticism. The senator's voting record and positions on the key issues of health care, gun control, and race relations became Gore's targets of opportunity. Drawing distinctions between himself and his opponent, Gore contrasted Bradley's comprehensive, big-government orientation with his own more tempered, incremental approach. This comparison reinforced, Gore's image as a moderate.

Once his campaign was reorganized, Gore ran impressively. He lashed out at Bradley's failure to seek reelection, his support of Reagan's initial budget, and his costly social policy proposals. By doing so, Gore achieved two objectives: to create doubts in the minds of Democrats about Bradley's partisan loyalties and his command of the issues; and to revitalize his own image as a fighter, an active leader not a passive follower as his vice presidential stereotype suggested.

Gore's strategy was to contest Bradley everywhere. Tapping the financial and personnel resources at his disposal, he was able to stage a multistate campaign. The concentration of Democratic primaries in early March worked to his advantage as did the absence of other contests between New Hampshire and Super Tuesday, the day on which nearly half of the Democratic delegates were to be selected. Focusing on traditional Democratic themes and issues, Gore maintained a heavy speaking schedule. As his campaign moved onto solid ground with the Democratic electorate, he too began to play it safe. He distanced himself from the news media, holding fewer news conferences and avoiding the off-the-cuff remarks that had gotten him into trouble in the past.

The strategy of campaigning widely, matching Bradley's spending in the big states, and appealing to core Democratic voters on the basis of traditional party issues, combined with the tactics of being less formal and seeming more comfortable with average Democratic voters proved successful. Gore whipped Bradley in every state, largely on the basis of a strong vote from self-declared Democrats, especially from organized labor. By the evening of March 7, the vice president was in a position to claim victory. He emerged from the primaries stronger than when he entered them. The party had coalesced around him. He had even rivaled Bill Clinton for the news media's attention in early March. But the glow from his victory was to be short-lived.

SUMMARY

The delegate selection process has changed dramatically since 1968. Originally dominated by state party leaders, it has become more open to the party's rank and file as a consequence of the reforms initiated by the Democratic Party. These reforms, designed to broaden the base of public participation and increase the representation of the party's electorate at its nominating convention, have affected the Republicans as well, even though the GOP has not chosen to mandate national guidelines for its state parties, as the Democrats have. Supreme Court decisions that give the national parties the authority to dictate rules, new state laws that conform to these rules, and public pressure to reflect popular sentiment and improve representation have led to a greater number of primaries and more delegates selected in them for both parties.

Public participation has increased somewhat although turnout levels have varied with the date of the contest, the level of intraparty competition, the amount of money spent, and other candidate-related factors, but is less than one-half of that in the general election. The delegates have been demographically more representative than those of the prereform era. Larger percentages of women and minorities have been chosen. The delegates seem to be more ideologically conscious and consistent in their views, however, than do rank-and-file partisans.

There have been other effects, some of them not beneficial to the parties. Candidacies have proliferated. Factions within the parties are more in evidence. These unintended consequences have generated still other reforms, such as the imposition of a window period and the creation of superdelegates, designed to produce more cohesiveness within the party without at the same time abolishing the original goals of reform. They have also been designed to strengthen the influence of party leaders and elected officials.

The strategy for seeking delegates has also been affected by the rules changes. The basic tenets of this strategy include:

1. Plan far ahead.
2. Concentrate efforts in the early contests.
3. Raise and spend big bucks early.
4. Gain media attention.
5. Develop a deep and wide organization.
6. Monitor public opinion.
7. Design and target a distinctive appeal.

Although tactical decisions on how to mobilize and allocate sufficient resources to build and maintain delegate support depend on the particular circumstances of individual candidates, the use of new technology, particularly in the arena of communications, has revolutionized presidential campaigning and shortened the time frame in which incidents, remarks, and events can make a difference. Computers are now used to map and track political advertising; targeted appeals are calibrated to arouse particular emotions in selective political communities; interactive campaigning on the Net and in town meetings is also standard fare. Even voting by mail and online is beginning to take hold. All of these technologies are expensive, another reason why having a large war chest has become increasingly important.

In general, there have been two successful prototypes for winning the nomination: the come-from-the-pack approach of the non-front-runners, and the out-front, big bucks, challenge-me-if-you-dare approach of the leading candidates.

Non-front-runners need stepping-stones to the nomination. Their initial goal must be to establish themselves as viable candidates. At the outset, the key is recognition. Over the long haul, it is momentum. Recognition is bestowed by the news media on those who do well in the early caucuses and primaries; momentum is achieved through a series of prenomination victories that demonstrate electability. Together, recognition and momentum compensate for what the non-front-runners lack in reputation and popular appeal. That is why non-front-runners must concentrate their time, efforts, and resources in the first few contests. They have no choice. Winning will provide them with opportunities; losing will confirm their secondary status.

For the front-runners, the task is different and easier. They have to maintain their position as likely nominees, not establish it. This purpose provides them with a little more flexibility at the outset, but it also requires a broad-based campaign with major resources raised and spent early. Front-runners must take advantage of their organizational and financial base to build a quick and insurmountable lead.

In the end, it is the ability to generate a popular appeal among the party's electorate that is likely to be decisive. Only one person in each party can amass a majority of the delegates, and that is the individual who can build a broad-based coalition. Although specific groups may be targeted, if the overall constituency is too narrow, the nomination cannot be won. That is why most candidates tend to broaden and moderate their appeal over the course of the prenomination process and continue to do so in the general election campaign.

 ## WHERE ON THE WEB?

The Nomination Campaign

- **Democracy in Action**
  http://www.gwu.edu/~action/P2004
  A Web site maintained by the Graduate School in Campaign Management of the George Washington University. Contains pertinent information and links to other sources.
- **Gallup Poll**
  http://www.gallup.org
  Check this site for up-to-date polling data.
- **National Journal**
  http://www.nationaljournal.com
  There are many news sources for following the presidential primaries and caucuses; the *National Journal's* site is one of the best.
- **New York Times**
  http://www.nytimes.com

The *New York Times* prides itself on being a paper of record. You will find much information on the policy positions and speeches of the candidates in this newspaper as well as the latest delegate count and prenomination polls.

- **Politics1**
  http://www.politics1.com
  An online guide to current politics with links to other relevant sites for the 2004 election.
- **Polling Report**
  http://www.pollingreport.com
  Summarizes public polls on the 2004 election.
- **Yahoo**
  http://www.yahoo.com
  A comprehensive listing of articles on the nomination and election.
- **WhiteHouse04**
  http://www.niu.edu/newsplace/whitehouse
  This site is maintained by Professor Ari Bass at the University of Northern Illinois. It lists articles, comedy, editorials, and links to other sites.

The Candidates

Listed below are the Web sites the candidates are using during their campaigns.

Republicans
- **George W. Bush**
  http://www.georgebush.com

Democrats
- **Carol Mosely Braun**
  http://www.carolforpresident.com
- **Howard Dean**
  http://www.deanforamerica.com
- **John Edwards**
  http://www.johnedwards2004.com
- **Richard Gephardt**
  http://www.dickgephardt2004.com
- **Bob Graham**
  http://www.grahamforpresident.com
- **John Kerry**
  http://www.johnkerry.com
- **Dennis Kucinich**
  http://www.kucinich.us
- **Joe Lieberman**
  http://www.joe2004.com
- **Lyndon LaRouche**
  http://www.larouchein2004.net
- **Al Sharpton**
  http://www.sharptonexplore2004.com

EXERCISES

1. Check the home pages of the candidates. Use the information from their Web sites to compare and contrast their positions on the most controversial issues in the campaign. Then compare the personal images that they have presented. On the basis of these comparisons, whom would you support and why?

2. Follow the news of the nomination campaign from the perspective of a major newspaper, television network, and news magazine (see Where on the Web? in Chapter 7, page 259). Is the coverage essentially the same? From which source did you learn the most about strategy and tactics? From which did you learn the most about the candidates themselves?

3. Analyze the nomination campaign on the basis of the candidates' basic appeals, and their strategies and tactics. Use Internet sources from the candidates, the news media, and public interest Web sites to obtain the information you need for your analysis.

SELECTED READING

Bartels, Larry M. *Presidential Primaries and the Dynamics of Public Choice.* Princeton, N.J.: Princeton University Press, 1988.

Greer, John G. *Nominating Presidents: An Evaluation of Voters and Primaries.* New York: Greenwood, 1989.

Gurian, Paul-Henri, and Audrey A. Haynes. "Campaign Strategy in Presidential Primaries, 1976–1988." *American Journal of Political Science* 37 (February 1993): 335–341.

Jamieson, Kathleen Hall, and Paul Waldman, eds. *Electing the President 2000: The Insider's View.* Philadelphia: University of Pennsylvania Press, 2001.

Magleby, David B. *Getting Inside the Outside Campaign.* Provo, Utah: Brigham Young University, 2000.

Mayer, William G., ed. *In Pursuit of the White House.* Chatham, N.J.: Chatham House, 2000.

———. "The Long Complicated Road to the White House." *PS: Political Science and Politics* 36 (April 2003): 151–202.

Norrander, Barbara. "Ideological Representativeness of Presidential Primary Voters." *American Journal of Political Science* 33 (August 1989): 570–587.

———. "The End Game in Post-Reform Presidential Nominations." *Journal of Politics* 62 (November 2000): 999–1013.

Polsby, Nelson W. *The Consequences of Party Reform.* New York: Oxford University Press, 1983.

Shafer, Byron E. *Quiet Revolution: The Struggle for the Democratic Party and the Shaping of Post-Reform Politics.* New York: Russell Sage Foundation, 1983.

Stanley, Harold W. "The Nominations: The Return of the Party Leaders," in *The Elections of 2000,* edited by Michael Nelson, 27–53. Washington, D.C.: Congressional Quarterly, 2001.

Woodward, Bob. *The Choice.* New York: Simon & Schuster, 1996.

NOTES

1. McCarthy's name was on the ballot, but the president's was not. The regular Democratic organization in New Hampshire had to conduct a campaign to have Democrats write in Johnson's name.

2. The groups that were initially singled out were Native Americans, African Americans, and youth. Subsequently, the list of affected groups has been altered by the addition of Hispanics, Asian/Pacific Americans, and women, and by the deletion of youth. In 1992, the party also added those with physical disabilities to the groups protected against discrimination.

3. Some states still hold a presidential preference vote with a separate election of delegates by a convention. Others connect the presidential vote and delegate selection on an at-large or district basis. By voting for a particular candidate or delegates pledged to that candidate (or both), voters may register their presidential choice and delegate selection at the same time and by the same vote. The number of these primaries has increased as a consequence of the rules changes.

4. Iowa and New Hampshire both have state laws that require their contests to be the first caucus and primary, respectively. They obviously gain advantages by doing so. The candidates come and visit with voters often. The news media also arrive in force to cover the beginnings of the next campaign. There is an economic gain as well. New Hampshire estimates that it took in $264 million from its 2000 primaries. "First in the Nation: The New Hampshire Primary; What It Means to the State and the Nation," published by the State of New Hampshire, 2000, 4.

   Democratic Party rules take these state laws into consideration by the exceptions granted to these two states. The perennial problem for the Democrats, however, has been that other states have also enacted legislation that schedules their nomination contests before the official period begins, thereby forcing Iowa and New Hampshire to move their selection date even further ahead—all in violation of party rules. After Democratic leaders in Michigan threatened to move their primary first in 2004, the chair of the Democratic National Committee agreed to appoint a party committee to revisit the Iowa and New Hampshire exemptions.

5. In 1984, the Democrats had raised the minimum vote needed to obtain delegates to 20 percent in caucuses and up to 25 percent in primaries. This change was designed to help nationally known candidates, such as Walter Mondale who was running that year for the Democratic nomination, and reduce the factionalizing effect that a large number of candidates could have on the party. After losing in 1980, the Democrats hoped the change would enable the eventual winner to emerge earlier, be a candidate of national prominence, and be better positioned to challenge the Republicans in the general election.

   Naturally, these changes hurt minority candidates such as Jesse Jackson, whose supporters were concentrated in districts with large minority populations. Although Jackson received votes in majority districts, he was unable to achieve the minimum required percentage in many of them. Thus, his 19 percent of the popular vote in 1984 translated into only 10 percent of the delegates. Owing to pressure from Jackson and others, the Democrats lowered the minimum threshold in 1988 to 15 percent and have kept it there since then.

6. A proposal by Jesse Jackson to decrease the number of PLEOs by eliminating the automatic inclusion of members of the party's national committee, however, was rejected by the very people who were to be excluded, the Democratic National Committee in 1990.

7. The incentive plan awarded 5 percent additional delegates to states that held their primaries or caucuses between March 15 and April 14, 7.5 percent more for holding their

election between April 15 and May 14, and 10 percent for holding it May 15 or later. The plan had few takers, however.

8. Advisory Commission on the Presidential Nomination Process, "A Review of the Republican Process: Nominating Future Presidents," Republican National Committee, May 2000.

9. Will Lester, "GOP Scuttles Primary Plan," Associated Press, July 29, 2000; <http://www.ap.com>.

10. In another decision by the Supreme Court, also involving open primaries, the power of parties (in this case, state parties) to establish rules for nominating candidates was affirmed. In December 1986 the Supreme Court, in the case of *Tashjian v. Republican Party of Connecticut* (107 S. Ct. 544, 1986), voided a Connecticut law that prohibited open primaries. Republicans, in the minority party at the time in Connecticut, had favored such a primary as a means of attracting independent voters. Unable to get the Democratic-controlled legislature to change the law, the state Republican Party went to court, arguing that the statute violated First Amendment rights of freedom of association. In a 5 to 4 ruling, the Supreme Court agreed, and struck down the legislation.

11. The formula Republicans use to determine the size of each state delegation is complex. It consists of three criteria: statehood (six delegates), House districts (three per district), and support for Republican candidates elected within the previous four years (one for a Republican governor, one for each Republican senator, one if the Republicans won at least half of the congressional districts in one of the last two congressional elections, and a bonus of four and one-half delegates plus 60 percent of the electoral vote if the state voted for the Republican presidential candidate in the last election).

12. Under the plan used since 1968 and modified in 1976, the Democrats have allotted 50 percent of each state delegation on the basis of the state's electoral vote and 50 percent on the basis of its average Democratic vote in the last three presidential elections. The rule for apportionment was challenged in 1971 on the grounds that it did not conform to the "one person, one vote" principle, but a court of appeals asserted that it did not violate the equal protection clause of the Fourteenth Amendment.

13. In states in which there were both Republican and Democratic primaries, turnout averaged almost 18 percent according to an analysis by the Committee for the Study of the American Electorate. Steven A. Holmes, "Many Stayed at Home," *New York Times,* September 1, 2000, A18.

14. Federal Election Commission, "2000 Presidential Primary Election Results," <http://www.fec.gov/pubrec/fe2000/2000presprim.htm>.

15. Linda L. Fowler, Constantine J. Spiliotes, and Lynn VaVreck, "The Role of Issue Advocacy Groups in the New Hampshire Primary," in *Getting Inside the Outside Campaign,* ed. David B. Magleby (Provo, Utah: Brigham Young University, 2000), 31.

16. Earl Black and Merle Black, *The Vital South: How Presidents Are Elected* (Cambridge, Mass.: Harvard University Press, 1992), 268.

17. Barbara Norrander, "Ideological Representativeness of Presidential Primary Voters," *American Journal of Political Science* 33 (August 1989): 570–587.

18. Walter Stone Jr., Lonna Rae Atkeson, and Ronald B. Rapoport, "Turning On or Turning Off? Mobilization Efforts of Participating in Presidential Nominations," *American Journal of Political Science* 36 (August 1992): 688.

19. James I. Lengle, "Divisive Presidential Primaries and the Party Electoral Prospects, 1932–1976," *American Politics Quarterly* 8 (1980): 261–277; James I. Lengle, Diana Owen, and Molly Sonner, "Divisive Nomination Campaigns and Democratic Party Electoral Prospects," *Journal of Politics* 57 (1995): 370–383.

20. Lonna Rae Atkeson, "Divisive Primaries and General Election Outcomes: Another Look at Presidential Campaigns," *American Journal of Political Science* 42 (January 1998): 256–271.

21. Thomas B. Edsall, "First Democratic Race Is for Cash," *Washington Post,* January 1, 2003, A1, A6.

22. S. Robert Lichter, Daniel Amundson, and Richard E. Noyes, *The Video Campaign: Network Coverage of the 1988 Primaries* (Washington, D.C.: American Enterprise Institute, 1988), 95–96.

23. See Peverill Squire, *The Iowa Caucus and the Presidential Nominating Process* (Boulder, Colo.: Westview Press, 1989).

24. Craig Allen Smith, "The Iowa Caucuses and Super Tuesday Primaries Reconsidered: How Untenable Hypotheses Enhance the Campaign Melodrama," *Presidential Studies Quarterly* 22 (Summer 1992): 524.

25. New Hampshire brags that its primary has been the first in the nation since 1920. "First in the Nation."

26. However, Professor Barbara Norrander also notes that in nomination contests between 1976 and 1988 some of the biggest spenders on the Republican side have also been the biggest losers. Pat Robertson and Robert Dole in 1988 are two examples. Norrander found that the Republicans who did win within this period did so regardless of how much money they spent. In short, it appears that the prospective losers tried to compensate for their secondary status by spending more, and it did not work. Barbara Norrander, "Nomination Choices: Caucus and Primary Outcomes, 1976–1988," *American Journal of Political Science* 37 (May 1993): 361.

27. Thomas B. Edsall and Dan Balz, "Edwards Returns Law Firm's Donations," *Washington Post,* April 18, 2003, A4.

28. "Campaign 2000—The Primaries," *Media Monitor* XIV (March/April 2000): 1–2.

29. Ibid., 2.

30. Terence Jeffrey, quoted in *Campaign for President: The Managers Look at '96,* Institute of Politics, Harvard University (Hollis, N.H.: Hollis Publishing, 1997), 7–8.

31. Annenberg Public Policy Center, "The Primary Campaign: What Did the Candidates Say, What Did the Public Learn, and Did It Matter?" University of Pennsylvania (March 27, 2000): 2–3.

32. Pew Research Center for the People & the Press, "Fewer See Choice of President as Important: Voter Turnout May Slip Again," part 2, (July 13, 2000).

33. Joan Shorenstein Center on the Press, Politics, and Public Policy, "Voter Involvement Index: State Rankings," Harvard University, <http://www.vanishingvoter.org>.

34. "Campaign 2000—The Primaries," 4.

35. Thomas E. Patterson and Robert D. McClure, *The Unseeing Eye* (New York: Putnam, 1976), 58.

36. Craig B. Holman and Luke P. McLoughlin, *Buying Time 2000* (New York: Brennan Center for Social Justice, NYU School of Law, 2001), 29.

37. Frank Bruni, "The Ad Campaign: Bush Discusses His Candidacy," *New York Times,* September 26, 1999.

38. Howard Kurtz, "Ad Watch," *Washington Post,* October 28, 1999, A11.

39. John Broder, "The Ad Campaign: Donning the Reagan Mantle," *New York Times,* February 26, 2000, A10.

40. Peter Marks, "Negative Campaigning 2000: The Other Guy Did It First," *New York Times,* January 29, 2000, A1, A9.

41. Adam Nagourney and Richard Pérez-Peña, "Bush and McCain Trade Bitter Criticism as Campaigns in New York Gather Steam," *New York Times,* March 3, 2000, A15.

42. Peter Marks, "The Ad Campaign: McCain Launches a New Salvo," *New York Times,* February 9, 2000, A14; Howard Kurtz, "Bush Hits Back on Campaign Reform," *Washington Post,* February 17, 2000, A9.

43. Richard A. Oppel Jr., with Richard Pérez-Peña, "The Power Broker: Role in Ads Puts Focus on Bush Friend," *New York Times,* March 6, 2000, A14.

44. Howard Kurtz, "Democratic Themes Dominate Airwaves," *Washington Post,* January 9, 2000, A8; Peter Marks, "In New Hampshire Ads, an Audible Warmth," *New York Times,* December 6, 1999, A1, A22.

45. Dante J. Scala notes that the Democratic candidates who have been most successful in New Hampshire are those whose campaigns built such partisan coalitions. Dante J. Scala, "Rereading the Tea Leaves: New Hampshire as a Barometer of Presidential Primary Success," *PS: Political Science and Politics* 36 (April 2003): 187–192.

46. Dick Morris, *Behind the Oval Office* (New York: Random House, 1997), 146–147.

47. Alison Mitchell, "More Complaints About Negative Phone Calls," *New York Times* February 13, 2000, A27.

48. Pew Research Center for the People & the Press, "The Tough Job of Communicating with Voters," February 5, 2000.

49. In a television interview, Gore took credit for "inventing the Internet" when he meant to say that he had been a principal advocate for extending its utility for the government and to the public. He had also claimed that he and his wife were the role models for Erich Segal's book, *Love Story,* a claim that Segal denied. Gore exaggerated his physical danger as a military reporter in Vietnam and his own accomplishments as a Tennessee journalist. He was also plagued by his representation that there was "no legal authority" which prevented him from making fund-raising calls from his White House office. "Transcript: Vice President Gore on CNN's *Late Edition,*" March 9, 1999, <http://cnn.com>; Katherine Q. Seelye, with John M. Broder, "Questions over Veracity Have Long Dogged Gore," *New York Times,* February 17, 2000, A22.

50. Adam Nagourney, "Tension Between Dean and Kerry Helps Recast Race for Democrats," *New York Times,* May 12, 2003, A1, 21; Adam Nagourney, "Edwards Makes Rural Voters a Focus of His '04 Campaign," *New York Times,* May 22, 2003, A23.

51. Annenberg Center, "The Primary Campaign," 1, 4–10.

52. "The 2000 Nominating Campaign," 6–11.

53. David Wilhelm as quoted in Royer, *Campaign for President: The Managers Look at '92* (Hollis, N.H.: Hollis Publishing, 1994), 77.

54. John Pavlik and Mark Thalhimer, "From Wausau to Wichita: Covering the Campaign via Satellite," in *Covering the Presidential Primaries,* ed. Martha FitzSimon (New York: Freedom Forum Media Studies Center, 1992), 41.

55. Ibid., 36–37.

56. Neil Munro, "The New Wired Politics," *National Journal* (April 22, 2000): 1260.

57. Hamilton Jordan, "Memorandum to Jimmy Carter, August 4, 1974," in Martin Schram, *Running for President 1976* (New York: Stein & Day, 1977), 379–380.

58. According to Larry M. Bartels, momentum is a product of personal preferences that are projected onto expectations. Bartels argues that momentum can best be achieved by a little-known candidate who scores unexpected successes in situations where there is no clear front-runner. What happens is that people who have little substantive information about this candidate project their own desires for an ideal candidate onto this new winner. This result increases expectations and contributes to momentum. Larry M. Bartels, "Expectations and Preferences in Presidential Nominating Campaigns," *American Political Science Review* 79 (1985): 804–815.

59. The McCain team included campaign director, Rich Davis, who had served as deputy director of the 1996 Dole campaign, political director John Weaver, a veteran of the 1988 Republican campaign, and Mike Murphy, a political strategist who also worked on Dole's presidential bid. Supplementing the campaign were an array of current and former members of Congress, experienced Washington hands, and policy advisers.

60. Alison Mitchell, "Birth and Death of the 'Straight Talk Express,' From Gamble to Gamble," *New York Times,* March 11, 2000, A8.

61. "Campaign 2000," 4.

62. Ruth Marcus and John Mintz, "Bush Spending Spree Shrinks GOP Cash Gap," *Washington Post,* February 21, 2000, A1, A6.

63. Schuyler Kropf, "Decisive Win Boosts Momentum," *Charleston Post & Courier,* February 20, 2000, A14, as referenced in Bill Moore and Danielle Vinson, "The South Carolina Republican Primary" in Magleby *Getting Inside,* 42.

64. Pat Robertson recorded a telephone message urging Michigan voters to select Bush and the Christian Coalition made 45,000–50,000 calls with Robertson's voice. David Magleby, "Issue Advocacy in the 2000 Presidential Primaries," in Magleby, *Getting Inside,* 14. In addition, Right to Life groups mailed letters to over 400,000 household in Michigan and operated phone banks, which played taped messages criticizing McCain's position on social issues important to the Christian right.

65. Mitchell, "Birth and Death," A8.

66. McCain later claimed that he had been using the words of Luke Skywalker at the end of *Star Wars.* David Von Drehle, "McCain Tries to Erase His 'Evil' Accusation," *Washington Post,* March 2, 2000, A7.

67. Arthur Sanders and David Redlawsk, "Money and the Iowa Caucus," in Magleby, *Getting Inside,* 27.

68. Fowler, et al., "Issue Advocacy in New Hampshire," in Magleby, *Getting Inside,* 30.

69. Richard L. Burke with James Dao, "Aides Fear That Bradley Let Iowa Momentum Slip Away," *New York Times,* January 21, 2000, A22.

70. Despite his emphasis on racial justice, he did not gain much African American support. He had no labor endorsements. The campaign made little attempt to appeal to Latino voters; no Spanish language messages appeared on his Web site.

71. Mike Allen, "Bradley Campaign's Lost Opportunities Mount," *Washington Post,* February 13, 2000, A12.

72. The *Washington Post* reported that a *Wall Street Journal* reporter covering Bradley found himself seated in front of the candidate on a commercial flight. The reporter introduced himself and asked for a chance to talk with the candidate. Bradley declined and moved his seat. Barton Gellman, Dale Russakoff, and Mike Allen, "Where Did Bradley Go Wrong?" *Washington Post,* March 4, 2000, A7.

73. In 2000, Senator Orrin Hatch dropped out after the Iowa caucus in which he received only 1 percent of the vote. Gary Bauer exited after New Hampshire performances generated little possibility that he could rival the principal Republican challengers. Forbes left after a disappointing performance in the third contest in Delaware, a state in which he had won four years earlier.

74. Bay Buchanan, quoted in Royer, *Campaign for President '92,* 24.

75. Republicans Robert Dornan and Allen Keyes fell into the pulpit candidacy category in 1996 as did Keyes and Bauer in 2000. Each wished to use the nomination campaign as a platform for his issue agenda and ideological perspective as well as a vehicle for extending his own name recognition and political influence.

76. Scott Reed, quoted in *Campaign for President: The Managers Look at '96,* 182.

77. Mike Allen and Dan Balz, "Bush's '04 Campaign Quietly Being Planned," *Washington Post*, March 3, 2003, A1.

78. The principal operatives included chief strategist Karl Rove, campaign manager Joe Allbaugh, and communications director Karen Hughes. Bush's policy advisory groups were led by Condeleezza Rice, a foreign policy expert who served on President Bush's National Security Council, Stephen Goldsmith, domestic adviser and former mayor of Indianapolis, and economist Lawrence Lindsay, who had worked in the Reagan and Bush administrations.

79. The following exchange between Karen Hughes, the campaign's director of communications, and Jay Carney, a reporter for *Time* magazine, illustrates the care with which the campaign treated the issue of "gay appointments."

> Hughes: He said, first of all, how would I know? That's not a question he asks.
> Carney: But someone who is openly gay.
> Hughes: It would depend on their agenda. He would expect them to share his philosophy . . . he views that as someone's private business.
> Carney: So the issue would not be his sexuality or her sexuality but whether or not they were promoting . . .
> Hughes: Again, that's not a question he asks. He's never asked that of prospective employees.
> Carney: But if they're out of the closet, if they're open. If he knew.
> Hughes: How would he know that? Based on rumor?
> Carney: If they have a boyfriend or girlfriend.
> Hughes: He would expect people who worked with him to agree with his philosophy and his approach.
> Carney: Right. But—you see what I'm saying?
> Hughes: You're trying to make me say it the way you want me to say it.
> Carney: So the question is, would he appoint somebody who is known to be gay?
> Hughes: It's not a question that he would ask.

Howard Kurtz, "Team Bush's Defensive Strategy," *Washington Post*, March 5, 2000, C1, 14.

80. Linguist Deborah Tannen noted the emotional lexicon that his language contained: "In a speech on tax cuts last month [December 1999], Mr. Bush managed to work in 'child' or 'children' 11 times. In a speech on faith-based initiatives last summer, it was a dozen times. In a talk in New Hampshire in November [1999], children recur like a mantra 35 times (not counting 'kids' and 'students') . . . It's not only the speeches on education that are studded with hearts. Speaking on farm policy in Iowa, Mr. Bush called agriculture 'the heart of our economy.' Regarding Veterans Day, he told a New Hampshire audience that we must impart veterans stories to the next generation to 'raise a monument in their hearts.' The speech on faith-based groups contained 7 'hearts' and 11 'loves.'" Deborah Tannen, "Bush's Sweet Talk," *New York Times*, January 20, 2000, A23.

81. "Excerpts from Bush's Campaign Speech," *New York Times*, November 1, 1999, A14.

82. Polls did reflect a drop in his support among Catholics after Bush was accused of not condemning the anti-Catholic rhetoric of the president of Bob Jones University. Lydia Saad, "Bush Support Down among Catholic Republicans," Gallup poll, March 3, 2000, <http://www.gallup.com/poll/release/pr000303.asp>.

83. Frank Bruni, "Using Signals and Cues to Project Bush's Image," *New York Times*, March 19, 2000, A24.

84. Terry M. Neal, "Bush Team Uses Mock Ads to Test Effect of Forbes Attack," *Washington Post,* October 12, 1999, A5.

85. Kurtz, "Team Bush's Defensive Strategy," C1.

86. Frank Bruni reported a part of a Bush speech on foreign policy, delivered in January in Sioux City, Iowa, as follows: "When I was coming up, it was a dangerous world and we knew exactly who the they were. It was us versus them and it was clear who them was. Today, we're not so sure who the they are, but we know they're there." Frank Bruni, "The Syntax: Bush Follows in the Missteps of His Father," *New York Times,* January 23, 2000, A17.

87. Richard L. Berke, "Clinton Admits to Concerns as Gore Campaign Stumbles," *New York Times,* May 14, 1999, A1.

88. In addition to Coelho, the principal operatives of the Gore campaign were campaign manager Donna Brazile, a veteran organizer; media strategists Carter Eskew, Bob Shrum, and Tad Devine, all of whom had worked on other Democratic campaigns; policy advisers Elaine Kamarck (domestic) and Leon Furth (foreign), both of whom had served as advisers on his vice presidential White House staff; and his eldest daughter, Karenna Gore Schiff.

89. They succeeded in cutting the top-heavy layers of political consultants, pollsters, and media advisers, but were stuck with the $60,000 monthly lease that they had taken out on their K Street offices.

SPRING INTERREGNUM: CONSOLIDATING VICTORY AND POSTURING FOR THE ELECTION

5

Caucuses and primaries start earlier and conventions occur later, leaving an increasingly long period from the time the nomination is effectively determined to the time when the nominee is officially "crowned" as the party's standard-bearer. This interregnum is an important one for the prospective nominees and for their parties. The nominees need to repair any damage that the competition inflicted on their image, policy stands, and partisan electoral coalition. The parties need to reenergize, reunify, and refocus their efforts on the forthcoming campaign.

THE NONCOMPETITIVE PHASE OF THE NOMINATION CAMPAIGN

Image Repair

The more negative the nomination campaign, the more likely that the nominee's personal image has been tarnished, that some of the policies which the nominee has proposed have been criticized, perhaps to the point of ridicule, and that rifts have developed within the party. Each of these problems will require attention and a public campaign to overcome them.

Candidates often have to be reintroduced to voters, in part because attention has fallen off since the competitive phase of the primaries, and in part, because their personal negatives are too high. Biographical ads, reinforced by information given to the press, and convention speeches given by distinguished leaders can alter a less-than-desirable image that remains after a bitter nomination campaign.

Bill Clinton faced this problem after winning the Democratic nomination in 1992. Savaged first by press allegations of womanizing, draft dodging, and smoking marijuana, and later by criticism of his centrist policy positions by his opponent, Jerry Brown, Clinton needed to recast his presidential image. To do so, his campaign designed a series of commercials that detailed the hardships and struggles that this poor boy from Arkansas encountered growing up and ultimately surmounted in his rise to political prominence. The ads, combined with talk show appearances in which the candidate reminisced about his upbringing, gradually muted Clinton's negative image.

The Clinton campaign was helped in its reconstructive efforts by the news media's focus on Ross Perot's reemergence into the presidential race, his third-party challenge to President George H. W. Bush, and the subsequent Republican attacks against him. In the words of pollster Stan Greenberg:

> We came out of the primaries in very difficult shape . . . our negatives were very high. I think the principal advantage we gained from Perot was his being on the scene in June and our having the space to use that period to rebuild our candidacy. Without Perot, we assumed that, as you had with Dukakis, . . . [the Republicans] would have been on attack in June and it would have been hard for us to rebuild in that period.[1]

Al Gore faced a different type of image problem in the spring of 2000. He needed to establish his leadership credentials and move out of Clinton's shadow. The primaries had not enabled him to do so fully, in part because Bradley had proven to be a weak challenger, and in part, because Clinton remained a very active and visible president. To gain stature, Gore also needed some of the credit for the successes of the administration of which he was a part, and to cut Bush down in size, making him seem more like his father during the economic recession of 1991–1992 than the image of the popular, reformist governor he and his handlers tried to project.

Gore, who had successfully improved his standing with the Democratic electorate during the nomination process by attacking Bradley, tried the same tactic with Bush, painting his opponent as a stereotypical Republican, whose policies benefited the rich and powerful such as big tobacco, big oil, and the National Rifle Association. Not only did he wish to tie Bush to special interests, he also wanted to demonstrate his own aggressiveness and strength in taking on these moneyed interests and conservative issue groups.

Bush's father had pursued a similar campaign strategy in the summer of 1988 to get himself out of the shadows of Ronald Reagan and overcome the wimpy image with which he had been saddled.[2] The elder Bush was successful, but Gore was not. In fact, the aggressive strategy backfired by reinforcing the unattractive aspects of his image, that of a no-holds-barred, partisan, a typical Washington politician.

After two months of sagging ratings and a campaign that seemed adrift, Gore tried to change his "fighting" image to one of a more noble and high-minded candidate. He assumed the high road, talked of his vision for America, and let others attack his opponent.[3] But his campaign lacked the money to run ads to reinforce this image prior to the Democratic convention.

Repositioning and Reprioritizing the Issues

In addition to readjusting their presidential image, nominees often have to reposition themselves after moving toward their party's ideological core during a hard-fought primary campaign. They have to move back toward the center and reprioritize issues for the general election. Repositioning and reprioritizing can be tricky business, however, since the news media and opposition party are sure to point out policy inconsistencies, and in doing so, raise the integrity issue.

George W. Bush faced this problem after his defeat of John McCain. Forced to go right to appeal to the conservative Republican base, Bush had to moderate his stands and soften his conservative image. To broaden his appeal, Bush moved toward the policy center. He accentuated the positive, stressing issues of compassion such as education, housing, Medicare, and Social Security—issues that had special appeal to Democrats, and especially to women voters, and which would help mute the impression left by the competitive primaries that he was a hard-core conservative. By promoting Democratic issues, Bush was following the same strategy that Clinton used so successfully in 1995–1996 when he adopted Republican issues of stepped-up crime prevention, a balanced budget, and improved defense.[4]

But Bush also distinguished himself from his Democratic opponent by running ads that focused on the ethical and moral lapses of the Clinton–Gore administration, ads which served indirectly to reinforce his reformer image.[5] He also emphasized the one policy issue on which most Republicans agreed—the need for a strong military—and deemphasized the social issues that divided Republicans—abortion, school prayer, and gay rights.

Just as important was the Texas governor's urging of an end to Washington's strident ideological politics. Bush's theme of working together and talking quietly with one another was intended to heal divisions within his own party as well as provide a contrast to the partisan Washington environment with which his opponent was associated. Although he attacked his Democratic rival, particularly noting Gore's penchant for exaggeration, his flip-flops on the issues, and the contradiction between his promise to eliminate soft money and his active fund-raising for the Democrats, Bush's overall message was more positive than negative. And this message was heightened by Bush's rhetoric and personal style: his conciliatory language, moderate tone, commonsensical proposals, and a folksy manner.

To support this friendly, down-to-earth image, the Bush campaign placed the governor in small-group settings, such as experimental schools for underperforming, underprivileged, or learning-disabled children, neighborhood programs or community centers for troubled teenagers, and assisted-living facilities for senior citizens. Bush quietly empathized with those who were having troubles, talked about his goals and values, and explained how his policies would improve their plight. During May and June, the campaign limited itself to only a few media-oriented events per day in the key battleground states.[6]

The messages delivered at Bush's staged events were supported by a national advertising campaign aired in the same key states by the Republican National Committee. Using soft money, much of which was raised by the candidate and his fund-raisers, the Republicans ran generic ads featuring the same policy positions that Bush was emphasizing: Social Security investment accounts, tax cuts, economic opportunities for minorities, and school vouchers. A similar generic advertising campaign, funded primarily by the party's soft money account, had been waged four years earlier on behalf of Senator Robert Dole and other Republican candidates.

Polls taken at the end of this interim period indicated that Bush had enhanced his leadership image. He had consolidated his Republican base, gained the endorsement of rival John McCain, and energized Republican contributors and rank-and-file supporters. Moreover, he had moderated his policy agenda, moved to the center of the political spectrum, and softened his social conservatism. One sign of his growing stature was the widening lead he enjoyed in the polls over Vice President Al Gore.

Healing Partisan Discord

A third task following a competitive nomination battle is to reach out to partisans who supported other candidates. The sooner such an effort is undertaken, the better since the news media will continue to highlight rifts in the party and potential problems for the campaign. A first step in this effort is to gain the endorsements, and hopefully active support, of one's primary opponents. Overcoming the bitterness often involves more than a handshake. Gestures are important. A prime time speech at the convention, an honorary role in the campaign, even the hint of a position in the new administration are some of the "consolation prizes" that may be offered.

George W. Bush faced such a reunification challenge following his victory over John McCain. But mending fences proved difficult at first because of the responses Bush had made in an interview with the *New York Times* on the heels of his Super Tuesday victories. When answering a question about whether McCain raised his awareness of reform issues, Bush said, "No, he didn't change my views," although he did go on to add that McCain "made me a better candidate. He forced me to play to my strengths better." When asked again whether there was anything McCain brought to light or on which he changed his opinion, Bush responded as he had previously, "No, not really. We agreed more than we disagreed."[7] Naturally McCain's supporters were not happy with Bush's remarks.

However, McCain had incentives to support the Republican nominee if only to improve his negative image among party leaders and some rank-and-file GOP partisans, a necessity if he were to make another run for presidency in four or eight years. But McCain also needed to maintain his standing as a reformer motivated by his strong beliefs, as an individual who would not buckle under to the political establishment, a man above the crowd, a person of heroic stature. Nonetheless, it was not until early May, almost two months later, that Bush and McCain got together to reconcile their differences.

The Prelude to the Conventions

Considerable planning and much hype go into the preconvention period. Media attention turns to the vice presidential selection, usually the only unknown item left before the big show. That choice is the presidential nominee's. The last time that a convention actually selected the vice presidential nominee rather than ratified the person whom the winning presidential candidate designated was in 1956 when Adlai Stevenson, the Democratic candidate, professed no choice between Senators John F. Kennedy and Estes Kefauver, both of whom were vying for the nomination. The convention chose Kefauver.

The selection of the vice presidential nominee is one of the most important decisions which the prospective nominee must make. It is a character judgment that reflects on the nominee. It indicates the candidate's level of confidence in himself and his penchant for seeking advice from others. Picking an experienced, well-respected person who might have been or could someday be a candidate for the presidency usually suggests a willingness to delegate and a desire to share some decisional responsibility; it could also signify the candidate's perception that additional electoral support will be necessary to win. In the past, vice presidential nominees have been selected primarily because of the strength they bring to the ticket. Creating a geographic and/or ideological balance has been viewed as both necessary and desirable.

Bill Clinton broke with that tradition in 1992 when he chose a fellow southerner and a senator who also had a reputation as a moderate, Al Gore, to reinforce his image as a New Democrat in contrast with the liberal Democrats of the 1970s and 1980s. George W. Bush's selection of Dick Cheney, a former White House chief of staff, a representative from Wyoming and member of the Republican House leadership, and defense secretary in his father's administration, brought experience, particularly in national security affairs, to the ticket, experience which Bush lacked as a state governor. The choice of a governing mate, more than a running mate, also broke with tradition and suggested an enhanced vice presidency in a Bush administration.

Because so much media attention is directed toward the choice, presidential nominees keep their decisions secret for as long as possible. They want to create a situation in which the announcement can be made with as much hoopla and favorable commentary as possible. This desire has often precluded adequate screening of the candidates for fear that the news media will find out the identity of the prospective choice before the presidential candidate announces it.

The worse case scenario of this charade occurred in 1972 when George McGovern selected Thomas Eagleton, a senator from Missouri, as his running mate. Although he had spoken with the Democratic governor of the state, the senator himself, and the Missouri press, McGovern had not been informed of Eagleton's hospitalization for depression and the shock treatments he received for it at the Mayo Clinic.[8] When this information was revealed by the media, McGovern was caught in a dilemma—he could admit he made a mistake and drop Eagleton from the ticket, looking weak and perhaps mean-spirited in the process, or he could indicate that it wasn't a mistake and stick with him. Initially, McGovern chose the latter strategy. However, when medical authorities suggested that the malady was serious and too risky for a person who might someday become president, McGovern was forced to drop him and select another person.

George H. W. Bush faced a similar dilemma in 1988. Although he had chosen Indiana senator, Dan Quayle, Bush was unaware of Quayle's mediocre record as a student or his family's help in getting him an appointment in the Indiana National Guard, which lessened the possibility of active duty service during the Vietnam War. Bush, who had been accused of being a "wimp," felt he could not back off when the going got tough and stayed with Quayle and won.

In addition to the vice presidential selection, the prospective nominee also must oversee the planning for the national nominating convention. One objective is to avoid any problems, especially factional divisions that carry over from the primaries or are generated by a dispute over policy. A unified convention is viewed as the most successful way to launch a presidential campaign. Candidates and their handlers go to great lengths to orchestrate public events leading up to the convention. Nothing is left to chance.

Thus George W. Bush let it be known that he opposed changes to the traditional positions the party took in its platform so as not to alienate any of the core Republican supporters and chose a running mate who was acceptable to all major party factions. Bush wanted an upbeat, people-oriented convention that emphasized positive imagery. As the poll leader going into the conventions, he and his staff did not want to rock the boat or break his momentum.

In contrast, Gore needed a boost from the convention. He needed to enhance his leadership image and differentiate himself from Clinton. At the same time, he wanted credit for the policy successes of the administration of which he was a part. The first step in achieving the leadership objective was his surprising choice of Senator Joseph Lieberman, a Democrat from Connecticut, as his running mate. The selection of the devout, orthodox Jewish senator captured media attention. Bush and Cheney fell from public view. Moreover, Gore won praise for his courageousness in choosing Lieberman; he helped insulate himself from the scandals of the Clinton administration by designating a vice presidential nominee who had become associated with moral and ethical issues, the first Democrat to criticize Clinton's behavior on the floor of the Senate. Gore also reinforced his own ideological perspective as a moderate by selecting a senator who was in many ways more conservative than he was.

Like Bush, Gore also wanted his convention to be a public relations springboard for himself and his party. He needed an event to establish his personal independence and a podium from which to articulate the themes he intended to emphasize in the general election. Democratic convention leaders obliged him, scripting and orchestrating their convention to achieve his desired effect.

NATIONAL NOMINATING CONVENTIONS

The Tradition

National nominating conventions were at one time important decision-making bodies. Conventions were used to decide on the party's nominees, platforms, and rules and procedures, as well as provide a podium for launching presidential campaigns. Today, however, conventions are theater, pure and simple. They are ritual, part of the American political tradition, but not nearly as newsworthy as they were in bygone days.

Prior to 1956, majorities were constructed within conventions to make the critical decisions. Party leaders, who exercised considerable control over the selection of their state delegations, debated among themselves. Once they agreed on the candidates, they directed their delegates to vote in favor of their particular choice.

The last brokered conventions occurred in 1952. That year, Democratic and Republican leaders wheeled and dealed in "smoke-filled rooms" to select Governor Adlai Stevenson of Illinois and General Dwight Eisenhower as their respective nominees. Since those conventions, the delegate selection process has dictated the nominees.

Another indication of the decline of the brokered convention has been first ballot phenomena that have characterized recent conventions. In fact, since 1924, when the Democrats took 103 ballots to nominate John W. Davis, a convention marked by much rancor, even fights among the delegates, there have been only four conventions (two Democratic and two Republican) in which more than one ballot has been needed to choose a presidential nominee. In 1932, the Democrats held four roll calls before they agreed on Franklin Roosevelt, and took three in 1952 to nominate Adlai Stevenson. In 1940, Republican Wendell Willkie was selected on the eighth ballot, breaking a deadlock among Thomas Dewey, Arthur Vandenberg, and himself. Eight years later, Dewey was nominated on the third ballot.

A variety of factors have reduced the convention's decision-making capabilities. The broadcasting of conventions by radio and later television has detracted from the delegates' ability to bargain with one another. It is difficult to compromise before a television camera, especially during prime time. Public exposure has forced negotiations off the convention floor and even out of "leaky" but no longer "smoke-filled" committee rooms.

Size is another factor that has affected the proceedings. Conventions used to be relatively small. In 1860, 303 delegates nominated Democrat Stephen Douglas, and 466 chose Republican Abraham Lincoln. Today, the participants run into the thousands. Table 5–1 lists the number of delegate votes at Democratic and Republican conventions since 1940. When alternates and delegates who possess fractional votes are included, the numbers grow even more. In 2000, the Republicans had 2,066 delegates and the same number of alternates, while the Democrats had 4,370 delegates, some casting fractions of a vote, and 610 alternates.

Because of the large number of delegates, divisions within the parties tend to be magnified. These divisions, in turn, have produced the need for more efficient control over the convention's operation. For the party leaders and the prospective nominee, the task has become one of orchestration; their goal is to conduct a huge pep rally replete with ritual, speeches, and films—a made-for-TV production. From the perspective of the party and its nominees, the convention now serves primarily as a launching pad for the general election. Finally, and most importantly, the party's electorate now determines the convention delegates, not the state party leaders and elected officials. This determination occurs well in advance of the convention, is publicly known, and preordains the outcome. As a consequence, conventions have effectively lost their decision-making power and instead become decision-ratifying bodies characterized more by pomp and circumstance and less by substance.

The Official Proceedings

Preliminary decisions on the convention are made by the party's national committee, usually on the recommendation of its chair and appropriate convention committees. An incumbent president normally exercises considerable influence over many of these decisions: the choice of a convention city, the selection of temporary and permanent convention officials, and the designation of the principal speakers.

Both the Democrats and the Republicans have traditionally turned to national party leaders, primarily members of Congress, to fill many of the positions. The technicalities of scripting and staging the event are left to entertainment professionals, media consultants, pollsters, and party officials with national campaign experience.

TABLE 5–1 🌿

DELEGATE VOTES AT NOMINATING CONVENTIONS, 1940–2004

Year	Republicans	Democrats
1940	1,000	1,100
1944	1,059	1,176
1948	1,904	1,234
1952	1,206	1,230
1956	1,323	1,372
1960	1,331	1,521
1964	1,308	2,316
1968	1,333	2,622
1972	1,348	3,016
1976	2,259	3,008
1980	1,994	3,331
1984	2,234	3,933
1988	2,277	4,160
1992	2,210	4,286
1996	1,990	4,289
2000	2,066	4,370
2004	2,200*	4,320

*Estimate.

Source: Richard C. Bain and Judith H. Parris, *Convention Decisions and Voting Records,* 2nd ed. (Washington, D.C.: Brookings Institution, 1973), Appendix C. Copyright © Brookings Institution, 1973. Reprinted by permission of Brookings Publications. Updated by the author from data supplied by the Republican and Democratic National Committees.

In choosing a site, many factors are considered: the size, configuration, and condition of the convention hall, transportation to and from it, financial inducements, the political climate, the geographic area, and the cultural ambiance of the city itself. These factors weighed heavily in the Democrats' choice of Boston for their 2004 convention and the Republicans' choice of New York City for theirs.[9]

Speeches. Over the years, both parties have organized their conventions with similar schedules, daily themes, and speeches (lots of them) by party leaders, elected officials, celebrities, and occasionally, ordinary citizens. Of these speeches, the keynote address and the formal acceptance of the nomination by the candidates and their running mates are usually the most important and newsworthy.

The keynote address, which occurs early in the convention and in past years used to kick it off, has been designed to unify the delegates, smoothing over any divisions that may have emerged during the preconvention campaign, and to rouse them and the public for the coming election. The address ritually trumpets the achievements of the party, eulogizing its heroes and criticizing the opposition for its ill-conceived programs, inept leadership, and general inability to cope with the nation's most pressing problems. The keynoter for the party that does not control the White House sounds a litany of failures and suggests that the country needs new leadership. Naturally, the keynoter for the party in office reverses the blame and praise. Noting the accomplishments of the administration and its unfinished business, the speaker urges a continuation of the party's effective leadership and policy successes.[10]

The tone of the speech, however, can vary considerably. In 1984, Governor Mario Cuomo of New York, the Democratic keynoter, sounded a sober theme. Describing the United States as a tale of two cities, he chided the Reagan administration for pursuing policies that benefited the rich at the expense of the poor. In contrast, Ann Richards, then treasurer of Texas, gave a more folksy, upbeat, and humorous address in 1988. Criticizing George H. W. Bush for being aloof, insensitive, and uncaring, she concluded sarcastically, "he can't help it. He was born with a silver foot in his mouth."[11] Richards's comment irritated George W. Bush, so much so, that he resolved to run against her for governor of Texas, a race he won.

The Republicans did not designate a keynote speaker at their 2000 convention. The Democrats did, Representative Harold Ford Jr. of Tennessee, Gore's home state.

In recent years, there have been other newsworthy speeches. Pat Buchanan gave one of his rousing campaign speeches on opening night of the 1992 Republican convention. Endorsing the president for reelection, Bush's former challenger unleashed a scathing attack on the Democrats and Bill Clinton. The delegates loved the speech, but the news media saw it as harsh and mean-spirited conservative rhetoric.[12] In contrast, former President Reagan's speech in which he effectively passed the torch to his vice president, George Bush, was lauded for its eloquence and optimism. President Clinton's address to the 2000 Democratic convention was also a pass-the-torch speech in which the president noted the accomplishments of his administration and pointed to Al Gore as the best person to continue that successful policy legacy.

In recent conventions it has also become customary to give the potential or actual first lady an opportunity to address the convention to provide an "inside" perspective on the character, qualifications, and achievements of the prospective nominee. Elizabeth Dole and Hillary Clinton both gave speeches at the 1996 conventions as did Laura Bush and Tipper Gore in 2000.

Committee Reports. The major committees, credentials, rules, and platform, usually report to the delegates early in the convention. Often the product of lengthy negotiations, these reports to the convention represent the majority's voice on the committees and are usually ratified without change by the convention delegates. For a minority to present its views, 25 percent of the committee must concur. Membership on the committees tends to reflect support for the candidates in the convention as a whole. Thus, when the majority is unified and effectively coordinated, there is little the minority can do.

Presidential and Vice Presidential Nominations. Another day traditionally is devoted to the presidential nomination and balloting. In early conventions, it was customary for delegates simply to rise and place the name of a candidate in nomination without a formal speech. Gradually, the practice of nominating became more elaborate. Speeches were lengthened. Ritual required that the virtues of the candidate first be extolled before the candidate's identity was revealed. Today, with public speculation beginning months before and the selection of the nominee a foregone conclusion, the practice of withholding the name has been abandoned.

Demonstrations normally follow the practice of placing a person's name in nomination. The advent of television, however, has changed the nature of these demonstrations. No longer spontaneous, they are now carefully staged and timed to indicate enthusiasm for the nominee but also to keep convention events moving during the prime-time viewing hours.

Once nominations have been made, the balloting begins. The secretary of the convention calls the roll of states in alphabetical order, with the chair of each delegation announcing the vote. A poll of the delegation may be requested by any member of that delegation. Beginning in 1988, the Democrats have used an electronic system to ensure a fast and accurate count. After the delegation is polled, the chair records the vote of the state on a terminal connected to the podium.

Formally selecting the vice presidential nominee usually is the next order of business. In their early years, nominating conventions evidenced some difficulty in getting candidates to accept the vice presidential nomination. Because of the low esteem in which the office was held, a number of prominent individuals, including Henry Clay and Daniel Webster, actually refused it. In Webster's words, "I do not propose to be buried until I am really dead and in my coffin."[13]

Today, the vice presidency is coveted, especially as a stepping-stone to the presidency. In the twentieth century alone, six vice presidents have become president through succession (either death or resignation); two, Richard Nixon and George H. W. Bush, have been elected to the presidency (although Nixon was not elected directly from the vice presidency); and three others, Hubert Humphrey, Walter Mondale, and Al Gore have been losing presidential candidates.

Despite the appeal of the vice presidency, it is almost impossible to run for it directly. There are no vice presidential primaries and no government matching funds for vice presidential candidates. Only one "vote" really counts—the presidential nominee's. Since the prospective nominee normally has sufficient delegates to control the convention, the presidential standard-bearer can and does dictate the selection. Although most delegates accept the recommendation, there have been a sprinkling of protest votes over the years by delegates who do not like the person selected or who wish to use the vice presidential nomination to signify their opposition to a policy position or perspective that the presidential nominee has adopted.

Acceptance Addresses. In 2000, both major parties' vice presidential nominees made their acceptance speeches on the third night of the convention leaving the fourth and final night to the presidential nominees and their principal addresses, the highlight for contemporary conventions and the event that has the largest viewing audience.

The custom of giving acceptance speeches by the presidential standard-bearers was begun in 1932 by Franklin Roosevelt. Before that time, conventions designated committees to inform the presidential and vice presidential nominees of their decisions. Journeying to the candidate's home, the committees would announce the selection in a public ceremony. The nominee, in turn, would accept in a speech stating his positions on the major issues of the day. The last major party candidate to be told of the nomination in this fashion was Republican Wendell Willkie in 1940.

Today, acceptance speeches can be occasions for great oratory—they are both a call to the faithful and an address to the country. They articulate the principal themes for the general election. Harry Truman's speech to the Democratic convention in 1948 is frequently cited as one that helped to fire up the party. Truman chided the Republicans for obstructing and ultimately rejecting many of his legislative proposals and then adopting a party platform that called for some of the same social and economic goals. He electrified the Democratic convention by challenging the Republicans to live up to their convention promises and pass legislation to achieve these goals in a special session of Congress that he announced he was calling. When the Republican-controlled Congress failed to enact that legislation, Truman was able to pin a "do-nothing" label on it and make that label the basic theme of his successful presidential campaign.

In 1984, Democratic candidate Walter Mondale made a mammoth political blunder in his acceptance speech. Warning the delegates about the United States budget deficit that had increased dramatically during Reagan's first term, Mondale said that he would do something about it if he were elected president: "Let's tell the truth. Mr. Reagan will raise taxes, and so will I. He won't tell you. I just did." Democratic delegates cheered his candor, directness, and boldness; the public did not. He and his party were saddled with the tax issue throughout the *entire* campaign.

The 2000 acceptance addresses continued the practice of reiterating themes and emphasizing priorities. George W. Bush used his address to reach beyond his core coalitional support. Bush stressed inclusiveness, compassion, and morality, saying he wanted to maximize opportunities for all Americans. He used words such as *promise, moral courage, responsibility,* and *opportunity* to emphasize his moderate tone and unifying spirit. The Republican candidate spoke of broad policy goals but provided few details.

Al Gore sounded a populist theme. After lauding the accomplishments of the last eight years of Democratic control of the White House, Gore proceeded to differentiate himself and his policy goals from those of the Clinton administration. "I stand here tonight as my own man," he said.[14] Gore then went on to provide a litany of policy objectives designed to extend the economic prosperity to those who had not benefited as much during the Clinton years—middle-class, working Americans. In contrast to Bush, Gore was program oriented and issue specific.

Before the current nominating system dictated the eventual nominees and gave them operational control over the convention, there were frequent internal controversies involving the party leadership, the successful nominees, and their delegates on one hand and the unsuccessful candidates and their supporters on the other. These disputes concerned the credentials of the delegates, the rules of the nomination process and the convention, and the party's campaign platform.

Intra- and Interparty Disputes

Credentials. All delegates must present proper credentials to participate at national nominating conventions. Disputes over credentials have occurred from time to time but not recently. Twice in the twentieth century, Republican conventions witnessed major credential changes that ultimately determined their nominee. William Howard Taft's victory over Theodore Roosevelt in 1912 and Dwight Eisenhower's over Robert Taft in 1952 followed from convention decisions to seat certain delegates and reject others.[15]

Democratic conventions also witnessed credentials fights. In 1968 and again in 1972, these challenges were based on allegations that certain party members had been excluded from caucuses and conventions, that certain state delegations did not possess sufficient minority representation, and that some of those delegations were chosen in a manner that did not conform to party rules.[16]

Rules. Rules govern the manner in which the convention is conducted; they also can affect the next delegate selection process four years down the road. In formulating the rules, there is often tension between the desire of the minority to be heard and the interest of the majority, especially the leadership, to run an efficient convention. A humorous incident at the 1956 Republican convention illustrates this tension. In the nomination for vice president, Richard Nixon was expected to be the unanimous choice. A movement to dump him from the ticket, led by perennial candidate Harold Stassen, had failed. When the roll of states was called for nominations, a delegate from Nebraska grabbed the microphone and said he had a nomination to make. "Who?" said a surprised Joseph Martin, chair of the convention, at this deviation from the script. "Joe Smith," the delegate replied.

Martin did not permit the name of Joe Smith to be placed in nomination, although the Democrats were later to contend that any Joe Smith would have been better than Nixon.

For the most part, convention rules have not caused much wrangling. Those that have generated the most controversy have concerned voting for a party's nominees. Until 1936, the Democrats operated under a rule that required a two-thirds vote for winning the nomination. James K. Polk's selection in 1844 was a consequence of Martin Van Buren's failure to obtain the support of two-thirds of the convention, although Van Buren had a majority. The two-thirds rule in effect permitted a minority of the delegates to veto a person they opposed.

Among the more recent rules controversies, two stand out. During the 1976 Republican convention, the Reagan organization proposed a rules change that would have required Gerald Ford to name his choice for vice president before the convention's vote for president, as his opponent, Ronald Reagan had done. Ford's supporters strongly opposed and subsequently beat this amendment. As a consequence, there was no way for Reagan to shake the remaining delegates loose from Ford's coalition.

The other occurred at the 1980 Democratic convention. At issue was a proposed requirement that delegates vote for the candidate to whom they were publicly pledged at the time they were chosen. Trailing Jimmy Carter by about six hundred delegates, Ted Kennedy, who had previously supported this requirement, urged an open convention in which delegates could vote their consciences rather than merely exercise their commitments. This change in the rules would have required rejection of the pledged delegate rule. Naturally, the Carter organization favored the rule and lobbied strenuously and successfully for it. The Democrats have subsequently repealed this rule, requiring instead that delegates reflect in good conscience the sentiments of those who elected them.

Platform. Platforms have always been an important part of nominating conventions. They are a collective statement of the party's principal positions and agenda for the fall campaign. As such, they have become targets of opportunity for those who seek to promote their issues and interests. The heterogeneous character of both major political parties has contributed to the battles over the content and wording of the platform. It has also forced the platform drafting process to become more open and provide greater opportunities for those who represent interests within the party to participate.

Although platforms contain rhetoric and self-praise, they also articulate goals and policy positions that differentiate one party from the other. In an examination of the Democratic and Republican platforms between 1944 and 1976, political scientist Gerald Pomper found that most of the differences were evident in the planks incorporated by one party but not by the other.[17] Over these years the Republicans, who were in the minority during that period, emphasized national security and general governmental matters, whereas the Democrats, the majority party, stressed economic issues, particularly those that pertained to labor and social welfare.

Party platforms have become more detailed and policy specific. They used to consist of broad goals and objectives. Today they are designed with the party's electoral coalition in mind. They tend to have something for every relevant group.

Beginning in 1988, the Democrats toned down their liberal rhetoric in an attempt to make their platforms more appealing to middle-class voters disaffected by the party's social policies in the 1970s and 1980s. In contrast, the Republicans have moved to the right, becoming more conservative in the 1980s and 1990s. The GOP position on abortion has been especially divisive for the party.

There have also been substantial differences in content between the party's platforms. (See Box 5–1, "Contrasts in the 2000 Republican and Democratic Party Platforms.") These differences in turn have produced different public policies because elected officials of both parties have a relatively good record of meeting their pledges. Although approximately three-quarters of party platforms are high-sounding rhetoric, about one-fourth contains fairly specific promises. Of these, Pomper found that almost 75 percent have been kept.[18]

Convention Strategies and Tactics

There are a number of prizes at nominating conventions. The platform contains some of them. The rules can also be important, but the big prize is the presidential nomination itself. When that is in doubt, all the efforts of the leading contenders must be directed at obtaining the required number of votes to be nominated. When it is not in doubt, the leading contenders can concentrate on uniting the party, articulating their themes, and converting the convention into a huge campaign rally for themselves. In 1976, the Reagan organization focused its attention on winning the nomination; in 1980, it sought to present a united front; in 1984, it orchestrated a coronation ceremony that was repeated by George Bush in 1988 and 1992, Bob Dole in 1996, and George W. Bush in 2000.

In recent Democratic conventions, the front-runners have tried to heal the wounds of the nomination contest by appealing to disaffected delegates to join them and the party for the fall campaign. Making peace with his principal opponent in 1998, the Reverend Jesse Jackson, Michael Dukakis conceded the rules changes and some of the platform proposals Jackson wanted in exchange for Jackson's public support of the Democratic ticket at the convention and during the campaign. In 1992, the Clinton campaign appealed to delegates who supported his opponents. One of those opponents, Jerry Brown, refused to release his delegates or endorse the Democratic ticket. As a consequence, the Clinton delegates refused to consider any of his proposals for reform and denied him a prime-time opportunity to address the convention. Clinton faced no disappointed nomination seekers in 1996, nor did Gore in 2000.

A key to success, regardless of the objective, is organization. Recent conventions have seen the operation of highly structured and efficient candidate organizations. Designed to maximize the flow of information, regulate floor activity, and anticipate and control roll call votes, these organizations usually have elaborate communications systems linking floor supporters to a command center outside the convention hall. Key staff members at the command center monitor reports, articulate positions, and make strategic decisions.

In addition to desiring a unified convention, candidates often have specific image goals. For Clinton in 1992, it was to reintroduce himself and discard the party's liberal label. In 1996, it was to present himself as a successful president and

---

BOX 5–1 🌿

CONTRASTS IN THE 2000 REPUBLICAN AND DEMOCRATIC PARTY PLATFORMS

REPUBLICANS	DEMOCRATS

Abortion

... the unborn child has a fundamental individual right to life which cannot be abridged. We support a human life amendment to the Constitution

   ... oppose using public revenues for abortion and will not fund organizations which advocate it.

The Democratic Party stands behind the right of every woman to choose ... it is a fundamental constitutional liberty that individual Americans—not government—can best take responsibility for making the most difficult and intensely personal decisions regarding reproduction.

Affirmative Action

We believe rights inhere in individuals, not in groups. We will attain our nation's goal of equal opportunity without quotas or other forms of preferential treatment.

We have increased funding for Civil Rights enforcement ... Al Gore has strongly opposed efforts to roll back affirmative action programs.

Campaign Finance Reform

We have one guiding principle. ... Will any particular proposal encourage or restrict the energetic engagements of Americans in elections? Stop the abuses of corporate and labor "soft" money contributions to political parties; enact "paycheck protection" ensuring that no union member is forced to contribute to anybody's campaign; preserve the right of every individual and group to express their opinions and advocate their issues.

We must restore Americans' faith in their own democracy by providing real and comprehensive campaign finance reform. The McCain–Feingold bill is the very first piece of legislation President Al Gore will submit to Congress. And then he will go further ... [with] tough new lobbying reform, publicly guaranteed TV times for debates and advocacy by candidates, and a crackdown on special interest issue ads.

Education—School Vouchers

We advocate choice in education, not as an abstract theory, but as the surest way for families, especially low-income families, to free their youngsters from the failings of dangerous schools and put them onto the road to opportunity and success.

What America needs are public schools that compete with one another and are held accountable for results, not private school vouchers that drain resources from public schools and hand over the public's hard-earned tax dollars to private schools with no accountability.

Energy

America needs a national energy strategy that will increase domestic supplies of coal, oil, and natural gas. Our country does have ample energy resources waiting to be developed. Environmental concerns are not at the heart of the matter.

From the Redwood forests to the Florida Everglades, ... we have protected millions of acres of our precious natural lands. We stopped development in America's last wild places ... Republicans see them as the playground of the powerful—there for big business to exploit with drilling and mining.

Guns
We defend the constitutional right to bear arms, and we affirm the individual responsibility to safely use and store firearms.

We need mandatory child safety locks, to protect our children. We should require a photo license ID, a full background check, and a gun safety test to buy a new hand-gun in America.

Health Care
We will promote a health care system that supports, not supplants, the private sector; that promotes personal responsibility in health care decisionmaking; and that ensures the least intrusive role for the federal government.

We must redouble our efforts to bring the uninsured into coverage step-by-step and as soon as possible. We should guarantee access to affordable health care for every child in America.

Patient's Bill of Rights
We believe that a quick and fair resolution to treatment disputes without going to court is the best result. However, as a last resort, we also support a patient's right to adjudicate claims in court to receive necessary medical care.

Americans need a real, enforceable Patient's Bill of Rights with the right to appeal decisions to an outside board, guaranteed coverage to emergency room care, and the right to sue when they are unfairly denied coverage.

Social Security
Personal savings account must be the cornerstone of restructuring [Social Security] . . . Choice is the key. Any new options to retirement security should be voluntary.

To build on the success of Social Security, Al Gore has proposed the creation of Retirement Savings Plus . . . savings accounts with a governmental match, . . . separate from Social Security.

Tax Cuts
. . . It's time to change the tax system, to make it simpler, flatter, and fairer for everyone. We . . . enthusiastically endorse the principles of Governor Bush's tax cut plan . . .

Democrats seek . . . tax cuts that are specifically targeted to help those who need them the most. These tax cuts would let families . . . save for college, invest in their job skills and life-long learning, pay for health insurance, . . .

Source: Adapted from the 2000 Republican and Democratic Party platforms, <http://www.nc.org/2000/2000platformcontents> and <www.dems2000.com/AboutThe Convention.html>.

as the person best able to lead the country into the twenty-first century. Bob Dole sought to redefine himself and his party as sensitive to the values, needs, and aspirations of the average American. In 2000, George W. Bush reinforced his centrist compassionate image while Al Gore stressed his personal independence and political popularism.

The Mediated Convention: Theater and News

Political conventions used to be major newsworthy events. Radio began covering national conventions in 1924 and television in 1956. Because conventions in the

1950s were interesting and unpredictable events in which important political decisions were made, they attracted a large audience, one that increased rapidly as the number of households having television sets expanded. During the 1950s and 1960s, about 25 percent of the potential viewers watched the conventions, with the numbers swelling to 50 percent during the most significant part of the meetings. The sizable audience made conventions important for fledgling television news organizations, which were beginning to rival newspapers for news coverage.

Initially, the three major networks provided almost gavel-to-gavel coverage. They focused on the official events, that is, what went on at the podium. Commentary was kept to a minimum.

The changes in the delegate selection process that occurred in the 1970s and 1980s had a major impact on the amount and type of television coverage as well as the size of the viewing audience. As the decision-making capabilities of conventions declined, their newsworthiness decreased, as did the proportion of households that tuned in and the amount of time spent watching them.

The major networks subsequently reduced their coverage. In 1992, they covered each of the conventions for a total of fifteen hours; in 1996, they reduced that coverage to twelve hours, and to eight and a half hours in 2000.[19]

Although cable and public television have extended their coverage, and the American public still feel that conventions serve a useful purpose, the overall audience watching the conventions has declined.[20] Surveys conducted by the Annenberg Public Policy Center and The Joan Shorenstein Center on the Press, Politics, and Public Policy found about half the television audience indicated that they did not see any of the conventions.[21] Of those who did watch some portion of the conventions, the majority of these viewers came upon the conventions while channel surfing, and for the most part watched for only a few minutes.[22]

The surveys revealed that convention watching varied with age. Those over fifty were four times as likely to tune in for an hour or more than those twenty-nine and under.[23] Partisans watched their own convention more than the opposition's convention.[24]

Party officials, concerned with the declining participation and interest of young people in partisan national politics, created Web sites to attract this next voting generation. They trumpeted the interactive character of their convention sites. In addition, thirty-five other Internet sites, dominated by news organizations, covered the conventions live. But "hits" on these news sites were down as well.[25]

In short, the big news of the 2000 nominating conventions was that despite the increasing number of ways in which the electorate could follow them, despite each party's hype and public appeal, despite the news coverage of the conventions, more people did not watch them than did.

The decline in the viewing audience has produced two opposite effects. It has caused the parties to increase their scripting and orchestration of their conventions in an attempt to create more compelling theater; it has also encouraged the press to hunt for news and engage in endless analysis to make the conventions more newsworthy. The result has been to create two simultaneous conventions: the one staged by the parties and the other reported by the press.

Theater. The choice of a site; the selection of speakers; and the timing, length, and content of their talks are all made with television in mind. One aspect of this theatrical orientation has been the use of a variety of entertainment formats to hold the delegates' and, especially, television viewers' interests: short speeches, film clips, and video biographies in addition to the pageantry, banners, and orchestrated cheers of the assembled throng. Another has been timing and sequencing events to occur during prime time and building up to the grand finale—the nominees' acceptance speeches.

A third feature of recent conventions has been the thematic content woven into the official proceedings. The Republicans scripted their 2000 convention to highlight certain policies and principles. Each day had a message and messengers, supplemented by a package of press releases, speeches, and other convention news available to anyone on the convention's Web site. On day one the message was that the Republican Party favored expanded opportunities for all Americans; no child was to be left behind. Improving education and extending health care were the primary vehicles by which this goal was to be accomplished. The candidate's wife, Laura Bush, a school librarian, and General Colin Powell, Chairman of the Joint Chiefs of Staff during the Gulf War and a proponent of volunteerism, especially mentoring needy children, served as symbols and speakers. On the second day, strength and security was the theme with addresses from John McCain, a Vietnam hero, Elizabeth Dole, initially a candidate herself for the 2000 nomination, and Dr. Condeleezza Rice, Bush's chief national security adviser. Keeping America prosperous and preserving the Social Security and Medicare systems was the focus of day three featuring speeches by a variety of small business entrepreneurs and vice presidential nominee, Dick Cheney. On the fourth day, the nominee, George W. Bush, was center stage with his acceptance speech as the main event.

The Democrats also orchestrated their convention although not as tightly as the Republicans. For the first two days, the Democrats focused on their contemporary presidential heroes. Day one was devoted to the accomplishments of the Clinton administration with both the first lady, who was running for the Senate from New York, and the president as major speakers. The Clintons then left the convention so as not to distract attention from the new nominees and their policies. The Kennedy legacy was featured on the second day of the Los Angeles convention. Forty years earlier, the last time the Democrats met in that city, John F. Kennedy had been nominated for president. Members of the Kennedy family including Senator Ted Kennedy and Caroline Kennedy Schlossberg, the former president's daughter, spoke about the Kennedy legacy. On the third day, the party featured women members of the House of Representatives, along with Dick Gephardt, the House minority leader, and an address by vice presidential nominee, Joseph Lieberman. The final day was reserved for Al Gore, who was introduced by his wife, Tipper, with his convention speech highlighting and ending the meeting.

Conventions have become faster paced and more varied than in the past, primarily to keep their viewing audience. From the standpoint of the parties, the more cogent the message and the more entertaining the proceedings, the more likely the convention will have a positive impact on the voters. Obviously, the press have a different objective and perspective.

AP/Wide World Photos

Al Gore kisses his wife, Tipper, after officially receiving the 2000 Democratic nomination. In that brief moment, Gore demonstrated his spontaneity, passion, and fidelity—personal virtues he wished to emphasize as he launched his presidential candidacy before millions of American viewers.

News. Conventions may be entertaining, but from the perspective of the press, most of what goes on is public relations, not news. As a consequence the thousands of correspondents covering the event must hunt for news beyond the official proceedings. Television cameras constantly scan the floor for dramatic events and human interest stories. Delegates are pictured talking, eating, sleeping, parading, even watching the convention on television. Interviews with prominent individuals, rank-and-file delegates, and family and friends of the prospective nominee are conducted. To provide a balanced presentation, supporters and opponents are frequently juxtaposed. To maintain the audience's attention, the interviews are kept short, usually focusing on reactions to actual or potential political problems. There are also endless commentary, prognostications, and forecasts of how the convention is likely to affect voters.[26] Once the conventions are over, however, they are rarely mentioned in the reporting of the campaign although clips from convention highlights, especially from the acceptance speeches of the nominees will reappear in their advertising.

Coverage inside the convention is supplemented by coverage outside the hall. Knowing this, groups come to the convention city and arena to air grievances and to protest. The most violent of these political demonstrations occurred in 1968 in Chicago, the city where the Democratic Party was meeting. Thousands of people, many of them students, marched through the streets and parks protesting U.S. involvement in the Vietnam War. Police set up barricades, blocking, beating, and arresting many of the protestors. Claiming that the events were newsworthy, the broadcast networks broke away from their convention coverage to report on these activities and show tapes of the bloody confrontation between police and protestors. Critics charged that the presence of television cameras incited the demonstrators and that coverage was disproportional and distracted from the proceedings. In response, CBS News reported that it had devoted only thirty-two minutes to these events out of its thirty-eight hours of convention coverage.[27]

At subsequent conventions, protests have occurred but have not received as much attention by the mainstream press. Demonstrations in Philadelphia and Los Angeles during the 2000 conventions were noted but not emphasized, nor did they seem to distract from the proceedings of either convention.

The networks' orientation, which highlights conflict, drama, and human interest, often clashes with the parties' desire to present a united and enthusiastic front to launch their presidential campaigns. The clash between these two conflicting goals has resulted in a classic struggle for control between the news media and politicians. The more convention managers are successful in orchestrating their meetings to achieve their objectives, the less newsworthy the news media find the conventions to be. In contrast, the more the press report on division, dissension, and turmoil, the less the conventions meet the parties' and their nominees' principal goals for launching their presidential campaign. The same conflict is evident in news coverage of minor party conventions as well although, from the perspective of the planners of these events, a principal goal is to obtain any live coverage at all. (See Box 5–2, "Minor Party Conventions.")

BOX 5–2 ⚜

MINOR PARTY CONVENTIONS

Minor parties also hold political conventions for the purpose of nominating candidates and promulgating their platform. In most cases these conventions are held with little fanfare and even less national media coverage. The absence of competition within the party combined with the improbability of winning the presidential election or even affecting its outcome explain the low visibility given to most of these events.

The Reform Party's conventions in 1996 and 2000 have been exceptions. Although they did not receive live coverage from the broadcast networks, they did from cable news and public affairs networks, such as CNN and C-SPAN, which covered some of their proceedings including the acceptance speech of the presidential nominee. The broadcast networks covered the conventions as items on the evening news. H. Ross Perot, the party's founder and financial backer, had much to do with the coverage the Reform Party's nomination process got in 1996, whereas the attraction in 2000 was the battle between supporters and opponents of Pat Buchanan, the former Republican who left that party to run as the Reform candidate.

In 1996, the Reform Party held a two-stage convention. At the first stage of the nomination process, Perot and his opponent, former Governor Richard D. Lamm of Colorado, were given an opportunity to address the assembled delegates. During the next week, partisans voted by regular mail or e-mail with the results announced at the second convention, which also provided another opportunity for the winning candidate, Perot, to announce his vice presidential selection and make his acceptance speech.

In 2000, there was also a mail ballot as well as a convention vote, but it was the organizational battle over Buchanan's candidacy in the months leading up to the convention that attracted media attention. The hard-ball tactics that Buchanan's supporters employed to oust state party officials who opposed his candidacy created deep divisions within the party and ultimately led to a walkout by delegates hostile to Buchanan. These angry delegates proceeded to hold their own convention, nominate their own candidates, and claim the Reform Party label as theirs while Buchanan's backers nominated him as their Reform Party candidate. The dispute ended up in the courts which had to decide which of these two sets of candidates should be listed as the Reform nominees for 2000. Similarly, the Federal Election Commission had to determine which of them was entitled to the $12.6 million the party was to receive on the basis of Perot's 1996 vote. The commission chose Buchanan.

The other minor party that received some national coverage in 2000 was the Green Party, which nominated consumer advocate and anticorporate crusader Ralph Nader. Holding its convention in June before those of the Republicans and Democrats, the Green Party gained coverage by virtue of Nader's reputation as an outspoken critic of corporate America and its special interest politics as well as early polls, which indicated that his candidacy could make a difference in the outcome of the Bush–Gore contest. In other words, Nader provided the party with visibility and the party gave him a pulpit from which to articulate his beliefs.

Assessing the Convention's Impact

Do national nominating conventions have an impact on the election? Most observers believe that they do. Why else would the major parties devote so much time, money, and effort to these events? Why else would party leaders and academics concerned with civic education bemoan the reduction of convention coverage by the broadcast networks? Why else would the parties conduct focus groups, consult poll data, and even tally hits on their convention Web sites and monitor e-mail responses?

Political scientists also believe that conventions matter. They have hypothesized that there is a relationship between convention unity and electoral success. Since 1968, the party that appears to have had the most harmonious convention has emerged victorious. It is difficult, however, to say how much or even whether the unity contributed to the result or simply reflected the partisan environment that fostered that particular outcome.

In the short run, conventions almost always boost the popularity of their nominees and decrease that of their opponents. This boost is referred to as the convention "bounce," which tends to average about a 6 percent gain in the public opinion polls. The only recent nominee who did not get a bounce was George McGovern in 1972. Table 5–2 indicates the bounces which nominating conventions since 1960 have given their party's nominees.

Bounces, however, can be short-lived as President Bush discovered in 1992, Robert Dole in 1996, and George W. Bush in 2000. Al Gore's bounce seemed to wipe away the gains which his Republican opponent made following the preceding postnomination period and the GOP convention. Gore's support rose about 8 percent in the public opinion polls. He had trailed Bush going into the Democratic convention and led him after it. George H. W. Bush got a similar boost from the Republican convention in 1988, moving him into a lead he never relinquished.

The importance of conventions for the nominees is that they allow them to define themselves and do so before a large audience. Thus, candidates such as George H. W. Bush and Al Gore, both vice presidents who were seen largely in the shadows of the more charismatic presidents with whom they served, finally had the opportunity to shine alone, and they did.

The long-term impact is more difficult to measure. Nonetheless, political scientists have suggested three major effects of conventions on voters: (1) the conventions heighten interest, thereby increasing turnout; (2) they arouse latent feelings, thereby raising partisan awareness; (3) they color perceptions, thereby affecting personal judgments of the candidates and their issue stands.[28]

Each of these effects is supported by survey data taken before, during, and after recent conventions. The Vanishing Voter and Annenberg surveys found a substantial rise in public interest in the campaign immediately before, during, and after the Republican and Democratic conventions of 2000 as well as more positive feelings toward the parties and their nominees.[29] As expected, partisans of each party responded more favorably during the week of their party's nominating convention.[30] The reactions of partisans shored up support for their party's nominees, which was reflected in election polls conducted after the conventions.[31] They also provided viewers with information; for those who watched, the conventions helped to clarify candidate images and policy positions.[32] In this way, they contributed to the knowledge necessary to making a more informed judgment. The Annenberg study on the 2000 conventions concluded:

> The number of voters feeling they have learned enough about the candidates to make an informed choice continues to climb, albeit slowly. Whereas at the beginning of the year only 20 percent felt they had learned enough, that number now stands at approximately 50 percent. The period of the conventions saw an increase of 10 percent in this figure.[33]

In short, conventions can have a powerful psychological impact on their viewers, making them more inclined to follow the campaign and vote for a party's candidates. They can energize participants. They can also have an organizational effect, fostering cooperation among the different and frequently competing groups within a party, encouraging them to submerge their differences and work toward a common goal.

TABLE 5–2

CONVENTION BOUNCES, 1968–2000

Year	Candidates (winner)	Last Poll before First Convention	Poll after First Convention (challenger/party)	Bounce for Challenger	Last Poll before Second Convention	Poll after Second Convention (incumbent/party)	Bounce for Incumbent
1968	Nixon (R)	40	45	+5	NA	43	—
	Humphrey (D)	38	29	—	NA	31	+7
	Wallace (AI)	16	18	—	NA	19	—
1972	Nixon (R)	53	56	—	57	64	+7
	McGovern (D)	37	37	0	31	30	—
1976	Carter (D)	53	62	+9	57	50	—
	Ford (R)	36	29	—	32	37	+5
1980	Reagan (R)	37	45	+8	45	38	—
	Carter (D)	34	29	—	29	39	+10
	Anderson (I)	21	14	—	14	13	—
1984	Reagan (R)	53	46	—	52	56	+4
	Mondale (D)	39	48	+9	41	37	—
1988	Bush (R)	41	37	—	42	48	+6
	Dukakis (D)	47	54	+7	49	44	—
1992	Clinton (D)	40	56	+16	56	52	—
	Bush (R)	48	34	—	37	42	+5
1996	Clinton (D)	52	48	—	50	55	+5
	Dole (R)	30	41	+11	38	34	—
	Perot (Ref.)	12	7	—	7	6	—
2000*	Gore (D)	39	37	—	39	47	+8
	Bush (R)	50	54	+4	55	46	—
	Others	6	5	—	2	5	—
	No opinion	5	4	—	4	2	—

*Likely voters.

NA = Not available

Source: Karlyn Bowman, American Enterprise Institute; updated by author from Gallup poll, "Gore Gains in Race for President as a Result of Democratic Convention," August 21, 2000; <http://www.Gallup.com/poll/release/pr0082.asp>.

Studies have also shown that convention watchers tend to make their voting decisions earlier in the campaign.[34] Whether they make those decisions because they watch the convention or whether they watch the convention because they are more partisan and politically aware, and have made or are making their voting decisions, is unclear, however. Nonetheless, a significant portion of the electorate claim that they decide for whom they will vote at the time of the convention. In 2000, that proportion was estimated to be 14 percent.

CHARACTERISTICS OF THE NOMINEES

The nominations of relatively obscure governors by the Democrats in 1976, 1988, and 1992 and a former movie actor and California governor by the Republicans in 1980 indicate that changes in the preconvention process have affected the kind of people chosen by their parties. In theory, many are qualified. The Constitution prescribes only three formal criteria for the presidency: a minimum age of thirty-five, a fourteen-year residence in the United States, and native-born status. Naturalized citizens are not eligible for the office.

In practice, a number of informal qualifications have limited the pool of potential nominees. Successful candidates have usually been well known and active in politics, and have held high government positions. Of all the positions from which to seek the presidential nomination, the presidency is clearly the best. Only five incumbent presidents (three of whom were vice presidents who had succeeded to the office) have failed in their quest for the nomination. It should be noted, however, that several others were persuaded to retire rather than face tough challenges.

Over the years, there has been a variety of paths to the White House. When the congressional caucus system was in operation, the position of secretary of state was regarded as a stepping-stone to the nomination if the incumbent chose not to seek another term. When national conventions replaced the congressional caucus, the Senate became the incubator for most successful presidential candidates. After the Civil War, governors emerged as the most likely contenders, particularly for the party that did not control the White House. Governors of large states possessed a political base, a prestigious executive position, and leverage by virtue of their control over their delegations.[35] Today, the vice presidency is seen as a stepping-stone to the presidential nomination.

There are other informal criteria, although they have less to do with qualifications for office than with public prejudices. Only white males have ever been nominated by either of the major parties although African Americans have sought the Democratic nomination. Until John F. Kennedy's election in 1960, no Catholic had been elected, although Governor Alfred E. Smith of New York was chosen by the Democrats in 1928. Joseph Lieberman's selection as Al Gore's running mate is the first time a Jewish American has been nominated for that position. Michael Dukakis was the first candidate whose ancestry could not be traced to northern Europe, a surprising commentary on a country that has prided itself for many years on being a melting pot. The selection of a woman, Geraldine Ferraro, by the Democrats in 1984 for their vice presidential nomination, the candidacy of Elizabeth Dole for her party's 2000 presidential nomination, and the appeal of General Colin Powell in 1996 as a potential Republican candidate and Hillary Rodham Clinton as a future Democratic candidate, however, have made gender and race seem less of a barrier today than they were in the past.

Public attitudes are changing. A poll taken after Lieberman's selection found an overwhelming percentage of those surveyed (88 percent) indicated that Lieberman's Jewish religion made no difference to them.[36] Gallup polls reveal a growing public tolerance toward electing people of various racial and religious backgrounds to the nation's highest office. A 1999 survey indicated that being a woman, an African American, or a Jew no longer automatically disqualifies an individual in the minds of most Americans. However, a significant proportion of the population would still not vote for an atheist or a homosexual for president. Table 5–3 presents the findings of Gallup polls over a sixty-year period.

Personal matters, such as health and family life, can also be factors. After Alabama governor George Wallace was crippled by a would-be assassin's bullet, even his own supporters began to question his ability to withstand the rigors of the office. As noted previously, Senator Thomas Eagleton was forced to withdraw as the Democratic vice presidential nominee in 1972 when his past psychological illness became public. Before George W. Bush announced Dick Cheney's selection as his running mate, he had his father, former President George Bush, inquire about Cheney's medical condition. Cheney, who had suffered three heart attacks in the 1980s, was described by his Houston doctors as in excellent health. Democratic candidates John Kerry and Bob Graham had much-publicized operations for cancer and heart disease, respectively, at the beginning of the 2003–2004 election cycle. Today, presidential and vice presidential candidates are expected to release detailed medical reports on themselves.

Family ties have also affected nominations and elections, as the father–son relationship between the Bushes demonstrates. There have been only two bachelors elected president, James Buchanan and Grover Cleveland.[37] During the 1884 campaign, Cleveland was accused of fathering an illegitimate child and was taunted by his opponents with "Ma, Ma, Where's my Pa? Gone to the White House, Ha! Ha! Ha!" Cleveland admitted responsibility for the child, even though he was not certain he was the father.

Until 1980, no person who was divorced had ever been elected. Andrew Jackson, however, married a divorced woman, or at least a woman he thought was divorced. As it turned out, she had not been granted the final court papers legally dissolving her previous marriage. When this information became public during the 1828 campaign, Jackson's opponents asked rhetorically, "Do we want a whore in the White House?"[38] Jackson and Cleveland both won. That a candidate has been divorced and remarried seems to have little impact or even gain much notoriety today.

Adultery is another matter. Senator Edward Kennedy's marital problems and his driving accident on Chappaquiddick Island, off the coast of Massachusetts, in which a young woman riding with the senator was drowned, were serious impediments to his presidential candidacy in 1980. Gary Hart's alleged "womanizing" forced his withdrawal in 1988, and made his reentry into Democratic presidential

TABLE 5–3 🏆

TOLERANCE IN VOTING FOR WOMEN AND MINORITIES
FOR PRESIDENT (PERCENTAGE WHO WOULD *NOT* VOTE FOR
A PERSON WITH CERTAIN CHARACTERISTICS)

Characteristic	Year			
	1937	1958	1978	1999
Women	64%	41%	19%	07%
African American	—	53	18	04
Jew	47	28	12	06
Catholic	30	24	04	04
Atheist	—	75	53	48
Homosexual	—	—	66	37

Source: Frank Newport, "Americans Today Much More Accepting of a Woman, Black, Catholic, or Jew as President," Gallup Organization, <http://www.gallup.com/poll/releases/pr990329.asp>, April 1, 1999. Reprinted by permission.

politics problematic. Similarly, the length of the period between Pat Robertson's marriage and the birth of his first son raised some eyebrows and was a topic of conversation and concern among some of his religious followers.

Bill Clinton's nomination in 1992, despite the allegations of marital infidelity, marijuana smoking, and draft dodging, and in 1996, despite a pending sexual harassment suit by an Arkansas employee and the ongoing Whitewater investigation, as well as George W. Bush's self-admitted binge drinking as a younger man suggest that the electorate is more concerned about contemporary conditions and behavior than they are with relationships and behavior that have occurred in previous years, especially in the distant past.[39]

The informal qualifications of the presidential nominee have in general been matched by those of the vice presidential candidate as well. (For lists of Republican and Democratic Party conventions and nominees, see Appendix E.)

SUMMARY

With the end of the competitive stage of the caucuses and primaries coming earlier and earlier, candidates who emerge victorious have to continue campaigning right up until their national convention even though their nomination may be secure. During this interregnum, which in 2000 lasted more than four months and which in 2004 may last longer, the winners must consolidate their base, unify their party, and gain the support and endorsements of their nomination opponents. In addition, they may have to raise money for the party, and if they did not accept federal funds, they also need to raise it for themselves. They have to plan their general election strategy, developing and testing the themes they wish to articulate and the personal images they want to project. Moreover, they have to stay in the news, avoid mistakes, and build their campaign organization. There is little rest for the weary.

As the nomination process now preordains the party's presidential candidate and control of the committees that set the rules, review the credentials, and draft the platform, the national nominating conventions have become more entertainment than news. Great effort goes into scripting and orchestrating the meetings to present a good show, one that will attract viewers, emphasize mainstream policy positions, and create or reinforce leadership images.

The parties still see their conventions as important events that provide a favorable environment for beginning their fall campaigns. From the perspective of convention planners, the goals are to convey unified partisans who enthusiastically and confidently support their nominees. From the perspective of the party, the goals are to raise the spirits and hopes of its workers, both delegates and the partisans at home, obtain even more donations, and mobilize the faithful for the fall campaign. From the perspective of the nominees, the goals are to demonstrate their broad-based policy appeal and strong leadership images.

The press covering the convention have different goals. Not oblivious to their public service function, they still need to maximize their viewing audience by reporting the convention as news, as well as presenting it as the party's public relations spectacular. To do this, they must find and report newsworthy events, those that are dramatic, divisive, and unexpected, provide analysis, and engage in endless prognosis about what it all means for the election and for the next government.

Although contemporary conventions are highly theatrical events, they do attract public attention, increase electoral awareness, and help shape perceptions of the candidates, parties, and their respective issue positions. Their impact varies with the attitudes and predispositions of those who watch or read about them. For partisans, conventions reinforce allegiances making party identifiers more likely to vote and work for their party's nominees. For those less oriented toward a particular party, conventions deepen interest in the campaign; in 2000, they also contributed to a more positive outlook about the candidates and their parties. In general, conventions provide the electorate with information with which to make a more informed voting decision; they also hasten that decision for a certain percentage of voters.

The changes in the nominating process have also affected the characteristics, qualities, and background of those gaining their party's nomination. They have enlarged the selection zone for potential standard-bearers. It is unlikely that a Democratic convention before 1972 would have chosen a McGovern, Carter, Dukakis, or even Clinton, or that a former movie actor and governor would have come as close as Reagan did to defeating President Gerald Ford for the Republican nomination in 1976. Moreover, the selection of a woman by the Democrats in 1984 and a Jew in 2000 as vice presidential nominees combined with the boomlet for General Colin Powell in 1996 and Elizabeth Dole's own candidacy four years later suggests that gender, religion, and race may no longer be the critical criteria they once were for presidential and vice presidential nominees. Times have changed; the electorate, reflecting the mores of the society, has become more tolerant. The selection zone has gotten larger.

WHERE ON THE WEB?

The political parties are obviously a good source of information about their nominating conventions. Here again are the sites for the major parties and the Green and Reform Parties.

- **Democratic National Committee**
  http://www.democrats.org
- **Green Party**
  http://www.greenparty.org
- **Reform Party**
  http://www.reformparty.org
- **Republican National Committee**
  http://www.rnc.org
  For other parties see:
- **Democracy Network**
  http://www.dnet.org

EXERCISES

1. Compare the Democratic and Republican conventions on the basis of their schedules, the tenor of their televised speeches, and their video presentations. Which did you find more interesting and why?
2. Compare the acceptance speeches of the major party candidates for the presidential and vice presidential nominations. On the basis of your comparison, indicate to what extent these speeches augured the principal appeals of the candidates in the general election. Compare these appeals to those of the minor party candidates.
3. Contrast the major party platforms with those of two third parties, one on the left of the political spectrum and one on the right. Are the major parties both centrist with most of their positions within the mainstream of American public opinion? With which of these platforms do you have the most agreement?
4. Looking back toward the last presidential campaign or forward to the next, indicate which parts of the Republican and Democratic Parties' platform positions were emphasized by the candidates and to whom were they emphasized. Which parts of their platforms did the candidates conveniently forget? On the basis of your analysis, which of the major party candidates seemed more loyal to his party in speeches, advertising, or debate responses? (You can obtain information about the candidates from their Web sites.)
5. Examine the inauguration address of the newly elected president and any other major addresses made within the first one hundred days in office to see which of the party's platform positions are highlighted and which are not. On the basis of your analysis, do you think that platforms are important agenda setters for the new administration?

SELECTED READING

Adler, Wendy Zeligson. "The Conventions on Prime Time." In *The Homestretch: New Politics,* edited by Martha FitzSimon and Edward C. Pease, 55–57. New York: The Freedom Forum Media Studies Center, 1992.

Cammarano, Joseph, and Jim Josefson, "Putting It in Writing: An Examination of Presidential Candidate Platforms in the 1992 Election." *Southeastern Political Review* 23 (June 1995): 187–204.

Davis, James W. *National Conventions in an Age of Party Reform.* Westport, Conn.: Greenwood Press, 1983.

Maisel, L. Sandy. "The Platform-Writing Process." *Political Science Quarterly* 108 (Winter 1993–1994): 671–698.

Pavlik, John V. "Insider's Guide to Coverage of the Conventions and the Fall Campaign." In *The Homestretch,* 40–54.

Shafer, Byron E. *Bifurcated Politics: Evolution and Reform in the National Party Convention.* Cambridge, Mass.: Harvard University Press, 1988.

Smith, Larry David, and Dan Nimmo. *Cordial Concurrence: Orchestrating National Party Conventions in the Telepolitical Age.* New York: Praeger, 1991.

NOTES

1. Stan Greenberg quoted in Charles T. Royer (ed.), *Campaign for President: The Managers Look at '92* (Hollis, N.H.: Hollis Publishing, 1994), 184–185.
2. In August, following the Republican convention, Bush criticized Democratic candidate Michael Dukakis for his softness on crime, his weak defense posture, his environmental record in Massachusetts, and his association with liberal policy and liberal groups.
3. Dan Balz and Terry M. Neal, "Suddenly Sunny Gore Lets Allies Rain on Bush," *Washington Post,* June 1, 2000, A4.
4. Alison Mitchell, "Bush Strategy Recalls Clinton on the Trail in '96." *New York Times,* April 18, 2000, A18.
5. Terry M. Neal and Ceci Connolly, "Bush, Gore Both Grab for Reform Mantle," *Washington Post,* March 13, 2000, A4.
6. Alison Mitchell, "Bush's Strategy Evokes Images of Rose Garden," *New York Times,* July 17, 2000, <http://www.nytimes.com>.
7. "Excerpts from Interview with Bush on Campaign Issues and Election Strategy," *New York Times,* March 16, 2000, A16.
8. George McGovern, conversation with the author.
9. In detailing its logistic requirements for the party's 2004 convention, the Democrats asked cities bidding for the convention for 17,000 hotel rooms, 125 air-conditioned buses, and control over the convention site for a three-month period, preceding and following the meetings.
10. Perhaps the most famous of all keynote addresses was William Jennings Bryan's. A relatively unknown political figure, Bryan, at the age of thirty-six, electrified the Democratic convention of 1896 with his famous "Cross of Gold" speech. His remarks generated so much enthusiasm that the delegates turned to him to lead them as their standard-bearer. He did, and lost.
11. Ann Richards, "Address to the Democratic Convention in Atlanta, Georgia, on July 19, 1988," as quoted in *Congressional Quarterly* 46 (July 23, 1988): 2024.

12. Buchanan had agreed to submit a copy of his speech to Bush's managers twenty-four hours in advance of delivery to ensure that it was consistent with the campaign's themes and did not preempt former President Ronald Reagan who was to follow Buchanan. Fearful that the campaign organization would leak the speech, however, Buchanan decided to submit one speech and give another address, one of his stump speeches which was shown only to convention coordinator Craig Fuller and faxed to Bob Teeter, Bush's pollster and strategist. Bay Buchanan, quoted in Royer, *Campaign for President*, 208.

13. Quoted in Malcom Moos and Stephen Hess, *Hats in the Ring* (New York: Random House, 1960), 157–158.

14. "Transcript of Gore's Speech," Associated Press, <http://wire.ap.org>, August 17, 2000.

15. In both cases, grassroots challenges to old-line party leaders generated competing delegate claims. The convention in 1912 rejected these challengers and seated the regular party delegates, producing a walkout by Roosevelt's supporters and giving the nomination to Taft. Forty years later, the delegates denied the nomination to Taft's son by recognizing the credential of delegates pledged to Eisenhower and rejecting those supporting Senator Taft.

16. The California challenge at the 1972 Democratic convention illustrates the last of these complaints. George McGovern had won the primary and, according to California law at the time, was entitled to all the delegates. The party's credentials committee, however, decided that the state's delegates should be divided in proportion to the popular vote because the commission that had revised the Democratic rules for 1972 (a commission McGovern initially chaired) had affirmed the principle of proportional voting, although it did not require states to change their law to conform to this principle until 1976. McGovern challenged the credentials committee ruling and won on the convention floor, thereby making his nomination all but certain.

17. Gerald M. Pomper, "Control and Influence in American Politics," *American Behavioral Scientist* 13 (November/December 1969): 223–228; Gerald M. Pomper with Susan S. Lederman, *Elections in America* (New York: Longman, 1980), 161.

18. Ibid., 161. One reason that platform promises have been kept is that elected officials participate in the drafting; in fact, they hold many of the key committee positions. For the party in power, the incumbent president seeking reelection usually takes the lead, exercising the most influence over the composition of the platform committee and the product it produces. For the party out of power, the chair of the national committee usually selects the leadership of the platform committee, and the successful nominee usually controls a majority of the delegates.

19. Thomas E. Patterson, "Lessons from the Last Convention," *Vanishing Voter*, Joan Shorenstein Center on the Press, Politics, and Public Policy, August 13, 2000, <http://www.vanishingvoter.org/releases/08-13-00conv-1.shtml>.

20. Gallup Poll, "Most Americans Think Conventions Serve a Useful Purpose," July 20, 2000, <http://www.gallup.com/poll/072100.asp>.

21. Kathleen Hall Jamison et al., "The Public Learned about Bush and Gore from Conventions; Half Ready to Make an Informed Choice," Annenberg Public Policy Center, August 25, 2000, 2; "GOP Convention Struggles for Audience," *Vanishing Voter*, August 11, 2000, <http://www.vanishingvoter.org/releases/08-25-00conv.shtml>.

22. Patterson, "Lessons from the Last Convention."

23. "GOP Convention Struggles."

24. Jamison et al., "The Public Learned about Bush and Gore from Conventions," 2.

25. PC Data Online, a firm that monitors traffic on news sites, reported a 14 percent drop in the number of people who accessed these sites during the conventions. Howard Kurtz,

"Web Coverage Does Not Spark Convention Interest, *Washington Post*, August 14, 2000, <http://www.washingtonpost.com/wp-dyn/articles/ A246142000Aug14.html>.

26. Convention viewers say that they find media's analysts less interesting than party-produced speeches, documentaries, and interviews.

27. "Republicans Orchestrate a Three-Night TV Special," *Broadcasting*, August 28, 1972, 12.

28. Thomas E. Patterson, *The Mass Media Election* (New York: Praeger, 1980), 72–74.

29. Jamison et al., "The Public Learned about Bush and Gore from Conventions," 2; "Voter Involvement Index," *Vanishing Voter*, August 20, 2000, <http://www.vanishingvoter. org/graphs/vi08-20-00.shtml>.

30. Jamison et al., "The Public Learned about Bush and Gore from Conventions," 2.

31. Gallup Poll, "Bush up 54% to 37% over Gore after GOP Convention," August 7, 2000, <http://www.gallup.com/poll/releases/pr000807.asp>; Gallup Poll "Gore Gains in Race for President as Result of Democratic Convention," August 21, 2000, <http://www.gallup. com/poll/releases/pr000821.asp>.

32. Jamison et al., "The Public Learned about Bush and Gore from Conventions," 3–5; "Conventions Boost Americans' Issue Awareness," *Vanishing Voter*, August 30, 2000.

33. Ibid.

34. Patterson, *Mass Media Election*, 103.

35. The House of Representatives has not been a primary source of nominees. Only one sitting member of the House, James A. Garfield, has ever been elected president, and he was chosen on the thirty-fifth ballot. In recent nomination contests, however, a number of representatives have sought their party's nomination. Representative Morris Udall finished second to Jimmy Carter in 1976; Representative John Anderson competed for the Republican nomination in 1980 before running as an independent candidate in the general election. In 1988, Representatives Jack Kemp and Richard Gephardt were candidates for their party's nomination. There were no serious House candidates for either party in 1992. In 1996, Representative Robert Dornan sought the Republican nomination while Speaker Newt Gingrich did not close the door on a potential draft movement for his nomination. The only House candidate in 2000 was Republican John Kasich of Ohio. Two House members, former minority leader Richard Gephardt and Dennis Kucinich, were candidates for the Democratic nomination in 2004.

36. Gallup Poll, "Positive Public Reaction to Gore's Choice of Lieberman as VP," August 8, 2000, <http://www.gallup.com/poll/releases/pr000808.asp>.

37. Historian Thomas A. Bailey reports that in his quest for the presidency, Buchanan was greeted by a banner carried by a group of women that read, "Opposition to Old Bachelors." *Presidential Greatness* (New York: Appleton-Century Crofts, 1966), 74.

38. Ibid.

39. Clinton feared that he would not have been renominated and reelected if the Monica Lewinsky affair had become public before the convention and general election campaign.

PART III

The Presidential Campaign

ORGANIZATION, STRATEGY, AND TACTICS

6

INTRODUCTION

Elections have been held in the United States since 1789; campaigning by parties for their nominees began soon thereafter. It was not until the end of the nineteenth century, however, that presidential candidates actively participated in the campaigns. Personal solicitation was viewed as demeaning and unbecoming of the dignity and status of the presidency.

Election paraphernalia, distributed by the parties, first appeared in the 1820s; by 1828, there was extensive public debate about the candidates. Andrew Jackson, and to a lesser extent, John Quincy Adams, generated considerable commentary and controversy. Jackson's supporters lauded him as a hero, a man of the people, "a new or second Washington"; his critics referred to him as "King Andrew the first," alleging that he was immoral, tyrannical, and brutal.[1] Adams was also subjected to personal attack. Much of this heated rhetoric appeared in the highly partisan press of the times.

The use of the campaign to reach, entertain, inform, and mobilize the general electorate began on a large scale in 1840. Festivals, parades, slogans, jingles, and testimonials were employed to energize voters. The campaign of 1840 is best remembered for the slogan, "Tippecanoe and Tyler too," promoting Whig candidates General William Henry Harrison, hero of the battle of Tippecanoe in the War of 1812, and John Tyler, and for its great jingles:

WHAT HAS CAUSED THIS GREAT COMMOTION?
(SUNG TO THE TUNE OF "LITTLE PIG'S TAIL")

What has caused this great commotion, motion, motion,
Our country through?
It is the ball a rolling on, on.

Chorus
For Tippecanoe and Tyler too—Tippecanoe and Tyler too,
And with them we'll beat little Van, Van, Van, [Martin Van Buren]
Van is a used up man,
And with them we'll beat little Van.[2]

The successful Whig campaign made it a prototype for subsequent presidential contests.

The election of 1840 was also the first in which a party nominee actually campaigned for himself. General William Henry Harrison made twenty-three speeches in his home state of Ohio.[3] He did not set a precedent that was quickly followed, however. It was twenty years before another presidential candidate took to the stump and then under the extraordinary conditions of the onset of the Civil War and the breakup of the Democratic Party.

Senator Stephen A. Douglas, Democratic candidate for president, spoke out on the slavery issue to try to heal the split that it had engendered within his party. In doing so, however, he denied his own personal ambitions. "I did not come here to solicit your votes," he told a Raleigh, North Carolina, audience. "I have nothing to say for myself or my claims personally. I am one of those who think it would not be a favor to me to be made President at this time."[4]

Abraham Lincoln, Douglas's Republican opponent, refused to reply, even though he had debated Douglas two years earlier in their contest for the Senate seat from Illinois, a contest Douglas won. Lincoln, who almost dropped out of public view when the campaign was under way, felt that it was not even proper for him to vote for himself.[5] He cut his own name from the Republican ballot before he cast it for others in the election.[6]

For their part, the Republicans mounted a massive campaign on Lincoln's behalf. They held what were called "Wide Awake" celebrations in which large numbers of people were mobilized. An account of one of these celebrations reported that

> the Wide-Awake torch-light procession is undoubtedly the largest and most imposing thing of the kind ever witnessed in Chicago. Unprejudiced spectators estimate the number at 10,000. Throughout the whole length of the procession were scattered portraits of Abraham Lincoln. Banners and transparencies bearing Republican mottoes, and pictures of rail splitters, were also plentifully distributed. Forty-three bands of music were also in the procession.[7]

Presidential candidates remained on the sidelines until the 1880s. Republican James Garfield broke the tradition by receiving visitors at his Ohio home. Four years later in 1884, Republican James Blaine made hundreds of campaign speeches in an unsuccessful effort to offset public accusations that he profited from a fraudulent railroad deal. Benjamin Harrison, the Republican candidate in 1888, resumed the practice of seeing people at his home, a practice that has been referred to as front-porch campaigning. Historian Keith Melder writes that Harrison met with 110 delegations consisting of almost 200,000 people in the course of the campaign.[8] William McKinley saw even more visitors over the course of his front-porch campaign in 1896. He spoke to approximately 750,000 people who were recruited and in some cases transported to his Canton, Ohio, home by the Republican Party.[9]

McKinley's opponent, William Jennings Bryan, actually traveled around the country making speeches. By his own account, he logged more than 18,000 miles and made more than six hundred speeches, and, according to press estimates, he spoke to almost 5 million people, nearly collapsing from exhaustion at the end of the campaign.[10]

In 1900, Republican vice presidential candidate Theodore Roosevelt took on Bryan, "making 673 speeches, visiting 567 towns in twenty-four states, and traveling 21,209 miles."[11] Twelve years later, ex-president Theodore Roosevelt, once again took to the hustings, only this time he was trying to defeat a fellow Republican president, William Howard Taft, for his party's nomination. Roosevelt won nine primaries, including one in Ohio, Taft's home state, but was denied the nomination by party leaders. He then launched an independent candidacy in the general election, campaigning on the Progressive, or "Bull Moose," ticket. His Democratic opponent, Woodrow Wilson, was also an active campaigner. The Roosevelt and Wilson efforts ended the era of passive presidential campaigning. The last front-porch campaign was waged by Warren G. Harding in 1920.

Harding's campaign was distinguished in another way; he was the first to use radio to speak directly to voters. This new electronic medium and television, which followed it, radically changed presidential campaigns. Initially, candidates were slow to adjust their campaign styles to these new techniques.[12] It was not until Franklin Delano Roosevelt that radio was employed skillfully in political campaigns. Roosevelt also pioneered the "whistle-stop" campaign train, which stopped at railroad stations along the route to allow the candidate to address the crowds that came to see and hear him. In 1932, Roosevelt, who personally took a train to Chicago to accept his nomination, visited thirty-six states, traveling some 13,000 miles in his presidential campaign. His extensive travels, undertaken in part to dispel a whispering campaign about his health—he had polio as a young man, which left him unable to walk or even stand up unaided—forced President Herbert Hoover onto the campaign trail.[13]

Instead of giving the small number of speeches he had originally planned, Hoover logged more than 10,000 miles, traveling across much of the country. He was the first incumbent president to campaign actively for reelection. Thereafter, with the exception of Franklin Roosevelt during World War II, personal campaigning became standard for incumbents and nonincumbents alike.

Harry Truman took incumbent campaigning a step further. Perceived as the underdog in the 1948 election, Truman whistle-stopped the length and breadth of the United States, traveling 32,000 miles and averaging ten speeches a day. In eight weeks, he spoke to an estimated 6 million people.[14] While Truman was rousing the faithful with his down-home comments and hard-hitting criticisms of the Republican-controlled Congress, his opponent, Thomas E. Dewey, was promising new leadership but providing few particulars. His sonorous speeches contrasted sharply and unfavorably with Truman's straightforward attacks.

The end of an era in presidential campaigning occurred in 1948. Within the next four years television came into its own as a communications medium. The number of television viewers grew from less than half a million in 1948 to approximately 19 million in 1952, a figure that was deemed sufficient in the minds of campaign planners to launch a major television effort. The Eisenhower presidential organization budgeted almost $2 million for television, and the Democrats promised to use both radio and television "in an exciting, dramatic way" in that election.[15]

The potential of television was evident from the outset. Republican vice presidential candidate, Richard Nixon, took to the airwaves in 1952 to reply to accusations that he had appropriated campaign funds for his personal use and had received money and other gifts from wealthy supporters, including a black-and-white cocker spaniel named Checkers. Nixon denied the charges but said that under no circumstances would he and his family give up the dog, which his children dearly loved. A huge outpouring of public sympathy for Nixon followed, effectively ending the issue, keeping him on the ticket, and demonstrating the impact television could have on a political career and a presidential campaign.

Television made mass appeals easier, but it also created new obstacles for the nominees. Physical appearance became more important as did oratory skill. Instead of just rousing a crowd, presidential aspirants had to convey a personal message and compelling image to television viewers.

Television had other effects as well. It eventually replaced the party as the principal link between the nominees and the voters. It decreased the incentive for holding so many election events—rallies, parades, speeches—since many more people could be reached through this mass medium. It also required that campaign activities and events be carefully orchestrated and scripted, keeping in mind how they would appear on the screen and what images they would convey to voters. Off-handed comments and quips were discouraged because they invariably got candidates into trouble.

The people who organized and ran campaigns were also affected. Public relations experts were called on to apply mass marketing techniques. Pollsters and media consultants supplemented and to some extent replaced old-style politicians in designing and executing strategies. Even the candidates seemed a little different. With the possible exception of Lyndon Johnson and Gerald Ford, both of whom succeeded to the presidency through the death or resignation of their predecessors, incumbents and challengers alike reflected the grooming and schooling of the age of mass communications. And where they did not, as in the cases of Walter Mondale, Michael Dukakis, and Robert Dole, they fared poorly.

This chapter and the one that follows discuss these aspects of modern presidential campaigns. Organization, strategy, and tactics serve as the principal focal points of this chapter, whereas news coverage, image and issue projection, and the impact of the media on campaigns are addressed in the next one.

The next section of this chapter describes the structures of modern presidential campaigns and the functions they perform. It examines attempts to create hierarchical campaign organizations but also notes the decentralizing pressures. The tensions between candidate organizations and the regular party structure are alluded to as is the relationship between the campaign organization and the new administration.

The basic objectives that every strategy must address are explored in the section that follows. These include designing a basic appeal, creating a leadership image, sometimes coping with the incumbency factor, and building a winning geographic coalition. The last section of the chapter deals with tactics, describing the techniques for communicating a candidate's message, orchestrating the campaign, targeting and timing appeals, and finally, turning out the voters on election day.

ORGANIZATION

Running the Campaign

Running a campaign is a complex, time-consuming, nerve-racking venture. It involves coordinating a variety of functions and activities, including advance work, scheduling, press arrangements, issue research, speech writing, polling and focus groups, media advertising and placement, finances and legal issues, and party and interest group activities. To accomplish these varied tasks, a large, specialized campaign organization is necessary.

All recent presidential campaigns have had such organizations with similar features. There is a chairperson who presides over the organization and acts as a liaison between the candidate, the party, and the public; a hands-on manager who oversees the operation; a political director and several deputies charged with supervising day-to-day activities; a press secretary, speechwriters, and a research team; usually an administrative head of the national headquarters; division chiefs for special operations; and a geographic hierarchy that reaches to the state and local levels. Every campaign also has its pollsters, media consultants, strategists, and grassroots organizers, plus an array of technical experts, including accountants and lawyers.

Within this basic structure, organizations have varied somewhat in style and operation. Most have been centralized, with a few individuals making the key strategic and tactical decisions; a few have been decentralized. Some have worked through or in conjunction with national and state party organizations; others have disregarded these groups and created their own field organizations. Some have operated from a comprehensive game plan; others have adopted a more incremental, design-it-as-you-go approach. In some, the nominees have assumed an active decision-making role; in others, the candidates defer to the principal campaign advisers who collectively make major strategic and tactical decisions.

The Goldwater (1964), Nixon (1972), Reagan (1984), Bush (1988), Clinton (1992 and 1996) and George W. Bush (2000) campaigns all exemplify the tight, hierarchical structure in which a few individuals control decision making and access to the candidate. In Goldwater's case, his chief advisers were suspicious of top party regulars, most of whom did not support the senator's candidacy. They opted for an organization of believers, one that would operate in an efficient fashion.[16]

The same desire for control and for circumventing the party was evident in Richard Nixon's reelection campaign in 1972. Completely separated from the national party, even in title, the Committee to Reelect the President (known as CREEP by its critics) raised its own money, conducted its own public relations (including polling and campaign advertising), scheduled its own events, and even had its own security division. It was this division, which operated independently from the Republican Party, that harassed the Democratic campaign of George McGovern by heckling his speeches, spreading false rumors, and perpetrating other illegal acts, including the attempted wiretapping of the Democratic National Committee headquarters at the Watergate Office Building.

The excesses perpetuated by individuals in this group illustrate both the difficulty of overseeing all the aspects of a large presidential campaign and the risk of placing nonprofessionals in key positions of responsibility. Had the more experienced Republican National Committee exercised greater influence over the presidential campaign, there might have been less deviation from accepted standards of behavior.

The Reagan and Bush (1988) efforts operated more closely with state Republican Party organizations than had either Goldwater's or Nixon's. Directed by separate campaign organizations, each was linked to the party at both the national and the state levels. Fund-raising efforts and grassroots activities were primarily party affairs, whereas the presidential campaign organization exercised most of the control over the basic strategy, thematic content of the campaign, relations with the media, resource allocation, and the scheduling and appearances of the presidential and vice presidential candidates.[17]

The George W. Bush campaign in 2000 also was a model of the well-run, well-coordinated effort. Four of Bush's closest friends and political advisors in his race for governor oversaw the campaign from its inception to its conclusion. Donald L. Evans functioned as the national finance chairman. After the money phase of the campaign was concluded, he served as campaign chairman. Karl Rove, who had planned Bush's challenge to Governor Ann Richards, was the campaign's principal political strategist, Joe Allbaugh, the day-to-day campaign manager, and Karen P. Hughes, director of communications and principal link to the news media (see Figure 6–1).

Democratic campaign organizations have tended to be looser in structure and more decentralized in operation than have the Republicans'. Until the 1970s, the Democrats had stronger state parties and a weaker national base. As a consequence, their presidential candidates tended to rely more heavily on state party organizations than did the Republicans. In recent years Democratic presidential campaigns have designated regional and state coordinators to oversee state party efforts on their behalf. These coordinators, placed on the payroll of the state parties to reduce administrative costs, also have served as intermediaries between the official party organizations and the campaign.

Although the organizations of Walter Mondale and Michael Dukakis had difficulty carrying out coordinated campaign efforts, the Clinton campaigns did not. Both his 1992 and 1996 efforts were well-run operations, with carefully designed strategic plans, and a "war room" for tactical operations and quick reactions to events. Both Clinton campaigns relied heavily on pollsters to monitor the public mood. And both depended on a media team to design and target advertising. Clinton himself was heavily involved in these efforts, particularly in the early phases of both campaigns. As president, he ran weekly strategy sessions during the 1995–1996 campaign period in which major issues were discussed and decisions made.[18]

The Gore 2000 campaign initially had organizational problems. Amid Bradley's challenge in 1999, Gore prodded by internal criticism, including that of the president, regrouped, moved to Tennessee, and hired a new campaign manager. These efforts bore fruit during the contested part of the nomination but tensions redeveloped when Gore fell behind Bush in the polls during the spring interregnum. As a consequence, Gore again changed his campaign manager, with William M. Daley, commerce secretary and architect of the Clinton administration's public relations campaign for the North American Free Trade Agreement (NAFTA), taking over for Tony Coelho. Daley imposed discipline on the campaign and helped his candidate regain the initiative by the end of the Democratic

FIGURE 6–1 ⚜

THE GEORGE W. BUSH CAMPAIGN ORGANIZATION IN 2000

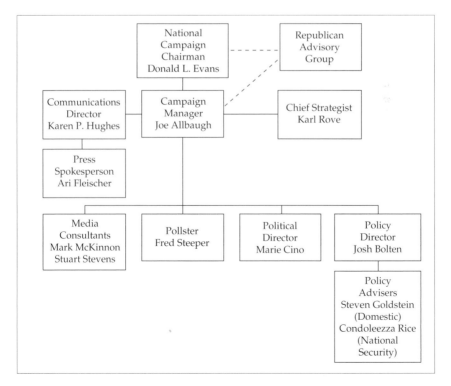

convention. Senior advisers in the Gore campaign included the vice president's college friend and media advisor, Carter Eskew; advertising manager, Bill Knapp, other political consultants, Robert Strum, Tad Devine, and Michael Donilon; and campaign manager, Donna Brazile. Figure 6–2 shows the principals of the Gore organization.

Transitioning to Government

How presidential campaigns are organized, who holds the key positions, and the organization's relationship to the party all have important implications for government. A campaign organization reflects a candidate's management style: a willingness to take advice, to delegate to others, and to make decisions and adhere to them or adjust them if the situation changes. Reagan's reliance on his campaign organization, his reluctance to second-guess his advisers, augured his White House staffing arrangement and his passive administrative style. In contrast, Clinton's penchant for details, his involvement in campaign strategic and tactical decisions, and his constant desire to assess the public mood before, during, and after he voiced his policy preferences were also reflected in the way in which he did business as president. Similarly, George W. Bush's hands-off style suggested the CEO management approach he assumed at the beginning of his presidency.

A second way in which campaigns affect governance is through the personnel who are recruited for key administration positions, particularly for those in the

FIGURE 6–2

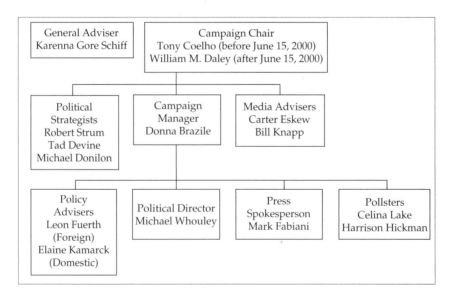

THE GORE CAMPAIGN ORGANIZATION IN 2000

White House. Many of the senior aides in the White House have also served in the inner circles of presidential campaigns, as have many junior aides. However, the success with which these campaign personnel have made the adjustment to White House staff has been mixed at best. In George W. Bush's case, chief political strategist, Karl Rove, and communications director, Karen Hughes, continued to be very influential in their roles in the new administration. Bush's chief policy advisers during the campaign, Josh Bolten, Condoleezza Rice, and Lawrence Lindsay, also were appointed to policy positions in the White House. Of this group, only Lindsay, the president's chief economic aide, was involuntarily terminated within the first two years.

The relationship between the candidate's organization and the party's organization also impacts on governance. Candidates who circumvent their party and its elected officials in the planning and conduct of their presidential campaigns, as Richard Nixon did in 1972, Jimmy Carter did in 1976, and, to a lesser extent, Bill Clinton did in 1992, find it more difficult to mobilize the necessary support in Congress to bridge the separation of powers and govern effectively. They have less inclination to build a strong party organization and more incentive to convert it into a personal following, responsive to their needs, particularly reelection. When the president leaves office, however, these supporters lose their patron and ultimately their position, although they may reappear in other campaigns or other administrations.

When the party loses a presidential campaign, the candidate's organization disintegrates, and the party, blamed in part for the defeat, must try to rebuild itself. Not only does this situation contribute to frequent turnover among national party leaders, but it weakens the party as a result, a scenario which affected the Democrats in 2001 and contributed to that party's defeat in the 2002 midterm elections.

STRATEGIC OBJECTIVES

Strategies are game plans, blueprints, calculated efforts to convince the electorate to vote for a particular candidate. They include a basic appeal as well as a plan for implementing it.

Certain decisions cannot be avoided when developing an electoral strategy. These decisions stem from the rules of the system, the costs of the campaign, the character of the electorate, and the environment in which the election occurs. Each decision involves identifying objectives, allocating resources, and monitoring and adjusting that allocation over the course of the campaign. That is what a strategy is all about: it is a plan for developing, targeting, and tracking campaign resources. Most strategies are articulated before the race begins; a few may be forged during the election itself. In 1984, Reagan strategists designed an elaborate plan well before the Republican convention. The Bush plan in 1988, the Clinton plans in 1992 and 1996, and the George W. Bush strategies in 2000 and 2004 were also designed before their respective conventions met to nominate the candidates.[19] Gore adjusted his during the campaign as did Humphrey in 1968, Dukakis in 1988, Bush in 1992, and Dole in 1996.

Designing a Basic Appeal

The first step in constructing a campaign strategy is designing a basic appeal. This appeal has two principal components: partisan images and key policy positions and priorities. The objective is to frame the electoral choice in as advantageous a manner as possible to the candidate and party.

Partisan Images. All things being equal, the candidates of the dominant party have an advantage that they try to maximize by emphasizing their partisan affiliation, lauding their partisan heroes, and making a blatant partisan appeal. When the Democrats were the majority, their candidates traditionally clothed themselves in the garb of their party. During the same period, the Republicans did not. Eisenhower, Nixon, and Ford downplayed partisan references, pointing instead to their personal qualifications and positions on certain types of issues. As the gap between the two parties narrowed, Republican candidates became more willing to point to their partisan label. Today both major party candidates wear that label proudly.

Identifying with the party is only one way in which the partisan orientations of the electorate are activated and reinforced. Recalling the popular images of the party is another. For the Democrats, common economic interests are still the most compelling link that unites their electoral coalition. Perceived as the party of the average person, the party that got the country out of the Great Depression, the party of labor and minority groups, Democrats have tended to do better when economic issues are salient as they were in 1992 and 1996.

Democratic candidates emphasize "bread-and-butter" issues, such as jobs, wages, education, and other benefits for the working and middle classes. The Democrats contrast their concern for the plight of the average American with the Republicans' ties to the rich and especially to business.

The Democrats' sympathy for the less fortunate, however, has been a mixed blessing in recent years. Beginning in the 1970s and continuing into the 1990s, this sympathy has been perceived by much of the electorate as antithetical to the interests of the middle class. Exploiting this perception, Republicans have repeatedly criticized their liberal "tax-and-spend," big government opponents.

Bill Clinton sought to reassert his party's middle-class appeal in his presidential campaigns. Calling himself a "New Democrat," Clinton took pains to distinguish his own moderate policy orientation from the more liberal views of his Democratic predecessors and the more conservative positions of his Republican opponents. He presented himself as a change-oriented candidate in 1992 and as a builder of progress in 1996. In contrast, Al Gore took a more populist approach in 2000, initially emphasizing his desire to help working families and later pitching his appeal to middle-class voters.

Whereas economic issues have tended to unite the Democrats, social issues have been more divisive. Since the 1970s, Republican presidential candidates have taken advantage of these differences by focusing on those that divide Democrats: school vouchers, private investment of Social Security funds, and programs that establish preferences on the basis of race (such as affirmative action) or that mandate benefits regardless of sexual orientation. In doing so, the Republicans have not only appealed to the fears and frustrations of moderate and conservative

Democrats but have reaffirmed their own support for the traditional American values of individual initiative, family responsibility, and local autonomy.

In 1992, and again in 1996, the Clinton campaign effectively countered this Republican imagery by taking policy positions that promoted family and community values, personal safety, and a less intrusive role for government. In 2000, it was the Republican candidate, George W. Bush, who occupied the political center, addressing the "Democratic" issues of education, health care, and Social Security with his own public–private sector policies. The issues of abortion, gun control, and to a lesser extent, the death penalty are ones that continue to offer clear-cut differences between the parties and for the most part, their nominees.

When foreign policy, national security, and more recently, homeland security are of major concern, Republican candidates have traditionally done better. This is why they tend to stress these issues in their campaigns. In 1952, Eisenhower campaigned on the theme "Communism, Corruption, and Korea," projecting himself as the candidate most qualified to end the war. Nixon took a similar tack in 1968, linking Humphrey to the Johnson administration and the war in Vietnam. Four years later, Nixon varied his message, painting George McGovern as the "peace at any price" candidate and himself as the experienced leader who could achieve peace with honor. Gerald Ford, though, was not nearly as successful in conveying his abilities in foreign affairs, in part because he was overshadowed by the expertise and statesmanship of his secretary of state and national security adviser, Henry Kissinger. Reagan, despite his own lack of experience in foreign affairs, pointed to the Soviet invasion of Afghanistan and to the Iranian hostage situation to criticize the weakness of the Carter administration in 1980, as well as to urge greater expenditures for defense; in 1984, he emphasized the increased defense capacity of the United States and to its success in containing the expansion of communism. Similarly, in 1988 George H. W. Bush cited his experience in foreign affairs and his personal acquaintance with many world leaders, although his emphasis on foreign policy became a liability four years later with the Cold War over, the Persian Gulf War concluded, and the public preoccupied with an economy in recession. Lacking his father's expertise in foreign affairs, George W. Bush did not stress foreign policy in his 2000 campaign but did in 2004 in the light of 9/11.

The general perception that the Democrats are weaker in foreign and military affairs has prompted some of their recent standard-bearers to talk even tougher than their opponents. In his 1976 campaign, Carter vowed that an Arab oil embargo would be seen by his administration as an economic declaration of war. In 1984, Walter Mondale supported the buildup of U.S. defenses, including Reagan's strategic defense initiative. In 1988, Dukakis spoke about the need for the United States to be more competitive within the international economic arena as did Clinton in 1992. Gore emphasized his own foreign policy experience in the House, Senate, and as vice president, pointing to his vote in favor of the resolution in 1991 that authorized the use of armed forces in the Persian Gulf.

Salient Issue Positions. The electoral environment affects the priorities and substance of a candidate's policy appeal. In 1992, the electorate was concerned mostly about the economy, particularly jobs and the federal budget deficit. In 1996, with the economy growing, unemployment low, inflation in check, and the stock market at a record high, the electorate in general expressed satisfaction with the country's economic condition, a situation that favored the incumbent. The salient issues in 2000 were how to improve education, provide tax relief, and put Social Security and Medicare on a firmer financial foundation.

In general, economic issues tend to be the most recurrent concerns in American elections. They "hit home" in a way that social and national security issues may not. A poor economy helps the party that is out of power and hurts an incumbent running for reelection. Ronald Reagan drove the economic problem home in 1980 with the question he posed at the end of his debate with President Jimmy Carter, a question directed at the American people: "Are you better off now than you were four years ago?" Similarly, James Carville, chief strategist of the 1992 Clinton campaign, kept a sign over his desk that read, "It's the economy, stupid." He did not want anyone in the Clinton organization to forget that the poor economy was the campaign's primary issue. Having a weak economy was a particularly severe problem for President George H. W. Bush in 1992 because he faced not one but two challengers who echoed the same theme—economic conditions had deteriorated and the Bush administration was to blame for them.

A strong economy should help the party in power. The economic progress that occurred during the Clinton administration muted Dole's criticism that the economy could do better and would if he were elected. Thus, it is surprising that Gore did not focus more attention on the economic progress that had been made during the previous eight years in his campaign. With his own polls indicating that the electorate credited the president, not the president and vice president, for the economic prosperity, with no effective economic message that tested well among the voters, and with his own desire to distance himself from President Clinton, Gore chose instead to emphasize his policy differences with Bush rather than his policy agreements with Clinton.[20] Only in the final weeks of the campaign did he return to the "prosperity now" theme as a reason for keeping him in office. By then it was too late to make much of a difference. On election day, voters saw both candidates as equally capable of maintaining the economic prosperity.[21]

Creating a Leadership Image

Regardless of the partisan imagery and thematic emphases, candidates for the presidency must stress their own qualifications for the job and cast doubt on their opponents'. They must appear presidential, demonstrating those personal characteristics and leadership qualities the voters consider essential.[22]

Accentuating the Positive. A favorable image, of course, cannot be taken for granted. It has to be created, or at least polished. Contemporary presidents are expected to be strong, assertive, and dominant. During times of crisis or periods of social anxiety, these leadership characteristics are considered absolutely essential. The strength that Franklin Roosevelt was able to convey by virtue of his successful bout with polio, Dwight Eisenhower by his military command in World War II, and Ronald Reagan by his tough talk, clear-cut solutions, and consistent policy goals contrast sharply with the perceptions of Adlai Stevenson in 1956, George

McGovern in 1972, Jimmy Carter in 1980, and Walter Mondale in 1984 as weak, indecisive, and vacillating.

When Gerald Ford and Jimmy Carter were criticized for their failure to provide strong leadership, their campaign organizations countered by focusing on their actions as president, emphasizing those situations in which they were in charge—giving orders, making decisions, announcing policies, negotiating agreements. George H. W. Bush tried to use the same strategy in 1992 as did Clinton in 1996. George W. Bush can also be expected to do so in 2004, pointing to his actions following September 11, 2001, the anti-terrorism campaign at home and abroad, especially the actions taken in Afghanistan and Iraq, as evidence of decisive, bold decision making.

For challengers, the task of seeming to be powerful, confident, and independent (one's own person) can best be imparted by a no-nonsense approach, a show of optimism, and a conviction that success is attainable. John Kennedy's rhetorical emphasis on activity in 1960 and Richard Nixon's tough talk in 1968 about the turmoil and divisiveness in the country helped to generate the impression of a take-charge personality. Kennedy and Nixon were seen as leaders who knew what had to be done and would do it.

George W. Bush took another tack in 2000. He talked quietly in moderate tones to distinguish himself from the strident rhetoric of Washington politicians and to give added credibility to his pledge to pursue a bipartisan approach if elected. In contrast, Gore was more aggressive, more partisan, more passionate, and more issue-oriented. He tried to present himself as the more knowledgeable and experienced candidate.

In addition to seeming tough enough to be president, it is also important to exhibit sufficient knowledge and skills for the job. In the public's mind, personal experience testifies to the ability to perform. In 1992, Bush was able to contrast his governing experience with that of his opponents, leaving Perot to emphasize his can-do qualities as a successful businessman and Clinton to emphasize his experience as governor.

Experience was not an issue in 1996, but in 2000 it was. Although Gore was seen as more knowledgeable than Bush, the latter was able to offset his opponent's advantage by virtue of his performance in the presidential debates, particularly in the second debate which focused on foreign policy. His substantive answers to questions about his policy proposals and how he would deal with potential international problems seemed to allay fears that he did not understand the issues, much less have the cognitive skills necessary to deal with them effectively.

Empathy is also an important attribute for presidential candidates. People want a president who can respond to their emotional needs, one who understands what and how they feel. As the government has become larger, more powerful, and more distant, empathy has become more important. Roosevelt and Eisenhower radiated warmth. Carter, Clinton, and George W. Bush were particularly effective in generating the impression that they cared, whereas Al Gore reached out to those at the lower end of the socioeconomic scale by the priorities he emphasized and the policy positions he took. By comparison, McGovern, Nixon, Dukakis, and Dole appeared cold, distant, and impersonal.

Candor, integrity, and trust emerge periodically as important attributes in presidential image building. Most of the time these traits are taken for granted. Occasionally, however, a crisis of confidence, such as Watergate or the Clinton impeachment, dictates that political skills be downplayed and these personal qualities stressed. Such crises preceded the elections of 1952, 1976, and 2000. In the first two of these elections, Dwight Eisenhower, a war hero, and Jimmy Carter, who promised never to tell a lie, both benefited from the perception that they were honest, decent men not connected with the "mess" in Washington. George W. Bush made much of the scandalous behavior in the Clinton administration during his nomination campaign, but much less during the general election campaign. However, he often repeated the line that brought him the most accolades before Republican audiences: "When I put my hand on the Bible, I will swear to not only uphold the laws of our land, I will swear to uphold the honor and dignity of the office to which I have been elected, so help me God."[23] In contrast, Gore pledged emphatically not to let the American people down.

Character is important in elections when character issues have preoccupied the administration currently in power. It also tends to be more important when less is known about the candidates—at the beginning of their presidential quest. It is less important for reelection because the electorate by then has a basis for evaluating the kind of president that person has made.

Highlighting the Negative. Naturally, candidates can be expected to raise questions about their opponents. These questions assume particular importance if the public's initial impression of the candidates is fuzzy, as it may be with outsiders who win their party's nomination. When Republican polls and focus groups revealed Dukakis's imprecise image in 1988, senior Bush advisers devised a strategy to take advantage of this situation and define Dukakis in ways that would discredit him. The strategy was based on the premise that the higher the negative perceptions of a candidate, the less likely that candidate would be to win.[24] Lee Atwater, architect of this strategy, put it this way: "When I first got into politics, I just stumbled across the fact that candidates who went into an election with negatives higher than 30 or 40 points just inevitably lost."[25]

In 1992, Bush also challenged the qualifications of his opponents. With Clinton's moderate policy positions making it difficult for Bush to paint his challenger as liberal as he had done to Dukakis, Bush chose to emphasize the issues of trustworthiness and candor. But here his campaign ran into a public reactions problem generated by adverse reactions to his negative Dukakis campaign four years earlier and to the allegations about Ross Perot that were leaked to the media by supporters of Bush. Fearing that his first negative commercials would be greeted by a "there he goes again" refrain by the press, the Bush campaign delayed their airing and then introduced them with a touch of humor to soften their effect.[26] Still, voters were leery.[27]

Unlike Dukakis, who chose initially not to dignify Bush's attacks by replying to them, Clinton helped defuse the attacks against him by reacting quickly and directly. This rapid reaction not only deflected criticism, but it also enabled the Clinton campaign to keep the media focus on their issue—the economy—not on the candidate's character.

Negativity has continued in each subsequent election. In 1996, the Clinton campaign unleashed a barrage of press releases, advertisements, and oppositional research in which Dole's extensive voting record in the Senate was criticized. Dole countered with more personal accusations. In 2000, Gore's credibility, particularly his tendency to exaggerate his own importance and embellish stories he told, became the focus of Republican attacks after the first and second presidential debates in which the Democratic candidate misspoke several times. In contrast, the Democratic criticism of Bush was based on his competence, not his character. Democrats alleged that confusion over details and factual errors indicated that Bush lacked a deep understanding of the issues. In the words of television correspondent Cokie Roberts, "The story line is Bush isn't smart enough and Gore isn't straight enough."[28]

In summary, candidates try to project images of themselves that are consistent with public expectations of the office and its occupant. Traits such as inner strength, decisiveness, competence, and experience are considered essential for the office, and others such as empathy, sincerity, credibility, and integrity are viewed as necessary for the individual. Which traits are considered most important vary to some extent with the assessment of the strengths and weaknesses of the incumbent. Challengers try to exploit an incumbent's vulnerabilities by emphasizing the very skills and qualities which the president is said to lack.

Candidates' campaigns almost always stereotype their opponent by associating them with negative party and personal images. Gore and his fellow Democrats described Bush as a conservative Republican whose policies threatened the Social Security and Medicare programs and would benefit the rich at the expense of the less fortunate. The Bush campaign painted Gore as a consummate liberal politician who would say and do anything to get elected.

Dealing with Incumbency

Claiming a leadership image requires a different script for an incumbent than for a challenger. Until the mid-1970s when the media became more critical of presidential performance, incumbents were thought to have an advantage. (See Box 6–1, "An Incumbency Balance Sheet.") Between 1900 and 1972, thirteen incumbents sought reelection and eleven won; and the two who lost, Taft in 1912 and Hoover in 1932, faced highly unusual circumstances. In Taft's case he was challenged by the independent candidacy of former Republican president, Theodore Roosevelt. Together, Taft and Roosevelt split the Republican vote, enabling Democrat Woodrow Wilson to win with only 42 percent of the total vote. Hoover ran during the Great Depression, for which he received much of the blame.

Following the 1972 election, however, incumbents have not fared as well. All have sought reelection, but only Reagan and Clinton have succeeded. Adverse political and economic factors help explain the more recent defeats. The worst political scandal in the nation's history and the worst economic recession in forty years hurt Ford's chances, as did his pardon of the person who had nominated him for the vice presidency, Richard Nixon. In 1980 and 1992, a weak economy, a loss of confidence in the president's leadership abilities, and an anti-Washington mood among the electorate contributed to Carter's and George H. W. Bush's losses.

Today incumbents are advantaged or disadvantaged based on their perceived performance in office. Having a good record contributes to a president's reelection potential just as a poor record detracts from it. Bad times almost always hurt an incumbent. A crisis, however, helps, at least in the short run. Rightly or wrongly, the public places most responsibility for economic conditions, social relations, and foreign affairs on the president. That a president may actually exercise little control over some of these external factors seems less relevant to the electorate than do negative conditions themselves, the desire that they be improved, and the expectation that *the president* do something about them.

Attributes such as personal favorability appear to be less important. Both Carter and George H. W. Bush had favorable personal ratings yet both were defeated in their reelection attempts. Clinton's favorability evaluation was much less positive, yet he was easily reelected in 1996. However, his highly negative ratings in 2000 may have hurt Gore, or so Gore feared and designed a strategy to separate himself from Clinton.

Building a Winning Geographic Coalition

In addition to designing a general appeal and addressing leadership/incumbency issues, a winning geographic coalition must be assembled. Since the election is decided by the Electoral College, the primary objective must always be to win a majority of the college, not necessarily a majority of the popular vote. In the words of George W. Bush's director of policy and media planning, Frank Dowd, "We never put together a plan to win the popular vote. We put together a plan in the states that we targeted based on winning the Electoral College vote."[29]

Electoral College strategies almost always require candidates to campaign in most of the large states with the most electoral votes. Failure to win a majority of these states makes it extremely difficult to put together a winning coalition, although George W. Bush managed to do so in 2000. The basic strategic consideration is how many resources should be expended in these states. The answer usually is a lot, probably even more than the proportional share of the vote these states have in the Electoral College.[30]

Critical to designing an Electoral College strategy is determining the most competitive states. These states assume added importance because of the winner-take-all method by which most states allocate their electoral vote. Polling is used to monitor a candidate's strength in these states as well as the nation as a whole.[31] As polls reveal preference shifts among registered and likely voters, candidates reschedule their campaign appearances and move their resources from state to state, shoring up support in some and building it in others. Resource calculations are made primarily on the basis of polling data, the relative strength or weakness of the party organization in the state, the number of electoral votes that are at stake, and the availability of funds.

In building their Electoral College coalitions, candidates start with their base—areas that have been traditionally favorable to their party's nominees. Following the Civil War, the Democrats could depend on the "Solid South" while Republicans were stronger in the Northeast. Beginning in the 1960s, these areas began to shift their partisan orientation. Conservative, white southerners, reacting

BOX 6–1 ❧

AN INCUMBENCY BALANCE SHEET

Incumbency can be a double-edged sword, strengthening or weakening a claim to leadership. Incumbents ritually point to their accomplishments, noting the work that remains, and sounding a "stay-the-course" theme; challengers argue that it is time for a change and that they can do better.

ADVANTAGES OF INCUMBENCY

Being president is thought to help an incumbent in the quest for reelection more often than not. The advantages stem from the visibility of the office, the esteem it engenders, and the influence it provides. The president is almost always well known. A portion of the population may even have difficulty at the outset in identifying challengers although the extended nomination process contributes to the name recognition of all the candidates in the general election.

Moreover, incumbents are generally seen as experienced and knowledgeable, as leaders who have stood the tests of office in the office. Such a perception benefits incumbents more often than not. Stability and predictability satisfy the public's psychological needs; the certainty of four more years with a known quantity is likely to be more appealing than the uncertainty of the next four years with an unknown one provided the performance in office for the past four years has been viewed as generally acceptable.

Translated into strategic terms, the public's familiarity and comfort with incumbents permits presidents running for reelection to highlight their opponent's lack of experience, and contrast it with their own experience and their record in office. Carter used a variation of this tactic in 1980. He emphasized the arduousness of the job in order to contrast his energy, knowledge, and intelligence with Reagan's. Clinton contrasted himself with his opponent in another way in 1996. He portrayed himself as the candidate for the future and his seventy-three-year-old opponent as the link to the past.

The ability of presidents to make news, to affect events, and to dispense the "spoils" of government can also work to their advantage. Presidents are in the limelight and can maneuver to remain there. Having a "bully pulpit" gives them an advantage in setting the campaign agenda in presidential as well as midterm elections. George W. Bush's emphasis on the war on terrorism and the need to ensure that certain nations, such as Iraq, do not possess biological, chemical, and nuclear weapons in the 2002 midterm elections illustrates how presidents can manipulate the environment to their political advantage.

All recent presidents who have campaigned for reelection have tried to utilize the symbolic and ceremonial presidency, signing legislation into law in the Rose Garden of the White House, meeting heads of state in Washington or their own capitals, making speeches and announcements, holding press conferences, honoring military and civilians—all behind the presidential seal. Clinton emphasized these presidential activities, giving rise to the term *constant campaign*. He all but obliterated the line between governing and campaigning. George W. Bush has done much the same.

Presidents have another trump card. Presumably, their actions can influence events. They try to gear economic recoveries to election years. They also use their discretionary authority to distribute the resources at their disposal, such as grants, contracts, and emergency aid. They must be careful, however, not to seem overtly partisan. Actions that appear to be solely or primarily for political purposes, such as Ford's pardon of Nixon in 1974 or announcements of juicy federal government contracts can backfire.

The incumbency advantages extend to vice presidents seeking their party's presidential nomination but not nearly as much to their general election campaign. Of the four incumbent vice presidents who tried to succeed to the presidency directly from the vice presidency—Nixon (1960), Humphrey (1968), George H.W. Bush (1988), and Al Gore (2000)—only Bush was successful.

The difficulty that incumbent vice presidents face is that they cannot exert leadership skills from a position of followership. To establish their leadership credentials, vice presidents need to get out of the president's shadow; they have to separate themselves from the president. If they do so on the basis of their policy differences with the administration, it becomes that much more difficult to claim and share the successes of that administration. George H. W. Bush dealt with this problem by stating that he would pursue Reagan's agenda but do so in a kinder and gentler way. Moreover, he refused to indicate positions he had taken or advice he had given to Reagan, thereby casting his fate with his popular predecessor and forcing the electorate to judge him in 1988 on the basis of the performance of the administration in which he served. Al Gore, on the other hand, articulated a popularist policy in contrast to the Clinton administration's more incremental, mainstream approach. Moreover, in his acceptance speech at the Democratic convention, Gore made a point of asking voters to support him on the basis of *his* policy goals, not Clinton's. "This election is not an award for past performance. I'm not asking you to vote for me on the basis of the economy we have. Tonight I ask for your support on the basis of the better, fairer, more prosperous America we can build together."[32]

DISADVANTAGES OF INCUMBENCY

Today these incumbency advantages can sometimes be offset by equally strong disadvantages, which stem from the dilemmas contemporary presidents face, the persistent media criticism they encounter, and the anti-Washington, antipolitician mood of the contemporary electorate.

In their campaigns for office, presidential candidates hype themselves, make promises, and create expectations. Once in office, however, they find these expectations difficult to meet. With the constitutional system dividing authority; the political system decentralizing power; and public opinion fluid, ambiguous, often inconsistent, and compartmentalized, it is difficult for presidents to build and maintain a governing consensus. Yet their leadership role demands that they do so—hence the gap between expectations and performance.

Persistent media criticism contributes to these difficulties. With radio and television talk-show hosts railing against them, their policies, and their behavior in office, with television and newspaper investigative reporters heightening public awareness of policy problems and inadequate governmental responses to them, with network news coverage generally more critical of incumbents, particularly during presidential campaigns, presidents find it hard to project a favorable leadership image, although Reagan was able to do so and Clinton gained high job approval ratings during his last five years in office.

negatively to the civil rights revolution, moved into the Republican camp in large numbers. Since 1960, the only Democratic presidential candidates who have been able to win in the South were southerners such as Jimmy Carter (Georgia) who carried much of the South in 1976 but not in 1980 and Bill Clinton (Arkansas) who won approximately half the southern states in 1992 and 1996. Although the increasing social conservatism of the Republican Party has helped that party establish a base in the South, it has also eroded Republican strength in the Northeast, a region that has become increasingly Democratic. With the Rocky Mountain region strongly Republican and the Pacific Coast states leaning Democratic, the focus of recent campaigns has been the Midwest, America's so called weather vane, a region that tends to reflect the country's mood.

Since 1968, Republicans who have won the presidency have concentrated their campaigns in the major battleground states in the Midwest plus California and New York. Victories in a majority of these states, when added to the Republican South and Rocky Mountain areas, have been sufficient to amass an Electoral College majority in six of the last nine elections.

The three Democratic wins, Carter in 1976 and Clinton in 1992 and 1996, were achieved in large part by narrowing the Republican advantage in the South and winning a majority of the large industrial states. When the Republicans are not able to take the South for granted, they must devote more resources to this area. Doing so enables the Democrats to compete more effectively by maximizing their flexibility in deciding where to campaign and how much time, money, and effort to spend.

In 2000, both parties focused their efforts in five key battleground states, an area that extended from Pennsylvania in the mid-Atlantic region to Ohio, Michigan, and Wisconsin in the Midwest to Florida in the South, although at one time or another nineteen states were in contention. Conceding California, Illinois, and New York to the Democrats, Bush's strategists believed that they needed to win at least three and perhaps four of these five targeted states to gain an Electoral College majority. In the end, they won only two, Ohio and Florida, but did better than expected in the traditional Democratic strongholds of Arkansas, Tennessee (Gore's home state), and West Virginia to eke out an Electoral College victory.

The concentration of both campaigns in these key battleground states is evident from the advertising buys of the candidates and their parties. The Brennan Center for Social Justice, in conjunction with faculty at the University of Wisconsin, calculated overall and individual state advertising during the presidential campaign beginning June 1, 2000. According to the center, most of the $167.5 million spent on television advertising was expended in Florida, Illinois, Iowa, Michigan, Missouri, Ohio, Oregon, Pennsylvania, and Wisconsin. Bush and the Republican National Committee also spent about $12 million in California compared only to $107,000 for Gore and the Democrats. The rest of the country did not see much of the advertising for the presidential campaign.[33]

Another factor contributing to the focus in 2000 was the third-party campaign of Ralph Nader. Democrats were so concerned about Nader's incursions into their liberal constituency that they launched a major campaign against him in the final two weeks, arguing that a vote for Nader in toss-up states was in reality a vote for Bush. As part of this effort, an email petition, circulated by some of Nader's past and current supporters, urged him to instruct his backers in the key, competitive states to vote for Gore. To counter the Democrat's anti-Nader push, the pro-Bush Republican Leadership Council ran $100,000 worth of ads quoting Nader's criticism of Gore in Oregon, Minnesota, and Wisconsin.[34]

TACTICAL CONSIDERATIONS

Whereas the basic objectives set the contours of the campaign strategy, tactical considerations influence day-to-day decisions and activities. Tactics are the specific ways by which strategic objectives are achieved. They involve techniques to communicate, target, and time the messages so that they have maximum impact. Unlike strategy, which can be planned well in advance, tactics change with the environment and events.

Occasionally candidates are criticized for overemphasizing tactics at the expense of strategy. This accusation was directed at Bob Dole in 1996 and, to a lesser extent, at Al Gore in 2000.[35] Candidates who fall behind in the polls, such as Dole and Gore, are more apt to change their tactics and policy appeals to find something that works. Take Gore during the presidential debates—confrontational and impolite during the first debate, placid during the second, and physically aggressive during the third.[36]

Reaching Voters

There are a variety of ways to convey a political message, including door-to-door canvassing, direct mail, and mass media. At the local level especially, door-to-door campaigning may be a viable option.

Personal contact is generally considered to have a greater influence on voters than any other kind of campaign activity.[37] It is most effective in stimulating voting. To a lesser extent, it may also influence the decision on how to vote. The problem with personal contact is that it is time-consuming, volunteer-intensive, and reaches a limited number of people.

The Kennedy organization in 1960 was one of the first to mount a campaign on the local level. Using the canvass as a device to identify supporters and solicit workers, Kennedy's aides built precinct organizations with the newly recruited volunteers. The volunteers, in turn, distributed literature, turned out the voters, and monitored the polls on election day. They were instrumental in Kennedy's narrow victory in several states. Organized labor, the Christian Coalition, and the NAACP used effective grassroots methods in 2000 to get their supporters out to vote.

In making contacts, candidate organizations usually rely on telephone banks and computerized mailing lists to identify likely supporters. The Perot campaign was particularly successful in using the telephone, specifically its toll-free number, to organize potential voters. Unable to turn to lists of registered voters or past supporters as the major parties could, Perot publicized his 800 number, and his organization recorded the telephone numbers of all callers, used their names and addresses to compile a geographic map of areas of potential strength, and then proceeded to target advertising toward these areas.

Direct mail has also been employed with increasing frequency to distribute information about candidates and their party and mobilize voters. For conveying a substantive message to a specific audience, direct mail can be extremely efficient, although its effectiveness varies with the level of education of the group to which it is directed. It tends to have greater impact on those who are less educated, particularly those who do not receive a lot of other mail.

Another option is the electronic media: radio, television, and the Internet. More costly than the telephone, radio and television have the advantage of reaching large numbers of people. Although messages cannot be personalized, they can be targeted on radio, cable, and local television to specific audiences, regionally and, on non-English-language cable stations, ethnically. (Media advertising is discussed in Chapter 7.)

The reach of radio and television, the size of their potential audiences, and their ability to direct messages to sympathetic listeners or viewers explain why an increasing proportion of expenditures by the campaigns of the presidential candidates are spent on the production and airing of this form of advertising. In 1976, total expenditures on all forms of media accounted for approximately half the campaign budget; in 2000 it was 60 percent.[38] Additionally the Democrats spent 44.3 percent of their soft money and the Republicans 32 percent of theirs on candidate-oriented issue ads in 2000.[39]

Developments in the communications media, specifically satellite technology, have also enabled candidates to design and project their messages to local audiences. They can remain in their studios and be interviewed by local anchors around the country. Electronic town meetings and press conferences have now become standard fare, as has the use of the Internet to raise money, enlist volunteers, provide information, and to the extent possible, mobilize the vote.

No matter how extensive a candidate's use of mass media may be, a certain amount of personal campaigning is still necessary. Appearances by presidential hopefuls generally create favorable news, generate excitement among partisans, and spur local turnout. The problem with personal appearances is that they are wearing, have questionable impact, and are not completely controlled even though extensive preparation goes into them.

Orchestrating the Campaign

Whether appearing in person or on television, much advance work is necessary. Nothing is left to chance. Jerry Bruno, who advanced Democratic presidential campaigns in the 1960s, described his tasks as an advance man, tasks that have not changed all that much over the years:

> It's my job in a campaign to decide where a rally should be held, how a candidate can best use his time getting from an airport to that rally, who should sit

next to him and chat with him quietly in his hotel room before or after a political speech, and who should be kept as far away from him as possible.

It's also my job to make sure that a public appearance goes well—a big crowd, an enthusiastic crowd, with bands and signs, a motorcade that is mobbed by enthusiastic supporters, a day in which a candidate sees and is seen by as many people as possible—and at the same time have it all properly recorded by the press and their cameras.[40]

Bruno's efforts are indicative of the great lengths to which modern campaigns go to prevent uncontrolled and unanticipated events from marring a presidential candidate's appearance.

Even with all the advance preparations, however, things can go wrong. If the crowds are thin, if the candidate is heckled, if a prominent public figure refuses to be on the platform with the candidate or a controversial one appears, or if the candidate makes a verbal slip, then the event may do more harm than good. Walter Mondale got off to an embarrassing start in 1984 when an early-hour Labor Day parade in which he was to appear drew relatively few onlookers. The news was not Mondale but the absence of spectators to watch him. Television cameras pictured Mondale walking down nearly empty streets in New York City. The message was clear—he sparked little enthusiasm.

Dole was plagued by poor advance work in 1996. Here's how *New York Times* reporter Adam Nagourney described some of the problems the campaign encountered in its closing days as it tried to generate momentum:

> The Republican candidate, an awkward public figure to begin with, these days often finds himself standing in front of small crowds, or shouting over a screechy or failing sound system, or watching as balloons drop or confetti shoots off in the middle of a speech, or taking the stage to such metaphorically challenging music as the "Mission Impossible" theme, or driving off in his limousine and leaving part [of] his motorcade behind.
>
> Sometimes the results are amusing: In Jacksonville, Fla., . . . Mr. Dole found himself speaking at a festive waterfront rally—a classic "photo op" backdrop indeed, except for one thing: just to one side, about fifteen scantily dressed women hung over a railing, taking in the action. Mr. Dole's aides had arranged to have their candidate speak outside a branch of the franchise Hooters.[41]

The arduous and exhausting schedules of modern campaigns have contributed to displays of emotion by candidates that have embarrassed them and damaged their public image, such as when Senator Edmund Muskie seemed to break into tears during a speech in New Hampshire when defending his wife from the attacks of William Loeb, publisher of the state's *Manchester Union Leader.* In the minds of some, the incident made Muskie look weak and not presidential.

Candidates have also made off-color or inappropriate remarks that have caused controversy. Not realizing a microphone in front of him was on, George W. Bush used a scatological metaphor to characterize a *New York Times* reporter to vice presidential candidate Dick Cheney, who, in turn, replied, "big time." Sixteen years earlier, Bush's father had used a similar epithet.[42]

Some one-liners have worked to a candidate's advantage, at least in the short run. When Republican vice presidential nominee Dan Quayle compared his Senate experience with John F. Kennedy's in his debate with Lloyd Bentsen, the Democratic candidate shot back, "I served with Jack Kennedy; I knew Jack Kennedy; Jack Kennedy was a friend of mine. Senator, you are no Jack Kennedy."[43] Quayle, shaken by Bentsen's blunt reply, remained on the defensive for the remainder of the debate. George H. W. Bush's "Read my lips" pledge not to raise taxes enhanced his popularity during the 1988 campaign but made it more difficult for him to find an acceptable solution to the problem of the budget deficit once in office. His repudiation of his own promise came back to haunt him during the 1992 campaign.

Targeting Messages

Candidates are normally very careful about their public utterances. Knowing that the press focuses on inconsistencies and highlights controversies, they tend to stick to a prepared script that coordinates themes, positions, pictures, and words. Reagan did so successfully in 1984. His campaign introduced a new theme every ten days to two weeks and keyed the president's speeches to it. Situations that might have distracted public attention or confused it were carefully controlled.

Speeches and policy statements are carefully constructed on the basis of survey research and focus group testing. They are also targeted to specific groups on the basis of these data. According to Bob Strum, senior adviser to Gore and veteran Democratic speechwriter, "Our targeting was driven almost entirely by Stan Greenberg's polling and Harrison Hickman's state-by-state polling, which told us what was going on in various states.[44]

Frequently code words are used to generate a particular response. The message is often compartmentalized. Groups get only those positions and priorities that the campaign has determined to be most in accord with their interests and beliefs. Other candidate stands and beliefs are not conveyed in these types of targeted messages. Such specialized, targeted messages can lead to unrealistic expectations and even perceptions of deception if the promises are not realized.

The new technology has facilitated computerized mailings, including emailings. Parties and interest groups purchase and maintain lists of their donors and others whose characteristics suggest that they would be sympathetic to the party or group's appeal. In its voter files, for example, the Republican National Committee has collected names, addresses, and relevant political and demographic data on 165 million voters.[45] The GOP lists, broken down by states, were distributed to state parties to raise money, as well as to target and turn out the vote on election day.

The use of the Internet has facilitated a new "activist" approach by parties and groups in which a steady stream of electronic messages are directed toward potential supporters with minimal cost. The danger with mass mailings on the Internet is that recipients may become irritated by all the unsolicited email, often referred to as "spam." To counter this problem, the Republican Web site and others that request email addresses of those who access sites often attach a clause which indicates that messages will be sent to those who supply their address.[46]

Timing Appeals

In addition to what to say, how to say it, and to whom, timing is also an important consideration. Candidates naturally desire to build momentum as their campaigns progress. The 1996 Clinton campaign was one of the most successful in adhering to a timed plan for communicating various messages to the voters. In the year before the election, the president emphasized his centrist and moderate positions, co-opting many of the Republicans' policy stands in the process. As the nomination campaign got under way, the president talked about family values and showcased himself in various presidential roles, in stark contrast with the Republican candidates who were criticizing one another's qualifications for the presidency. During the general election campaign, Clinton remained on his presidential pedestal, emphasizing the accomplishments of his administration and his desire to build a "bridge to the future."

In the 2000 election, Bush allocated his resources evenly over the course of the campaign whereas Gore spent more heavily in the final weeks. However, the Republican National Committee, which had more money on hand than did its Democratic counterpart, made up the difference by running ads on Bush's behalf.

Turning Out Voters

When all is said and done, it is the electorate that makes the final judgment. Who comes out to vote can be the critical factor in determining the winner in a close election. Although turnout is influenced by a number of variables, including the demographic characteristics and political attitudes of the population, registration laws and procedures, the kind of election and its competitiveness, and even the weather (see Chapter 3), it is also affected by the campaign itself.

On balance, lower turnout has hurt the Democrats more than the Republicans, because a larger proportion of Democratic Party identifiers are less likely to vote. Thus, a key element in the strategy of most Democratic candidates since Franklin Roosevelt has been to maximize the number of voters by organizing get-out-the-vote drives, particularly among core Democratic groups.

Traditionally, the party organizations at the state and local levels, not the candidate's central headquarters, mount these drives. A party divided at the time of its convention can seriously damage its chances in the general election. A case in point was the Humphrey campaign of 1968. Humphrey received the nomination of a party that took until late October to coalesce behind his candidacy, too late to register a large number of voters for the November election. Had it not been for organized labor's efforts in registering approximately 4.6 million voters, Humphrey probably would not have come as close as he did.

Whereas Humphrey's loss in 1968 can be attributed in part to a weak voter registration drive, Carter's victory in 1976 resulted from a successful one which the Democratic National Committee coordinated and financed. With the support of organized labor, Democrats outregistered Republicans. Labor's efforts in Ohio and Texas contributed to Carter's narrow victory in both states. A successful program to attract African American voters also helped increase Carter's margin of victory.

Both sides engaged in a massive grassroots effort to get out the vote in 2000 in the battleground states. According to Karl Rove, Bush's principal political strategist, "Our goal was to place 70 million phone calls in the last week of the campaign and we beat that by about 15 million. Our mail volume in the final week of the campaign was 111,544,186 pieces of mail, . . . 16,500,000 pieces of literature dropped door-to-door in the last two weeks, 1,234,500 yard signs, 1,501,500 bumper stickers."[47] Not to be outdone, the Democrats fielded an army of 40,000 volunteers to make personal contacts with potential Democratic voters and mailed an estimated 50 million letters.[48] And they were rewarded with a large turnout on election day.

Interest groups played a large role in these efforts. The NAACP spent $9 million to raise African American turnout in the key battleground states such as Florida, where 952,000 African Americans voted in 2000 compared to 527,000 in 1996.[49] This organization launched a targeted advertising campaign on television's Black Entertainment Network (BET) and in newspapers and radio that catered to the African American community. A telephone campaign featuring recorded announcements from President Clinton and African American leaders and a ministerial effort from the pulpits of black churches also urged members of this racial group to vote. The NAACP went so far as to register over 11,000 prisoners incarcerated at county jails in the South in the hopes of increasing turnout.[50]

The NAACP was not alone. The National Rifle Association and their adversaries, gun control advocates, pro-life and pro-choice groups, business associations, labor unions, environmental organizations, and a host of other groups all worked to mobilize their supporters in 2000 and will be active in 2004 as well. Labor Union leaders have pledged $20 million to mobilize nonunion voters, particularly African Americans, Latinos, and women in 2004 to defeat George W. Bush. They have created a 527 committee, Partnership for American Families, to do so.[51]

SUMMARY

Throughout much of the nineteenth century, presidential campaigns were run by the parties on behalf of their nominees. The goal was to energize and educate the electorate with a series of public activities and events. Beginning in the 1840s, but accelerating in the 1880s, presidential candidates became increasingly involved in the campaign. By the 1920s, they had become active participants, using radio, later television, and more recently the Internet, to reach as many voters as possible. To some extent, the electronic media has replaced the parties as the critical link between candidates and voters.

Advances in transportation and communications have made campaigning more complex, more expensive, and more sophisticated. These advances require considerable activity by the candidates and their staffs. Campaign strategy and tactics are now more closely geared to the technology of contemporary politics and run by the professionals of that new technology: pollsters, media consultants, direct mailers, grassroots organizers, lawyers, accountants, and a host of other specialists. Their inclusion in the candidate's organization has made the coordination of centralized decision making critical. It has also produced at least two separate organizations that need to be coordinated, one very loosely tied to the party's national committee and the other more tightly controlled by the candidates and their campaign staffs.

The job of campaign organizations is to produce a unified and coordinated effort. Most presidential campaigns follow a general strategy based on the prevailing political attitudes and perceptions of the electorate, the reputations and images of the nominees and their parties, and the geography of the Electoral College. The strategy includes designing a basic appeal, creating a leadership image, dealing with incumbency (if appropriate), and allocating campaign resources in the light of the Electoral College.

In projecting their basic appeal, Democratic candidates have emphasized their party label and those "bread-and-butter" issues that have held their coalition together since the 1930s. Republican candidates, on the other hand, did not emphasize partisanship until the 1980s, focusing instead on domestic and foreign policy problems. They also stressed character issues.

Part of the strategy of every presidential campaign is to project an image of leadership. Candidates do this by trumpeting their own strengths and exploiting their opponent's weaknesses. They try to project those traits that the public desires in their president, traits which are endemic of the office and resonate with the public mood of the election period.

An established record, particularly by presidents seeking reelection, shapes much of that leadership imagery. Depending on the times, that record may contribute to or detract from the candidates' reelection potential. In good times, incumbents have an advantage; in bad times, they do not. Being president—making critical decisions, exercising the powers of the office—is viewed as evidence of the leadership skills that presidential candidates have to demonstrate.

When allocating resources, the geography of the Electoral College must always be considered. Each party begins with a base of safe states. In the 1980s, that base was thought to be larger for the Republicans than for the Democrats. Population movements to the South and the West resulted in a regional advantage for the Republicans, one that allowed them greater flexibility in designing their geographic strategy. In the 1990s, however, the Democrats seemed to gain an advantage in the Northeast and Pacific Coast. Today about one-half of the states are truly competitive. Neither of the major parties has a lock on the Electoral College.

The candidates' strategies influence the conduct of their campaigns, but their tactics tend to have greater and more direct effect on day-to-day events. Key tactical decisions include what communication techniques are to be used, when, and by whom. They also include what appeals are to be made, how, when, and to whom.

Other than the belief that flexibility and rapid responses are essential, it is difficult to generalize about tactics. Much depends on the basic strategic plan, the momentum of the campaign, external conditions, and the unfolding of events. In the end, the methods that mobilize the electorate by getting people excited about a candidate are likely to be of the greatest benefit in turning out and influencing the vote. Much of the campaign is filtered through the news media. The next chapter explores this mediation and its impact on the election.

WHERE ON THE WEB?

Many of the *Where on the Web* sites listed in Chapter 4 will be useful for the general election as well.

- **Campaigns and Elections**
  http://www.campaignline.com
  Posts articles that have appeared in the magazine *Campaigns and Elections.*
- **CNN/All Politics: Elections 2004**
  http://CNN.com/ALLPOLITICS
  A combined site for CNN and *Time* magazine, this site contains articles and information on the presidential campaign.
- **C-SPAN**
  http://www.cspan.org
  This site has C-SPAN programming on the campaign as well as candidate appearances, speeches, student surveys, and political debates.
- **Gallup Poll**
  http://www.gallup.org
  Check this site for up-to-date polling data.
- **National Journal**
  http://www.nationaljournal.com
  There are many news sources for following the presidential primaries and caucuses. The *National Journal's* site is one of the best.
- **New York Times**
  http://www.nytimes.com
  The *New York Times* prides itself on being a paper of record. You will find much information on the policy positions and speeches of the candidates in this newspaper as well as the latest delegate count and prenomination polls.
- **Politics1**
  http://www.politics1.com
  An online guide to current politics with links to other relevant sites for the 2004 election.
- **Polling Report**
  http://www.pollingreport.com
  Summarizes public polls on the 2004 election.
- **Yahoo**
  http://www.yahoo.com/elections
  A comprehensive listing of articles on the nomination and election.
- **WhiteHouse04**
  http://www.niu.edu/newsplace

This site is maintained by Professor Ari Bass at the University of Northern Illinois. It lists articles, comedy, editorials, and links to other sites.

EXERCISES

1. Assess how the candidates targeted their appeals in the most recent presidential election. What appeals have they directed toward their partisans, especially to the principal groups in their party's traditional electoral coalition, and how have they dealt with independents and others, including those who supported third-party candidates?
2. Indicate the initial geographic strategies of the major party candidates in 2000 and then how those strategies changed over the course of the campaign. Now compare these strategies to those that should be employed in 2004.
3. What are the principal differences in the tactics which the major candidates have employed? Which of these tactics seem to work best and which did not? What do these tactics suggest about the mood of the electorate?

SELECTED READING

Jamieson, Kathleen Hall, and Paul Waldman, eds. *Electing the President 2000: The Insiders' View.* Philadelphia: University of Pennsylvania Press, 2001.

McCubbins, Mathew D., ed. *Under the Watchful Eye: Managing Presidential Campaigns in the Television Era.* Washington, D.C.: Congressional Quarterly Press, 1992.

Melder, Keith. *Hail to the Candidate: Presidential Campaigns from Banners to Broadcasts.* Washington, D.C.: Smithsonian Institution Press, 1992.

Morris, Dick. *Behind the Oval Office.* New York: Random House, 1997.

Nader, Ralph. *Crashing the Party: Taking on the Corporate Government in an Age of Surrender.* New York: St. Martin's Press, 2002.

Ornstein, Norman, and Thomas Mann, eds. *The Permanent Campaign and Its Future.* Washington, D.C.: AEI/Brookings, 2000.

"Special Issue: 2000 Presidential Elections," *Presidential Studies Quarterly,* 33 (March 2003): 5–187.

Tenpas, Kathryn Dunn, *Presidents as Candidates.* New York: Garland, 1997.

Thomas, Evan, et al. *Back from the Dead.* New York: Atlantic Monthly Press, 1997.

Troy, Gil. *See How They Ran: The Changing Role of the Presidential Candidate.* New York: Free Press, 1991.

White, Theodore H. *The Making of the President: 1960.* New York: Atheneum, 1988.

———*The Making of the President, 1964.* New York: Atheneum, 1965.

———*The Making of the President, 1968.* New York: Atheneum, 1969.

———*The Making of the President, 1972.* New York: Atheneum, 1973.

———*America in Search of Itself: The Making of the President, 1956–1980.* New York: Harper & Row, 1982.

Woodward, Bob. *The Choice.* New York: Simon & Schuster, 1997.

NOTES

1. Keith Melder, *Hail to the Candidate: Presidential Campaigns from Banners to Broadcasts* (Washington D.C.: Smithsonian Institution Press, 1992), 70–74.
2. Ibid., 87.
3. Ibid., 88.
4. Quoted in Marvin R. Weisbord, *Campaigning for President* (New York: Washington Square Press, 1966), 45.
5. Historian Gil Troy writes that Lincoln's avoidance of anything that smacked of political involvement was in fact a political tactic that he used throughout the campaign, emphasizing passivity and partisanship. Gil Troy, *See How They Ran: The Changing Role of the Presidential Candidate* (New York: Free Press, 1991), 66.
6. Weisbord, *Campaigning for President*, 5.
7. Quoted in Melder, *Hail to the Candidate*, 104.
8. Ibid., 125.
9. Keith Melder, "The Whistlestop: Origins of the Personal Campaign," *Campaign and Elections* 7 (May/June 1986): 49.
10. William Jennings Bryan, *The First Battle* (1896; reprint, Port Washington, N.Y.: Kennikat Press, 1971), 618.
11. Melder, *Hail to the Candidate*, 129.
12. Weisbord, *Campaigning for President*, 116.
13. Franklin Roosevelt had been disabled by polio in 1921. He wore heavy leg braces and could stand only with difficulty. Nonetheless, he made a remarkable physical and political recovery. In his campaign, he went to great lengths to hide the fact that he could not walk and could barely stand. The press generally did not report on his disability. They refrained from photographing, filming, or describing him struggling to stand with braces.
14. Cabell Phillips, *The Truman Presidency* (New York: Macmillan, 1966), 237.
15. Stanley Kelley, *Professional Public Relations and Political Power* (Baltimore: Johns Hopkins Press, 1956), 161–162.
16. Karl A. Lamb and Paul A. Smith, *Campaign Decision Making: The Presidential Election of 1964* (Belmont, Calif.: Wadsworth, 1968), 59–63.
17. Bush's organization in 1988 has received considerable praise for its tight-knit structure and efficient operating style. A small circle of advisers, each with designated areas of responsibility, ran the campaign and interacted with the nominee. By contrast, his 1992 organization was disjointed, uncoordinated, and internally competitive, with three separate groups, the White House, the reelection committee, and the campaign's media operation, vying for power. The Dole organization in 1996 was also not as tightly organized nor as efficiently run as the Reagan–Bush campaigns of the 1980s.
18. There was, however, a clash of personalities at the outset of the 1996 Clinton campaign. The principal antagonists were chief strategist Dick Morris along with the campaign operatives he brought on board and senior White House staffers who saw their roles as advisers and felt their access to the president threatened by the Morris group. However, these differences were muted by the apparent success of the Clinton campaign, the president's steady rise in the polls, and the joint strategy sessions which the president ran. The friction ended with Morris's resignation from the campaign after allegations of his weekly liaison with a Washington "call girl" became public. However, the strategic plan, which Morris had developed, continued to guide the campaign.
19. In the words of James Carville, principal Clinton strategist in 1992:

> By the time the convention had come, we had spent a lot of time, a lot of money, a lot of research on determining what it was that we wanted to do. By mid-June, . . . we had a pretty good idea of the things that we needed to accomplish, of the nature and depth of our problems and how we wanted to solve them and accomplish our objectives. . . . Strategically, we knew 85 percent of what we wanted to do by late June.

James Carville, quoted in Charles T. Royer, ed. *Campaign for President: The Managers Look at '92* (Hollis, N.H.: Hollis Publishing, 1994), 194.

20. "Anything that we tried taking credit for the economy at that point, we found just did not work. It was not believable. In fact, it reinforced the sense that he [Gore] was exaggerating and taking credit for things that were not real." Stanley Greenberg in Kathleen Hall Jamieson and Paul Waldman, eds. *Electing the President 2000: The Insider's View* (Philadelphia: University of Pennsylvania Press, 2001), 90.

21. Although Gallup polls taken throughout the election cycle showed voters' preferences on the candidates evenly divided as far as economic issues were concerned, the VNS exit poll indicated that of the 18 percent of the electorate who thought the economy was the most important issue, 59 percent voted for Gore compared to 37 percent for Bush and 2 percent for Nader.

22. An excellent examination of presidential traits appears in Benjamin I. Page, *Choices and Echoes in Presidential Elections* (Chicago: University of Chicago Press, 1978), 232–265. The discussion that follows in the text draws liberally from Professor Page's description and analysis.

23. George W. Bush, "Acceptance Speech at the Republican National Convention," <http://www.georgebush.com> August 3, 2000.

24. Following the Republican convention in August, when the public was just beginning to compare the candidates and form their initial impression of the nominees, Bush unleashed his anti-Dukakis campaign, painting his opponent as a free-spending liberal, soft on crime, weak on defense, and short on experience—a Democrat in the tradition of such unsuccessful and discredited Democratic candidates as George McGovern, Jimmy Carter, and Walter Mondale. Dukakis chose initially not to reply to Bush's attacks. His failure to do so compounded his problem, allowing the Republicans to shape early public perceptions of the Democratic nominee. By the time Dukakis did respond, his negative image had been established in the minds of many voters.

    The Dukakis experience served as a lesson to future presidential candidates.

25. Quoted in Thomas B. Edsall, "Why Bush Accentuates the Negative," *Washington Post,* October 2, 1988, C4.

26. Fred Steeper, in Royer, *Campaign for President,* 192.

27. A survey conducted by the Times Mirror Center for the People & the Press in early October 1992 found that 50 percent of those who saw the Bush advertisements felt that they were not truthful compared with 35 percent for the viewers of Clinton's ads. Times Mirror Center for the People & the Press, "Campaign '92: Air Wars," October 8, 1992, 2.

28. Cokie Roberts in Howard Kurtz and Terry M. Neal, "Bush Team Devised Truth Trap That's Tripping Gore," *Washington Post,* October 15, 2000, A11.

29. Matthew Dowd in Jamieson and Waldman, *Electing the President,* 45.

30. Political scientist Steven J. Brams and mathematician Morton D. Davis devised a formula for the most rational way to allocate campaign resources. They calculated that resources should be spent in proportion to the "3/2's power" of the electoral votes of each state. To calculate the 3/2's power, take the square root of the number of electoral

votes and cube the result. They offer the following example: "If one state has four electoral votes and another state has sixteen electoral votes, even though they differ in size only by a factor of four, the candidates should allocate eight times as much in resources to the larger state." In examining actual patterns of allocation between 1960 and 1972, Brams and Davis found that campaigns generally conformed to this rational allocation rule. "The 3/2's Rule in Presidential Campaigning," *American Political Science Review* 68 (1974): 113.

31. Matthew Dowd in Jamieson and Waldman, *Electing the President,* 45.
32. Al Gore, "Acceptance Speech to the Democratic National Convention," <http://www.algore2000.com>, August 17, 2000.
33. Craig B. Holman and Luke P. McLoughlin, "Buying Time," (New York: Brennan Center for Justice, 2001), 45, <http://www.brennancenter.org/tvads2000.html>.
34. Laura Meckler, "GOP Group to Air Pro-Nader TV Ads," Associated Press, <http://www.ap/20001028>, October 28, 2000.
35. During the Republican primaries and caucuses, Dole emphasized his Senate leadership role in contrast to the less impressive resumes of his challengers; after he had effectively sewn up the nomination and the Senate got mired in controversy, Dole changed his tactical focus and resigned from the Senate to become "Citizen Dole." When the citizenship role did not close the gap with an incumbent president, Dole turned to substantive issues, specifically, his proposal to cut income taxes by 15 percent. When the tax issue failed to generate the desired response, the Dole campaign changed its focus to other policy issues. Failing again to gain much leverage from these issues, Dole turned his attention to the president, first emphasizing Clinton's liberalism and then, his "character issue." Dan Balz, "In Challenger's Quest, Tactics More Prominent Than Strategy," *Washington Post,* October 25, 1996, A1, 18.
36. Clinton had used a similar tactic against Dole, moving toward him in their debate when he sensed that Dole was about to unleash a character attack against him.
37. Lynn Vavreck, Constantine J. Spiliotes, and Linda Fowler, "Making Contact: The Effects of Retail Politics in the New Hampshire Primary." See also Robert Huckfeldt and John Sprague, *Citizens, Politics, and Social Communications* (New York: Cambridge University Press, 1995); Paul Allen Beck, Russell J. Dalton, Steven Greene, and Robert Huckfeldt, "The Social Calculus of Voting: Interpersonal, Media, and Organizational Influences on Presidential Choices," *American Political Science Review* 96 (March 2002), 61.
38. Holman and McLoughlin, "Buying Time,"40.
39. Ibid., 68.
40. Jerry Bruno and Jeff Greenfield, *The Advance Man* (New York: Morrow, 1971), 299.
41. Adam Nagourney, "Disorders of All Kinds Plague Dole Campaign," *New York Times,* October 25, 1996, A1, 29. It was reports such as Nagourney's that prompted Dole to lash out at the *New York Times* for its liberal bias against him.
42. Another well-reported incident, this one involving Vice President Nelson Rockefeller, occurred in 1976. It too was precipitated by heckling. The Republican vice presidential candidate of that year, Senator Robert Dole, accompanied by Rockefeller, was trying to address a rally in Binghamton, New York. Constantly interrupted by the hecklers, Dole and then Rockefeller tried to restore order by addressing their critics directly. When this approach failed, Rockefeller grinned and made an obscene gesture. The vice president's response was captured in a picture that appeared in newspapers and magazines across the country, much to the embarrassment of the Republican ticket.
43. Lloyd Bentsen, quoted in "Transcript of the Vice Presidential Debate," *Washington Post,* October 6, 1988), A30.

44. Robert Strum as quoted in Jamieson and Waldman, *Electing the President,* 63–64.
45. John Mintz and Robert O'Harrow Jr., "Software Digs Deep Into Lives of Voters," *Washington Post,* October 20, 2000, A6.
46. John Mintz, "Political Groups Scramble to Find E-Mail Addresses of Likely Backers," *Washington Post,* October 22, 2000, A21.
47. Karl Rove in Jamieson and Waldman, *Electing the President,* 218–219.
48. Thomas B. Edsall, "Parties Use 'Ground War' as Close Race Nears End," *Washington Post,* October 30, 2000, A1, 16.
49. Susan Schmidt and Joan Mintz, "Voter Turnout Up Only Slightly Despite Big Drive," *Washington Post,* November 9, 2000, A35.
50. David Firestone, "Drive Under Way to Raise Turnout of Black Voters," *New York Times,* October 29, 2000, A1, 22.
51. Thomas B. Edsall, "Labor Targets Non Union Voters," *Washington Post,* February 27, 2003, p. A04.

MEDIA POLITICS

7

INTRODUCTION

Media and politics go hand-in-hand. The press has served as an outlet for divergent political views from the founding of the Republic. When political parties developed at the end of the eighteenth century, newspapers became a primary means for disseminating their policy positions and promoting their candidates.

This early press was contentious and highly adversarial, but it was not aimed at the masses. Written for the upper, educated class, newspapers contained essays, editorials, and letters that debated economic and political issues. It was not until the 1830s that the elitist orientation of the press began to change. Technological improvements, the growth in literacy, and the movement toward greater public involvement in the democratic process all contributed to the development of the so-called penny press, newspapers that sold for a penny and were directed at the general public.

The penny press revolutionized American journalism. Newspapers began to rely on advertising rather than subscriptions as their primary source of income. To attract advertisers, they had to reach a large number of readers. To do so, newspapers had to alter what they reported and how they reported it.

Prior to the development of the penny press, news was rarely "new"; stories were often weeks old before they appeared and were rewritten or reprinted from other sources. With more newspapers aimed at the general public, a higher premium was placed on gathering news quickly and reporting it in an exciting, easy-to-read manner.

The invention of the telegraph helped in this regard, making it possible for an emerging Washington press corps to communicate information to the entire country. What was considered news also changed. Events replaced ideas, human interest stories supplemented the official proceedings of government, drama and conflict were featured.

Stories of crime, sex, and violence captured the headlines and sold papers, not essays and letters on public policy. Joseph Pulitzer's *New York World* and William Randolph Hearst's *New York Journal* set the standard for this era of highly competitive "yellow journalism."[1]

Not all newspapers featured sensational news. In 1841, Horace Greeley founded the *New York Tribune,* and ten years later Henry Raymond began the *New York Times.* Both papers appealed to a more-educated audience interested in the political issues of the day. After a change in ownership, the *New York Times* became a paper of record. Operating on the principle that news is not simply entertainment but valuable public information, the *Times* adopted the motto, "All the news that's fit to print." It published entire texts of important speeches and documents and detailed national and foreign news.

Toward the middle of the nineteenth century, newspapers began to shed their advocacy role in favor of more neutral reporting. The growth of news wire services, such as the Associated Press and United Press, and of newspapers that were not tied to political parties, contributed to these developments.

As candidates became more personally involved in the campaign, they too became the subject of press attention. By the beginning of the twentieth century, the focus had shifted to the nominees, so much so that at least one candidate, Alton Parker, Democratic presidential nominee for 1904, angrily criticized photographers for their unyielding efforts to take pictures of him while he was swimming in the nude in the Hudson River.[2] Despite the intrusion into their personal lives, candidates began taking advantage of the press's interest in them, using "photo opportunities" and news coverage to project their image and extend their partisan appeal.

With the advent of radio in the 1920s and television in the 1950s, news media coverage of campaigns changed once again. Radio supplemented the print media. Although it did not provide regular news coverage, radio excelled at covering special events as they were happening. The 1924 presidential election was the first to be reported on radio; the conventions, major speeches, and election returns were broadcast live that year. During the 1928 election, both presidential candidates, Herbert Hoover and Alfred E. Smith, spent campaign funds on radio advertising.

Radio lost its national audience to television in the 1950s, but remained a favorite communications medium of candidates seeking to target their messages to specific groups in specific locations. A cheap and accessible electronic medium, radio continues to be used extensively, particularly during the nomination phase of the electoral process.

The influence of television on presidential elections was first felt in 1952. The most important news event of that presidential campaign was a speech by General Dwight Eisenhower's running mate, Richard Nixon. Accused of obtaining secret campaign funds in exchange for political favors, Nixon defended himself in a television address. He denied accepting contributions for personal use, accused the Democratic administration of being soft on communism, criticized his campaign opponents, and vowed that he would never force his children to give up their dog, Checkers, who had been given to the Nixon family by political supporters. The emotion of the speech, and particularly the reference to Checkers, generated a

AP/Wide World Photos

President Coolidge Poses with Native Americans President Coolidge used "photo ops" to attract attention in an otherwise dull campaign in 1924.

favorable public reaction, ended discussion of the campaign funds, kept Nixon on the Republican ticket, and demonstrated the power of television for candidates in their campaigns.

Paid television advertising by the political parties also first appeared in the 1952 presidential campaign. The marketing of candidates as if they were commercial products revolutionized the electoral process, particularly the strategy and tactics of the campaign. It enabled those seeking office to craft and project their image as well as attack their opponents' and to do so before a large viewing audience.

Campaigns have now become made-for-TV productions. Rallies and speeches are staged as media events, and on-air interviews are also part and parcel of the electoral process. Political advertising, designed to reinforce positive and negative candidate and party images, regularly consume more than half of the candidates' campaign budgets.

Nor has television broadcasting become the last word. Communication satellites, laser fiber optics, integrated circuits for high-speed transmission of digital images and data, and the Internet have opened additional channels for communicating during campaigns, and candidates are now beginning to take advantage of them. All the presidential campaigns today have Internet addresses that provide information about the candidates, their positions, and their campaigns.

This chapter examines these developments and their impact on presidential electoral politics. The first section discusses traditional "hard" news coverage of campaigns. It examines how network news organizations interpret political events and how candidates react to that interpretation. The "soft" news-entertainment format is explored in the second section. Here the chapter describes the techniques that candidates have used in recent campaigns to circumvent the national press corps. The third section turns to another news-entertainment feature—presidential debates. It describes their history, structure, staging, and impact on the public. Political advertising is the subject of the fourth section, in which some of the most successful advertisements are described, the increasing emphasis on negativity examined, and the effect of advertising on the electorate's perceptions of the candidates assessed. The final section looks at the media's cumulative impact on voting choice.

TRADITIONAL COVERAGE: HARD NEWS

The modus operandi of news reporting is to inform and interest the public. But the press does so with its own professional orientation—one that affects what is covered and how it is covered. Political scientist Thomas E. Patterson argues that the dominant conceptual framework in which the election is reported is that of a game. The candidates are the players and their moves (words, activities, images) are seen as strategic and tactical devices to achieve their principal goal—to win. Even their policy positions are frequently evaluated within this gaming framework, described as calculated attempts to appeal to certain political constituencies. Although Patterson argues that the gaming aspect of electoral politics is most pronounced at the beginning of the presidential selection process, he sees it as an organizing principle for the press throughout the entire election cycle.[3]

Why do media use the game, often referred to as a "horse race," as a primary focus? The answer is entertainment. Races are exciting. Viewing elections as a game heightens viewers' interest. Heightened interest, in turn, increases the size of the audience and, of course, the profits, since advertising revenue is based on the estimated number of people watching, hearing, or reading a particular program or paper.

There is another reason. The game format lends an aura of objectivity to reporting. Rather than presenting subjective accounts of the candidates' positions and their consequences for the country, this format encourages the news media to present quantitative data on the public's reaction to the campaign. Public opinion surveys reported as news are frequently the dominant story during the primaries and caucuses, sharing the spotlight with other campaign issues, such as the candidates' character, strategies, and tactics, during the general election.

Covering campaigns as if they were sporting events is not a new phenomenon. In 1976, Thomas Patterson found about 60 percent of television election coverage and 55 percent of newspaper coverage was devoted to the campaign as a contest.[4] Michael J. Robinson's and Margaret Sheehan's analysis of the *CBS Evening News* during the 1980 election revealed that five out of six stories emphasized the competition.[5]

What seems to be different today is the increasing emphasis placed on the game and the decreasing attention given to policy debate. Robinson and Sheehan found that the *CBS Evening News* devoted an average of only ninety seconds per program in 1980 to issues of policy, approximately 20 to 25 percent of the total election coverage.[6] In 1984, no policy question received more attention than did Geraldine Ferraro's finances or Ronald Reagan's age.[7] Although policy issues received more coverage in 1988, the focus on policy declined four years later, a surprising finding in the light of the economic recession and concerns about budget deficits, business competitiveness, and health care in that election.[8] In 1996, the networks devoted less than one-third of campaign coverage on their evening news shows to policy issues during the Republican primaries but almost half of it to policy thereafter. The horse race aspect that dominated coverage during the primary period declined after that—undoubtedly a product of Clinton's large lead in the polls.[9] The absence of a close race discouraged the press from giving as much coverage to the 1996 election as it did in 1992.

Although there was a close contest in 2000, the amount of election coverage on the evening news shows actually declined. Less time was given to the presidential campaign by the major television broadcast networks on these news programs than in previous elections, 12 percent less than in 1996 and 53 percent less than in 1992.[10] The focus on the horse race aspect of the election continued, however. (See Figure 7–1.)

FIGURE 7–1

FOCUS OF CAMPAIGN COVERAGE, 1992–2000

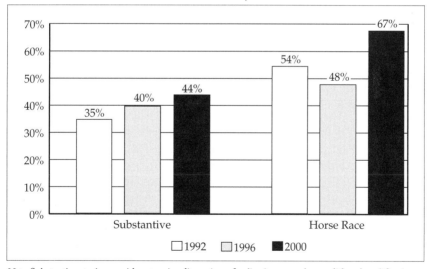

Note: Substantive stories provide extensive discussion of policy issues or the candidates' qualifications or professional background, or both. Horse race stories focus on who's ahead, who's behind, and candidate election strategies. Both substantive policy issues and election strategies/horse race topics may be found within the same story. Based on 622 stories from August 31, 1992 to October 25, 1992; 391 stories from September 2, 1996 to October 27, 1996; and 340 stories from September 4, 2000 to October 29, 2000 from the ABC, CBS, and NBC evening news.

Source: Stephen Hess, "Hess Report on Campaign Coverage in Nightly Network News," (November 7, 2000) Brookings Institution <http://www.brookings.edu/gs/projects/hessreport/week9.htm>. Copyright © Brookings Institution. Reprinted with the permission of Brookings Publications.

The Bad News Syndrome

Once the campaign begins, the principal candidates get approximately the same amount of coverage.[11] Contrary to popular belief, incumbents seeking reelection do not usually dominate the election news[12] although in 1996, Clinton did.

Incumbents tend to receive more negative coverage than challengers. In 1980, Jimmy Carter was treated more harshly than Ronald Reagan, and in 1984, Reagan was treated more harshly than Walter Mondale. Vice President George Bush running for president in 1988 fared poorly as well, as did his Democratic opponent, Michael Dukakis. Each received two negative comments for every positive one.

Much the same pattern emerged in 1992. In their analysis of network evening news coverage in 1992, S. Robert Lichter and his associates at the Center for Media and Public Affairs found that 69 percent of the evaluations of President George H. W. Bush—his campaign, his positions, his performance, his general desirability—were negative compared to 63 percent of all the comments about Clinton and 54 percent for Perot.[13]

Bill Clinton got better television coverage on the evening news in 1996. In fact, it was the best coverage he received during his first term as president with positive assessments outnumbering negative ones. Robert Dole, on the other hand, got more negative coverage, contributing to his accusation and the Republicans' perception that the press exercises a liberal, Democratic bias.

The bad news syndrome continued in 2000 although it was not quite as bad as in previous elections. In September, two out of three evaluations of George W. Bush were negative compared to more balanced coverage for Gore. After September, however, Gore received about as much negative coverage as Bush did. Overall, 65 percent of the comments about Bush were negative compared to 62 percent for Gore.[14] (See Figure 7–2.)

What is the reason for the generally bad press that candidates receive? Does it really indicate an ideological bias? Most academic experts do not believe that it does, pointing out that conservatives have been treated no better or worse than liberals although studies have also shown that reporters and correspondents tend to be more liberal and Democratic while the owners and their editors are more Republican and conservative.[15]

Ideological bias on election reporting is less pronounced than professional bias that shapes what is news. A fresh face winning and an experienced candidate losing are news; an experienced one winning and a familiar one losing are not. Similarly, the first time a candidate states a position, it is news; the second time it is old news; the third time it is not news. Since candidates cannot give new speeches every time they make an address, the news media that cover the candidates look for other things to report.

Verbal slips, inconsistent statements, and mistakes often become the focus of attention. Kiku Adatto found that "only once in 1968 did a network even take note of a minor incident unrelated to the content of the campaign."[16] In recent elections, however, there is much more frequent reporting of trivial slips. Roger Ailes, media director for George Bush's 1988 campaign, explained this phenomenon in the following manner:

Let's face it, there are three things that the media are interested in: pictures, mistakes, and attacks. That's the one sure way of getting coverage. You try to avoid as many mistakes as you can. You try to give them as many pictures as you can. And if you need coverage, you attack, and you will get coverage.

It's my orchestra pit theory of politics. If you have two guys on stage and one says, "I have a solution to the Middle East problem," and the other guy falls in the orchestra pit, who do you think is going to be on the evening news?[17]

FIGURE 7–2 🎗

GOOD NEWS VERSUS BAD NEWS IN CAMPAIGN 2000

GORE	Positive	Negative
Week 1	45%	55%
Week 2	56	44
Week 3	22	78
Week 4	60	40
Week 5	38	62
Week 6	19	81
Week 7	33	67
Week 8	35	65
Average	38	62

BUSH	Positive	Negative
Week 1	21%	79%
Week 2	47	53
Week 3	NA	NA
Week 4	39	61
Week 5	32	68
Week 6	37	63
Week 7	50	50
Week 8	29	71
Average	35	65

━━━ Positive ───── Negative

Note: Statistics on the percent of positive and negative evaluations based on total number of evaluations in the stories. Explicitly negative and positive statements by nonpartisan sources were considered when judging whether coverage was negative or positive. Based on 340 stories from September 4, 2000 to October 29, 2000 from the ABC, CBS, and NBC evening news. During Week 3 there were too few evaluations in the TV networks evening news for George W. Bush to report meaningful results. Between September 4 and October 27, 2000, PBS's *NewsHour with Jim Lehrer* had 57 percent positive and 43 percent negative evaluations of Bush, and 56 percent positive and 44 percent negative evaluations of Gore (based on evaluations in 177 stories).

Source: Stephen Hess, "Hess Report on Campaign Coverage in Nightly Network News," (November 7, 2000) Brookings Institution <http://www.brookings.edu/gs/projects/hessreport/week9.htm>. Copyright © Brookings Institution. Reprinted with the permission of Brookings Publications.

The news media's penchant for reporting embarrassing misstatements encourages the candidates not to be spontaneous, not to be candid, above all not to make mistakes. But it also forces candidates to acknowledge errors, misstatements, and unbecoming episodes in their past to try to minimize any negative fallout. In 2000, Al Gore admitted making factual errors during the first presidential debate; George W. Bush conceded that he had once been arrested for drunk driving many years earlier.

A candidate's failure to provide the news media with information, pictures, or even the pose they need can be a source of admonishment. Take the comment that ABC correspondent Sam Donaldson made to Michael Dukakis, who was playing a trumpet with a local marching band in the midst of his 1988 presidential campaign. Donaldson reported, "He played the trumpet with his back to the camera." As Dukakis played the Democratic victory tune, "Happy Days Are Here Again," Donaldson could be heard saying off-camera, "We're over here governor."[18]

Television news has an additional bias. As an action-oriented, visual medium, its content must move quickly and be capable of projecting a strong visual image on a screen. Television emphasizes pictures and deemphasizes words; less attention is devoted to what candidates say and more to how people react to their words and images. That is why campaign speeches are laden with sound bites and catch phrases, such as "Where's the beef?" "It is morning in America," "Read my lips— No new taxes," "a bridge to the twenty-first century," and "compassionate conservatism."

From the candidates' perspectives, the bad news is magnified by the fact that they do not get the opportunity to tell their own stories in their own words on the news that is broadcast by the major networks. The average length of a quotation from candidates on the evening news in 1968 was 42.3 seconds. In 1988, it was 9.8 seconds; in 1992, it was 8.3 seconds. During the 1996 Republican primaries and caucuses, it dropped even further, averaging only 7.2 seconds. There was a slight increase during the 1996 general election to 8.2 seconds, but still, according to Lichter and associates, journalists were on the air six times longer than were the candidates.[19]

Much the same pattern was evident in 2000. The average sound bite on the evening news was 7 seconds for the major party candidates, with Gore averaging a second more than Bush. In the average news story, correspondents were on camera seven times longer than were the candidates.[20] The bottom line is that it is the networks' anchors and correspondents, not the candidates, who present election news to the voters.

The Story Line

In addition to these presumptions about the nature of news and the format in which it is portrayed, there is also a framework into which that news is fitted. According to Patterson, a dominant story line emerges and much of the campaign is explained in terms of it. In 1992, it was Pat Buchanan's surprising showing against Bush that was news, not Bush's easy wins over his Republican rival; it was the conservative-controlled Republican convention and platform that garnered the headlines, not the adulation that greeted Bush and his running mate, Dan Quayle; it was the president's inability to turn the election around, to "hit a home run" during his debates with Clinton and Perot that was news rather than Bush's plans for the future or even the character issues he raised about his opponents. In Patterson's words:

> Bush's bad press was mainly a function of journalistic values. The news form itself affected both the content and the slant of most of his coverage. Bush's story was that of a reelection campaign in deep trouble—much like the story of a baseball team that was favored to win the pennant but stumbled early and never regained its stride.[21]

Patterson describes this story line as the likely-loser scenario.[22] It was the story of the Dole campaign in 1996. Portrayed as a weak opponent, hopelessly trailing the incumbent president, Dole's position in the race was used as the basis for evaluating and assessing the status of his campaign and how his strategy and tactics were or were not working. Unfortunately for Dole, that evaluation was harsh. The news media repeatedly referred to his struggling campaign and his attempts to "jump-start" it. Thus, the horse race metaphor contributed to the likely-loser scenario into which the press fit the story of the Dole campaign.

For Clinton, the story line was just the opposite. It was that of the front-runner who had a large lead and who had skillfully maneuvered to keep it. In this particular story, the press attributed Clinton's lead and inevitable success to a beneficial economic environment, superior resources, especially the perquisites of the presidency, and an extremely well-organized and well-run campaign. The news media's depiction of Ronald Reagan's 1984 presidential campaign was presented in a similar manner and provides another illustration of the press's use of the front-runner script.

Two other narratives, according to Patterson, are the bandwagon in which one candidate builds a larger and larger lead over the course of the campaign as people join the bandwagon and the opposite scenario in which the front-runner loses ground. In the first scenario, the image of strong and decisive leadership generates support; in the second, the image of weak and vacillating leadership contributes to the erosion. Jimmy Carter's primary spurt in 1976 provides an illustration of the bandwagon; his decline in the general election exemplifies the losing-ground story.[23]

The story line in 2000 focused on the closeness of the race, attributed in part to the weaknesses of both candidates: Gore's personal shortcomings and Bush's lack of depth on the issues. A variant on the competition theme toward the end of the campaign was the spoiler scenario for Ralph Nader. If Gore lost, it was Nader's fault.

Patterson's point is that the press fit the news of the campaign into the principal story rather than create a new story from the changing events of the campaign. Naturally, the perceptions of the news media affect the electorate's understanding of what is happening.

Impact of the News Media

What impact does the style and substance of election news coverage have on the voters? Studies of campaigning in the 1940s indicated that the principal effect of the print media was to activate predispositions and reinforce attitudes rather than to convert voters. Newspapers and magazines provided information, but primarily to those who were most committed. The most committed, in turn, used the information to support their beliefs. Weeding out opposing views, they insulated themselves from unfavorable news and from opinions that conflicted with their own.[24]

With the bulk of campaign information coming from the print media in the 1940s, voters, especially partisan voters, tended to minimize cross-pressures and to strengthen their own preexisting judgments. In contrast, the less committed also had less incentive to become informed. They maintained their ignorance by avoiding information about the campaign. The format of newspapers and magazines facilitated this kind of selective perception and retention.

Television might have been expected to change this situation because it exposed the less committed to more information and the more committed to other points of view. Avoidance became more difficult, although the use of remote control devices has rendered viewers less captive to the picture on a particular channel than they were when television first began to cover presidential campaigns.

Television news also compartmentalizes more than the print press. The evening news fits a large number of stories into a thirty-minute broadcast (which includes only twenty-three minutes of news). Of necessity, this time frame restricts the coverage that can be given to each item. Campaign stories average ninety seconds or less on the evening news, the equivalent of only a few paragraphs of a printed account. Their brevity helps explain why viewers do not retain much information from this type of television coverage.

Nonetheless, television news is still influential if only because more people follow presidential campaigns on television than through any other medium. It is the prime source of news for approximately two-thirds of the population. Newspapers are a distant second, with only about 20 percent of the population, but the most informed voters, listing them as their principal source of news. Radio and magazines trail far behind.

Television news helps set the agenda for the campaign. Its emphasis or lack of emphasis on certain issues affects the content of the debate, the attention paid by candidates to specific policy and character issues, and to some extent, the kinds of responses they have to provide. Media expert Michael J. Robinson believes that this agenda-shaping function directly affects the political elites. He argues that the press influences how political elites "relate" to the mass public and how those elites communicate political options.[25] In this way the news media affect the conduct of the campaign, which in turn influences the decisions of the electorate.

The news media may have a direct influence on voters as well. They provide information that colors public perceptions of the candidates and parties, particularly the candidates' qualifications for leadership. From the perspective of those running for office, this coverage is harsh and the reporters and commentators are adversarial. The candidates' motives are questioned, their speeches are summarized into a very few points or sound bites, their misstatements are highlighted, their character frailties emphasized, and their policy positions criticized and often portrayed as inconsistent, or even hypocritical.

Yet even with all the negative coverage, most candidates conclude that critical coverage is better than no coverage at all. Attention conveys legitimacy; it is an indication that the media take a candidate seriously. That is why candidates try their utmost to get coverage and to try to shape it in a favorable way.

But they also try to reach around the national press corps to appeal to their audiences directly. Since the 1990s, one of the methods for circumventing critical press coverage involves appearances on talk-entertainment shows, the nontraditional news media.

NONTRADITIONAL COVERAGE: SOFT NEWS

The use of a soft news format was pioneered by Ross Perot on television and Jerry Brown on radio in 1992. This new format provides a candidate-friendly environment in which to engage the electorate. Appearances on the morning and evening television news-talk shows (such as CBS's *The Early Show*, ABC's *Good Morning America*, NBC's *Today*, CNN's *Larry King Live*) and syndicated programs on these and other networks, including MTV, have now become commonplace.

Even incumbent presidents are expected to use this medium in their quest for reelection. President George H. W. Bush initially resisted in 1992, and when he finally consented to talk show interviews, he appeared ill at ease, especially on MTV. Bill Clinton was just the opposite. His appearance on the *Arsenio Hall Show* before the Democratic convention in 1992, wearing sunglasses and playing his saxophone, portrayed him as a "real cool guy," someone with whom the audience could identify. For Perot, talk show appearances constituted much of his "live" campaign, beginning with his announcement that he might run for president on the *Larry King Live* show in 1992 and again in 1996.

The candidates made the rounds in 2000. George W. Bush did much to strengthen his appeal among women with an appearance on *Oprah;* Al Gore had previously appeared on Oprah Winfrey's popular talk show. Both candidates taped parodies of themselves for a special election edition of *Saturday Night Live* as well as joked with the late-night comedians. Democratic vice presidential candidate, Joseph Lieberman, also went on the talk-entertainment circuit, but his counterpart, Republican Dick Cheney, did not. Cheney limited his appearances to shows with a news discussion format in which he felt more comfortable.

The use of the talk-entertainment format has several advantages for candidates. They are treated more like celebrities than politicians. The hosts tend to be more cordial and less adversarial than news commentators and reporters. Moreover, the audience is different. People who watch these shows tend to be less oriented toward partisan politics; thus they may be more open to the information presented by the candidates who appear on these programs, and correspondingly, more influenced by them.

AP/Wide World Photos

Clinton on the *Arsenio Hall Show* To reach larger, less politically involved audiences in 1992, presidential candidates appeared on entertainment shows. Here Bill Clinton plays his saxophone for Arsenio Hall. This appearance, like one on MTV, contrasted the younger, "swinging" Clinton with George Bush—a contrast that worked to Clinton's advantage.

Variations of the talk-entertainment format are town meetings and call-in programs in which candidates answer questions posed by average citizens. By interacting with everyday people, presidential candidates can demonstrate their responsiveness, sincerity, and empathy with the problems everyday people face. Bill Clinton was particularly effective in such a setting during his two presidential campaigns.

There are other benefits of the soft news format. For one thing, it distances candidates from the aggressive "gotcha" style of reporting in which national correspondents frequently engage. Instead of being asked very specific, often tricky, "hardball" questions, that focus on personality, image, horse race issues, and contradictions and ambiguities in the candidates' policy positions, interviewers and audience or call-in participants tend to ask "softer" questions that are more straightforward, issue-oriented, and easier to answer, questions which may even have been screened in advance by program producers. And the candidates can give longer answers that are broadcast in their entirety rather than in one or two sound bites. George W. Bush spoke for thirteen minutes on a single appearance on the *Late Show with David Letterman* in October—longer than the total time he appeared on the evening news of three television broadcast networks during the *entire* month of October. Similarly, Gore appeared on Letterman's show in September for more time than he appeared on the three evening news shows during that whole month combined.[26] Another advantage of doing the talk-entertainment circuit is that the candidates' appearances themselves may be news-worthy, thereby generating an even larger impact for the candidates when clips of their comments are rebroadcast or summarized on the news. Nor are the expenses associated with appearances on these shows comparable to the costs of staging a major media event or even designing, testing, and airing an advertisement.

The larger audience, the higher comfort level, and the greater ability of candidates to project their desired images by presenting seemingly spontaneous but often carefully crafted answers suggest that the soft news format will continue to be used by presidential campaigns to circumvent the national press corps and reach a portion of the general public directly.

PRESIDENTIAL DEBATES

Debates represent another "entertainment" component of presidential campaigns, one which candidates, particularly those who are behind, find useful. Candidates see debates as an opportunity to improve their own images and damage their opponents'. Unlike most of their campaign rhetoric—speeches, statements, and responses to questions—debates are live and unedited, although the formats limit the time for responses and the candidates' answers are usually carefully crafted and rehearsed. Nonetheless, debates give those running for office greater latitude to present their thoughts as they wish them presented, a reason that candidates like them.

The news media also like the debate format because it generates interest and facilitates comparison among the candidates. A debate is a newsworthy event that fits within the game motif.

The public likes debates because they are more exciting than staged campaign events and canned stump speeches. Debates provide voters with vital information. They generate increased interest in the campaign. They are a spectacle to be seen and heard.

The first series of televised debates occurred in 1960. John Kennedy used them to counter the impression that he was too young and inexperienced. Richard Nixon, on the other hand, sought to maintain his stature as Dwight Eisenhower's knowledgeable and competent vice president and the obvious person to succeed his boss in office.

In the three elections that followed, Lyndon Johnson and then Nixon, both ahead in the polls, saw no advantage in debating their opponents and refused to do so. Gerald Ford, however, trailing Jimmy Carter in preelection polls in autumn 1976, saw debates as his best opportunity to win in November. The Carter camp, on the other hand, saw them as a means of shoring up support. In 1980, the rationale was similar. From Reagan's perspective, it was a way to reassure the electorate about himself and his qualifications for office. For Carter, it was another chance to emphasize the differences between himself and Reagan, between their parties, and between their issue and ideological positions.

By 1984, presidential debates had become so much a part of presidential campaigns that even incumbents could not avoid them without making avoidance a major campaign issue. Thus, Ronald Reagan was forced by the pressures of public opinion to debate Walter Mondale, even though he stood to gain little and could have lost much from their face-to-face encounter. And in the 1992 election, George Bush's initial refusal to accept a plan for a series of campaign debates put forth by the Commission on Presidential Debates, a nonpartisan group that had organized the 1988 presidential and vice presidential debates, hurt him politically. Bill Clinton chided Bush repeatedly for his refusal to debate. Democrats dressed as chickens appeared at his campaign rallies. President Bush finally relented, telling his handlers, "I am tired of looking like a wimp."[27]

The issue in 1996 and again in 2000 was not whether to debate but whom to include. In 1992, Ross Perot and his running mate, Admiral James Stockdale, were invited to participate, and they did, to Perot's advantage but not to Stockdale's. In 1996, Perot and his running mate, Pat Choate, were not asked. The Bipartisan Commission on Presidential Debates, composed of five Democrats and five Republicans, concluded that Perot's candidacy was not viable, that he had no chance to win the election even though his name appeared on the ballot in all fifty states and the District of Columbia. The commission based its decision on Perot's standing in the polls, which was about 5 percent at that time, and on the judgment of a small number of political scientists and journalists, surveyed by the commission's staff and advisory council, who unanimously concluded that Perot not only could not win the election but would not carry a single state.[28]

The commission employed similar reasoning in 2000. It established three criteria for inclusion in the debates: a candidate had to meet the test of constitutional eligibility (be a natural born citizen, thirty-five years of age or older, and a resident of the United States for at least fourteen years), be on the ballot in enough states to have a chance of winning a majority of the electoral votes, and additionally, be organized in a majority of the congressional districts within the state, and demonstrate a sufficient level of electoral support by receiving an average of 15 percent or more in public opinion polls. Neither Ralph Nader nor Pat Buchanan came close to reaching the minimum level of support in the polls. As a consequence they were excluded.

By bringing the candidates together on the same stage at the same time, the debates become major campaign stories, routinely covered by the news media—stories that attract many viewers, more than any other single event of the entire campaign although there has been a decline since 1984 in the percentage of households watching presidential debates. (See Table 7–1.)

Although presidential debates have now become part of the American political tradition, their number, scheduling, and format are still subject to arduous negotiation between the principal contenders and their staffs. In these negotiations each side naturally wishes to maximize its advantages. Candidates who are ahead in the polls when these negotiations occur, usually the incumbent, call the shots. Thus, President Carter refused to include independent John Anderson in the 1980 debate; in 1984, President Reagan set the parameters for the debates

TABLE 7–1 🏵

Presidential Debates, 1960–1996

Year		Number of Debates	Average Estimated Size of the Television Audience (in millions)	Percent of Households Watching
1960	Kennedy v. Nixon	4	77	60
1976	Carter v. Ford	4*	65	51
1980	Carter v. Reagan	1	81	59
1984	Mondale v. Reagan	3*	66	46
1988	Dukakis v. Bush	3*	66	36
1992	Bush v. Clinton v. Perot	4*	66	42
1996	Clinton v. Dole	3*	40	29
2000	Gore v. G. W. Bush	4*	38†	26

*Includes one vice presidential debate.

†The average for just the three presidential debates in 2000 was 40.6 million.

Sources: Estimates of audience sizes for 1960–1992, "How Many Watched," *New York Times,* October 6, 1996, A25. Copyright © 1996 by the *New York Times.* Reprinted by permission. Estimates for 1996, "Debate Ratings Beat Baseball," Associated Press, October 17, 1996. Copyright © 1996 by the Associated Press. Reprinted by permission. Estimates for 2000 based on ratings by Nielsen Media Research as reported in the *New York Times,* October 19, 2000, A22. Copyright © 2000 by the *New York Times.* Reprinted by permission. Percentage of households reported in Thomas Patterson, *The Vanishing Voter* (New York: Random House, 2002), 122.

with Mondale, as did Vice President Bush for Dukakis in 1988. It was a different story, however, in 1992. With President Bush trailing in the polls, the campaign moving into the late-September–early-October period, and Clinton making an issue of Bush's refusal to debate, the president could not dictate the terms and had to accept a compromise that included formats that he and his advisers initially opposed.

Similarly, in 1996 with Clinton well ahead in the polls and sitting in the driver's seat, the Dole campaign had little choice but to accept the schedule, format, number, and length of the debates that Clinton's handlers proposed. The most important consideration for Dole was that Perot not be included. Dole wanted to present himself as the sole alternative to Clinton. He also wanted to extend the debates as long as possible. The reason was simple. Once the last debate was concluded, he did not want the press to write that the election was effectively over and write his obituary.[29]

The Commission on Presidential Debates proposed four 90-minute debates in 2000, three involving the presidential candidates and one, the vice presidential nominees. Al Gore accepted immediately, but George W. Bush did not. Instead, Bush proposed debates on two network talk shows, *Meet the Press* and *Larry King*

Live, and wanted only to participate in one of the commission's debates. With Gore enjoying a better reputation as a skilled and knowledgeable debater than Bush, the press interpreted the Republican candidate's counterproposal as an attempt to make the debates less formal, limit the size of the viewing audience, and reduce their impact on the electorate.[30] Although the vice president had stated that he would debate his opponent in any venue, including news shows, he refused to accept Bush's invitation unless and until the governor agreed to accept the bipartisan commission's entire debate proposal, which Bush eventually did.

Preparation

To get ready for the debates candidates take time out of their busy campaign schedules to go over briefing books that their aides compile, view videotapes of their opponents, and engage in mock debates with stand-ins playing their opposite number. This extensive preparation is designed to ensure that there are no surprises, that the candidates anticipate the questions and provide thoughtful answers that are consistent with their previous statements and advertising, and that they make no gaffes or misstatements that can be used against them by the press or by their opponents.

In addition to the concern about substance and rhetoric, campaign media consultants are also concerned about style—how candidates look, how they speak, and how they interact with the questioners and with their opponents. Kennedy and Carter talked faster than their opponents to create an action-oriented image in the minds of the viewers. Both tried to demonstrate their knowledge by citing many facts and statistics in their answers. Ford and Reagan spoke in more general terms, expressing particular concern about the size and structure of government. Reagan's wit and anecdotes in 1980, Bush's manner in 1988, and Perot's down-to-earth language and self-deprecating humor in 1992 conveyed a human dimension with which viewers could identify in contrast to their opponents' less "identifiable" responses. Dukakis was especially hurt by his reply to the question of whether he would favor an irrevocable death penalty for a person who raped and killed his wife. His matter-of-fact, rambling response sealed his technocratic, iceman image. When George W. Bush was asked about capital punishment in the first debate of the 2000 campaign, he appeared to relish Texas's record as number one in executions. The governor's manner, noted by the press, prompted a question in the third debate about whether Bush was proud of Texas's executions. Sounding much more contrite, Bush answered "no" but defended his decisions on individual death penalty appeals.

Despite the appearance of spontaneity, debates are highly scripted, carefully orchestrated events. The candidates are coached and rehearsed. They often sound like their stump speeches and ads. Over the course of the debates, there are times when candidates sound like a tape or CD repeating itself. Although most debate participants prepare extensively for them, Richard Nixon in his first debate with Kennedy, and James Stockdale in the 1992 vice presidential debate did not and suffered by comparison with their more polished opponents.[31]

Strategy and Tactics

Much calculation goes into debate strategy and tactics. Candidates need to decide which issues to stress and how to stress them; how to catch their opponents off guard or goad them into an error; whether and how to respond to a personal attack and to criticism of their policy positions. In 1992, Clinton emphasized the need to change policy. In 1996, he took credit for his policies and the good times that followed from them. In 1992, he was critical of Bush on the issues, especially the economy; in 1996, he took the high road as president.

Clinton had three broad objectives in his 1992 debates: stay focused on the economy, respond to any personal attack, and ignore Perot. Since he was in the lead, Clinton wanted to avoid making a big mistake. To present a knowledgeable, presidential image, he cited statistics and specific policy proposals and swiftly responded to any personal attacks against him. In one particularly effective response to Bush's imputation about his patriotism for protesting against the Vietnam War as a Rhodes scholar at Oxford University in Great Britain, Clinton said:

> When [Senator] Joe McCarthy went around this country attacking people's patriotism, he was wrong. . . . And a senator from Connecticut stood up to him named Prescott Bush. Your father was right to stand up to Joe McCarthy; you were wrong to attack my patriotism. I was opposed to the war, but I love my country.[32]

Bush looked away from his Democratic opponent and down at the podium as Clinton uttered these words about his father, suggesting to many viewers that Clinton's response hit home. Clinton was extremely persuasive in their second town meeting–style debate as well, empathizing with questioners and directing his responses to them. Bush seemed ill at ease and tentative in his responses. In contrast, his tentativeness reinforced the image that Democrats were trying to project, the president "just didn't get it." At one point near the end of the debate, television cameras caught him looking at his watch, thereby conveying the impression that he was uncomfortable and just wanted out.

In 1996, Clinton took a very different tack from the one he assumed four years earlier. To look, sound, and act presidential, Clinton did not engage in personal criticism about his opponent. He stuck to policy issues and ignored those that pertained to trust and ethical conduct. When Dole raised questions of personal integrity, Clinton moved closer and looked directly at him.

Dole was in a far more difficult position. Trailing the president in the polls, he had to make the case for change and for himself. To make matters worse, he had to overcome a reputation for being mean-spirited while doing so. In the first debate, Dole tried to achieve his objective by focusing on substantive policy issues, reiterating the arguments and policy appeals he had made on the campaign trail. In the second debate, still far behind in the polls, he raised the issue of trust and character, presenting himself as a person who keeps his word and suggesting that the president did not keep his. When Clinton did not take the bait and respond, there was little more Dole could do.

A strategic goal of most candidates during debates is to overcome any negative perceptions about them that have developed and, at the same time, magnify their positive attributes. For George W. Bush in 2000, this meant demonstrating his command of the issues, communication skills, and leadership potential. For Al Gore, the task was to contrast his knowledge and experience with his opponent's, distinguish his brand of Democratic popularism from Bush's more conservative posture, and convey that he had the strength of character, passion, and people skills to govern effectively.

Bush achieved his strategic goals; Gore did not. Going into the debates with low public and media performance expectations, Bush countered the "gravitas" issue by presenting policies in greater detail than he had in his stump speeches; he overcame allegations that he was prone to verbal slips and incoherency by employing well-tested words and phrases memorized from his speeches and ads, and offering to initiate a new spirit of bipartisanship and cooperation.

Although Gore did well in differentiating his policy positions from those of his Republican opponent, his aggressive manner and misstatements served to undermine his presidential image. In the first debate his sighs and expressions of dismay during Bush's responses produced a negative public reaction, particularly among women. In the words of Bush adviser, Matthew Dowd, "His 'sighs' and bearing made him look like he wasn't a nice person, and at points, when he answered questions, he lectured. He actually did more damage to himself than we did to him."[33]

Gore was careful not to make the same mistakes again. In the second debate he was on his best behavior, so much so that his placid and nonconfrontational style seemed disingenuine to those accustomed to his more aggressive debate posture. In the third debate, he took the offensive again, at one point even walking toward Bush and standing over him. In their comments and advertising following the debates, Republicans pointed to Gore's impatience, embellishments, and aggressiveness as evidence of his political, win-at-all-costs mentality.

Normally, the vice presidential debate is not nearly as consequential as the presidential one. Fewer people watch it since it involves the number two players on the teams. But the debate can raise or allay doubts about the vice president's capacity to fill in, if something were to happen to the president. In 1988, the vice presidential debate worked to Dan Quayle's disadvantage when his performance confirmed rather than challenged the impression that he was not up to the job. In 1992, Admiral James Stockdale, Perot's running mate, seemed unprepared which left doubts in voters' minds whether he (and by implication, Perot) were qualified for the country's top two jobs. In 1996, Jack Kemp floundered on foreign affairs.[34] No such concerns were evident about either vice presidential nominee during their one debate in 2000.

Evaluation and Impact

Before the debates begin, there is considerable media hype that helps generate expectations of how the candidates will do. For the poll leader, these expectations are high; for the candidate who is behind, they are lower; similarly, an incumbent president is often expected to outshine a challenger. When expectations are not realized, public opinion may shift a little; although if a contest is close, it is unlikely that a small shift will make a difference in the final outcome.

In 2000, Gore was deemed the more experienced and knowledgeable of the two major candidates. He was expected to do better than Bush in the debates. The low expectations gave Bush an advantage that his smooth, virtually mistake-free performance maximized.

The impact of the debates is not evident until several days following them. Instant voter reaction, reported by the news media, does not take into account press reactions, spin by the candidate's handlers, and ads that point to misstatements and question positions taken during the debate. The post-debate campaign can shift the perceptions of the electorate.

The news media evaluate debates in terms of the winner–loser scenario. The campaigns try to affect this evaluation through the use of "spin doctors," luminaries who are made available to the media following the debate. They also gear their advertising to positions that were stated and especially to misstatements that may have been made. The Republicans were particularly effective in spinning the first debate in 2000 to their advantage. In the words of Carter Eskew, close adviser and friend of Al Gore:

> [T]he Bush team did a really good job, fair and square, of capitalizing and jumping on the so-called misstatements the Vice President made in the [first] debate. Our senior team went off to Kentucky brain-dead, having not had any sleep, and said to our press operation, "Well you take care of this one, this is just a one-day thing. It'll be fixed." It wasn't. It became a very difficult thing for us to deal with, and became the public's perception of the first debate.[35]

The debates of 2000 were not the only ones in which spin, commentary, and advertising make a difference. The same was true in 1976 when in the course of a foreign policy debate, President Ford stated that the Soviet Union did not dominate the communist countries of Eastern Europe when in fact it did. News analysts made much of this faux pas, and Ford did not recant his comments for three days. In the interim his image, which had been initially enhanced by the second debate, was seriously damaged.[36] The debate reinforced the impression of many that he was just not up to the job.

There are usually only slight shifts in opinion in the days following debates because their principal effect is to solidify support, particularly among partisans. Those who are more involved are more likely to watch the debates; those who are more knowledgeable are more likely to learn from them; those who are more partisan are more apt to be convinced by them. People root for their own candidates.

Debates tend to reconfirm initial perceptions and predilections. Such reinforcement occurred in 1984 despite a shaky performance by President Reagan in his first debate with Walter Mondale and again in 1988. In 1992 and 1996, Clinton maintained his lead although Perot's support shot up as a consequence of his participation in the 1992 debates. (See Table 7–2.)

TABLE 7-2 🌿

THE IMPACT OF PRESIDENTIAL DEBATES ON ELECTORAL SUPPORT, 1992–2000

1992

Dates	Bush	Clinton	Perot	Other/Undecided
September 28–30	35%	52%	7%	6%
October 8–10	33	51	10	6
October 13–15	34	47	13	6
October 21–22	31	43	18	8
October 24–25	34	43	17	6

Debate dates: October 11, 13 (vice presidential), 15, and 19.

1996

Dates	Clinton	Dole	Perot
September 29	52%	37%	5%
October 8	54	38	5
October 13	54	39	4
October 16	54	41	5
October 17	50	40	6
October 18	52	41	5

Debate dates: October 6, 9 (vice presidential), and 16.

2000

Dates	Gore	Bush	Nader	Buchanan
October 1–3	49%	41%	2%	1%
October 4–6	41	48	4	1
October 7–9	44	47	3	1
October 10–12	45	45	3	—
October 13–15	44	47	3	—
October 16–18	39	49	5	—
October 19–21	41	50	3	1

Debate dates: October 3, 5 (vice presidential), 11, and 17.

Sources: 1992 figures are based on the *Gallup Poll Monthly* (September and October, 1992); 1996 figures are based on ABC News tracking poll of likely voters; 2000 figures from Gallup Poll of likely voters, <http://www.gallup.com> October 23, 2000.

For weaker partisans and independents, the debates can increase interest and can clarify, color, or even change opinions about the candidates. Before debating, Kennedy was thought by many to be less knowledgeable and less experienced than Nixon; Carter was seen as an enigma, as fuzzier than Ford; Reagan was perceived to be more doctrinaire and less informed than his first Democratic opponent, President Carter; Perot was seen as self-serving, autocratic, and arrogant; and in 2000, Democrats contended that George W. Bush was not up to the task, not sufficiently knowledgeable and experienced to be president.

Although the debates did not help Mondale, Dukakis, and Dole overcome their negative perceptions, they did help Kennedy, Carter, Reagan, and George W. Bush overcome theirs. In close races, such as in 1960, 1976, and 2000, debates can and did make a difference.

The case of 2000 is illustrative of the impact that debates can have. Trailing his Democratic opponent going into the debates, Bush led Gore coming out of them. Overall, a Gallup poll estimated that Bush gained about 7 percent in the polls during and after the period in which the debates were held. According to Gallup, Bush's largest gain was among independents and women. Gore had sizable leads among both groups before the first debate, but following the last he was behind among independents and barely ahead among women.

CAMPAIGN ADVERTISING

Candidates are marketed much like any commercial product. Advertising is used to gain attention, make a pitch, and leave an impression. The goal, of course, is to get the electorate to do something—vote for a specific candidate on election day.

Media consultants specializing in political advertising are hired to supplement regular campaign staff. Often referred to as "media gurus," this small group of savvy professionals designs, produces, and targets the advertisements as well as buys time on different stations to air them. Each campaign normally retains a political media consulting firm to coordinate its advertising program. In 2000, the Democratic presidential ads were produced by the firm of Squier, Knapp, and Dunn, which had also designed the advertising for the Clinton 1996 campaign. Bill Knapp oversaw the effort with help from Carter Eskew, a friend and adviser to Gore. Mark McKinnon, a Texas-based media consultant, who had worked on Bush's gubernatorial campaigns and previously for Democratic candidates, created the advertising for Bush's 2000 presidential effort, assisted by a team of Washington political consultants. The Republican National Committee's advertising was coordinated by another firm, Cold Harbor Films and its principal Alex Castellanos, who had previously worked on other Republican campaigns.

Designing and airing campaign ads constitutes the principal expense of contemporary presidential campaigns. The 2000 election campaign was no exception. Of the approximately $135 million allocated to the major party candidates, $70.8 million was devoted to advertising. But that was only part of the total presidential advertising. For the first time, the parties spent more than the candidates, a total of $81.4 million, on their presidential campaigns. When group expenditures for issue ads ($15.2 million) are included, the total amount comes to a whopping $167.5 million.[37]

The Republicans enjoyed a slight advantage in overall advertising expenditures. Bush and the Republican National Committee combined to spend $86 million compared to $64 million for Gore and the Democratic National Committee.[38] However, nonparty group expenditures were heavily in Gore's favor with such organizations as Planned Parenthood, handgun control, the Sierra Club, and the AFL-CIO outspending such organizations as the National Rifle Association, pro-life, and industry and trade groups by about 6 to 1. Nevertheless, $4.7 million more was spent by or for Bush than Gore.[39]

Techniques and Timing

Advertising allows candidates to say and do what they want. The trick is to make it look real. Candidate-sponsored clips are not unbiased, and the public knows it. The trick is to make sure that the words and pictures convey the message which the campaign has carefully calibrated on the basis of its voter research. To refine advertisements and improve the odds that they project the desired messages which in turn produce the desired effects, they are pretested before focus groups. In fact, every one of the 538 ads that the Gore campaign aired went through the pretest/retest process.[40]

The most effective ads are those that reinforce the news. If ads become news, so much the better. Take the Democrats' 1964 ad suggesting that Barry Goldwater might get the country involved in a nuclear war. Designed to reinforce the impression that Goldwater was a trigger-happy zealot who would not hesitate to unleash nuclear weapons against a communist foe, the ad pictured a little girl in a meadow plucking petals from a daisy. She counted to herself softly. When she reached nine, the picture froze on her face, her voice faded, and a stern-sounding male voice counted down from ten. When he got to zero there was an explosion, the little girl disappeared, and a mushroom-shaped cloud covered the screen. Lyndon Johnson's voice was heard: "These are the stakes—to make a world in which all of God's children can live, or go into the dark. We must either love each other, or we must die." The ad ended with an announcer saying, "Vote for President Johnson on November 3. The stakes are too high for you to stay home."

The commercial was run only once. Goldwater supporters were outraged and protested vigorously, but their protestations actually kept the issue alive. In fact, the ad itself became a news item, and parts of it were shown on television newscasts. The Democrats had made the point, and the news media helped reinforce it.

A daisy girl look-alike advertisement was aired in several battleground states in 2000 by a nonprofit, Republican-oriented group from Texas. Like its famous predecessor, the ad featured a young girl plucking the petals of a daisy, a countdown, and a nuclear explosion. The message was that the Clinton–Gore administration had jeopardized the nation's security by providing nuclear secrets to China in exchange for campaign contributions, thereby giving China the capacity to unleash a nuclear attack against the United States. The ad ended with the words, "Don't take a chance, please vote Republican."[41]

LBJ Library Collection

Campaign Advertising The "daisy girl" from the infamous campaign commercial for Lyndon Johnson, just before she was seemingly annihilated by an atomic explosion.

A public outcry followed the airing of this advertisement. Democrats denounced it as outrageous and irresponsible. The Bush campaign, fearing a backlash, disavowed responsibility and urged the group sponsoring the ad to pull it. They did, but not before it had become a news item as well, thereby heightening the attention it received from the press. Unlike the original daisy girl ad, however, the 2000 version did not reinforce campaign themes or messages, and thus had little discernible impact on the electorate.

Media presentations must appear to be authentic. When candidates are placed in situations in which they do not fit, the visual media can do more damage than good. Such was the case when Michael Dukakis's staff created a photo opportunity in which their candidate wore an army helmet and rode in a combat-ready tank. The objective of the advertisement was to demonstrate Dukakis's support for the military and for a strong national defense policy. The situation, however, was so contrived and the candidate looked so silly that the Republicans countered with a commercial in which a scene from the Dukakis ad was actually featured along with information about the Democratic candidate's opposition to a long list of military programs and weapons systems.

Political commercials take many forms. Short spots are interspersed with other commercials in regular programming. Longer advertisements that preempt part of the standard broadcast fare and full-length productions, such as interviews, documentaries, and campaign rallies, have also been employed, perhaps less so in recent elections because of their expense. The primary benefits of the short spots are that they make a point, are cheaper to produce and air, and are usually viewed by a larger audience. Longer programs, which may go into greater detail about the candidate's career, qualifications, and beliefs, are generally seen by fewer people, although Ross Perot's novel media campaign in 1992 attracted and maintained a sizable audience even though most of his programs lasted thirty minutes or longer. In 1996, he was less successful. His audience was only about one-third the size of the one he had in 1992.

In addition to length, scheduling is also a critical consideration for campaign advertisers. For the candidate who appears to be ahead, the advertising should appear at a steady rate over the course of the campaign. Nixon in 1968 and 1972, Carter in 1976, Clinton in 1992 and 1996, and George W. Bush in 2000 followed this practice. Reagan in 1984, Bush in 1988 and 1992, and Gore in 2000 did not. Each decided to increase their advertising buys as the campaign progressed.

Most advertising content is sequenced as well. At the outset, it is necessary to provide biographical information about family, experience, and qualifications for the office. The Clinton biographical ads were particularly effective in 1992. His biography, entitled "The Man from Hope," presented the personal Clinton from his childhood in Hope, Arkansas, the town in which he was born and initially raised, to his governorship of that state. The film used the town's name to convey Clinton's optimism and his life story to demonstrate his ability to achieve his dreams and the country's.

Both Al Gore and George W. Bush, who had run biographical ads in their 2000 nomination campaign, continued and supplemented those ads at the beginning of the general election campaign. The Gore ads stressed the candidate's career as a journalist, his service during the Vietnam War, and his twenty-four years of public service as a representative, senator, and vice president. Bush's ads pointed to his popularity as governor of Texas and his ability to bring people together.

Once the personal dimension has been established, the policy orientations of the candidates and their priorities for the coming years are articulated. In this phase of advertising, themes are presented and policy positions noted. In the third stage, the candidate frequently goes on the offensive by running a series of ads in which the reasons not to vote for the opponent are stressed. Candidates who are behind frequently use the earlier stages to "go negative."

The 2000 campaign contained an especially heavy dosage of negative advertising in its final weeks. According to a study by the Brennan Center for Social Justice at New York University, nearly 90 percent of the candidate ads in the three weeks before the election were negative.[42] The advertising campaign had come full circle. From initially trumpeting their candidate's strengths, the campaigns ended by blasting their opponent's weaknesses. The choice had come down to who was the lesser of two evils.

Targeting

Targeting is a critical component of political advertising. It enables campaigns to direct their messages to particular groups within the electorate and to do so in the most efficient manner.

Most presidential campaigns go to great lengths to place their advertising where it will do the most good, taking the Electoral College into account when doing so. Clinton targeted his 1996 ads toward twenty-four key states, very similar in composition to the group he targeted four years earlier. A little less than half the ads ran in five of the largest, most competitive states: California, Florida, Michigan, Pennsylvania, and Ohio. Since Clinton advertised early and often, his media consultants avoided the big and expensive news media markets in New York, Washington, D.C., and Los Angeles in the hope that this unusually early advertising campaign would not become a campaign issue. It didn't. Only two stories about Clinton's ads appeared in the mainstream press during this period.[43]

Dole also targeted his ads toward key states. The problem was that the designation of his key states changed over the course of the campaign. At the outset, Dole focused on the Midwest and mid-Atlantic states. When his polls showed little gain from the advertising, he shifted about $4 million to his California budget, thereby wasting much of the effort and money that had been put into the earlier states. The advertising shifted in content as well, as the campaign struggled to find wedge issues.

Targeting was even more concentrated in 2000 with both candidates and their parties dueling over the airways in the battleground states. Initially the Gore campaign focused on seventeen states and Bush on twenty-three. Both campaigns relied on their public opinion polls to gauge the continuing competitiveness of the states and the impact of their advertising efforts. States that became less competitive over the course of the campaign, such as Ohio for the Democrats and Illinois for the Republicans, were dropped from the targeted list. Gore ran more ads than Bush by using the less expensive day spots which have a larger female audience.

Images and Messages

The name of the game is image making. With the emphasis on leadership, three dimensions of presidential qualities are usually stressed: one has to do with character and persona; another with issue positions and basic values; and a third with essential leadership skills—vision, charisma, decisiveness, and the capacity for getting things done.

Positivity. Positive campaign advertisements emphasize the strengths of a candidate. For presidents seeking reelection, or even vice presidents running for the top office, one of those strengths is clearly experience in high office. Incumbents' advertising pictures them in a variety of presidential roles. One of Jimmy Carter's most effective 1980 commercials showed him in a whirl of presidential activities ending as darkness fell over the White House. A voice intoned, "The responsibility never ends. Even at the end of a long working day there is usually another cable addressed to the chief of state from the other side of the world where the sun is shining and something is happening." As a light came on in the president's living quarters, the voice concluded, "And he's not finished yet." Ronald Reagan in 1984 and George Bush in 1992 used a variation of the president-at-work ad.

Comparisons are also important. Although all candidates must demonstrate their presidential qualities, they also need to distinguish themselves from their opponents. In 1976, Carter emphasized his unusual leadership abilities. His slogan, "A leader, for a change," as well as his less formal appearance and even his decision to use green as the color of his literature in contrast to the traditional red, white, and blue, conveyed "freshness" and set him apart from old-style Washington politicians in general and the two Republican presidents who preceded him in particular. In 1980, Reagan stressed different kinds of solutions to the nation's old and persistent policy problems, as did Perot in 1992. Perot's ads that year were among the most distinctive ever seen in a presidential campaign. Their amateurish quality was purposely designed to set them apart from the slick, smooth, professional commercials of his Republican and Democratic opponents. It was precisely this contrast that Perot wished to convey to the American people. His ads in 1996 lacked the visual appeal and uniqueness of those he aired in 1992. In 2000, Bush's ads emphasized his likeability and trustworthiness; Gore's stressed his knowledge, experience, and his caring and crusading spirit as a fighter for the working class. Both candidates' organizations ran more positive than negative commercials until the final two weeks of the campaign, but their national party organizations went negative earlier.

Negativity. Ads that exploit an opponent's weaknesses by focusing on character deficiencies, issue inconsistencies, or false leadership claims are referred to as confrontational, attack, or negative ads. This type of advertising has increased since the 1970s.

Negative campaigning, of course, is nothing new. In fact, it is as old as presidential electoral politics. George Washington was called a philanderer and a thief; Andrew Jackson was accused of marrying a prostitute; at the outset of the Civil War, Abraham Lincoln was charged with being illegitimate and black; Theodore Roosevelt was said to be a drunkard; Herbert Hoover, a German sympathizer during World War I; and Franklin D. Roosevelt, a lecher, lunatic, and a closet Jew whose real name was Rosenfeldt.

What seems to be different today is the increasing emphasis placed on these negative ads by the candidates; the extent to which they seem to have affected the tenor, agenda, and issues of the campaign; and the widely held belief that they have had a major impact on the perceptions of the electorate.

Instead of playing to a candidate's strengths, negative advertising exploits the opposition's weaknesses, using ridicule and stereotyping to drive home a point. As early as 1952 when political advertising first appeared on television, negative commercials were used to highlight potentially vulnerable positions and images of the opposition. And they have continued to do so.

One of the most successful and repeated negative commercials, "the people-in-the-street ad," features interviews with ordinary citizens who are asked about the candidates. The comments usually are edited to highlight a message, and the ads sound like news. In Ford's 1976 ads, for example, most of the people inter-viewed were from Carter's home state of Georgia. "He [Carter] didn't do any-thing," stated one man from Atlanta. "I've tried, and all my friends have tried, to remember exactly what Carter did as governor, and nobody really knows." The commercial concluded with an attractive woman, also from Georgia, saying, in a thick southern accent, "It would be nice to have a President from Georgia—but not Carter." She smiled. The ad ended.

Negative advertising has been used extensively in recent campaigns. In 1988, researchers estimated that anywhere from 40 to 60 percent of all the advertising broadcast was negative.[44] What distinguished the negative ads of 1988 from those of previous campaigns was that they played on the fears and anxieties of the American people; they primed racial attitudes and reinforced racial steoretypes.[45]

One ad in particular evoked a strong, emotional response. Directed against Michael Dukakis, it featured a mug shot of Willie Horton, an African American prisoner who had raped a white woman while on a weekend furlough from a Mas-sachusetts jail. Aimed at those who were fearful of crime, of African Americans, and of liberals and their "do-good" social policies, the ad placed Dukakis squarely in the liberal, do-gooder camp.

Sponsored by a political action committee supporting Bush, this commercial was supplemented by other PAC ads featuring relatives of the victims of Horton's crimes, including a man whose wife had been raped by Horton and a woman whose brother had been stabbed by him. More than $2 million was spent on speak-ing tours for these people who were personally touched by Horton's horrendous acts.[46] The Bush campaign produced ads of its own to reinforce the crime issue.[47]

The cumulative impact of these crime ads was to leave the impression that Michael Dukakis released hardened criminals who then recommitted heinous crimes on innocent victims. By the end of the campaign, 25 percent of the elec-torate knew who Willie Horton was, what he did, and who furloughed him; 49 percent thought Dukakis was soft on crime.[48] The ads achieved their intended effect.

The amount of negative advertising remained extensive in 1992. L. Patrick Devlin's analysis of candidate advertising in that election found that almost 70 percent of Clinton's ads were negative compared with 56 percent of Bush's. In all, Devlin reports that about half of the presidential ads were negative.[49] In 1996, Devlin found that two out of every three Dole ads was negative. Clinton used only four all negative ads against Dole. One, "Wrong in the Past," went through a litany of popular education and health care programs that Dole ostensibly opposed. The announcer ended the ad by repeating the theme, "Bob Dole, wrong in the past, wrong for our future." According to Professor Devlin, this ad was shown 6,780 times in seventy-five media markets.[50]

Most of Clinton's ads were not totally negative, however. They were ads that compared Dole to Clinton, to Dole's obvious disadvantage. But they were very powerful precisely because they were not perceived as negative.[51] Clinton's media advisers were aware that negative ads had taken a toll on voters.

In the negative ads of 2000, Democrats challenged George W. Bush's record in Texas, accused him of being a captive of special interests, and chided him for proposing policies that would help the rich, bankrupt Social Security, and take away badly needed funds from the public schools for private school vouchers. Republicans, in turn, characterized Al Gore as a proponent of big government, big spending, and big give-away programs. Gore's credibility was sharply challenged at the end of the campaign as were Bush's qualifications for the nation's top job. (See Box 7–1, "The Air Wars of 2000.")

Since the 1988 election the public has become more leery of the negative ads. Part of their skepticism stems from the legacy of negative advertising, particularly in that year. Part of it also results from ad watching by major news organizations. Large newspapers, news services, and networks now regularly assign reporters to cover advertising and examine the accuracy of its claims. There has been a steady increase in this type of coverage.

Impact. People get a lot of information from advertisements, both positive and negative, even *more* than they get from the news. Thomas Patterson and Robert McClure found that voters in 1972 did not learn and retain much information about the substantive issues from television news. They concluded:

1. Most election issues are mentioned so infrequently that viewers could not possibly learn about them.
2. [M]ost issue references are so fleeting that they could not be expected to leave an impression on viewers.
3.   [T]he candidates' issue positions generally were reported in ways guaranteed to make them elusive.[52]

Their findings, which occurred during the era of television journalism when the ABC, CBS, and NBC news organizations dominated the air waves and commanded public attention, have not been refuted by contemporary scholars. Even though there are many alternative sources of news about the campaign available to the electorate, there is little evidence to suggest these alternative sources have produced a more informed public. In fact, recent studies continue to suggest that people learn more from the advertisements about the candidates and their issue positions than they do from the news itself.[53]

If negative ads inform voters, do they also make them more cynical, especially when combined with negative news coverage of the campaign? According to two political scientists, Stephen Ansolabehere and Shanto Iyengar, they do. Their experimental studies on negative ads found that these ads adversely affected turnout, increased cynicism, and decreased feelings of efficacy, especially for those with no partisan allegiances. In other words, the ads were a turnoff; people who saw them lost interest in voting.[54]

Other political scientists, however, are not so sure. In fact, much of the theoretical and empirical evidence suggests quite the opposite effect, that negative ads stimulate turnout. By providing hard-hitting information about the candidates, the commercials strike an emotive chord in many voters, thereby increasing their incentive to vote.[55] This evidence is consistent with the judgments of media professions that negative ads really "work."

BOX 7–1

THE AIR WARS OF 2000: ADVERTISING STRATEGIES

GEORGE W. BUSH

Bush tried to present himself as a different kind of Republican, a "compassionate conservative." To convey such an image, his campaign commercials focused on Bush himself, his concern for the everyday problems people face, his interaction with those from all walks of life. Bush's policy emphases were tailored to present him as a caring Republican, not as the mean-spirited, business-oriented elitist that the Democrats tried to stereotype him and his Republican backers as.

Bush was prominently featured in his ads. Research by Bush's media team indicated that Bush's personal appearance had a positive effect. According to Russ Schriefer, a member of the inner circle, "We found early on that the best person we had to promote the message was the governor.[56]

One of the major differences between the Bush campaign and others that preceded it was the relatively small number of ads used, only twenty-six in all. About half of them were done in Spanish as well as English; a few used a combination of Spanish and English in the same ad. The campaign made a conscious effort to target Latino communities with Spanish-language ads in California, Florida, Nevada, Pennsylvania, and New Mexico in which Bush's nephew, who is part Latino, was also featured.[57] In one such ad, Bush appeared with his extended family and also with people in the Latino community and spoke for himself:

> Where I come from cultural diversity isn't something you read about. It's something you see every day. In my core, it's family. I'm proud of the Latino blood that flows in the Bush family. Latinos contribute so much. In return they deserve the full promise of American life. With reforms that say this is your country—this is your home.[58]

Initially, most of the campaigns' ads were positive, trumpeting Bush's leadership qualities. In one of his earliest ads, the governor was presented in casual clothes sitting alone, then talking with common people, and finally, spending time with his wife and family. In the ad, Bush said:

> I think that there's a lot of cynicism today in America because of broken promises. I believe most people expect the best out of elected officials, and when elected officials disappoint them, it creates a cynical environment.
>
> Secondly, I believe oftentimes campaigns resort to mud throwing and name-calling. And Americans are sick and tired of that kind of campaigning. What they want to hear is what's on people's minds and where the candidates' hearts are. I'm going to run a campaign that is hopeful and optimistic and very positive.[59]

Most of Bush's ads followed a similar format in which the candidate would be seen first alone, then interacting with people, and at the end, alone or with his family. Bush himself did the voice-overs for the ads.

As the campaign progressed, an increasing number of negative ads were designed and aired. Intended to reinforce Gore's character flaws and liberal policy positions, these ads raised questions about the type of president the Democrat would make. One of the most effective of these ads, "Trust" was played throughout the entire campaign. It showed Bush in an open-neck shirt talking to the camera.

I believe we need to encourage personal responsibility so that people are accountable for their actions. And I believe in government that is responsible to the people.

That's the difference in philosophy between my opponent and me. He trusts government. I trust you.

I trust you to invest some of your own Social Security money for higher returns.

I trust local people to run their own schools. In return for federal money, I will insist on performance. And if schools continue to fail, we'll give parents different options.

I trust you with some of the budget surplus. I believe one-fourth of the surplus should go back to the people who pay the bills. My opponent proposes targeted tax cuts only for those he calls the right people. And that means half of all income tax payers get nothing at all.

We should help people live their lives, but not run them. Because when we trust individuals, when we respect local control of schools, when we empower communities, together we can ignite America's spirit and renew our purpose.[60]

The Republican National Committee ads were even more negative than those of the Bush campaign. During and after the presidential debates, they focused on the credibility issue. The ads featured some of Gore's biggest bloopers: his visit to the Buddhist temple in 1996 and his statement that said he invented the Internet. Most of these ads used a female commentator:

There's Al Gore, reinventing himself on television. Like I'm not going to notice. Who's he going to be today? The Al Gore who raises money at a Buddhist Temple or the one who promises campaign finance reform?[61]

One of the most controversial ads aired by the RNC contained a subliminal flash frame with the word *RATS* written on it. Since the frame could not be distinguished when the ad was shown at its normal speed, critics contended that the ad's sponsors intended a subliminal message, associating Gore and government bureaucrats, the subject of the ad, with a much disliked rodent. Republicans denied the allegation, pointing out that the letters were simply the last four of the word bureauc*rats*. Nonetheless, the ad was pulled after one showing and the issue continued to be the subject of media scrutiny and Democratic protests.[62]

AL GORE

Although the Gore team tested and aired many more ads than did the Bush campaign, about three times as many, they ran them in fewer states. Designed with specific areas in mind, Gore's ads emphasized issues relevant to that population: Social Security and Medicare in Florida, environmental issues in Washington and Oregon, education in Iowa, jobs in Michigan, and health issues in West Virginia and Nevada, the state to which high-level nuclear waste was to be sent.

The Gore advertising campaign was more distinctively cycled than Bush's. Following the Democratic convention and continuing through the summer, biographic/documentary ads were used to try to define Gore as his own person. At the end of September 2000, the Gore campaign began airing a commercial that tied Gore's populism to his experience as a fighter for his beliefs and values. Pictured first in an Army uniform in Vietnam, then with his family, and finally interacting with everyday people, the announcer listed Gore's commitments and achievements:

Vietnam veteran. Father of four. Married thirty years. Al Gore will fight for families.

Tax cuts for middle-class families, including a $10,000-a-year tax deduction for college tuition.

Continued welfare reform with time limits, work requirements.

Forced deadbeat parents to take responsibility for their children.

A crime victim's bill of rights to protect victims, not just criminals.[63]

Unlike the spokesman's role that Bush assumed in his ads, Gore did not take an active speaking role in his. In fact, he spoke in only twelve of his seventy-five ads.

Gore's depiction, however, was extremely positive, a caring person who would go out of his way to help others. Health care was one of the issues that Gore's ads trumpeted, including his support for a patient's bill of rights. One of his health care ads fueled public outrage at the insensitivity of some HMOs by telling of the predicament of the Malone family whose son had suffered brain damage as a result of medical misjudgments during his birth. Denied private nursing care by the family's HMO even though that care had been prescribed by a doctor as necessary to sustain the child's life, the mother and father turned to others for help. The case was brought to the attention of the vice president who pitched in. Here are excerpts from the ad:

Mrs. Malone: We had gotten to the point of complete desperation.
Announcer: Al Gore heard the story, and fought back.
Mrs. Malone: He [Gore] told the insurance company. "Don't do this. Don't cut this child's coverage."
Announcer: Al Gore got the Malone family the help they needed. But knowing that all families need protection from HMO abuses, he's fighting for a real Patient's Bill of Rights.
Mrs. Malone: Even if he fought half as hard for the people of our country, as he did for my son . . . nobody loses.[64]

The Gore campaign aired more negative ads than the Bush campaign did. In striking out at Bush, Gore's handlers had three principal objectives: to diminish Bush's role as governor of Texas, to question his preparation and readiness to be president, and to typecast him as a conservative Republican in bed with big business, special interests, and the rich.[65]

The anti-governor ads, following a strategy that Bush's father had used successfully against his 1988 opponent, Michael Dukakis, and unsuccessfully against Bill Clinton, focused on the environment, the imposition of the death penalty, and the low minimum wage. Here's an excerpt from one of them:

They say oil and water don't mix. Nowhere is that more true than in Texas. After seventeen years in the oil business, George Bush ran for governor, then passed law to let big polluters regulate themselves. Today Texas is number three in water pollution, number one in air pollution.[66]

Bush chose not to respond to most of the ads that criticized his governorship.

Other Gore ads were directed at Bush's policy positions, particularly in the domestic area. Social Security was a major issue for the Democrats.

What happens when you promise the same money to two different groups of people? According to the *Wall Street Journal,* George W. Bush is promising young workers a trillion dollars from Social Security to put in private investments. That would cut Social Security benefits for seniors. Bush is also promising seniors that same trillion for their Social Security checks. So what happens when Bush promises the same to young workers and to seniors?
Answer: One promise gets broken.
Next question: Which one?[67]

What the Gore ads did not do was attack Bush personally although it was not for lack of trying. According to Bill Knapp, Gore's advertising director, "We had ad after ad making fun of him—showing his sound bite goofs, showing he's stupid, showing he's a smart aleck—and the voters just rejected it. They thought they were out of context and unfair.[68]

Only toward the end of the campaign did the Democrats find a gaffe that worked. During a campaign appearance Bush had said, "[T]hey want the government to control Social Security like it's some kind of federal program," but opinion on Bush had solidified by this point, and the ad had only a limited effect.

The Democratic National Committee aired even more negative ads than did the Gore campaign, fifty-two in all, targeting Republican positions and candidates. They even went after Dick Cheney, trying to diminish his favorable image by pointing to his very conservative voting record as a member of Congress from Wyoming. These anti-Cheney ads had little effect and were soon dropped.

PAT BUCHANAN AND RALPH NADER

Third-party candidates also spent money on television advertising but nowhere near the amount that the major parties and their candidates spent. Of the almost $13 million that the Reform Party received, mostly from a federal grant, about $10 million was expended on advertising. Buchanan's ads were designed to gain attention for his candidacy, to be remembered since there was not enough money to show them repeatedly, and to highlight Buchanan's strong policy stands, particularly his "America first" theme.

One Buchanan ad, intended to appeal to blue-collar workers, opened with a man eating a spaghetti dinner and choking on a meatball. Dialing 911 for help, he hears a recorded message that English is no longer the official language. "For Spanish, press 1; for Korean, press 2." An announcer contrasted Buchanan's fidelity to America's Anglo-European heritage to Bush and Gore's multiculturalism. By the end of the ad the man was on the floor, a dog licking his face, and the recorded message saying, "For Swahili, press 12."[69]

Nader's ads were not as dramatic as Buchanan's. As an antiestablishment candidate, Nader sought to contrast his pristine, consumer advocacy to Bush's and Gore's politics as usual. In doing so, he presented news clips of Bush and Gore as an announcer incanted the selling of the presidency: "Grilled tenderloin for fund-raiser, $1,000 a plate; campaign ads filled with half-truths, $10 million; promises to special interests, $10 billion."[70]

THE CUMULATIVE IMPACT OF THE MEDIA

The time, money, and energy spent on media by the candidates suggest that the mass media have a major impact on campaigns and elections. Why else would so many resources be devoted to them? Yet it is difficult to document the media's precise effect on voting behavior.

Much of the candidates' concern focuses on news coverage. The negativism of the press, the tendency to highlight inconsistencies and misstatements, even the propensity to interpret rather than report events, has led many people, especially candidates, to conclude that this coverage is biased, has adversely affected their campaigns, and unduly influences the results of the election.

Are the media, particularly the news media, really that powerful? Do they affect voter choice? The answer is probably yes, although their impact may depend on the level of public knowledge, strength of partisan attitudes of the electorate, and the initial judgments voters make even before the campaign begins. For knowledgeable partisans, the primary media effect is to reinforce rather than challenge their inclinations to support their party's nominees.

With the decline of strong partisanship in the electorate and the increase in the number of independents, the audience that may be affected during the general election has become larger and is potentially more malleable for a longer period. In 2000, 8 percent of likely voters had not made up their minds for whom to vote by the last week of the campaign according to a survey conducted by the Pew Research Center for the People & the Press.[71]

For those without strong partisan identities, an increasing proportion of the electorate, and those who are marginally interested in the election, the news media provide valuable information, according to the Annenberg Public Policy Center and The Joan Shorenstein Center on the Press, Politics, and Public Policy.[72] This information shapes perceptions of the candidates, parties, and issues and may also motivate people to vote. In general, the media are apt to be more influential during the early part of the election cycle when less is known about the candidates than at the end.

Despite the distortion and bias, voters believe that they have enough information to make a voting decision. When asked if they learned enough from the 2000 campaign to make an informed choice, 83 percent of voters said yes.[73] How much information people *really* need to do so is a question that has been subject to continual debate.[74]

SUMMARY

The mass media have a profound effect on presidential politics: on the organization, strategy, and tactics of the campaign; on the distribution of resources; and directly or indirectly on the electorate's voting decisions. That is why so much of presidential campaign is devoted to media-related activities.

The news media see and report the campaign as a game, fitting statements, events, and activities into various story lines. Their schema highlights drama and gives controversial statements and events the most attention but also downplays deep discussions of policy issues. They also play up personalities and give dispro-portionate attention to blunders, factual errors, personal exaggerations, and slips of the tongue; they focus on conflict and emphasize the contest.

Candidates naturally try to improve on this coverage. They orchestrate their campaigns for the news media. They choose their words carefully, minimize spon-taneity, include sound bites in their speeches, create good visual images, and do all they can to prevent embarrassing situations from occurring. But even with all this preparation and staging, the news of their campaign may not be accurate or com-plete, and from the candidates' perspective, it is never good enough.

For this reason candidates also try to circumvent the national news media to reach the voters directly. People like to be entertained, so candidates have resorted to various entertainment formats to convey a message, project an image, and ener-gize their supporters. In the past, parades, rallies, and other campaign events were the principal vehicles by which these objectives were achieved. Today, radio and television news interviews, media-driven events, talk-entertainment shows, late-night comedy programs, town meetings, and presidential debates are the most fre-quently used devices to gain and maintain attention from a sizable segment of the population.

The soft news-entertainment programs have been particularly amenable to a conversational dialogue with the electorate, a dialogue that may itself become a news event. Within this less hostile format, candidates can be more expansive, seemingly more responsive, and better able to display their positive personal attributes. Town meetings are also useful in this respect. They have the additional advantage of allowing candidates to interact directly with the audience, to demon-strate their understanding of the people's problems and empathy for those who suffer from them, and to present solutions on a level that the average person can understand and appreciate.

Debates constitute still another entertaining, educational opportunity, partic-ularly for candidates who need to enhance their personal images, convey their pol-icy positions, and demonstrate their communication skills, command of the issues, and commitment to their goals. Not only do debates permit candidates to present their positions on contemporary issues in their own words and often to a large audience, but they also facilitate comparisons with their opponents. The news media play a role here as well, covering the debates and often participating in them, reporting the public's reaction as well as their own evaluations, and then integrating the debate into the ongoing campaign story.

Paid advertising is a fourth device, one that candidates and their parties have used extensively to sell themselves and their ideas to the voters. The techniques that they employ, the strategies and tactics they use, even the people who design and target the ads come from the advertising profession.

In recent presidential campaigns, more than half of the candidate's budgets was spent on media, primarily on the production, airing, and targeting of advertis-ing. Although political commercials tap both positive and negative leadership dimensions, the amount of negativity has increased. Voters have become increas-ingly leery about the claims of the ads, though advertisements still seem to have an impact.

Most communications analysts believe that media campaigns are important because they inform the electorate. They may energize supporters. They can affect perceptions of the candidates, parties, and issues, which in turn can influence vote choice. For strong partisans, the cumulative impact of the media is to reinforce predispositions and existing political attitudes; for weaker partisans and independents, however, the impact can also be to alter opinions and help individuals arrive at an informed voting decision. Although one election campaign does not usually change partisan attitudes on a permanent basis, it may cause them to shift, and over a period of time, to change.

The proportion of the electorate whose voting choice is actually influenced by hard and soft news coverage, presidential debates, and candidate advertising is difficult to assess. But campaign managers take no chances. In a close election, influencing even a small number of voters can change the outcome. And from the candidates' and their managers' perspectives, that outcome is what the presidential election is all about.

WHERE ON THE WEB?

In addition to the media outlets mentioned in previous chapters, here are some others to explore.

- **Alliance for Better Campaigns**
  http://www.bettercampaigns.org
  A public interest group that promotes high standards of media coverage and citizen involvement.
- **Associated Press**
  http://www.ap.org
  The largest news service in the United States. It provides fast-breaking information on its wire service and Web site.
- **Center for Media and Public Affairs**
  http://www.cmpa.com
  Conducts studies on television coverage of the campaign and the "spin" that the candidates and their stands on the issues get.
- **Commission on Presidential Debates**
  http://www.debates.org
  This is the group that plans the debates, selects the cities, decides which candidates can participate, and moderates the discussion format between the principal candidates. Provides transcripts of past and present presidential debates.
- **The Freedom Forum**
  http://www.freedomforum.org
  This site provides information on freedom of the press issues, with links to the Newseum, the Media Studies Center, and the First Amendment Center.
- **Newspaperlinks.com**
  http://www.newspaperlinks.com
  Provides links to the online editions of local newspapers across the country.
- **The Pew Research Center for the People & the Press**
  http://www.people-press.org

A nonpartisan research organization sponsored by the Pew Charitable Trusts that surveys public opinion on politics and on media coverage.
- **Politics Online**
http://www.politicsonline.com
A good source to access presidential campaigning on the Internet.
- **Washington Post**
http://www.washingtonpost.com
A good source of information about the campaign and the mind-set of the Washington political establishment.

EXERCISES

1. Contrast the advertisements of the presidential candidates on the basis of their messages, presentations, and target groups. Note also the media on which the advertisements ran. These ads should be available on the candidates' Web sites.
2. Check the accuracy of the ads you have discussed in question one. Major newspapers such as the *New York Times* and the *Washington Post* and news networks assess some of the campaign advertising and their assessments can be obtained on their Web pages.
3. Compare the amount of television coverage given to the horse race and to issues of candidate personality, policy, and strategy and tactics by examining the analysis performed by the Center for the Media and Public Affairs, <http://www.cmpa.com>. Do you feel the coverage was balanced or unbalanced? Did it provide voters with sufficient information to make an intelligent judgment on election day? Did the press display an ideological bias?
4. Take any major event in the presidential campaign and compare coverage of it by a national newspaper, television broadcast network, a national news magazine, and a major source of information on the Internet. Which coverage was better? Why?
5. View one of the presidential debates and note the principal points the candidates wished to make. If elected, did the candidate follow through on the positions he advocated? (These tapes should be available in the C-SPAN archives and at the Commission on Presidential Debates Web site, <http://www.debates.org>.)

SELECTED READING

Ansolabehere, Stephen, and Shanto Iyengar. *Going Negative.* New York: Free Press, 1995.

Buchanan, Bruce. *Renewing Presidential Politics: Campaigns, Media, and the Public Interest.* Lanham, Md.: Rowman & Littlefield, 1996.

Cappella, Joseph N., and Kathleen Hall Jamieson. *Spiral of Cynicism.* New York: Oxford University Press, 1997.

Davis, Richard, and Diana Owen. *New Media and American Politics.* New York: Oxford University Press, 1998.

Devlin, L. Patrick. "Contrasts in Presidential Campaign Commercials of 1992." *American Behavioral Scientist* 37 (November 1993): 272–290.

———. "Contrasts in Presidential Campaign Commercials of 1996." *American Behavioral Scientist* 40 (August 1997): 1058–1084.

———. "Contrasts in Presidential Campaign Commercials of 2000." *American Behavioral Scientist* 44 (August 2001): 2338–2369.

Farnsworth, Stephen J., and S. Robert Lichter. *The Nightly News Nightmare: Network Television Coverage of Presidential Elections, 1988–2000.* Lanham, Md.: Rowman & Littlefield, 2003.

Goldstein, Ken, and Paul Freedman. "Campaign Advertising and Voter Turnout: New Evidence for a Stimulation Effect." *The Journal of Politics* 64 (August 2002): 721–740.

Hart, Roderick. *Campaign Talk: Why Elections Are Good for Us.* Princeton, N.J.: Princeton University Press, 2000.

Holman, Craig B., and Luke P. McLoughlin. *Buying Time 2000: Television Advertising in the 2000 Federal Elections.* New York: Brennan Center for Social Justice at New York University, 2001.

Iyengar, Shanto, and Donald Kinder. *News That Matters: Television and American Opinion.* Chicago: University of Chicago Press, 1987.

Jamieson, Kathleen Hall. *Everything You Think You Know about Politics and Why You're Wrong.* New York: Basic Books, 2000.

———. *Packaging the Presidency: A History and Criticism of Presidential Campaign Advertising.* Oxford: Oxford University Press, 1996.

———. *Dirty Politics: Deception, Distraction, Democracy.* Oxford: Oxford University Press, 1996.

———. and David S. Birdsell. *Presidential Debates.* New York: Oxford University Press, 1988.

Kaid, Lynda Lee, and Anne Johnston. "Negative versus Positive Television Advertising in U.S. Presidential Campaigns, 1960–1988." *Journal of Communications* 41 (Summer 1991): 53–64.

Kerbel, Matthew Robert. *Edited for Television: CNN, ABC, and the American Presidential Campaign.* Boulder, Colo.: Westview Press, 1998.

Kraus, Sidney. *Televised Presidential Debates and Public Policy.* 2nd ed. Mahwah, N.J.: Erlbaum, 2000.

Mayer, William G. "In Defense of Negative Campaigning." *Political Science Quarterly* III (Fall 1996): 437–455.

Patterson, Thomas E. *Doing Well and Doing Good: How Soft News and Critical Journalism Are Shrinking the News Audience and Weakening Democracy—And What News Outlets Can Do about It.* Cambridge, Mass.: Joan Shorenstein Center on the Press, Politics, and Public Policy, 2000.

———. *Out of Order.* New York: Knopf, 1993.

Schroeder, Alan. *Presidential Debates: Forty Years of High-Risk TV.* New York: Columbia University Press, 2000.

West, Darrell M. *Air Wars: Television Advertising in Election Campaigns, 1952–2000,* 3rd ed. Washington, D.C.: Congressional Quarterly, 2001.

NOTES

1. The term *yellow journalism* comes from the comic strip, "The Yellow Kid," which first appeared in Joseph Pulitzer's *New York World* in 1896. The kid, whose nightshirt was colored yellow in the paper, was an instant hit and sparked a bidding war for the comic strip between Pulitzer and William Randolph Hearst. Although the strip's popularity lasted only a few years, the competition between these two media titans continued for decades.

2. David Stebenne, "Media Coverage of American Presidential Elections: A Historical Perspective," in *The Finish Line: Covering the Campaign's Final Days*, ed. Martha FitzSimon (New York: Freedom Forum Media Studies Center, 1993), 83.

3. Thomas E. Patterson, *Out of Order* (New York: Knopf, 1993) 53–133.

4. Thomas E. Patterson, "Television and Election Strategy," in *The Communications Revolution in Politics*, ed. Gerald Benjamin (New York: Academy of Political Science, 1982), 30.

5. Michael J. Robinson and Margaret A. Sheehan, *Over the Wire and on TV: CBS and UPI in Campaign '80* (New York: Russell Sage Foundation, 1983), 148.

6. Ibid., 146.

7. Thomas E. Patterson and Richard Davis, "The Media Campaign: Struggle for the Agenda," in *The Elections of 1984*, ed. Michael Nelson (Washington, D.C.: Congressional Quarterly, 1985), 119.

8. "Clinton's the One," *Media Monitor* (November 1992): 2.

9. "Dole's Summer Doldrums," *Media Monitor* (July/August 1996): 2; "Take This Campaign—Please," *Media Monitor* (September/October 1996): 2–3.

10. Surprisingly, the morning talk and news entertainment shows provided greater coverage. Stephen Hess, "Hess Report on Campaign Coverage in Nightly Network News," Brookings Institution, November 11, 2000, <http://www.brookings.edu/GS/Projects/HessReport/week9.htm>.

11. Not only do the news media focus more on the candidates than their policies, but they focus primarily on the major party candidates. When running for their party's nomination, candidates receive coverage roughly in proportion to their popular standing, with the front-runners getting the most attention. After the conventions are over, it becomes primarily a two-person contest. Minor party and independent candidates tend to receive little, if any, attention, the exceptions being John Anderson in 1980, Ross Perot in 1992, and Ralph Nader in 2000.

12. James Glen Stovall, "Incumbency and News Coverage of the 1980 Presidential Campaign," *Western Political Quarterly* 37 (December 1984): 628.

13. Although partisan sources were equally harsh on the candidates of the other major party, they were not as harsh on Perot, reflecting perhaps the Republican and Democratic strategies not to criticize him in public. Nonpartisan sources, people who might be considered experts or just plain voters, were more positive about Clinton than Bush. Among both partisan and nonpartisan sources, Perot received the best press. "Clinton's the One," 3–4.

14. Hess, "Hess Report." Another study, this one commissioned by the Project for Excellence in Journalism, found that while the spin was more negative than positive, Bush actually got better coverage than Gore. Jeff Leeds, "Study Finds Negative Media Political Coverage—Especially for Gore." *Los Angeles Times*, November 1, 2000, <http://www.latimes.com/news/politics/elect2000/pres/news2>.

15. S. Robert Lichter, Stanley Rothman, and Linda S. Lichter, *The Media Elite* (Bethesda, Md.: Adler & Adler, 1986).

16. Kiku Adatto, "The Incredible Shrinking Sound Bite," *New Republic* (May 28, 1990): 22.

17. Quoted in David R. Runkel, ed., *Campaign for President: The Managers Look at '88* (Dover, Mass.: Auburn House, 1989), 136.
18. Quoted in Adatto, "Sound Bite," 22.
19. "Take This Campaign—Please," 2.
20. Center for Media and Public Affairs, "Journalists Monopolize TV News."
21. Thomas E. Patterson, *Out of Order*, 106.
22. Ibid., 119–120.
23. Ibid., 118–119.
24. Paul Lazarsfeld, Bernard Berelson, and Hazel Goudet, *The People's Choice* (New York: Columbia University Press, 1948); Bernard Berelson, Paul Lazarsfeld, and William McPhee, *Voting: A Study of Opinion Formation in a Presidential Campaign* (Chicago: University of Chicago Press, 1954).
25. Michael J. Robinson, "Mass Media and the Margins of Democratic Politics: Non-Transformations in the USA," (unpublished paper, March 1993), 81–83.
26. Center for Media and Public Affairs, "Journalists Monopolize TV News."
27. Peter Goldman, Thomas M. DeFrank, Mary Miller, et al., *Quest for the Presidency: 1992* (College Station: Texas A&M Press, 1994), 535.
28. Perot complained bitterly, first appealing to the Federal Communications Commission and then instituting legal action to prevent the debates from being held if he could not participate. Although he failed to stop the debates, he used his exclusion to emphasize one of his campaign themes—the self-serving nature of the two-party system and the need to reform it. The reason that Perot was so agitated was that participating in the debates was part of his campaign strategy. He had boosted his popularity significantly in 1992 by his performance in the presidential debates and hoped to do so again in 1996.
29. Tony Fabrizio, Dole's pollster, quoted in *Campaign for President: The Managers Look at '96.* (Hollis, N.H.: Hollis Publishing, Harvard University Institute of Politics, 1997), 171.
30. The other networks indicated that they would not carry news shows of their competitors; hence, the debates on regularly scheduled programs would reach a much smaller audience than would the Commission's debates.
31. Nixon had closeted himself alone in a hotel before his first debate with Kennedy. He received only a ten-minute briefing. Moreover, he had bumped his knee on a car door going into the television studio and was in considerable pain. Theodore H. White, *The Making of the President, 1960* (New York: Atheneum, 1988), 285.
32. Quoted in "Campaign '92: Transcript of the First Presidential Debate," *New York Times* (October 12, 1992), A16.
33. Matthew Dowd in Kathleen Hall Jamieson and Paul Waldman, *Electing the President 2000: The Insiders' View* (Philadelphia: University of Pennsylvania Press, 2001), 22.
34. Moreover, Kemp was not particularly critical of the vice president or president, something a challenger has to be to make the case for change. His performance so dismayed Republican strategists who were watching it on television that Haley Barbour, the chair of the Republican National Committee was heard to remark, "I told you we should have kept the ball game [the National League playoffs] on one channel!" Haley Barbour, quoted in Evan Thomas, *Back from the Dead* (New York: Atlantic Monthly Press, 1997), 184.
35. Carter Eskew in Jamieson and Waldman, *Electing the President*, 71.
36. Surveys taken at the conclusion of the debate indicated that a majority of people believed Ford had won. After the media played up the Eastern Europe comment and the public had a chance to digest it, the reaction was almost the opposite. By more than two to one, Carter was perceived to be the winner.

37. Craig B. Holman and Luke P. McLoughlin, *Buying Time 2000: Television Advertising in the 2000 Federal Elections* (New York: Brennan Center for Social Justice at New York University, 2001), 40–41. The Brennan Center study is based on a data set that tracked advertisements in the seventy-five major media markets for the 2000 campaign, almost 1 million ads (970,410). Of these, about one-third (302,450) were presidential ads with the vast majority aired during the general election campaign; the rest were shown during the nominations. Most of the ads targeted the key battleground states with the exception of Texas and New York.
38. Ibid., 45.
39. Ibid.
40. Carter Eskew in Jamieson and Waldman, *Electing the President,* 67.
41. Leslie Wayne, "Infamous Political Commercial Is Turned on Gore," *New York Times,* October 27, 2000, A26.
42. Holman and McLoughlin, *Buying Time,* 54–56.
43. Dick Morris, *Behind the Oval Office* (New York: Simon & Schuster, 1996), 139.
44. Lynda Lee Kaid and Anne Johnston, "Negative versus Positive Television Advertising in U.S. Presidential Campaigns, 1960–1988," *Journal of Communications* 41 (Summer 1991): 54.
45. Nicholas A. Valentino, Vincent L. Hutchings, and Ismail K. White, "Cues That Matter: How Political Ads Prime Racial Attitudes During Campaigns," *American Political Science Review* 96 (March 2002), 75–88.
46. M. Hailey, "Crime Victims Condemn Dukakis," *Austin-American Statesman,* October 11, 1988, B3.
47. The most potent of these Bush ads, called "Revolving Door," saw inmates walking through a revolving door of a prison with the announcer warning:

    As governor, Michael Dukakis vetoed mandatory sentences for drug dealers. He vetoed the death penalty. His revolving-door policy gave weekend furloughs to first degree murderers not eligible for parole. While out, many committed other crimes like kidnapping and rape. And many are still at large. Now Michael Dukakis says he wants to do for America what he's done for Massachusetts. America can't afford that risk!

    L. Patrick Devlin, "Contrasts in Presidential Campaign Commercials of 1988," *American Behavioral Scientist* 32 (March/April 1989): 389.
48. Edwin Diamond and Adrian Marin, "Spots," *American Behavioral Scientist* 32 (March/April 1989): 386.
49. L. Patrick Devlin, "Contrasts in Presidential Campaign Commercials of 1992," *American Behavioral Scientist* 37 (November, 1993): 288.
50. L. Patrick Devlin, "Contrasts in Presidential Campaign Commercials of 1996," *American Behavioral Scientist* 40 (August 1997): 1064.
51. The public perceived Clinton's 1996 campaign as less negative than his 1992 campaign according to a national survey conducted right after the election by Princeton Survey Research Associates for the Pew Research Center for the People & the Press. Here's the question and the responses:

    Compared to past presidential elections, would you say there was more mud slinging or negative campaigning in this campaign or less mud slinging or negative campaigning in this campaign?

	1992	**1996**	**2000**
More	68	49	34
Less	6	36	46
Same			
(volunteered response)	14	12	16
Don't Know	2	3	4

Pew Research Center, "Voters Side with Bush for Now," November 14, 2000, Q24.

52. Thomas E. Patterson and Robert D. McClure, *The Unseeing Eye* (New York: Putnam, 1976), 58.

53. Craig Leonard Brians and Martin P. Wattenberg, "Comparing Issue Knowledge and Salience: Comparing Reception from TV Commercials, TV News, and Newspapers," *American Journal of Political Science* (February 1996): 172–193.

54. Stephen Ansolabehere and Shanto Iyengar, *Going Negative: How Political Advertisements Shrink and Polarize the Electorate* (New York: Free Press, 1995), 147–150.

55. Ken Goldstein and Paul Freedman, "Campaign Advertising and Voter Turnout: New Evidence for a Stimulation Effect," *Journal of Politics* 64 (August 2002), 122–123. See also Steven Finkel and John Geer, "A Spot Check: Casting Doubt on the Demobilizing Effect of Attack Advertising," *American Journal of Political Science* 42 (June 1988), 573–595; Paul Freedman and Ken Goldstein, "Measuring Media Exposure and the Effects of Negative Campaign Ads," *American Journal of Political Science* 43 (September 1999), 1189–1208; Kim Fridkin Kahn and Patrick Kenney, "Do Negative Campaigns Mobilize or Suppress Turnout? Clarifying the Relationship between Negativity and Participation," *American Political Science Review* 93 (December 1999), 877–890; Martin Wattenberg and Craig Brians, "Negative Campaign Advertising: Demobilizer or Mobilizer?" *American Political Science Review* 93 (December 1999), 891–900.

56. Russ Schriefer in L. Patrick Devlin, "Contrasts in Presidential Campaign Commercials of 2000," *American Behavioral Scientist*, 44 (August 2001), 2343.

57. Lionel Sosa in Jamieson and Waldman, *Electing the President*, 159.

58. George W. Bush Campaign Committee Web site, <http://www.georgebush.com>.

59. Ibid.

60. Ibid.

61. Devlin, "Contrasts in Campaign Commercials of 2000," 2350. On Halloween, the Bush campaign released an ad entitled "Nonsense" that focused on the misstatements Gore made in support of his programs and misrepresentations of Bush's. The ad pictured Gore in a pharmacy, then froze on a *Washington Times* headline, "Aides Concede Gore Made Up Story" superimposed on the screen; the picture then returned to Gore and the word *nonsense*. The scene shifted to Bush with workers and then back to Gore in his debate with Bill Bradley. At this point an announcer said:

> Remember when Al Gore said his mother-in-law's prescription cost more than his dog's? His own aides said the story was made up. Now Al Gore is bending the truth again. The press calls Gore's Social Security attacks "nonsense."
>
> Governor Bush [plan] sets aside $2.4 trillion to strengthen Social Security and pay all benefits.
>
> Gore: "There has never been a time in this campaign when I have said something untrue."
>
> Announcer: Really?
>
> George W. Bush Campaign Web site, <http://www.georgebush.com>.

62. Devlin, "Contrasts in Campaign Commercials of 2000," 2350.

63. Al Gore Campaign Web site, <http://www.algore2000.com>.

64. Ibid.

65. Knapp in Jamieson and Waldman, *Electing the President*, 165–167.

66. Devlin, "Contrasts in Campaign Commercials of 2000," 2359.

67. Gore Campaign Web site, <http://www.algore2000.com>.

68. Bill Knapp in Devlin, "Contrasts in Campaign Commercials of 2000," 2355.

69. Ibid., 2361–2361.

70. Ibid., 2362–2363.

71. Pew Research Center for the People & the Press, "Popular Vote a Toss-up: Final Reelection Poll," November 6, 2000.

72. Annenberg Public Policy Center, "Conventions Increase America's Appetite for News about Presidential Race," University of Pennsylvania, August 13, 2000; "Americans Learned Much about Convention Positions after First Two Debates," October 10, 2000, <http://www.appcpenn.org>. Joan Shorenstein Center on the Press, Politics, and Public Policy, "Conventions Boost Americans' Issue Awareness," Harvard University, August 30, 2000; "News Coverage Propels Election Interest," September 20, 2000; "Debates Boost Issue Awareness Slightly, but Most Americans Are Still Uninformed about Candidates' Policies," October 26, 2000, <http://www.vanishingvoter.org>.

73. Pew Research Center for the People & the Press, "Despite Uncertain Outcome, Campaign 2000 Highly Rated," November 16, 2000.

74. For a very interesting article on this subject see Larry M. Bartels, "Uniformed Votes: Information Effects in Presidential Elections," *American Journal of Political Science* 40 (February 1996): 194–230.

PART IV

THE
ELECTION

UNDERSTANDING PRESIDENTIAL ELECTIONS

8

INTRODUCTION

Predicting the results of an election is a favorite American practice. Politicians do it; the news media do it; even the public tries to anticipate the outcome far in advance of the event. It is a form of entertainment—somewhat akin to forecasting the winner of a sporting contest.

Presidential elections are particularly prone to such predictions. National surveys report on the opinions of the American public at frequent intervals during the campaign. On election night, television news commentators project a winner before most of the votes are counted. Election day surveys of voters exiting from the polls assess the mood of the electorate and present the first systematic analysis of the results. Subsequently, more in-depth studies reveal shifts in opinions and attitudes.

Most predictions and analyses of the electorate based on survey data are not conducted solely for their entertainment or news value, although many are. They also provide important information to candidates running for office and to those who have been elected. For the nominees, surveys of public opinion indicate the issues that can be effectively raised and those that should be avoided. They also suggest which audience might be most receptive to specific policy positions. For the successful candidates, analyses of voter preferences, opinions, and attitudes provide an interpretation of the vote, indicate the range and depth of public concern on the key issues, and signal the amount of support newly elected presidents are likely to receive as they begin their administration.

This chapter examines the presidential vote from four perspectives. The first looks at the political, economic, and social environment as a precursor to the vote. It examines models that political scientists have used to explain and predict voting behavior and the controversy those models generated in 2000 by their unanimous forecast of a Gore victory.

The second section deals with snapshots of the public at different points during the campaign. It discusses national polls, describes their methodologies, and evaluates their effects. The news media's election eve forecasts and analyses are also described.

The third section turns to an examination of the vote itself. After discussing election day surveys, it reports on the National Election Studies, which have been conducted since 1952. These studies, which are surveys of the national electorate before and after the election, provide basic data that scholars have used to analyze elections and understand voting behavior. The principal findings of these analyses are summarized for each presidential election since 1952.

The final section of the chapter turns to the relationship between campaigning and governing, between issue debates and public policy making, between candidate evaluations and presidential style. Do the campaign issues determine the form of agenda building? Does the projected or perceived image of the candidates affect the tone of the presidency or the actions of the one who is elected? Can an electoral coalition be converted into a governing party? Does the selection process help or hinder the president in meeting the expectations it creates? These questions are explored in an effort to determine the impact of the election on the operation of the presidency, the behavior of the president, and the functioning of the political system.

PREDICTING PRESIDENTIAL ELECTIONS

Political scientists have had a long running debate about how much campaigns really matter. Do they dictate, influence, or have relatively little impact on election outcomes?

There are two principal schools of thought. One argues that campaigns usually do not matter all that much, that the environment in which elections occur shapes the electorate's judgment and augurs the results of the vote. The other position is that campaigns can be decisive, particularly when the electorate is closely divided. These contending positions are not necessarily inconsistent with one another, but they do reflect differences in the perceptions of what are the most important influences on voting—economic, social, and political conditions or attitudes, issues, and personalities?

Formal Models

Those in the environment-conditions-the-results school have constructed formal models by which they forecast election outcomes. They identify critical variables that measure or reflect the economic, social, or political environment in which an election occurs, place these variables in their model, and use them to predict the percentage of the vote that the winning candidate should receive. To ensure that they have the right combination of factors in their model, the researchers usually test its accuracy on the basis of how their models would have forecast the vote in past elections.

Quantifiable economic data are generally available for analysis. Per capita growth of the gross domestic product (GDP), the rise or fall in personal incomes, the rate of inflation, even the level of unemployment are indicators of the state of the economy, and presumably reflect how people evaluate that state.

Relevant political factors include the public's approval of the president. A high approval rating normally indicates general satisfaction with the administration, a condition that would help an incumbent running for reelection. Factors that might mitigate the impact of high job approval ratings include fatigue with the incumbent president or party in power and/or a personal dislike of one or both of them. Clinton had strong performance but weak favorability ratings as the 2000 elections approached. Although 54 percent of the electorate approved of the job he was doing, a majority also had an unfavorable opinion of him personally. Which of these two factors was the more important in affecting the vote Vice President Al Gore received in 2000? World peace, international opinion of the United States within the international community, and protection of American interests abroad may also be relevant considerations for a presidential election.

In short, the models make an assumption that voters will make a retrospective voting decision to stay the course if times are good and they are satisfied or change the course if times are bad and they are unhappy.

Peace, prosperity, and control of the presidency all favored the Democrats in 2000, or so the modelers thought. Meeting in late August at the annual convention of the American Political Science Association, all of them predicted a Gore victory. They estimated that he would receive anywhere from 52.8 to 60.3 percent of the vote. What happened? Why were the modelers wrong?

Some critics attributed the incorrect estimates of the final popular vote to ideological bias. They see political scientists as liberal-leaning and Democratic— hence the favorable forecast for Gore. Others, however, contended that the 2000 election was unique, or at least different from previous elections. Perhaps the economy didn't help the Democrats because the prosperity had lasted too long; people had gotten used to it. The electorate believed that either of the candidates could and would continue the good economic times into the future. Or perhaps, a good economy is not nearly as beneficial to the party in power as a bad economy is harmful. Gore's inability or unwillingness to take credit for the successful economic policies of the Clinton years may also have been a factor.

What about Clinton's high approval ratings? Did Gore distance himself too much from Clinton to bask in the approval of the administration? Did Clinton's personal excesses and the persistent news about them tire the public and fuel a desire for a change? There is some evidence that it did.[1]

Did the models measure the wrong variables or did the 2000 campaign matter more than previous campaigns? Perhaps the strategies and tactics of the major party candidates did not balance one another. Bush may have been more advantaged by his strategy than Gore was by his. Besides, Gore did win the popular vote, so the models did predict the right outcome even though they overestimated Gore's percentage of the two-party vote.

In their postmortems following the election, the modelers pointed to a variety of factors that impaired their collective judgment: They used the wrong combination of variables; they calculated presidential approval but not Clinton's personal unfavorability; they overemphasized economic factors and underestimated moral and social ones; and finally, they failed to consider the uniqueness of the 2000 election and the 2000 campaign. Dr. Christopher Wlezien concluded an analysis of why his and other models did not capture the final result with greater accuracy with the following admonition:

> All that forecasting models can offer well in advance of an election is some sense of the advantage or disadvantage candidates have as the campaign begins. They offer a starting point of sorts, not the final resting place. Campaigns matter. They always have and always will. If this wasn't already clear before the 2000 election, it is now.[2]

Public Opinion Polls

In addition to using formal models to forecast the vote, political scientists and journalists also depend heavily on public opinion surveys to predict election outcomes and gain information about the political views of the electorate. The public is naturally interested in who is going to win. The news media and candidates are obsessed with the answer to the question of who will win for obvious reasons. In focusing on the campaigns, the news media report who is ahead, how the candidates are perceived, and what issues are dividing the voters. In forging a winning coalition, candidates and their organizations need to know how the electorate is reacting to them and their issue positions. Waiting for this information until after the election is over is obviously too late. That is the reason there are so many public opinion polls.

In recent elections, there have been literally hundreds of polls.[3] Published in newspapers, broadcast by the television networks, and available online, they monitor daily shifts in perceptions, opinions, and anticipated voting decisions of the electorate. Polls also provide the major party campaigns with information about how their messages are being received, the type of appeals that seem to resonate most effectively with different groups of voters, and the electoral opportunities which present themselves over the course of the campaign.

Although the number of polls has mushroomed in recent years, polling itself is not a new phenomenon. There have been nationwide assessments of public opinion since 1916. The largest and most comprehensive of the early surveys were the straw polls conducted by the *Literary Digest,* a popular monthly magazine. The *Digest* mailed millions of ballots and questionnaires to people who appeared on lists of automobile owners and in telephone directories. In 1924, 1928, and 1932, the poll correctly predicted the winner of the presidential election. In 1936, it did not: A huge Alfred Landon victory was forecast, and a huge Franklin Roosevelt victory followed.

What went wrong? The *Digest* mailed 10 million questionnaires over the course of the campaign and received 2 million back. As the ballots were returned, they were tabulated. This procedure, which provided a running count, blurred shifts in public opinion that may have been occurring over the course of the campaign. But that was not its only problem. The principal difficulty with the *Digest*'s survey was that the sample of people who responded was not representative of the voting public. Automobile owners and telephone subscribers were simply not typical voters in 1936, since most people did not own cars or have telephones. This distinction mattered more in 1936 than it had in previous years, because of the Great Depression. There was a socioeconomic cleavage within the electorate. The *Literary Digest* sample did not reflect this cleavage; thus its results were inaccurate.

While the *Digest* was tabulating its 2 million responses and predicting that Landon would be the next president, a number of other pollsters were conducting more scientific surveys and correctly forecasting Roosevelt's reelection. The polls of George Gallup, Elmo Roper, and Archibald Crossley differed from the *Digest*'s in two principal respects: they were considerably smaller, and their samples approximated the characteristics of the population as a whole, permitting more accurate generalizations of public opinion to be made.

The *Digest* went out of business, but Gallup, Roper, and Crossley continued to poll and to improve their sampling techniques. In 1940, Gallup predicted Roosevelt would receive 52 percent of the vote; he actually received 55 percent. In 1944, Gallup forecast a 51.5 percent Roosevelt vote, very close to his actual 53.2 percent. Other pollsters also made predictions that closely approximated the results. As a consequence, public confidence in election polling began to grow. (See Table 8–1.)

The confidence was short-lived, however. In 1948, all major pollsters forecast a victory by Republican Thomas E. Dewey. Their errors resulted from poor sampling techniques, from the premature termination of polling before the end of the campaign, and from incorrect assumptions about how the undecided would vote.

In attempting to estimate the population in their samples, the pollsters had resorted to filling quotas. They interviewed a certain number of people with different demographic characteristics until the percentage of these groups in the sample resembled that percentage in the population as a whole. Simply because the percentages were approximately equal, however, did not mean that the sample was representative of the population. For example, interviewers avoided certain areas in cities, and their results were consequently biased.

Moreover, the interviewing stopped several weeks before the election. In mid-October, the polls showed that Dewey was ahead by a substantial margin. Burns Roper, son of Elmo Roper, polling for *Fortune* magazine, saw the lead as sufficiently large to predict a Dewey victory without the need for further surveys. A relatively large number of people, however, were undecided. Three weeks before the election, Gallup concluded that 8 percent of the voters had still not made up their minds. In estimating the final vote, he and other pollsters assumed that the undecided would divide their votes in much the same manner as the electorate as a whole. This assumption turned out to be incorrect. Most of those who were wavering in the closing days of the campaign were Democrats. In the end, most of them voted for Truman or did not vote at all.

The results of the 1948 election once again cast doubt on the accuracy of public opinion polls. Truman's victory also reemphasized the fact that surveys reflect opinion at the time they are taken, not necessarily days or weeks later. Opinion and voter preferences may change.

To improve the monitoring of shifts within the electorate, pollsters changed their method of selecting people to be interviewed. They developed more effective means of anticipating who would actually vote. They polled continuously to identify more precisely and quickly any shifts that occurred in public sentiment and reactions to campaign events. They also extended their surveys to the day before the election to get as close to the time people actually vote as they could. Obviously, the closer to election day the more likely the poll should come close to forecasting the actual results. Public opinion has solidified; more people have made up their minds; and pollsters can usually anticipate what their decision will be on election day.

These changes, plus the continued refinement of the questions, have produced better and more accurate polls, particularly in the one hundred days before the election. Between 1936 and 1950, the average error of the final Gallup preelection poll was 3.6 percent; since then it has usually been less than 2 percent.[4] Other polling organizations have also experienced high levels of accuracy. Table 8–2 lists the final preelection polls and results in 2000.

TABLE 8–1 🌺

GALLUP POLL ACCURACY RECORD, 1936–2000

Year	Gallup Final Survey	Election Results	Deviation
2000	46.0% Gore; 48.0% Bush	48.2% Gore, 48.0% Bush	-2.9%
1996	52.0 Clinton	50.1 Clinton	+1.9
1992*	49.0 Clinton	43.2 Clinton	+5.8
1988	56.0 Bush	53.9 Bush	-2.1
1984	59.0 Reagan	59.1 Reagan	-0.1
1980	47.0 Reagan	50.8 Reagan	-3.8
1976	48.0 Carter	50.0 Carter	-2.0
1972	62.0 Nixon	61.8 Nixon	+0.2
1968	43.0 Nixon	43.5 Nixon	-0.5
1964	64.0 Johnson	61.3 Johnson	+2.7
1960	51.0 Kennedy	50.1 Kennedy	+0.9
1956	59.5 Eisenhower	57.8 Eisenhower	+1.7
1952	51.0 Eisenhower	55.4 Eisenhower	-4.4
1948	44.5 Truman	49.9 Truman	-5.4
1944	51.5 Roosevelt	53.3 Roosevelt	-1.8
1940	52.0 Roosevelt	55.0 Roosevelt	-3.0
1936	55.7 Roosevelt	62.5 Roosevelt	-6.8

*The Ross Perot candidacy created an additional source of error in estimating the 1992 presidential vote. There was no historical precedent for Perot, an independent candidate who was accorded equal status to the major party nominees in the presidential debates and had a record advertising budget. Gallup's decision to allocate none of the undecided vote to Perot, based on past performance of third-party and independent candidates, resulted in this overestimation of Clinton's vote.

Source: Gallup poll, <http://www.gallup.com/poll/trends/ptaccuracy.asp>, April 4, 1999; updated by Gallup poll, "Popular Vote in Presidential Race Too Close to Call," November 7, 2000, <http://www.gallup.com/poll/releases/pr00110.asp>. Reprinted by permission.

Very close elections in 1960, 1968, and 1976, however, resulted in several pollsters making wrong predictions. In 1980, the size of Reagan's victory was substantially underestimated in some nationwide polls; in 1992 and 1996, Clinton's margin was overestimated, whereas in 2000 Gore's was underestimated by some pollsters (see Table 8–2).

Why do pollsters under- or overestimate the results? Although opinions can change between a poll and the actual vote, that change should be small since most pollsters now conclude their surveys the day before the election. There are, however, two other variables that pollsters must consider: turnout and undecided voters. Who is likely to vote, whether the undecided will vote, and if so, for whom are factors that can result in a discrepancy between the sample result and the popular vote.

Anticipating likely voters is a tricky business, more so, the further the time from election day. Simply asking people whether they plan to vote is not sufficient because more people will say that they intend to vote than actually do so.[5] People do not want to admit that they may not vote, or that something may interfere with their doing so. Thus, pollsters usually ask a battery of questions to determine the likelihood of the respondent actually voting: Are you currently registered to vote? Did you vote in the last election? By the way, where do people vote around here?

Similarly, it is necessary for pollsters to anticipate who is really undecided, whether they will vote, and if so, for whom. The wording of preference questions can be critical. Researchers at Harvard's Shorenstein Center found that presenting people with a list of choices and asking them for whom they would vote if the election were held today results in a lower percentage of undecideds than if they are given the additional option of choosing an alternative response such as "or haven't you picked a candidate yet?"[6]

TABLE 8–2 ⚜

ACCURACY OF THE FINAL PREELECTION POLLS, NOVEMBER 6, 2000

Poll*	Bush	Gore	Nader	Buchanan/Others
Actual results	47.9	48.4	2.7	1
CBS	44	45	4	1
CNN/*USA Today*/Gallup	48	46	4	1
IBD/CSM/TIPP†	47.9	46	3.7	—
Reuters/MSNBC/Zogby	46	48	5	1
Voter.com	50	45	3.5	—

*All polls include the allocated undecided vote.

†*Investor's Business Daily, Christian Science Monitor,* TIPP poll conducted by TechnoMetrica Market Intelligence.

Source: Polling Report, <http://www.pollingreport.com/election.htm>.

As election day approaches, pollsters need to allocate the undecided vote if they are to accurately forecast the results. If their allocation formula proves to be incorrect, then their sample is likely to deviate from the actual vote. This happened in 2000 when some pollsters split the undecided vote between Gore and Bush. As a consequence they failed to capture the extent of the late surge for Gore.[7] Similarly in 1992, pollsters made an incorrect judgment about the Perot vote. Based on the experience of other third-party and independent candidates whose support had declined as election day neared, pollsters underestimated the popular vote that Perot received. Not only did Perot's support not decline, but his campaign succeeded in attracting a large number of first-time voters whose turnout was difficult to predict. Nader also experienced a small surge of support at the end of the campaign.

Typically, most voters decide well before the campaign's final week. In fact, in a normal election, one-half to two-thirds of the electorate make their decision before or during the national nominating conventions. If most people decide before Labor Day, the polls conducted in September are likely to be close to the final election results. And they have been. In "trial heats" conducted by the Gallup organization, the candidate who was ahead in early September won in eleven of fourteen elections between 1948 and 2000. During this period, the person ahead at the end of September won all but two of these elections, Truman and Gore being the only exceptions.[8]

Television Forecasts

Forecasts continue right to the end, until all the votes are tabulated. The final projections are presented by the major television networks during the night of the election. In broadcasting the results the news media have three objectives: to report the vote, to forecast the winners, and to analyze the returns, and do so ahead of the others.

Beginning in the 1980s, the major networks and news services established a consortium to pool their resources in reporting the vote count. Thousands of reporters were assigned to precincts and county election boards around the country to communicate the presidential, congressional, and gubernatorial votes as soon as they are tallied.

If all the news media wished to do were report the results, this type of reporting would suffice. But they wish to do more. They want to analyze the vote and explain its meaning. To do so, they consolidated their data-gathering into an operation that also conducted a large exit poll in which thousands of people were surveyed after they left their voting places. Beginning in 1992, this organization, known as the Voter News Service (VNS), has conducted a large exit poll following the national election.[9]

Here's how exit polls work. A large number of precincts across the country are randomly selected. The random selection is made within states in such a way that principal geographic units (cities, suburbs, and rural areas), size of precincts, and their past voting records are taken into account. Approximately 1,200 representatives of the polling organization administer the poll to voters who are chosen in a systematic way (for example, every fourth or fifth person) as they leave the voting booths. Voters are asked to complete a short questionnaire (thirty to forty items) that is designed to elicit information on their voting choices, political attitudes, and candidate evaluations and feelings, as well as their demographic characteristics. Several times over the course of the day, the questionnaires are collected, tabulated, and their results telephoned to a central computer bank and analyzed.

A variety of statistical models are used to compare the returns from the precincts to those of past elections and to returns from other parts of the state. The sequence of the votes, the order in which they are received, is also considered in the analysis. Then, after most or all of the election polls in a state have been completed, the findings of the exit poll are broadcast. Over the course of the evening the networks adjust the VNS data to reflect the actual results as they are tabulated.

The exit poll is usually very accurate. Because it is conducted over the course of the day, there is little bias that would under- or overrepresent certain types of voters who cast their ballots at different times of the day. Moreover, only voters are sampled and in large numbers, thereby reducing the error to much less than that of the national surveys conducted before the election. In addition, the exit poll provides a sample of sufficient size to enable analysts to discern the attitudes, opinions, and choices of smaller groups and subgroups (such as white southern Protestants, African American males, and unmarried, college-educated women) within the electorate. In 2000, 13,130 people exiting hundreds of polling places around the country participated in this survey. (See Table 8–3, pages 286–287.)

Early projections of the winner on election night based on exit polling have generated considerable criticism, primarily on the grounds that they discourage turnout and affect voting in areas in which the polls are still open. This controversy was heightened in 1980. When the early returns and polls conducted for the networks and major newspapers all indicated a Reagan landslide, the networks projected his victory early in the evening while voting was still occurring in some parts of the country. At 9:30 P.M. eastern standard time (EST), President Jimmy Carter appeared before his supporters and acknowledged defeat before a national television audience. Almost immediately Carter's early announcement incurred angry protests, particularly from defeated West Coast Democrats, who alleged that the president's remarks discouraged many Democrats from voting. It is difficult to substantiate their claim, however.[10] Researchers who have studied the impact of the 1980 television projections on voting have found a small reduction in turnout in the West, but little evidence of vote switching or turnout bias toward or against the projected winner as a result of the early projections.[11]

The minimal effect of the election reporting on the outcome of the election seems to be related to the fact that relatively few people watch the broadcasts and then vote. Most people vote first and watch the returns later in the evening. Perhaps this pattern of voting and then watching or listening to the returns explains why George H. W. Bush's projected victory on the networks in 1988 before the polls closed on the West Coast did little to change the results in three out of four Pacific states (Washington, Oregon, and Hawaii) that voted for Michael Dukakis. Nonetheless, sensitivity to the criticism that early returns affect turnout and voting behavior led the networks to agree prior to the 1992 election not to project winners in any election within a state until its polls had closed. In states with different time zones, a majority of its polls have to close before winners would be projected.

The networks amended their pledge to make a national prediction in 1996 even as people were voting on the West Coast. Promptly at 9 P.M., EST, they forecast a Clinton victory. In anticipation of this early forecast, Republicans bitterly criticized the practice of calling the election before the polls had closed and warned of possible legislation to prevent it from happening again. No such legislation has been enacted, however.

Another prediction controversy in which speed and accuracy collided occurred in 2000. Early in the evening of the election (7:50 P.M., EST), the television broadcast networks forecast a victory for Al Gore in Florida on the basis of exit polls even though residents in the central time zone living in the Florida Panhandle were still voting. The announcement elated Democrats. However, as the evening wore on, a discrepancy was noted between the actual returns and the exit polls. On the basis of this discrepancy, CNN retracted its prediction of a Gore victory. The other networks quickly followed suit. At 2:16 A.M. (EST), the Fox News channel declared Bush the winner on the basis of tabulated returns. Again, the other networks quickly followed.

Hearing the news, Vice President Gore called Governor George W. Bush to concede the election and was on his way to make a public announcement to his supporters. Before he did so, however, he learned that the election was still too close to call. Gore then telephoned Bush again and retracted his concession while the networks retracted their prediction of a Bush victory.[12] In the end, the closeness of the Florida vote combined with the voiding of thousands of improperly punched ballots precluded a valid exit poll prediction.

After much controversy over the inaccurate predictions of the Florida elections results in 2000, the VNS did a substantial overhaul of their analytic models. In the 2002 midterm elections, the new system failed. Poll takers could not get through on the phone lines and the analysis could not be completed. The VNS organization subsequently went out of business.

INTERPRETING THE ELECTION

In addition to predicting the results, the television networks also provide instant analyses of results on election night. This analysis, based primarily on exit polls, relates voting decisions to the issue positions, ideological perspectives, and partisan preferences of the electorate. Patterns among demographic groups, issue stands, and electoral perceptions and choices are noted and used to explain why people voted for particular candidates.

Although exit polls present a detailed picture of the electorate on election day (see Table 8–3), they do not provide a longitudinal perspective. To understand changes in public attitudes and opinions, it is necessary to survey people over the course of the campaign, asking the same questions and, if possible, reinterviewing the same people before and after they vote. The nationwide polls conducted by Gallup, Zogby, Pew, and the major news organizations often repeat questions, but they do not do so with the same respondents. The National Election Studies do.

They reinterview and repeat some of the same questions they posed to the same people earlier.[13] This interview–reinterview technique has enabled social scientists to discern opinion changes and the factors that have contributed to them over the course of the campaign. The wealth of data that these studies have produced has served as a basis for political scientists to construct theories of why people vote as they do.

Models of Voting Behavior

There are two basic models of voting behavior: the *prospective*, which emphasizes the issues and looks to the future; and the *retrospective*, which emphasizes the candidates and their parties and looks to the past.[14]

In the prospective voting model, voters compare their beliefs and policy preferences with those of the parties and their nominees. They make a determination of which party and which candidates espouse positions that are closer to their own and thus would more likely pursue those positions if elected. In other words, voters make a judgment on the prospects of obtaining future policy they desire based on the current positions of the candidates and the parties and the policies they promise to pursue.

In the retrospective voting model, voters also make a judgment about the future but do so primarily on the basis of the parties and their candidates' performance in the past. How they evaluate that performance is critical to the voting choice they will make on election day. In other words, history serves as a prologue for the future in the retrospective voting model although voters also factor into the equation their anticipation of how candidates will perform, once in office.

Of the factors considered in performance evaluations, external conditions—how good or bad things seem to be—are almost always a major part of that analysis. If the economy is strong, society harmonious, and the nation perceived as secure and at peace, people assume that their leaders, particularly the president, must be doing a good job. If conditions are not good, then the president gets much of the blame.[15] Thus, the key question that voters ask themselves when making a retrospective evaluation is: Am I and my country better off now than before the party now in power and its candidates won control of the White House?

If an incumbent president or even vice president is running, then this retrospective judgment should be closely related to the voting decision. If, however, there is no incumbent seeking reelection (such as in 1952), then the retrospective judgment is less relevant for voters but partisan affiliation remains important.

Another component of retrospective voting decisions involves a comparison between the principal contenders. Which of them is more likely to do well in the future?[16] It is not sufficient to assess only the current administration, even if the president is seeking reelection, if the candidate for the opposition is thought to be markedly better or worse. Thus, in any one voting decision, voters weigh the parties and candidates' past performance as well as the promise offered by the challengers and their party for the future.

In both models, partisanship is apt to be an important influence on the evaluations people make to arrive at their voting decision. As noted in Chapter 3, political attitudes are relatively stable. They can be changed, but how quickly and under what circumstances has been subject to some dispute.[17] What a partisan orientation does is to provide voters with a lens through which campaigns can be filtered, candidates and issues evaluated, and electoral judgments made.

In the retrospective model, partisanship itself is the consequence of evaluations of the past performance of parties. It therefore functions as a summary judgment of how the parties and the candidates have performed, and as a basis for anticipating how they will perform in the future. Partisans who make a retrospective evaluation are more apt to rate presidents of their party more favorably and those of the other party less favorably. Similarly, partisans tend to be closer to their candidate's positions on the issues than to the opponent's.

Since the identification people have with political parties is the most stable and resilient factor affecting the voting decision, it is considered to be the single most important long-term influence on voting. Orientations voters have toward the candidates and issues are short-term factors that fluctuate from election to election. If strong enough, they can, of course, cause people to vote against their partisan inclinations or, over time, cause those inclinations to change. For those who resist these changes, however, their partisan identities serve as an inducement and a rationalization for supporting the party and its candidates.

Since a majority of the electorate continues to identify with a political party or leans in a partisan direction, the candidate of the dominant party should have an advantage—all things being equal. But all things are never equal. Candidates change, issues change, the public mood changes, and even the partisan identity of voters can shift over time. Thus, it is important to understand how the electorate evaluates these changes, how people feel about the candidates, how they perceive and evaluate candidates and their issue stands, and how the electorate's perceptions and evaluations affect their voting decisions and the election outcomes.[18] The next sections discuss the interplay of these components in presidential elections since 1952.

1952–1956: The Impact of Personality

In 1952, the Democrats were the dominant party, but the Republicans won the presidential election and gained a majority in both houses of Congress. The issues of that election—the fear of communism at home and abroad, the presence of corruption in high levels of government, and United States involvement in the Korean War—benefited the GOP, as did the popularity of its presidential candidate, former General Dwight D. Eisenhower. These short-term factors offset the Democrats' longer-term, partisan advantage and enabled the Republicans to win.[19] The electorate saw the Republicans as better able to deal with the problems of fighting communism, promoting efficiency in government, and ending the war. Eisenhower was also perceived in a more favorable light than his opponent, Adlai Stevenson. Although the public still regarded Democrats as more capable of handling domestic problems, the appeal of Eisenhower, combined with the more favorable attitude toward the Republican Party in the areas of foreign affairs and government management, resulted in the victory of the minority party's candidate.

President Eisenhower's reelection four years later was also a consequence of his personal popularity, not his party's. Eisenhower was positively evaluated by voters. His opponent, Adlai Stevenson, was not. The Republicans did not win control of Congress, however, as they had in 1952. Their failure to do so in 1956 testified to the continuing partisan advantage that the Democrats enjoyed among the American electorate during this period.

1960–1972: The Increasing Importance of Issues

Beginning in 1960, the issues of the campaign seemed to play a more important role in the election's outcome than they had since the New Deal realignment. Noneconomic policy issues undercut the impact of a partisanship forged since the 1930s on economic ties. In general, these issues contributed to the defection of Democrats from their party's presidential candidates in 1960, 1968, and 1972 and to defections by Republicans (and southern Democrats) in 1964.

John Kennedy's Catholicism was a primary concern to many voters in 1960 and helps explain the closeness of that election. Despite the Democrats' dominance within the electorate, Kennedy received only 115,000 more votes than Richard Nixon, 0.3 percent more of the total vote. Kennedy's Catholicism cost him votes. He lost about 2.2 percent of the popular vote, or approximately 1.5 million votes, because he was a Catholic.[20] The decline in Democratic voting was particularly evident in the heavily Protestant South. Outside the South, however, Kennedy picked up Democratic votes because of the massive support he received from Catholics. Almost 80 percent of the Catholic vote, 17 percent more than the Democrats normally obtained, went to Kennedy. In fact, the concentration of Catholics in the large industrial states may have contributed to the size of his Electoral College majority.[21]

Although Kennedy barely won in 1960, Lyndon Johnson won by a landslide four years later. Short-term factors also explain the magnitude of the Johnson victory.[22] Barry Goldwater was perceived as a minority candidate within a minority party, ideologically to the right of most Republicans. Moreover, he did not enjoy a favorable public image, as Johnson did. Policy attitudes also favored the Democrats, even in foreign affairs. Goldwater's militant anticommunism scared many voters. They saw Johnson as the peace candidate.

Goldwater's strong ideological convictions, coupled with his attempt to differentiate his policy positions from Johnson's, undoubtedly contributed to greater issue awareness. Although most policy-conscious voters had their views on the issues reinforced by their partisan attitudes, two groups within the electorate did not. White southern Democrats, fearful of their party's civil rights initiatives, cast a majority of their votes for Goldwater, and northern Republicans, who disagreed with their candidate's policy positions, voted for Johnson. For the first time since the New Deal realignment, five states in the solidly Democratic South (plus Goldwater's home state of Arizona) went Republican, auguring the major regional realignment that was to occur.

The impact of a new set of foreign policy and social issues that divided the Democrats began to be evident in 1968. With the Vietnam War, urban riots, campus unrest, and civil rights dividing the nation and splitting the Democratic party, partisan desertions increased. The Democratic share of the vote declined 19 percent, while the Republican proportion increased 4 percent. The third-party candidacy of George Wallace accounted for much of the difference.

Wallace's support was much more issue based than was that of Democrat Hubert Humphrey or Republican Richard Nixon. The Alabama governor did not have as much personal appeal for those who voted for him as did his policy positions.[23] Unhappy with the Democratic Party's handling of a wide range of social issues, white Democratic partisans, particularly in the South but to a limited degree in the urban North as well, turned from their party's presidential candidate, Hubert Humphrey, to vote for Wallace, who received 13.5 percent of the vote. Had Wallace not run, the Republican presidential vote undoubtedly would have been larger, since Nixon was the second choice of most Wallace voters.

The results of the 1968 presidential election thus deviated from the partisan alignment of the electorate. The voters made a retrospective judgment. A significant number of them had grievances against the Democratic Party and against Lyndon Johnson's conduct of the presidency. This included many Democrats who voted for Wallace and, to a much lesser extent, for Nixon. A decline in the intensity of partisanship and a growth in the number of independents contributed to the amount of issue voting that occurred in 1968. Had it not been for the Democrats' large partisan advantage and the overwhelming African American vote that Humphrey received, the presidential election would not have been nearly so close.

The trend away from partisan presidential voting for the Democratic candidate continued in 1972. With a nominee who was ideologically and personally unpopular, the Democrats suffered their worst presidential defeat since 1920. Richard Nixon enjoyed a better public image than George McGovern. He was seen as the stronger presidential candidate. The electorate reacted to him personally in a positive manner, although less so than in 1960.[24] McGovern, on the other hand, was viewed negatively by non-Democrats and neutrally by Democrats. These perceptions, positive for Nixon and negative for McGovern, contributed to Nixon's large victory, as did his stands on most of the issues. Most of the electorate saw the Republican standard-bearer as closer to their own positions than the Democratic candidate. McGovern was perceived as liberal on all issues and ideologically to the left of his own party. Thus, Democrats defected in considerable numbers, but Republicans did not.[25]

1976–1996: The Evaluation of Performance

1976. Issue differences narrowed in 1976. Neither Gerald Ford nor Jimmy Carter emphasized the social and cultural concerns that played a large role in the previous presidential contest. Both focused their attention on trust in government and on domestic economic matters. In the wake of Watergate and a recession that occurred during the Ford presidency, it is not surprising that these issues worked to the Democrats' advantage.

Carter was also helped by a slightly more favorable personal assessment than that given to Ford.[26] The latter's association with the Nixon administration, highlighted in the public mind by his pardon of the former president, his difficult struggle to win his own party's nomination, and his seeming inability to find a solution to the country's economic woes adversely affected his image as president.

Nonetheless, Ford was probably helped more than hurt by being the incumbent. He gained in recognition, reputation, and stature. He benefited from having a podium with a presidential seal on it. His style and manner in the office contrasted sharply with his predecessor's—much to Ford's advantage. As the campaign progressed, his presidential image improved.[27] It just did not improve quickly enough to allow him to hold on to the office.

With sociocultural issues muted and the Vietnam War over, economic matters divided the electorate along partisan lines. This shift put the candidate of the dominant party back into the driver's seat. Democrats had more faith in their party's ability to improve the economy. Carter won primarily because he was a Democrat and secondarily because his personal evaluation was more favorable than Ford's. Carter was also helped by being a southerner. He received the electoral votes of every southern state except Virginia. In an otherwise divided Electoral College, this southern support proved to be decisive.

1980. When Carter sought reelection in 1980, being a Democrat, an incumbent, and a southerner was not sufficient. Poor performance ratings overcame the advantage that partisanship and incumbency normally bring to a president of the dominant party. In 1976, Carter was judged on the basis of his potential *for* office. In 1980, he was judged on the basis of his performance *in* office. As the results of the election indicate, that judgment was very harsh. Carter's vote fell behind his 1976 percentages in every single state, and in approximately half the states it dropped at least 10 percent. Why did he lose so badly?

Personal evaluations of Carter and assessments of his policies were not nearly as favorable as they had been four years earlier. Starting the campaign with the lowest approval rating of any president since the ratings began in 1952, Carter saw his performance in office approved by only 21 percent of the adult population in July 1980. Personal assessments of Ronald Reagan were also low, although, in contrast to Carter's ratings, they became more favorable as the campaign unfolded.

Economic conditions also seemed to benefit Reagan. Concerns about the economy, persistently high inflation, large-scale unemployment, and the decreasing competitiveness and productivity of American industry all worked to the advantage of the party out of power. For the first time in many years, the Republicans were seen as the party better able to invigorate the economy, return prosperity, and lower inflation. The Democrats, and particularly Carter, were blamed for the country's economic problems.

Dissatisfaction with the conduct of foreign affairs, culminating in frustration over the Soviet Union's invasion of Afghanistan and especially the failure of the United States to obtain the release of American hostages held in Iran, contributed to Carter's negative evaluation and to changing public attitudes toward defense spending and foreign affairs. In 1980, most Americans supported increased military expenditures, a position with which Reagan was closely identified, combined with a less conciliatory approach and a tougher, more militant posture in dealing with problems abroad.

These issues, together with the negative assessment of Carter as president, explain why he lost. Twenty-seven percent of the Democrats who had supported Carter in 1976 deserted him four years later. Approximately 80 percent of these deserters voted for Reagan. They represented all ideological groups, not just conservatives. And Carter's share of the independent vote declined substantially.

John Anderson, a former Republican member of Congress, also ran in 1980 as an independent. He was a protest candidate who drew equally from Democrats and Republicans. Anderson was unable, however, to attract a solid core of supporters. Nor was he able to differentiate his policy positions sufficiently from Carter's and Reagan's to generate an issue-oriented vote. In the end, his failure to win any electoral votes and only 6.5 percent of the popular vote demonstrated the resiliency of the major parties and the legitimacy that their labels provided candidates for national office.

In summary, Carter was repudiated by the voters because of how they retrospectively evaluated his presidency. In 1980, it was Reagan who appeared to offer greater potential. He won primarily because he was the option that had become acceptable. He did not win because of his ideology or his specific policy positions. Although there was a desire for change, there was little direct ideological or issue voting.[28] Nor did Reagan's personal appeal in 1980 contribute significantly to his victory.[29]

1984. Four years later, Reagan's personal appeal did contribute, however. In 1984, voters rewarded President Reagan for what they considered to be a job well done with a huge victory. What factors contributed to Reagan's impressive victory?

Ideology did not work to Reagan's advantage in 1984 any more than it did in the previous election. In 1984, the average voter considered himself or herself to be a moderate, holding issue positions slightly closer to the liberal Mondale than to the conservative Reagan.[30] This moderate perspective, however, did not easily translate into presidential voting. As a consequence, it did not adversely affect Reagan; nor did it help Mondale.

There was a potential for issue voting in 1984. The electorate did perceive a choice between the two candidates on a range of domestic matters. But it was conditions more than positions that seemed to influence the electorate's judgment. A resurgent economy, strengthened military, and renewed feelings of national pride brought the president broad support. Although voters agreed with Mondale more than with Reagan on many of the specific problems confronting the nation, they viewed Reagan as the person better able to deal with them.

Leadership was a dominant concern. Voters evaluated Reagan much more highly than Mondale in this regard. Reagan was seen as the stronger and more independent of the two candidates, less beholden to special and parochial interests. When leadership was combined with the ability to deal with the most pressing problems and a very favorable personal evaluation of Reagan, the president won hands down. It was a retrospective vote. The electorate supported Reagan primarily for his performance in office. In other words, they voted *for* him in 1984 just as they had voted *against* Carter four years earlier.

1988. The trend of retrospective voting continued in 1988. George Bush won because the electorate evaluated the Reagan administration positively, associated Bush with that administration, and concluded that he, not Michael Dukakis, would be better able and more likely to maintain the good times and the policies that produced them.[31] That Bush was not as favorably evaluated as Reagan had been four years earlier partially accounts for his narrower victory.[32]

Partisanship affected voting behavior more in 1988 than it had in any election since 1960.[33] In the past, a high correlation between partisan identities and voting behavior had worked to the Democrats' advantage. In 1988, it did not. An increase in Republican allegiances and a decline in Democratic ones produced an almost evenly divided electorate. There were slightly more Democrats but greater turnout and less defection among Republicans. In the end neither candidate enjoyed a partisan advantage, but among independents, Bush held a solid lead.

Ideological orientations worked to reinforce partisan voting patterns in 1988, with Republican candidate Bush winning overwhelmingly among Republicans and conservatives and Democratic candidate Dukakis doing almost as well among Democrats and liberals. The problem for Dukakis, however, and any liberal for that matter, is that the proportion of the electorate that considers itself liberal has declined substantially. In 1988, almost twice as many people who voted consid-ered themselves conservative rather than liberal.

In addition to ideology and party, issues affected voting behavior in 1988; however, they did not work primarily to benefit either candidate. With neither partisanship nor issues producing a clear advantage, the retrospective evaluation of the Reagan presidency seems to have been the deciding factor, the one that best explains the election outcome.[34] Sixty percent of the electorate approved of how Reagan had handled his job, and of them, almost 80 percent voted for Bush.[35]

1992. Four years later, however, Bush was judged on his own performance in office, and that judgment was negative. Bush received only 37.4 percent of the popular vote in a three-person contest and 168 electoral votes (only 31 percent of the total). His 1992 vote declined among every population group.

With the economy in recession, budget and trade deficits rising, and layoffs of white-collar managers and blue-collar workers dominating the news, people were fearful about their economic future. Blaming the president for these unsatisfactory economic conditions, voters turned to the challenger and his promises for change.

Clinton was clearly helped by his partisan affiliation. With slightly more Democrats in the electorate than Republicans, Clinton received the votes of three out of four Democrats. For the first time since 1964, Republican defections actu-ally exceeded those of Democrats. Turnout, which traditionally benefits Republi-cans, was neutralized in 1992. Democratic turnout was up and Republican turnout was down.

TABLE 8–3

PORTRAIT OF THE AMERICAN ELECTORATE, 1992–2000 (IN PERCENTAGES)

Percentage of 2000 Total		1992			1996			2000*		
		Clinton	Bush	Perot	Clinton	Dole	Perot	Bush	Gore	Nader
	Total vote	43%	38%	19%	49%	41%	8%	48%	48%	3%
48	Men	41	38	21	43	44	10	53	42	3
52	Women	46	37	17	54	38	7	43	54	2
81	Whites	39	41	20	43	46	9	54	42	3
10	Blacks	82	11	7	84	12	4	9	90	1
07	Hispanics	62	25	14	72	21	6	35	62	2
02	Asians	29	55	16	43	48	8	41	55	3
65	Married	40	40	20	44	46	9	53	44	2
35	Unmarried	49	33	18	57	31	9	38	57	4
17	18–29 years old	44	34	22	53	34	10	46	48	5
33	30–44 years old	42	38	20	48	41	9	49	48	2
28	45–59 years old	41	40	19	48	41	9	49	48	2
22	60 and older	50	38	12	48	44	7	47	51	1
05	Not high school graduate	55	28	17	59	28	11	38	59	1
21	High school graduate	43	36	20	51	35	13	49	48	1
32	Some college education	42	37	21	48	40	10	51	45	3
24	College graduate	40	41	19	44	46	8	51	45	3
18	Postgraduate education	49	36	15	52	40	5	44	52	3
54	White Protestant	33	46	21	36	53	10	56	42	2
26	Catholic	44	36	20	53	37	9	47	50	2
04	Jewish	78	12	10	78	16	3	19	79	1
14	White born-again Christian†	23	61	15	26	65	8	80	18	1
26	Union household	55	24	21	59	30	9	37	59	3
07	Family income under $15,000	59	23	18	59	28	11	37	57	4
16	$15,000–$29,999	45	35	20	53	36	9	41	54	3

24	$30,000–$49,999	41	38	21	48	40	10	48	49	2
25	over $50,000	40	42	18	44	48	7	51	46	2
13	over $75,000	36	48	16	41	51	7	52	45	2
15	over $100,000	—	—	—	38	54	6	54	43	2
	Family's financial situation is									
50	Better today	24	62	14	61	35	3	36	61	2
38	Same today	41	41	18	46	45	8	60	35	3
11	Worse today	61	14	25	27	57	13	63	33	4
23	From the North	47	35	18	55	34	9	39	56	3
26	From the Midwest	42	37	21	48	41	10	49	48	2
31	From the South	42	43	16	46	46	7	55	43	1
21	From the West	44	34	22	48	40	8	46	48	4
35	Republicans	10	73	17	13	80	6	91	8	1
27	Independents	38	32	30	43	35	17	47	45	6
39	Democrats	77	10	13	84	10	5	11	86	2
20	Liberals	68	14	18	78	11	7	13	80	6
50	Moderates	48	31	21	57	33	9	44	52	2
29	Conservatives	18	65	17	20	71	8	81	17	1
67	Employed	42	38	20	48	40	9	48	49	2
33	Unemployed	56	24	20	49	42	8	48	47	3
09	First-time voters	48	30	22	54	34	11	43	52	4
57	Approve of Clinton's performance	—	—	—	—	—	—	20	77	2
41	Disapprove of Clinton's performance	—	—	—	—	—	—	88	9	2
40	Continue Clinton's policies	—	—	—	—	—	—	11	87	2
46	Be more conservative	—	—	—	—	—	—	85	13	1
10	Be more liberal	—	—	—	—	—	—	35	56	7

*N = 13,130.

†Includes all Protestants in 2000.

Source: Voter News Service. 1992–1996 data from the *New York Times*, November 10, 1996, 28. Copyright © 1996 by the *New York Times*. Reprinted by permission. 2000 data supplied to the author.

Still, Clinton's partisan advantage could have been offset by a lopsided vote of independents against him. Independents who constitute more than one-quarter of the electorate. In the 1980s, that vote had strongly favored the Republicans. In 1992, it did not. Independents divided their support among the three candidates, with Clinton the plurality victor at 38 percent and Perot and Bush splitting the rest. (See Table 8–3.) In four years, Bush had lost one-third of the independent vote, thereby dooming his reelection.

Nor did ideology work to the president's advantage as it had in previous elections. Although liberals and conservatives continued to support Democratic and Republican candidates respectively, Perot cut into both votes, dropping Bush's support among conservatives 15 percent from his 1988 level. Moreover, Clinton did comparably better among moderates than previous Democratic candidates had done, substantially leading Bush and Perot among this group.

Although Bush was credited with a successful foreign policy, the lower salience of foreign policy issues undercut Bush's achievements in this policy realm and even served to highlight his inattention to domestic matters. The economy was the principal issue and Clinton its principal beneficiary.

Among the traditional support groups Clinton continued to enjoy an advantage among women, Jews, African Americans and Hispanics, and lower-income, less-educated voters. The generational cleavages evident in past presidential elections were muted in 1992 with the youngest cohort of voters, those eighteen to twenty-nine years old, voting for Clinton at about the national average. Clinton also received a plurality of the male vote, the first time a Democratic candidate had done so since 1976. The only demographic groups that continued to vote for Bush were the wealthy; white Protestants, especially born-again Christians; and those voters who identified themselves as homemakers. Perot's numbers were fairly steady among demographic groups. He did comparatively better among men than women, among the young than the old, and among independents than partisans.

Clinton won a solid victory. Even though he received only 43 percent of the vote, his popular vote margin over the president was 5.6 percent. In the Electoral College, he won thirty-two states and the District of Columbia for a total of 370 votes, demonstrating how the Electoral College can enlarge the margin of victory for the winning candidate.

Had Perot not run, it is unlikely that the results of the election would have been any different. Exit polls of Perot voters indicate that they would have divided their votes fairly evenly between Clinton and Bush although the number voting would undoubtedly have declined. Among nonvoters surveyed, Clinton received at least as much support as he did among voters. In a two-person contest, however, Clinton would have received a larger mandate.

1996. By 1996, domestic concerns were still dominant, but the economy was stronger, crime had decreased, and the nation remained at peace—all conditions that favor incumbents. Voters responded accordingly, reelecting the Democratic president and the Republican congressional majority. Clinton's popular and electoral vote exceeded his 1992 totals, although the regional composition of his vote remained essentially the same as it had been four years earlier.

Despite misgivings about some aspects of the president's character, notably his personal integrity, honesty, and willingness to stand up for his beliefs, voters saw Clinton as more caring, more in touch with the times, and more visionary than his Republican opponent. But it was the nation's economy, not the president's character, that proved to be the critical factor in determining the outcome of the election. Those who perceived themselves to be better off (about one-third of the electorate) supported the president; those who saw themselves as worse off (about 20 percent) supported his opponents.

Democrats stayed with the president and Republicans with their candidate. Clinton, however, did better than either of his opponents among independent voters. Similarly, he won a majority of the votes of people who identified themselves as moderates; as expected, liberals voted disproportionately for Clinton and conservatives for Dole. It is interesting to note that strictly on the issues, the public was slightly closer to Dole's positions on the key issues than to Clinton's. But Clinton's performance evaluation and his leadership potential easily overcame these issue positions in the minds of the voters, much as they had twelve years earlier when an electorate, closer to Mondale on the issues, voted overwhelmingly for Reagan.[36] Leadership triumphs in presidential electoral politics.

The demographic groups that shifted most in their support of the president were women and younger voters. The gender gap was the largest in the nation's history. For the first time, a majority of women voted for one candidate and a plurality of men for another. And despite the Democrats' appeal to the elderly on the basis of the Medicare issue, it was youth who gave the president greater support than any other age cohort.

Hispanic voters contributed significantly to Clinton's victory. Alarmed by Republican attempts to limit immigration, deny government benefits to legal aliens, and oppose bilingual education, Hispanics voted in record numbers and overwhelmingly for Clinton. African Americans remained as strongly Democratic as they had in previous elections.

Cleavages were also evident among secular and sectarian voters. Regular churchgoers, particularly religious fundamentalists, voted Republican. Mainstream Protestant groups were less supportive of the Republicans. Those who did not profess a religion or practice it on a regular basis were much more Democratic and likely to vote for Clinton.

In short, the 1996 election was a referendum on the Clinton presidency, and Clinton won. Not only did the electorate evaluate his first term favorably, but they saw the president as more capable of understanding and handling the challenges of the 1990s and building a bridge to the twenty-first century than either Dole or Perot.

2000: The Anticipation of Future Performance

Although the 2000 election could have been another referendum on the Clinton presidency, it was not for many voters. Vice President Al Gore's decision to emphasize the differences between himself and Governor George W. Bush rather than contrast the economic, social, and international conditions at the end of 2000 with those of 1992, the last time the Republicans controlled the White House, focused the attention of the electorate on the future not the past. Encouraging voters to make more of a prospective choice than a retrospective judgment turned out to be a poor strategic decision for the vice president.

Nonetheless, many of the same voting patterns emerged in 2000 as were evident in previous presidential elections, particularly those of the 1990s. (See Table 8–3.) The electorate was clearly and evenly divided. Parity between the major parties contributed to this division. Partisans overwhelmingly supported their party's nominee while independents were almost evenly split between Bush and Gore. However, Gore did not fare as well among Democratic voters, especially weak Democrats, as Clinton had four years earlier.[37] Gore's failure to embrace the policies of the Clinton administration may have had something to do with his decline in support from his own party.

A large, persistent gender gap even increased in size to 11 percent in 2000, with a majority of women supporting Gore and Lieberman and a majority of men backing Bush and Cheney. The principal gender policy differences concerned the role of government with women favoring a larger role in the economic and social arena than men.[38]

Other core groups within the parties' traditional electoral coalitions also voted in record proportions along party lines: African Americans, Latinos, and organized labor for the Democratic candidates and the Christian Coalition for the Republicans. The efforts of the Bush campaign to appeal to minority voters, seemed to have little impact.

There was also a regional divide, with Gore doing well in the Northeast and Pacific Coast, Bush in the South and Rocky Mountain areas, and the agricultural heartland in the Midwest. The vote in the other regions of the country was more evenly split between the two candidates.

Religious voting trends continued as well. Jews voted heavily for Gore and his Jewish running mate, Joseph Lieberman; Catholics gave Gore slightly more support than Bush, largely as a consequence of a strong Hispanic vote. Protestants preferred Bush, particularly those who considered themselves members of the religious right. As in other recent elections, there was also a sectarian-secular divide; the more regular the voters' attendance at religious services, the greater the likelihood of their voting Republican.

The division within the electorate was also evident in the issue and ideological preferences of Bush and Gore voters. Those who wanted more conservative policies than those of the Clinton administration, particularly those who thought tax cuts should be the number one priority, supported Bush. Most Gore voters favored a continuation of Clinton's policies and saw Social Security solvency as the primary issue. Nonetheless, Bush succeeded in moderating Gore's advantage on social issues by emphasizing his compassion and differentiating his conservatism from that of the congressional Republicans.[39]

Bush's vote varied directly and Gore's indirectly with income and education levels, with the exception of those with a postgraduate education who leaned toward Gore. Contributing to the size of Bush's vote was the increasing proportion of upper-income voters (with family incomes of $50,000 or more) who cast ballots in 2000—53 percent versus 39 percent in 1996.

As expected, the way in which people evaluated the Clinton administration and President Clinton personally carried over to their 2000 presidential vote.[40] Those who had supported Clinton in 1996 and those who approved his performance in office cast ballots for Gore; those who did not vote for Clinton in the previous election, including two out of three Perot voters, and those who disapproved of his job performance went for Bush.

Did severing his ties with the Clinton administration help or hurt Gore? Gore's pollsters contended that they had no choice. Their surveys and focus groups indicated that the president was a liability, that he turned off swing voters, and that the electorate was tired of his scandal-plagued administration and wanted a change. However, Clinton did energize Democrats. There were states in which his active campaigning might have made a difference, states such as Arkansas and Florida. The debate over Bill Clinton's influence on the 2000 election is likely to continue, particularly if Senator Hillary Clinton seeks the presidency in the future.[41]

The third-party candidacies of Ralph Nader and Pat Buchanan attracted much less attention and support than in the years when Perot ran on the Reform Party ticket. Neither candidate had funds that were comparable to Perot's in 1992 or even 1996. However, the closeness of the 2000 election enhanced the influence of these third-party candidates, especially Nader's.[42] In retrospect, had Nader not been on the Florida ballot, Gore would have probably won that state and thereby the Electoral College. In the exit polls, 70 percent of those who said that they voted for Nader indicated that they would still have voted had he not run. Of this group, Gore was preferred over Bush by a margin of 2 to 1. Using this calculus, Gore would have received 22,747 more votes than Bush in Florida, enough to give him a victory in that state.

In short, the nation's bitter political divisions during the Clinton presidency were also evident in the vote for his successor. These partisan divisions fueled the political controversy over the Florida vote that followed the election. Were it not for the strong economy, the general contentment of the society, and people's optimism about the future, these divisions might have generated the same level of intensity within the population as they had among the political elites in Washington during the 1990s. Fortunately, however, they did not, and the electorate was able to get over its angst from the Florida vote controversy as the new president took office and began to exercise power. Politics returned to normal until 9/11.

CONVERTING ELECTORAL CHOICE INTO PUBLIC POLICY

The President's Imprecise Mandate

It is not unusual for the meaning of the election to be ambiguous. The reasons that people vote for presidents vary. Some do so because of their party affiliation, some because of issue stands, some because of their assessment of the candidates' potentials or their past performance. For most people, a combination of factors contributes to their voting decision. This combination makes it difficult to discern exactly what the electorate means, desires, or envisions by its electoral choice.

The president is rarely given a clear mandate for governing. For a mandate to exist, the presidential candidates must take discernible and compatible policy positions, and the electorate must vote for them because of those positions. Moreover, the results of the election must be consistent. If there is a discrepancy between the popular and the electoral vote or if one party wins the White House and another wins the Congress—the rule not the exception since 1968—it is difficult for a president to claim a mandate for governing.

Few elections meet the criteria for a mandate. Presidential candidates usually take a range of policy positions, often waffle on a few highly divisive and emotionally charged issues, may differ from their party and its other candidates for national office in their priorities and their stands, and rarely have coattails long enough to sweep in others with them. In fact, they may run behind their congressional candidates, as most recently elected presidents have.

Mandates may not exist, but that has not prevented presidents from claiming them. They do so largely for political reasons. Winning a large popular and electoral vote and gaining control of Congress creates opportunities and expectations that a newly elected president might want to seize in order to change national policy. Such an incentive would be enhanced if the victor defeated an incumbent.

Professor Patricia H. Conley argues that the elections of 1952, 1964, and 1980 encouraged the winners to claim a policy mandate. Eisenhower's campaign promise to go to Korea, Goldwater's strong opposition to Johnson's domestic legislative program, and Reagan's rejection of the ideology, policies, and programs of the Carter administration provided the electorate a clear choice of policy direction. The winners' sizable victories were interpreted as mandates for these presidents to pursue their policy goals.[43]

The election results in 1948 and 1992 were not quite as clear, according to Conley, but they still offered Truman and Clinton opportunities to claim a mandate and use it as evidence of popular support.[44] Democratic majorities in both houses of Congress furthered the claim that the voters had made a policy choice in their electoral decisions. Clinton's failure to achieve many of his promises, such as to cut middle-class taxes, stimulate the economy, "change welfare as we know it," reform the nation's health care system, and eliminate discrimination on the basis of sexual orientation, shows the flip side of a mandate claim—the magnification of failure, of not meeting expectations that the newly elected president has heightened.

George W. Bush was careful not to claim a mandate in 2000 as he pursued his campaign promises. However, prior to 9/11, he had achieved only one of them that required legislation—a large tax cut. Other proposals, such as a new energy policy, education policy, military restructuring and revitalizing, even his faith-based initiative had been stymied. For Bush the bar was low and so, initially, were the results.

In short, election interpretations can contribute to political outcomes, at least in the short run. The longer the time that elapses after the election the less that election can serve as a guide to priorities and policy decisions for the government.

Presidents must adapt to changing times. Their refusal to do so can result in an embarrassing defeat that weakens them politically. A case in point was the Clinton administration's resistance in 1993 to dropping its principal campaign promise to stimulate the economy even though the economy was improving. Similarly, Clinton clung to his comprehensive program to reform the health care system even though public support for it waned. In both cases he got out of touch with a public mood, which had changed since the election.

Party Platforms, Campaign Pledges, and the New Agenda

Assuming that party is an influence on voting behavior, what cues can presidents cull from their partisan connection in defining their programmatic mandate? As described in Chapter 5, party platforms normally contain a large number of positions and proposals, but there are problems in using the platform as a guide for a new administration. First and foremost, presidential candidates may not have exercised a major influence on the platform's formulation. Second, they may have had to accept certain compromises in the interests of party unity. It is not unusual for a nominee to disagree with one or several of the platform's positions or priorities. Carter personally opposed his party's abortion stand in 1980 and had major reservations about a \$12 billion jobs program that the Democratic platform endorsed. Dole made little mention of the Republican Party's abortion plank once his 1996 campaign began.

In addition to containing items the president-elect may oppose, the platform may omit some items that the new president favors, particularly if they are controversial. There was no mention of granting amnesty to Vietnam draft dodgers and war resisters in the 1976 Democratic platform, although Carter had publicly stated his intention to do so if he was elected.[45]

On the other hand, presidential nominees usually do exercise influence over the contents of the platform, as did Gore in 2000, Clinton in 1992 and 1996, and Bush and Dukakis in 1988. Surprisingly, George H. W. Bush did not put as much of his imprint on the 1992 Republican platform even though his delegates controlled the platform committee; his son George W. Bush did, however, in 2000 and will again in 2004.

There is a correlation between campaign promises, party platforms, and presidential performance. Political scientist Jeff Fishel found that from 1960 to 1984 presidents "submitted legislation or signed executive orders that are broadly consistent with about two-thirds of their campaign pledges." Of these, a substantial percentage were enacted into law, ranging from a high of 89 percent of those proposed during the Johnson administration to a low of 61 percent during the Nixon years.[46] Although these figures do not reveal the importance of promises, their scope, or their impact, they do suggest that, in general, campaign platforms and candidate pledges are taken seriously by those in power. They provide a foundation from which an administration's early policy initiatives emanate.[47]

Expectations and Performance

When campaigning, candidates also try to create an aura of leadership, conveying such attributes as assertiveness, decisiveness, compassion, and integrity. Kennedy promised to get the country moving, Johnson to continue the New Frontier–Great Society programs, Nixon to "bring us together," and George H. W. Bush to maintain the Reagan policies that produced peace and prosperity for the eight previous years but to do so in "a kinder and gentler" way. In 1992, Clinton pledged policy change in a moderate direction and an end to gridlock between Congress and the presidency; in 1996, he promised to build a bridge to the twenty-first century. In 2000, George W. Bush promised to defuse the strident partisan political climate in Washington.

These promises created performance expectations. In the 1976 election, Jimmy Carter heightened these expectations by his constant reference to the strong, decisive leadership he intended to exercise as president. His decline in popularity stemmed in large part from his failure to meet these leadership expectations. In contrast, Reagan's high approval before, during, and after his reelection indicated that most of the public believed that he had provided the strong leadership he had promised in his 1980 and 1984 campaigns. Clinton's job ratings in 1996 and thereafter also suggest public approval for his performance in office although not necessarily for some of his personal behaviors he displayed.

All new administrations, and to some extent most reelected ones, face diverse and often contradictory desires. By their ambiguity, candidates encourage voters to see what they want to see and believe what they want to. Disillusionment naturally sets in once a new president begins to make decisions. Some supporters feel deceived, while others may be satisfied.

One political scientist, John E. Mueller, has referred to the disappointment groups may experience with an administration as "the coalitions of minorities variable." In explaining declines in popularity, Mueller notes that presidents' decisions inevitably alienate parts of the coalition that elected them. This alienation, greatest among independents and supporters who identify with the other party, can produce a drop in popularity over time, although as the Reagan and Clinton presidencies demonstrate, such a drop is not inevitable, particularly if good times prevail.[48]

The campaign's emphasis on personal and institutional leadership also inflates expectations. By creating the aura of assertiveness, decisiveness, and potency, candidates help shape public expectations of their performance in office. Most presidents contribute to the decline in their own popularity by promising more than they can deliver. The question is, can the promise of leadership be conveyed during the campaign without creating unrealistic and unattainable expectations for the new president? For most candidates, especially challengers, the answer seems to be no.

The Electoral Coalition and Governing

Not only does the selection process inflate performance expectations and create a set of diverse policy goals, it may decrease the president's power to achieve them. The political muscle of the White House has been weakened by the decline in the power of party leaders, the growth of autonomous state and congressional electoral systems, and the decentralization and compartmentalization of power within the government.

Today, presidential candidates are largely on their own. They essentially designate themselves to run. They create their own organizations, choose the top people to run them, mount their own campaigns, win their own delegates, and set their own convention plans. They pay a price for this independence, however. By winning their party's nomination, candidates gain a label and some organizational support. But in the general election, they must supplement that support with their own campaign organization as well as expand their prenomination electoral coalition.

If elected, they must broaden their appeal and expand the coalition still further. One of Clinton's worst political mistakes during his first term in office was the emphasis he placed on homosexual rights on the second day of his administration, thereby fulfilling a campaign promise but alienating a portion of his electoral constituency in the process. With only 43 percent of the electorate voting for him in 1992, Clinton could ill afford to antagonize some of his supporters so soon.

The personalization of the presidential electoral process has serious implications for governing. To put it simply, it makes coalition building more difficult. The electoral process provides newly elected presidents with fewer political allies in the states and in Congress. It makes their partisan appeal less effective. It fractionalizes the bases of their support.

Personality politics has created a fertile environment for interest group pressures. Groups vie for the nominee's attention and favor during the campaign and for the president's after the election is over. This group struggle, a cause and consequence of the decentralization and compartmentalization of power in government, provides a natural source of opposition and support for almost any presidential action or proposal. It enlarges the arena of policy making and contributes to the multiplicity of forces that converge on most presidential decisions.

Finally, the democratization of the selection process has widened the separation among state, congressional, and presidential elections. Moreover, the anti-Washington, antigovernment mood of the electorate, evident since the mid-1970s, has given outsiders, who are less experienced in national politics and may as a result be less able to meet the demands of the office when they first assume it, an electoral advantage. Carter in 1976 and Clinton in 1992 made much of the fact that they did not owe their nomination to the power brokers within their own party nor did they owe their election to members of Congress. George W. Bush also distanced himself from congressional Republicans. Carter and Clinton's electoral ploy soon became a governing handicap. Almost as soon as they took office, they had difficulty getting Congress to follow their lead. Bush, on the other hand, dealt effectively with the Republican Congress, but ran into trouble after Senator Jeffords's defection and the Democrats took over control of the Senate.

Personality Politics and Presidential Leadership

What are presidents to do under these circumstances? How can they lead, achieve their goals, and satisfy pluralistic interests at the same time? Obviously, there is no set formula for success. Forces beyond the president's control may affect the course of events. Nonetheless, presidents would be wise to follow certain maxims in their struggle to convert promises into performance and perhaps also to get reelected.

1. They must identify and limit their own priorities rather than have the priorities forced on them by others. Their priorities should be consistent, well focused, and achievable within the current political environment.

2. They must build and rebuild their own issue coalitions rather than depend solely or even primarily on existing partisan or ideological divisions to support most of their goals. In an age of parity between the major parties and divided partisanship within government, it doesn't make political sense to hew to a partisan line all or even most of the time. With unified government and greater party cohesion in Congress, it makes more sense.

3. They must be flexible enough to adjust to changing conditions and public moods yet consistent enough to provide direction and stability in their policy orientation and credibility for their words. People want to know the direction in which their president is heading.

4. They must take an assertive stand rather than let rhetoric and actions speak for them. They must be sensitive to public opinion but try to mold that opinion as well. Leadership often requires interpreting public opinion and making policy decisions that are consistent with it, although the president must not be perceived as a captive of the polls.

5. Finally, they must grow and learn in office utilizing the status of their position to enhance their personal esteem in the eyes of the public and the lessons of the past as guides to the future. To counter the increasingly negative media coverage, the White House must be a source of good news, good pictures, and credit-producing events for the president. Advisors should remain in the shadows.

Priority setting is a necessary presidential task. Without it, an administration appears to lack direction and leadership. People question what presidents are doing and have difficulty remembering what they have done. The absence of clear, achievable priorities at the beginning of the Carter administration, combined with the president's perceived inconsistency in some of his economic and foreign policy decisions, affected Carter's approval ratings in the public opinion polls and contributed to his defeat four years later.

The Reagan administration understood the lessons of the Carter experience, but the Clinton administration did not, at least not initially. Reagan limited the issues, controlled the agenda, and, most importantly, focused the media on his principal policy objectives during his first term in office. Clinton did not. He had too many goals, too little public support, and took on too much himself. All of these factors adversely affected his leadership image and his opportunities to achieve his policy objectives during his first two years in office. But to his credit, Clinton learned from this experience and became more focused in his words, decisions, and actions after that.

George W. Bush maintained his initial focus on cutting taxes, reforming education, and rebuilding the military. But it was the events of 9/11 and its aftermath that really oriented the president and defined his role during his first term in office.

Presidents have discretion in deciding on their priorities. Reagan used this discretion at the beginning of his first term when he jettisoned his conservative social agenda in favor of major economic reforms. George H. W. Bush chose to emphasize foreign policy and deemphasize domestic issues in the first three years of his administration, despite his campaign's emphasis on domestic concerns. Clinton stuck with his principal priority of stimulating the economy (even though the economy was recovering) but added a host of other policies from deficit reduction to child immunization to ending discrimination against homosexuals in the military to comprehensive health care and welfare reform. By doing so, he overwhelmed Congress and dissipated much of its energy and his public support. George W. Bush was careful not to overload the Congress, but he had few accomplishments to trumpet as well until the events of September 11th strengthened his hand and fortified his resolve.

Beyond establishing priorities and positions, presidents have to get them adopted. Their electoral coalition does not remain a cohesive entity within the governing system. The inevitable shifting of that coalition forces them to build and rebuild their own alliances around their policy objectives. Constructing these alliances requires organizing skills different from those used in winning an election.

Public appeals are often necessary to maintain a high level of support on potentially divisive national issues and to use that support to influence those in power to back the president's initiatives. The Reagan administration effectively marshaled public support in 1981 and 1982 by taking to the airwaves to explain his program to the American people and rally them behind it, particularly his budget and tax proposals. The White House then orchestrated the public's favorable response, directing it toward members of Congress. George H. W. Bush and Bill Clinton initially were much less successful in convincing the public to support controversial domestic policies, but Clinton was able to gain support for his trade policies (NAFTA and GATT) and mobilize opposition to Republican budget proposals in 1995 and 1996.

In addition to building an external coalition, presidents need to employ other inducements and tactics to convince public officials, who have their own constituencies and must be responsive to them, to back presidential policy. This effort requires time, energy, and help. The president cannot do it alone.

As campaign organizations are necessary to win elections, so, too, are governing organizations necessary to gain support for presidential policies. Several offices within the White House have been established to provide liaison and backing for the president on Capitol Hill, in the bureaucracy, and with interest groups and the public. By building and mending bridges, presidents can improve their chances for success. They can commit, convince, cajole, and otherwise gain cooperation despite the constitutional and political separation of institutions and powers.

Unlike winning the general election, making and implementing public policy are not all-or-nothing propositions. Assessments of performance are based on expectations, somewhat as they were in the elections. Part of the image problem all presidents face is the contrast between an idealized public conception of the institution's powers with the president's actual ability to get things done in normal times. The gap between expectations and performance explains why presidents need a public relations staff and why constant campaigning seems inevitable today.

If presidents cannot achieve their goals, they can at least look good trying, and perhaps they can even claim partial success. Finally, they can always change their public priorities to improve their batting averages. Public appeals may or may not generate support within the governing coalition, but they can boost support outside it, and create political capital that they can use later on.

SUMMARY

Americans are fascinated by presidential elections. They want to know who will win, why the successful candidate has won, and what the election augurs for the next four years. Their fascination stems from four interrelated factors: elections are dramatic; they are decisive; they are participatory; and they affect future policy and leadership.

Using past elections as a guide, political scientists have tried to construct models to anticipate how the electorate will react to economic, political, and to a lesser extent, social conditions. The models provide formulas for calculating the percentage of the vote the winning candidate will receive based on a combination of quantifiable indicators such as per capita GDP, level of unemployment, rate of inflation, and popularity of the president. In the past, these models have been reasonably accurate; in 2000, they were not, substantially overestimating the size of Gore's popular vote victory.

Whatever the reasons for the models' inaccuracy, most political scientists still agree that campaigns do matter, that they can affect voting behavior and thereby alter the conventional wisdom of who is likely to win.

To see how campaigns affect the electorate, researchers monitor public opinion over the course of an election. They do so by analyzing data from national and state opinion polls of likely voters. Polls are also important to candidates for discerning what to emphasize and how to maximize the impact of an appeal.

National opinion polls have become fairly accurate measures of the public mood and candidate preferences at the time the polls are taken. They provide data that can be employed to help explain the meaning of an election: the issues that are most salient, the positions that are most popular, and the hopes and expectations that are initially directed toward the elected leaders of government.

The personality of the candidates, the issues of the campaign, and the evaluation of the administration that has controlled it have dominated recent elections and the voting decisions of the electorate. Singularly and together, these factors, along with partisanship, explain the outcome of the vote. In 1960, it was Kennedy's Catholic religion that seemed to account for the closeness of the popular vote despite the large Democratic majority in the electorate. In 1964, it was Goldwater's uncompromising ideological and issue positions that helped provide Johnson with an overwhelming victory in all areas but the deep South. In 1968, it was the accumulation of grievances against the Democrats that spurred the Wallace candidacy and resulted in Nixon's triumph. In 1972, ideology, issues, and the perception of McGovern as incompetent split the Democratic Party and culminated in Nixon's landslide. In 1976, however, partisanship was reinforced by issue, ideological, and personal evaluations to the benefit of the dominant party's nominee. But in the next two elections, it was not. Dissatisfaction with Carter's performance in 1980 and satisfaction with Reagan's in 1984 overcame the Democrats' decreasing numerical advantage within the electorate, leading voters to cast their ballots for Reagan as the person they thought would be best qualified to lead. By 1988, the Democrats had appeared to lose their partisan advantage. The issues in that election, although important, did not favor one candidate at the expense of the other. This left the retrospective evaluation of the Reagan years as the critical factor, an evaluation that was positive.

In a certain sense, the 1992 election was a rerun of 1980. The incumbent was rejected on the grounds that his performance in dealing with the nation's most pressing issue, the economy, was unsatisfactory. Almost two-thirds of the electorate voted against the incumbent president. Of the other two candidates, Clinton was elected primarily because of his partisan affiliation and the public's perception of him as a moderate. That he came from the South, chose Gore as his running mate, and ran an excellent, highly focused campaign all contributed to his victory. Perot ran a strong race for an independent candidate in that election, but independent candidates are disadvantaged within the electorate because they lack a solid base of support and within the Electoral College because of the winner-take-all system used by most of the states to cast their electoral votes. These disadvantages, combined with Perot's early withdrawal and later reentry and his lack of experience in the public sector, were just too great to overcome.

If the 1992 election was a rejection of Bush, the 1996 election marked an approval of Clinton. The president easily won reelection. His share of the popular vote increased by 6 percent; he received slightly more electoral votes as well with the geographic bases of his coalition remaining largely the same. Helped by a stronger economy, a skilled campaign, and effective use of the presidential office, Clinton augmented his partisan support from Democrats with a successful appeal to moderates and to independent voters. Women in particular were attracted to his candidacy, whereas men slightly favored his Republican opponent. In general, Clinton was seen as the more caring, more energetic, more visionary candidate, the one who was more likely to understand contemporary challenges and future needs.

Partisan divisions, issue differences, and mixed performance evaluations of the Clinton presidency carried over into the 2000 election, although the focus tended to be more on future policies and leadership than on past performance. The electorate was evenly divided about the candidates, the direction in which they wanted to move the country, and the priorities and policies they wished to pursue. Disputes over the vote count and the discrepancy between the popular and electoral vote heightened these divisions, clouded the election mandate, and undercut the good will that the victor normally receives after the results are in and the new administration begins to take shape.

The public has a diverse and inflated set of expectations after the election. That they may be conflicting, unrealistic, or in other ways unattainable matters little for a new president. Presidents are expected to lead, to achieve, and to satisfy the interests of a heterogeneous coalition. Their failure or success depends in large part on their ability to fulfill these expectations.

The election provides them with an open-ended mandate that means different things to different people, including the presidents themselves, but usually does not provide them with the political clout to get things done. This situation has presented serious governing problems for recent presidents, none more serious than those following the 2000 election. To overcome these problems, presidents must establish their own priorities, construct their own governing alliances, provide a sense of direction while flexibly moving among policy options, mold but be sensitive to public opinion, and use their office to enhance their image and their programs' chances for being enacted into law. It is not an easy task but one that presidents are expected to undertake.

WHERE ON THE WEB?

Public Opinion

Access the latest polls about the election from the following sites:

- **Gallup Organization**
  http://www.gallup.com
- **CBS News Poll**
  http://www.CBSNews.com
- **The Pew Research Center for the People & the Press**
  http://www.people-press.org
- **Roper Center for Public Opinion Research at the University of Connecticut**
  http://www.lib.uconn.edu/Roper Center
- **Zogby International**
  http://www.zogby.com

Election Results

The Web sites of most major news organizations will have the unofficial results as collected by the Associated Press just as soon as the election is over and the results have been tabulated. These results may not include absentee ballots, which are counted later or the results of any vote challenges. The official results are available from the Federal Election Commission, <http://www.fec.gov>, later in the year. For presidential election results by states from 1860–2000 see *Atlas of U.S. Presidential Elections* <http://www.uselectionatlas.org>.

Election Analysis

Most major news organizations carry the final election exit poll on their Web sites. In addition, data from the National Election Studies conducted by the Center for Political Studies at the University of Michigan, <http://www.umich.edu/nes>, are made available to faculty and students at universities and colleges that are members of the Inter-University Consortium for Political and Social Research about six months after the election is completed.

EXERCISES

1. Look at polls over the course of the election and try to explain opinion shifts on the basis of events in the campaign or in the country as a whole. You can obtain a graph of Gallup polling over the course of the election at that organization's Web site.

2. Compare the results of several national polls at different points in the election cycle to determine how the results contrast and compare to one another. If the polls show different results for the same period, try to ascertain who the respondents were (the general public, the electorate, registered voters, or most likely voters), whether they were asked the same questions, how many people were surveyed, and whether the results were within the margin of error of the polls.

3. After the election has concluded, access the large exit poll that will appear on the Web sites of the major news networks. Analyze the election results on the basis of this poll. In your analysis, note how major demographic groups voted, what the major issues were, how important partisanship and ideology seemed to be, and the feelings voters had toward the candidates and their parties.

4. On the basis of the results of the presidential election (or if the election is not over, the anticipated results), write a memo for the winning candidate explaining the meaning (mandate) of the election for governance. In your memo indicate what the people expect the new president to do and the order in which new priorities should be tackled.

SELECTED READING

Abramson, Paul R., John H. Aldrich, and David W. Rohde. *Change and Continuity in the 2000 Elections.* Washington, D.C.: Congressional Quarterly, 2002.

Bartels, Larry M. et al. "Al Gore and George Bush's Not-So-Excellent Adventure." *PS* 34 (March 2001): 9–75.

Conley, Patricia Heidotting. *Presidential Mandates: How Elections Shape the National Agenda.* Chicago: University of Chicago Press, 2001.

Dahl, Robert A. "Myth of the Presidential Mandate." *Political Science Quarterly* 105 (Fall 1990): 355–372.

Erikson, Robert S. "The 2000 Presidential Election in Historical Perspective."*Political Science Quarterly* 116 (Spring 2001): 29–52.

Fiorina, Morris. *Retrospective Voting in American National Elections.* New Haven, Conn.: Yale University Press, 1981.

Fishel, Jeff. *Presidents and Promises.* Washington, D.C.: Congressional Quarterly, 1985.

Ladd, Everett Carll. "The 1992 Vote for President Clinton: Another Brittle Mandate?" *Political Science Quarterly* 108 (Spring 1993): 1–28.

———. "1996 Vote: The 'No Majority' Realignment Continues." *Political Science Quarterly* 112 (Spring 1997): 1–28.

Miller, Arthur H., and Martin P. Wattenberg. "Throwing the Rascals Out: Policy and Performance Evaluations of Presidential Candidates, 1952–1980." *American Political Science* Review 79 (1985): 359–372.

Pomper, Gerald M., F. Anthony Corrado, E. J. Dionne Jr., et al. *The Election of 2000.* New York: Chatham House, 2001.

———. "The 2000 Election: Why Gore Lost." *Political Science Quarterly* 116 (Summer 2001): 201–223.

Popkin, Samuel L. *The Reasoning Voter.* Chicago: University of Chicago Press, 1991.

Wattenberg, Martin P. *The Rise of Candidate-Centered Politics.* Cambridge, Mass.: Harvard University Press, 1991.

Wayne, Stephen J., and Clyde Wilcox, eds. *The Election of the Century and What It Tells Us about the Future of American Politics.* New York: M. E. Sharpe, 2002.

NOTES

1. Polls indicated that the public was tired of Clinton. The Pew Research Center for the People & the Press found that 36 percent agreed with the statement, "I am tired of all the problems associated with the Clinton administration" in August 1999. One year later the percentage that agreed increased to 48 percent. Pew Research Center for the People & the Press, "Issues and Continuity Now Working for Gore," September 14, 2000.

2. Christopher Wlezien, "On Forecasting the Presidential Vote," *PS* 34 (March 2001), 30. For an extended discussion by the modelers of what went wrong, see the March 2001 edition of *PS*, 9–75 and Christopher Wlezien, "Presidential Election Polls in 2000: A Study in Dynamics," *Presidential Studies Quarterly* 33(March 2003): 172–187.

3. Robert S. Erikson and Christopher Wlezien, "The Timeline of Political Campaigns" (paper presented at the annual meeting of the American Political Science Association, Boston, September 3–6, 1998), Table 1.

4. Professors Erikson and Wlezien analyzed election polls from 1944 to 1996. They found less variation among the polls in the last one hundred days before the election. They attribute this consistency to the "polarization of underlying preferences [of the electorate] during the campaign." Erikson and Wlezien, "The Timeline of Political Campaigns," 10.

5. In a postelection survey taken after the 2000 election by the National Election Studies, 72 percent of the respondents claimed that they voted compared to 51.3 percent of the actual voting-age population. The bogus claims may be a consequence of two factors: the belief that people should vote affected the answer to the question, Did you vote in the last election? Also most of the respondents had been interviewed prior to the election, had agreed to a postelection interview; perhaps they did not want to let the surveyor down by admitting that they did not vote.

6. Joan Shorenstein Center on the Press, Politics, and Public Policy, "One in Seven Likely Voters Still Undecided on a Presidential Candidate," Harvard University, October 18, 2000, <http://www.vanishingvoter.org>.

7. The results of Gallup's final unallocated poll was 47 percent for Bush, 45 percent for Gore, 4 percent for Nader, less than 1 percent for Buchanan, and 4 percent undecided. Anticipating that half of the undecided would not vote, Gallup split the remaining 2 percent between Bush and Gore. Either because more than half the undecided voted and/or voted more heavily for Gore, the final Gallup poll underestimated Gore's vote by more than 2.5 percent.

8. James E. Campbell and Kenneth A. Wink, "Trial-Heat Forecasts of the Presidential Vote," *American Politics Quarterly* 18 (July 1990): 257. Updated by author.

9. The results are telephoned to a center, which feeds them into a central computer. Each of the networks (ABC, CBS, NBC, FOX, and CNN) and the print media that participate in the consortium have terminals indicating what the exit polls are reporting, but retain their own experts to analyze the data as it is being reported.

10. In general, turnout declined more in the East and Midwest than it did in the far West in 1980. Even if there was a decline after Carter's concession, there is little evidence to

suggest that Democrats behaved any differently from Republicans and Independents. Hawaii, the last state to close its polls, voted for Carter.

11. Raymond Wolfinger and Peter Linquiti, "Tuning In and Turning Out," *Public Opinion* 4 (February/March 1981): 57–59. Harold Mendelsohn and Irving Crespi, *Polls, Television, and the New Politics* (Scranton, Penn.: Chandler, 1970), 234–236.

12. Sandra Sobieraj, "The Story Behind the Near-Concession." Associated Press, November 8, 2000, <http://www.ap.org>.

13. Normally, respondents are interviewed two months before and two months after the election.

14. Morris P. Fiorina, *Retrospective Voting in American National Elections* (New Haven, Conn.: Yale University Press, 1981).

15. Presidents will not be blamed for natural disasters or even acts of terrorism over which they have no control, but they will be evaluated on how quickly and effectively they react to the event, empathize with the victims, and provide federal assistance.

16. This view of retrospective voting was advanced by Anthony Downs, *An Economic Theory of Democracy* (New York: Harper & Row, 1957). Downs suggests that people evaluate the past performance of parties and elected officials in order to anticipate how they will perform in the future compared with their opponents.

17. Among political scientists there are two schools of thought. One believes that partisan change results from revolutionary events and government actions to deal with them. These events and policies divide and realign the electorate. The Depression of the 1930s and the Roosevelt administration's New Deal policies resulted in such a realignment along economic lines with the Democrats becoming the majority party. The civil rights movement of the 1950s and 1960s, the Democrats' embrace of that movement, and the civil rights and voting rights laws that were enacted, led to a new division within the electorate, particularly in the South, that led to the Republicans gaining ascendancy in that region of the country and also cutting into Democratic support among blue-collar workers in the major industrial areas.

There have been no major realigning events since that time, yet partisan attitudes have continued to shift, prompting some to postulate that partisan loyalties are also subject to evolutionary change. As the product of a collective body of political experience, these attitudes can strengthen or weaken as a consequence of how well the parties deal with contemporary conditions and events and how well they reflect the public moods and beliefs.

However partisanship takes hold, both schools of thought agree that party allegiances do affect voting behavior; the stronger the allegiances, the greater the effect.

18. For a very interesting, albeit sophisticated article on the impact of emotions on learning, perceptions, and voting see George E. Marcus and Michael B. Mackuen, "Anxiety, Enthusiasm, and the Vote: The Emotional Underpinnings of Learning and Involvement during Presidential Campaigns," *American Political Science Review* 87 (September 1993): 672–685.

19. For an analysis of the components of the 1952 presidential election, see Angus Campbell, Philip E. Converse, Warren E. Miller, and Donald Stokes, *The American Voter* (New York: Wiley, 1960), 524–527.

20. Philip E. Converse, Angus Campbell, Warren E. Miller, and Donald E. Stokes, "Stability and Change in 1960: A Reinstating Election," in *Elections and the Political Order*, ed. Angus Campbell, Philip E. Converse, Warren E. Miller, and Donald E. Stokes (New York: Wiley, 1966), 92.

21. Kennedy's Catholicism may have enlarged his Electoral College total by 22 votes. See Ithiel de Sola Pool, Robert P. Abelson, and Samuel Popkin, *Candidates, Issues, and Strategies* (Cambridge, Mass.: MIT Press, 1965), 115–118.

22. For a discussion of the 1964 presidential election, see Philip E. Converse, Aage R. Clausen, and Warren E. Miller, "Election Myth and Reality: The 1964 Election," *American Political Science* Review 59 (June 1965): 321–336.

23. Philip E. Converse, Warren E. Miller, Jerrold G. Rusk, and Arthur C. Wolfe, "Continuity and Change in American Politics: Parties and Issues in the 1968 Election," *American Political Science Review* 63 (December 1969): 1097. Wallace claimed that there was not "a dime's worth of difference" between the Republican and Democratic candidates and their parties. He took great care in making his own positions distinctive. The clarity with which he presented his views undoubtedly contributed to the issue orientation of his vote. People knew where Wallace stood.

24. Warren E. Miller and Teresa E. Levitin, *Leadership and Change* (Cambridge, Mass.: Winthrop, 1976), 164.

25. Arthur H. Miller, Warren E. Miller, Alden S. Raine, and Thad A. Brown, "A Majority Party in Disarray: Policy Polarization in the 1972 Election," *American Political Science Review* 70 (1976): 753–778.

26. Arthur H. Miller and Warren E. Miller, "Partisanship and Performance: Rational Choice in the 1976 Presidential Elections" (paper presented at the annual meeting of the American Political Science Association, Washington, D.C., September 1–4, 1977).

27. Ibid., 99.

28. Ibid., 7; Warren E. Miller, "Policy Directions and Presidential Leadership: Alternative Interpretations of the 1980 Presidential Election" (paper presented at the annual meeting of the American Political Science Association, New York: September 3–6, 1981).

29. According to Arthur H. Miller and Martin P. Wattenberg in their paper, "Policy and Performance Voting in the 1980 Election" (presented at the annual meeting of the American Political Science Association, New York, September 3–6, 1981), 15: "Reagan was the least positively evaluated candidate elected to the presidency in the history of the National Election Studies, which date back to 1952."

30. Paul R. Abramson, John H. Aldrich, and David W. Rohde, *Change and Continuity in the 1984 Elections* (Washington, D.C.: Congressional Quarterly, 1986), 171–180.

31. J. Merrill Shanks and Warren E. Miller, "Alternative Interpretations of the 1988 Election" (paper presented at the annual meeting of the American Political Science Association, Atlanta, Georgia, August 31–September 3, 1989), 58.

32. Paul R. Abramson, John H. Aldrich, and David W. Rohde, *Change and Continuity in the 1988 Elections* (Washington, D.C.: Congressional Quarterly, 1990), 195.

33. Ibid., 212.

34. J. Merrill Shanks and Warren E. Miller, "Partisanship, Policy, and Performance: The Reagan Legacy in the 1988 Election," *British Journal of Political Science* 21 (April 1991): 129–197.

35. Abramson, Aldrich, and Rohde, *Change and Continuity in the 1988 Elections,* 193, 195, and 198.

36. Paul R. Abramson, John H. Aldrich, and David W. Rohde, *Change and Continuity in the 1996 Elections,* (Washington, D.C.: Congressional Quarterly, 1998), 190.

37. Paul R. Abramson, John H. Aldrich, and David W. Rohde, *Change and Continuity in the 2000 Elections* (Washington, D.C.: Congressional Quarterly, 2002), 191.

38. Kris Kanthak and Barbara Norrander, "Change and Continuity in the Gender Gap" (paper presented at the conference on Assessing the Vitality of Electoral Democracy in the U.S.: The 2000 Election, Ohio State University, March 7–10, 2002).

39. Arthur H. Miller and Thomas F. Klobucar, "The Role of Issues in the 2000 Presidential Election," *Presidential Studies Quarterly* 33 (March 2003): 101–124.

40. Herbert Weisberg and Timothy Hill, "The Succession Presidential Election of 2000: The Battle of the Legacies" (paper presented at the conference on Assessing the Vitality of Electoral Democracy in the U.S.: The 2000 Election, Ohio State University, March 7–10, 2002).

41. Martin P. Watlenberg, "The Clinton 2000 Effect in Perspective: The Impact of Retiring Presidents on Their Parties' Chances of Retaining the White House," *Presidential Studies Quarterly* 33 (March 2003): 164–171; Margaret Tseng, "The Clinton Effect: How a Lame-Duck President Impacted His Vice President's Election Prospects," in *The Election of the Century and What It Tells Us About the Future of America Politics,* ed. Stephen J. Wayne and Clyde Wilcox (New York: M. E. Sharpe, 2002), 200–216.

42. For an excellent discussion on the influence of third-party candidates, see Samantha Luks, Joanne M. Miller, and Lawrence R. Jacobs, "Who Wins? Campaigns and the Third Party Vote," *Presidential Studies Quarterly* 33 (March 2003): 9–30.

43. Patricia Heidotting Conley, *Presidential Mandates: How Elections Shape the National Agenda* (Chicago: University of Chicago Press, 2001), 77–115.

44. Ibid., 116–145.

45. Another limitation to using a platform as a guide to the partisan attitudes and opinions of the public is that many people, including party rank and file, are unfamiliar with most of its contents. The platform per se is not the reason people vote for their party's candidates on election day.

46. Jeff Fishel, *Presidents and Promises* (Washington, D.C.: Congressional Quarterly, 1994), 38, 42–43.

47. One reason campaign promises are important is that they are part of the public record; candidates and parties can be held accountable for them. Another is that they represent the interests of a significant portion of the population. To gain public approval, presidents must respond to these interests. In addition, organized groups, to whom promises have been made, have clout in Congress and in the bureaucracy. Presidents can either mobilize these groups to help them achieve their campaign promises or be thwarted by them if they fail to do so. George Bush ran into this problem in 1990 when he recanted on his pledge not to raise taxes. Conservative Republican members of Congress, who opposed tax increases in their own campaigns for office, voted against the budget compromise that contained a tax increase, a compromise that the president supported.

48. John E. Mueller, *War, Presidents, and Public Opinion* (New York: Wiley, 1973), 205–208; 247–249.

CHAPTER ⚜

9

REFORMING THE ELECTORAL SYSTEM

INTRODUCTION

The American political system evolved significantly in the second half of the twentieth century. Party rules, finance laws, and media coverage are now very different from what they were before the 1960s. The composition of the electorate has changed as well, with the expansion of suffrage to all citizens eighteen years of age or older and the reduction of legal obstacles to voting. In addition, the Electoral College certainly does not function in the manner in which it was originally designed. Have these changes been beneficial? Has the system been improved? Are further structural or operational adjustments desirable? These questions have elicited a continuing, and sometimes spirited, debate.

Critics have alleged that the electoral process is too long, too costly, and too burdensome, that it wears down candidates and numbs voters, resulting in too many personal accusations and too little substantive discussion of the issues, too much name-calling and "sound bite" rhetoric, and too little real debate. They have said that many qualified people are discouraged from running for office and much of the electorate is uninformed, uninterested, and uninvolved. Other criticisms are that the system benefits special interests, encourages factionalism, weakens parties, overemphasizes personality and underemphasizes policy, and that it is unduly influenced by the news media. It has also been contended that voters do not receive the information they need to make an intelligent, informed decision on election day.

In contrast, proponents argue that the political system is more democratic than ever. More, not fewer, people are involved, especially at the nomination stage. Candidates, even lesser-known ones, now have an opportunity to demonstrate their competence, endurance, motivation, and leadership capabilities. Parties remain important as vehicles through which the system operates and by which governing is accomplished. Those who defend the process believe voters do receive as much information as they desire and that most people can and do make informed and rational judgments.

The old adage "where you stand influences what you see" is applicable to the debate about electoral reform. No political process is completely neutral. There are always winners and losers. To a large extent the advantages that some enjoy are made possible by the disadvantages that others encounter. Rationalizations aside, much of the debate about the system, about equity, representation, and responsiveness, revolves around a very practical, political question: Who gains and who loses?

Proposals to change the system need to be assessed in the light of this question. They should also be judged on the basis of how such changes would affect the operation of the political system and influence governance. This chapter discusses some of these proposals and the effect they could have on the road to the White House. The chapter is organized into two sections: one dealing with the more recent developments and proposals in party rules, campaign finance, and media coverage; and the other examining the long-term, democratic issues of participation and voting.

MODIFYING RECENT CHANGES

Party Rules

Of all the changes that have recently occurred in the nomination process, the reforms governing the selection of delegates continue to engender controversy and constant fine-tuning. Designed to encourage grassroots participation and broaden the base of representation, these reforms have also lengthened the nominating period, made the campaign more expensive, generated candidate-based organizations, weakened the influence of state and local party leaders, converted conventions into coronations, and loosened the ties between the parties and their nominees. All of these consequences have made governing more difficult.

Since 1968, when the Democrats began to rewrite their rules for delegate selection, the parties have suffered from these unintended repercussions. Each succeeding presidential election has seen reforms to the reforms, modifications that have attempted to reconcile expanded participation and representation with the traditional need to unify the party and have it play a consequential role in the national campaign. Although less reform conscious than the Democrats, the Republicans have also tried to steer a middle course between greater rank-and-file involvement and more equitable representation on the one hand and the maintenance of successful electoral and governing coalitions on the other.

How to balance these often competing goals has been a critical concern. Those who desire greater public participation have lauded the trend toward having more primaries and a larger percentage of delegates selected in them. Believing that the reforms have opened up the process and made it more democratic, they favor the continued selection of pledged delegates based on the proportion of the popular vote their candidate receives. In contrast, those who believe that greater control by state and national party leaders is desirable argue that the reforms have gone too far. They would prefer fewer primaries, a smaller percentage of delegates selected in them, more unpledged delegates participating in the nominating conventions, and a larger role for state and national party organizations in the entire presidential campaign.

Stronger party advocates appear to be in the ascendancy. Democratic Party rules have consistently sought to limit participation in its primary elections to registered or self-declared Democrats, although such restrictions are difficult to enforce in states that allow voters to request the ballot of either party (open primaries). Crossover voting by the partisans of one party in the other's primary became a particularly contentious issue in the 2000 nominations when John McCain and Bill Bradley directed their appeals to independent and independent-minded partisan voters.

From a party's perspective, the issue of crossover voting is critical to control of its own nominations. To allow nonpartisans to participate dilutes the influence of party regulars and creates the possibility for selecting a nominee who does not best reflect the interests, needs, or ideological views of most of the rank and file. A particular fear is that adherents of the other party will cross over to vote for the weaker candidate in order to enhance their own nominee's chances in the general election. There is little empirical data to support this fear, however.

From the perspective of the citizenry, on the other hand, a primary closed to all but registered partisans precludes much of the population from participating and reduces the incentive for these voters to become informed and get involved. Moreover, parties can benefit from an open primary system if it leads to its recruitment of more active supporters or makes their nominees more electable.

Another rules issue concerns the allocation of votes in primaries. Since 1992, the Democrats have used a straight proportional voting system that allocates pledged delegates according to the proportion of the popular vote a candidate receives. The Republicans permit the states to decide on the method of allocation, which could be proportional or winner-take-all within districts or on an at-large basis.

Proportional voting more closely reflects the view of a state's primary electorate, but it also could have the effect of extending the nomination and delaying a consensus on the eventual nominee, and cost more money. The more disunified the party is going into its nominating convention, the weaker its candidates are likely to be in the general election, or so the thinking has been within the national leadership of both major parties.[1]

There has been widespread public support for shortening the nomination campaign, which Professor Thomas E. Patterson has argued "disrupts the policy process, discourages the candidacies of responsible officeholders, and wears out the voters."[2] It also diverts public attention from issues of government to campaign-related controversies. Moreover, Patterson notes that a long campaign generates more negative news about the candidates as it progresses, thereby souring voters on the choices they have on primary day.[3]

Several proposals have been made for addressing this issue. Some have even been introduced in the form of legislation in Congress. One would limit the period during which primaries or caucuses could be held; a second would cluster primaries and caucuses, forcing states in designated regions or as groups to hold their elections on the same day; a third would create a national primary.

Having an official period during the spring of the election year for primaries and caucuses has been suggested as a way to reduce the impact the early contests have had on the nomination. A second but equally important objective has been to reduce the news media's influence on public opinion during these initial stages of the process.

The Democratic Party has attempted to achieve these goals since 1984 by imposing its own window period during which primaries and caucuses could be held. Opposition from several states, however, including Iowa and New Hampshire, has forced the party to grant them exceptions to the imposed time frame, much to the consternation of other states. The exceptions, in turn, continue to produce the problem that generated the proposal in the first place—the holding of early contests that receive extensive media coverage and for that reason are disproportionally important to the candidates, and do not accurately reflect sentiment within the party. This problem, in turn, has encouraged other states to move their primaries toward the beginning of the window period, thereby compressing the nomination process and starting the campaign earlier and earlier in the election cycle.

The Republicans faced the same problem as the Democrats. With no specified time frame imposed on their state parties, the GOP has encountered even more front-loading than the Democrats with many of the same unhappy consequences.

Front-loading creates inequities. It gives greater influence to those states that hold their contests earlier and less to those that hold them later. To the extent that partisans in the early states are not representative of the party's rank and file, they can generate momentum for a candidate who may not be the first or most acceptable choice for the party as a whole.

Front-loading helps well-known and well-financed candidates. Conversely, it hurts long shots who now must raise more money more quickly and must also enter more contests before they have had ample opportunity to demonstrate their electability. The stepping-stones to the nomination have become more compressed, as a result lessening the prospects that a non-front-runner can win the nomination.

Front-loading moves the campaign forward, well into the year before the general election. Not only does it lengthen the nomination process, it also shortens its competitive phase. In 2000, the competitive period lasted only six weeks. Thus candidates have to begin their quest for the nomination earlier, and if successful, continue it longer.

From the perspective of a democratic political system, perhaps the most serious consequence of front-loaded campaigns is that the decisive stage of the nomination process occurs before most people are paying attention to it. By the time the party's electorate tunes in, many of the candidates may have dropped out.[4]

Moreover, there is little incentive for the public to stay attentive or even turn out to vote in later primaries after the nomination has been effectively determined.

Inequitable state representation and declining participation were two of the reasons that both major parties established commissions to examine the impact of their nomination procedures on the party, its candidates, and its partisan electorate. After a series of public forums, the Republican Advisory Commission proposed scheduling changes that would have reversed the adverse impact of front-loading with primary dates established by state size, the least populous states going first. The larger states objected to the plan, fearing that the nomination would be settled before they voted. The proposal was scuttled by the Republican Rules Committee. The Democratic Party simply caved in to the front-loading dilemma. It has permitted causes and primaries to be held one month earlier in 2004, beginning the first Tuesday in February, with Iowa and New Hampshire even earlier.

Regional primaries, however, had been evolving since 1988 when southern Democrats, unhappy over the national party's liberal tilt, convinced their state legislatures to hold their nominating contests on the second Tuesday in March. Most of them have continued to do so. Meanwhile states in the Northeast, with the exception of New Hampshire, have moved their contests to the first Tuesday of the presidential nomination cycles and several of the Midwestern states now schedule theirs on the third Tuesday of that month. Despite this movement toward regional primaries, the front-loading of the system has worked to undercut the benefits of a regionalized process.

The case for regional primaries is based on the assumption that such a system would be more equitable for the states and provide more focus for the candidates. As long as the regions adopted some plan to rotate their nomination dates, which they do not do at present, over a period of time each area would be able to exercise approximately equal influence over the selection of a party's nominees. Moreover, candidates would be forced to address regional concerns and appeal to regional interests. A nomination that extended to the four regional primaries would probably ensure that the winning candidate had broad-based geographic support, the kind of support that is necessary to win in the Electoral College.

But regionalization is not without its critics who fear that it would exacerbate sectional rivalries, encourage local or area candidates, and produce more organizations to rival those of the state and national parties. Moreover, like straight proportional voting, a regional primary system could impede the emergence of a consensus candidate, thereby extending the process to the convention and increasing, not decreasing, costs, time, and media attention.

In addition, regional primaries help the best-organized and best-financed candidates, such as Bill Clinton and George H. W. Bush in 1992, Bob Dole in 1996, and Al Gore and George W. Bush in 2000. They make it more difficult for candidates who lack a national reputation and a huge war chest to compete in regions outside their own.

Another option, and the one that represents the most sweeping change, would be to institute a national primary. Although leaders of both major parties, including members of the reform commissions, have opposed this idea and

Congress has been cool to it, the general public seems to be more favorably disposed. Gallup polls taken over the last two decades indicate that about two-thirds of the electorate prefers such an election to the present system.[5]

Most proposals for a national primary call for it to be held in the late spring or early summer, followed by party conventions. Candidates who wished to enter their party's primary would be required to obtain a certain number of signatures. Any aspirant who won a majority would automatically receive the nomination. In some plans a plurality would be sufficient, provided it was at least 40 percent. In the event that no one received 40 percent, a runoff election would be held several weeks later between the top two finishers. Nominating conventions would continue to select the vice presidential candidates and to decide on the platforms.

A national primary would be consistent with the "one person, one vote" principle that guides most aspects of the U.S. electoral system. All participants would have an equal voice in the selection. No longer would those in the early, small primary and caucus states exercise disproportionate influence.

It is also likely that a national primary would stimulate turnout. The attention given to such an election would provide greater incentives for voting than currently exists, particularly in those states that hold their nomination contests after the apparent winner has emerged. A national primary would probably result in nomination by a more representative electorate than is currently the case.

A single primary election for each party would accelerate a nationalizing trend. Issues that affect the entire country would be the primary focus of attention. Thus, candidates for the nation's highest office would be forced to discuss the problems they would most likely address during the general election campaign and would most likely confront as president.

Moreover, the results of the election would be clear-cut. The person with the most votes would be the winner. The media could no longer interpret primaries and caucus returns as they saw fit. An incumbent's ability to garner support through the timely release of grants, contracts, and other spoils of government might be more limited in a national contest, but it would not be eliminated entirely. On the other hand, such an election would undoubtedly discourage challengers who lacked national reputations. No longer could an early victory catapult a relatively unknown aspirant into the position of serious contender and jeopardize a president's chances for renomination. In fact, lesser-known candidates, such as George McGovern, Jimmy Carter, Michael Dukakis, and even Bill Clinton in 1992, might find it extremely difficult to raise money, build an organization, and mount a national campaign. John McCain would have had more difficulty challenging George W. Bush if he had had to campaign in all fifty states.

From the standpoint of the major parties, a national primary would further weaken the ability of their leaders to influence the selection of the nominee. Successful candidates would probably not owe their victory to party officials. Moreover, a postprimary convention could not be expected to tie the nominee to the party, although it might tie the party to the nominee, at least through the election. The trend toward personalizing politics would probably continue.

Such nominees, if elected, might also find governing much more difficult. They could not count on the support of party leaders if those leaders played little or no role in the candidate's nomination. Party leaders and members of Congress who have no stake in the election of the president would be hard to mobilize and quick to jump ship should the president get into political difficulty.

Whether a national primary winner would be the party's strongest candidate is also open to question. With a large field of contenders, those with the most devoted or ideological supporters might do best. On the other hand, candidates who do not arouse the passions of the diehards but who are more acceptable to the party's mainstream might not do as well. Everybody's second choice might not even finish second, unless a system of approval voting or cumulative voting were used.[6] Approval or cumulative voting systems, however, complicate the election, confuse the result, undercut its legitimacy, and perhaps add to its costs.

In addition to weakening the party, a national primary could lessen the ability of states to determine when and how their citizens would participate in the presidential nomination process, thereby undercutting the federal system of nominations. Finally, a national primary would in effect produce two presidential elections every four years. Could public attention be maintained throughout such an elongated election cycle? Could sufficient money be raised? Could the candidates' grassroots organizations handle such a task, not once but twice? These questions have tempered widespread political support for such a plan despite the general appeal of the idea to the public.

Finance Laws

Closely related to the delegate selection process are the laws governing campaign finance. First enacted in the 1970s in reaction to secret and sometimes large illegal bequests to candidates, to the disparity in contributions and spending among the candidates, and to the spiraling costs of modern campaigns, particularly television advertising, these laws were designed to improve accountability, reduce spending, subsidize nominations, and fund the general election. Some of these objectives have been achieved, but in the process other problems have been created.

The laws have taken campaign finance out of the back rooms and put much of it into the public spotlight. They have also, however, created a nightmare of compliance procedures and reporting requirements. Detailed records of practically all contributions and expenditures of the presidential campaign organizations must now be kept and periodically reported to the Federal Election Commission.[7] Good accountants and attorneys, specializing in election law, are now as necessary as pollsters, image makers, and grassroots organizers.

But there were loopholes in the laws that party and nonparty groups, such as the Christian Coalition, the National Rifle Association, and pro- and antiabortion groups, trade associations, labor unions, and business groups exploited to their political advantage. The solicitation of soft money for issue advocacy ads effectively undercut the federal limits on individual contributions and campaign expenditures. The amount people could donate to the candidates for their party's nomination was limited by law, but not the amount they could contribute to their party's soft-money account, to nonparty groups, or the amount they could spend independently (or on themselves were they to run and not accept federal funds).

The McCain–Feingold bill sought to end this legal subterfuge by banning the national parties from raising soft money and running issue ads in which their candidates were mentioned by name thirty days or less before a primary and sixty days or less before the general election. Nonparty groups were also subject to the issue advocacy restriction. The constitutionality of the law was immediately challenged by opponents of the legislation, and in May 2003 a three-judge federal panel found parts of the law unconstitutional, thereby setting the stage for Supreme Court consideration of the matter in the fall of 2003 as the primary campaign was underway.

An important goal of federal funding has also not been met. Expenditures on behalf of the major party candidates, which are equal in theory, have not been equalized in practice. The Republicans are still able to raise more during the nomination phase and during the general election. Control of the White House helped the Democrats raise more soft money, enabling them to close this money gap in the 1990s, but without the perquisites of power and the soft money loophole, the Republican advantage can be expected to increase in the years ahead. Issue advocacy advertising and disbursements to their state parties to run get-out-the-vote campaigns are still permitted under the law; state parties can even raise soft money so long as they do not spend it on federal campaigns, although the distinction between state and federal campaigns tends to be lost when conducting partisan mobilization and voter turnout drives.

Nor has federal legislation curbed the increase in campaign expenditures, which has exceeded the rate of inflation. On the contrary, the need to supplement increasing expenditures for fund-raising, media, polling, and other important campaign activities has actually increased the amount of money that the campaign organizations believe that they must raise and spend to compete effectively. This need has forced presidential candidates to spend more time fund-raising and has encouraged them to shift as many of their campaign costs as possible to the national and state parties in the general election. Supplemental campaigns by nonparty groups are becoming increasingly important and may actually be enhanced by the new law's soft-money restrictions placed on the national parties.

The increase in the individual contribution limits from $1,000 to $2,000 should help the candidates during the nomination phase and the parties during the general election. But outside groups can also be expected to play an increasingly vital role. Particularly troublesome have been efforts by both national parties to "suggest" to PACs (Democrats to organized labor; Republicans to business groups and allegedly also to the Christian Coalition) and to individuals of both political persuasions how to spend their money most effectively, going so far as to suggest which commercials to buy, from whom, and when to air them.

PAC contributions and PAC spending on electoral activities constitute another very contentious issue, at least from the perception of the general public. PAC contributions can be limited by prohibiting or reducing the amount of money that they can give, but PAC contributions are not the problem in presidential elections. Spending is the problem and it cannot be constrained so long as the Supreme Court's *Buckley v. Valeo* decision stands. That decision equates campaign spending with freedom of speech, which is protected by the First Amendment. If individual and group spending were seen as the use of personal property in political campaigns, restrictions might not encounter the same constitutional proscriptions that they do with free speech.

So long as group activity is protected by the First Amendment, there is little Congress can do to deal with the "I-owe-you" problem that a newly elected administration faces. Increased federal funding might help, but there is already a shortfall in the election fund which is expected to worsen in the coming years. Besides, the limits placed on candidates who accept these funds are becoming increasingly burdensome to those candidates. Congress could raise the amount taxpayers can allocate to that fund, but there is still the problem of the declining percentage of taxpayers who are willing to check the box that allocates their taxes to the fund. More money for elections would leave less for other government expenses, not a happy prospect in an age of budget deficits.

There are other things that Congress could do. It could enact legislation requiring television stations that operate over the public airways to allow candidates free time to respond to political advertising, debate, or simply state their policy positions. Candidates might also get reduced rates for mailing campaign literature to the voters. But these proposals are opposed by profit-making media and would require a federal subsidy if they applied to the U.S. Postal Service, much less private carriers such as United Parcel Service (UPS) and Federal Express.

Moreover, a law that forced the media to provide free time might even be counterproductive, reducing rather than increasing the amount of public communications during the campaign. Television and radio stations would undoubtedly be discouraged from selling time to nonparty groups and individuals if they were under obligation to provide it free to the person or party who was the object of the commercial. A decrease in media advertising would reduce the information available to the public and increase the electorate's dependence on the candidates and the news media.

Besides, in point of fact, the appearance of candidates on talk-entertainment shows beginning in 1992 and the proliferation of all-news cable channels have given major candidates more "free" time to respond to questions about their policy positions and personal character. But it has also given the producers, hosts, and commentators on these shows subtle ways of influencing the electorate through the wording and sequencing of their questions to the candidates and even by their choice of whom to interview and when to do so.

The campaign finance quandary at its most basic level is one of competing social needs that have generated contradictory political goals. Freedom of speech implies the right to advance beliefs by contributing to the candidates and party of one's choice and spending independently on their behalf. In a democratic political system, however, a system in which the vote and presumably the voice of all citizens should be equal, the wealthy should not have an advantage. Yet appeals to a large segment of the electorate are very expensive. How to ensure that candidates have sufficient funds, that freedom of speech is protected, and political equality is promoted—*all without partisan advantage*—are issues that have and will continue to perplex Congress and the judiciary in the years ahead.

News Media Coverage

A third significant change in the electoral process concerns the way in which information about the campaign is communicated to the voters. Beginning in the 1950s, television became the principal medium through which candidates made their appeals and by which voters obtained information. Since then, television's emphasis on the contest, the drama, and the style of candidates has affected every nook and cranny of the campaign from public perceptions of the candidates and the parties to the judgment of the electorate on election day.

Changes in party rules and finance laws have also contributed to the media's impact. The increasing number of primaries and caucuses have provided the news media with greater inducements to cover these events and interpret their results. The desire of the parties to obtain maximum exposure for their nominating conventions has resulted in simultaneous conventions, the "official" ones at the podium, carefully orchestrated by the parties to benefit their nominees in the eyes of the public, and the unofficial ones, mediated by the news media, designed to interest and entertain viewers and readers with behind-the-scenes reporting and analysis.

The limited money available to presidential candidates who accept federal funding has also increased the importance of news about their campaigns and may have contributed to the news media's impact on the voters. Today candidates do not leave their coverage to chance. They attempt to influence it by carefully releasing favorable information and "spinning" the news to their advantage, by staging events and designing speeches in sound bite friendly formats, and by paying for many commercial messages.

Is the coverage adequate? Do voters receive sufficient information from the news media to make an intelligent decision? Many students of democracy believe they do not. Academicians, especially, have urged that greater attention be paid to policy issues and less to the game format of who is ahead, most likely to win, and why. One proposal would have the networks and wire services assign special correspondents to cover the issues of the campaign, much as they assign people to report on its color, drama, and personal aspects. Another would be to place greater emphasis on campaign coverage itself and assess the accuracy of the statements and advertising claims of the candidates as some newspapers, such as the *Washington Post* and the *New York Times,* and major television networks have begun to do on a regular basis.

In addition to criticizing the news media's treatment of the issues and its watchdog function in the campaign, academicians and others have frequently called into question the amount and accuracy of election reporting. The Federal Communications Commission has ruled that if the networks provide free time to some candidates, they must provide equal time to all running for the same position, including those of fringe parties. This "equal time" provision has in fact resulted in little or no free time, although coverage of debates between candidates for their party's nomination, and later between candidates of the major parties in the general election, is permitted. In 1996, for the first time the major networks gave the candidates limited time to use as they wished before the election. Networks are also required to be impartial in their coverage. Station licenses can be challenged and even revoked if biases are consistently evident in the presentation of the news.

Other than requiring fairness, preventing obscenity, and ensuring that public service commitments are met, there is little the government can do to ensure adequate coverage without impinging on the constitutional protections of freedom of the press. The news media are free to choose which elections and candidates to emphasize, what kind and how much coverage to provide, how to interpret the results of primaries and caucuses, and even to predict who will win before the election is concluded. And these freedoms tend to be exercised with public programming desires in mind. Not only do corporations that own media affiliates engage in constant private polling to discern the interest of the viewing, listening, and reading public, but people "vote" every day when they turn on a particular program on radio or television or buy a particular newspaper or magazine.

There is much that candidates can do, however, to affect the coverage they receive. If their words are unreported or not reported correctly, or if their ideas are misinterpreted or their motives suspected by the national news, they can seek other mass media formats for reaching the general public as they have done by using the entertainment and talk shows. They can also employ satellite technology to reach local and regional audiences directly and thereby circumvent the national networks and news services. And they can agree to other "competitive" formats that will get national coverage because they fit into the game motif that the news media use.

Another media-related issue is the election night projections based on exit polling data that the networks air before all voting has been completed. Since 1964, when a Lyndon Johnson landslide was predicted before the polls on the West Coast had closed, proposals have been advanced to limit or prohibit these glimpses into the immediate future. Beginning in 1984, the networks promised not to forecast the outcome in any state until a majority of its polls had closed. This voluntary restriction does not rectify the problem of having different time zones nor preclude a national prediction from being made before voting is completed in the continental United States.

Proposals to deal with the election night projection issue include one that would establish a uniform hour at which voting ends in the continental United States or another to terminate the current process entirely and replace it with a national system of mail ballots or eventually voting on the Internet. These proposals have also encountered criticism. Could the networks be expected to wait until voting ended across the nation, given the competitive character of news reporting?

Even if there was a uniform closing hour for the entire country, there still would be no guarantee that early forecasts, based on exit polls, could be eliminated. Moreover, a law, such as the one the House of Representatives passed in 1989 that would have forced thirty-nine states to change their voting hours, reduces their constitutional prerogative to conduct elections for federal officials. Eight states, including California, would have had to reduce the hours during which people could vote, conceivably contributing to lower turnout while others would have increased hours and correspondingly increased costs. A mail ballot, such as the one used in Oregon, might be possible in the nation as a whole although it might also be more vulnerable to fraud than the system that currently exists.

In addition to the obvious First Amendment problems that would be generated by restricting what and when the news could report about the election, there is another more general media-related issue. People enjoy the election night broadcasts. After a lengthy campaign, workers and sympathizers are eager to learn the results and to celebrate or commiserate, whereas the public desires the ritualistic conclusion that the reporting and analysis of the results on election night provide.

Moreover, exit polls have considerable value in the information they provide about the beliefs, attitudes, and motivations of the voters. Much of the initial analysis of presidential elections and their meaning is based on that poll data. In a democracy, it is essential to get as clear a reading of the pulse of the electorate as possible.

ENHANCING ELECTORAL CHOICE

Turnout

Although suffrage has expanded, a gap remains between those eligible to vote and those who actually do so. This gap, which will always exist in a system that does not compel voting, widened during the last forty years. In 1996, more than half those eligible chose *not* to vote; it remained low in 2000, 51.3 percent.

The decline in the intensity of partisan allegiances, the shift from party-centered to candidate-centered campaigns, the growing levels of mistrust and lower confidence in public officials, and the weakening sense of efficacy on the part of many people have all contributed to lower turnout and produced a "disconnect" between American citizens and their political system. That disconnect threatens to undermine the legitimacy of American electoral institutions and reduces the ability of elected officials to build and maintain a cohesive governing majority.

Low turnout in a free and open electoral system has been a source of embarrassment to the United States and of concern to its political leaders. How can a president legitimately claim a public mandate with the electoral support of so few of those who are eligible to vote? In the last four presidential elections, the winning candidate has received the votes of only about one-quarter of the voting-age population. Can a government still claim to be representative and democratic if almost half the population chooses not to participate in elections for public officials and only one out of four votes for the winning candidate?

A variety of legal, institutional, and political obstacles must be overcome if turnout is to increase. Congress addressed some of these problem areas in 1993 when it enacted legislation to ease registration procedures and in 2002 when it provided for provisional voting for those whose registration was challenged. The 2002 law also requires states to automate their voter registration.

Other proposals to make registration automatic, as it is in many European countries, or extending it to election day itself, as is already permitted in a few states, have also been advanced. Counties or states, which have facilitated registration in these ways, have considerably higher levels of turnout than those that do not.

Another proposal to enhance turnout would make election day a national holiday or move election day to Veterans Day, which comes later in the month. Presumably either change would prevent work-related activities from interfering with voting as much as they do now for the bulk of the population. Many countries follow the practice of holding their elections on a holiday or Sunday. The problem here is that an additional national holiday would cost employers millions of dollars in lost revenue and productivity, with no guarantee that turnout would increase, and veterans would probably oppose having politics obscure the meaning that the holiday was intended to have for the end of hostilities in the two World Wars. For workers in certain service sectors, the holiday might be a workday anyway.

Some states have extended the period for voting up to twenty-one days prior to the election to increase the number of voters. Others have enacted a "no fault" absentee ballot system for those who find it difficult or inconvenient to get to the polls on election day. Under a liberalized absentee voting procedure, any eligible voter can obtain an absentee ballot, no questions asked. Twenty states currently provide one or both of these options, and voting turnout in them has increased.[8]

Oregon has gone so far as to institute a mail ballot. After experimenting with voting by mail in a special election for Senate and later in the presidential primaries of 1996, Oregonians voted in favor of a ballot initiative that permanently institutes this method of voting beginning in 2000. Turnout in Oregon has exceeded the national average in those elections in which mail balloting has been used.[9]

But extending the voting period and balloting by mail are not without their costs. Fear of fraud if the ballots get into the wrong hands is one concern. Voting without all pertinent information is another. People who vote early do so without knowing what may be revealed at the end of the campaign. And for the candidates themselves, there is the added cost of mailing thousands of sample ballots or other information to voters and appealing to them to use them when voting. Nonetheless, the benefit of increasing turnout has motivated more states to modify their single-day, geographically based voting tradition.

Perhaps the most radical proposal for the United States would be to compel people to vote: to force them to go to the polls or cast an absentee ballot. Penalties would be imposed on those who refused to do so. Australia, Belgium, and Chile require voting and their turnout is very high. One obvious problem with forcing people to vote is the compulsion itself. Some may be physically or mentally incapable of voting. Others may not care, have little interest, and have very limited information. They might not even know the names of the candidates. Would the selection of the best-qualified person be enhanced by the participation of uninformed, uninterested, uncaring voters? Might demagogy be encouraged, or even slicker and more simplistic advertising designed? Would government be more responsive and more popular, or would it be more prone to what British philosopher John Stuart Mill referred to as "the tyranny of the majority?" Finally, is it democratic to force people to vote? If the right to vote is an essential component of a democratic society, then what about the right *not* to vote? Should it be protected as well?

In addition to easing or removing legal obstacles or creating a legal requirement to vote, there have been other kinds of suggestions for encouraging more people to participate. One is to change the electoral system itself to provide more incentives for those in the minority by increasing the likelihood that their vote would produce tangible results. Instituting proportional representation for Congress or in the apportionment of electoral votes could produce this effect; directly electing the president might also do so. In these cases those in the minority would have greater incentive to vote than they do under the current system. Winner-take-all voting, which occurs in single-member legislative districts and in most states in the Electoral College, discourages turnout in noncompetitive areas.

Systemic changes, however, are difficult to accomplish. They upset the established political order and are likely to generate opposition from those who fear change, resistance from those who like and gain from the current arrangement, or support from those who believe that they will benefit more if the system is modified in a certain way. Moreover, reforming the electoral system in this manner would require a constitutional amendment, which is always more difficult than enacting legislation. As a consequence, these proposals are not likely to be implemented in the short run nor in the absence of other changes.

Creating a more hospitable and engaging electoral climate is another way to increase turnout. If parties were strengthened, if their organizations were more broad-based, if they encouraged more participatory politics by providing more information to voters and more grassroots activities, turnout would likely be enhanced. But revitalizing the parties has proven to be extremely difficult, particularly in the current era in which so many people are turned off by partisan politics. Moreover, changes in the nomination process have weakened, not strengthened party structures, although organizational control over money and other campaign resources has begun to reverse that effect.

We have already referred to another potential arena of change—the communications industry. If candidates had greater access to the media, if they were given free time in addition to the time they purchased, if advertising were less expensive, if there were more debates during prime time, if candidates appeared on more interactive programs and more general entertainment formats, then more of the public might become engaged in the campaign and thus would turn out to vote rather than tune out, which unfortunately has been the case for far too many people today.[10] Greater exposure, however, might also numb the electorate; entertainment formats often emphasize style over substance and might trivialize the campaign. More television exposure might result in the election of more media celebrities and fewer civic-minded political leaders.

Educating the people on the merits of participating and the responsibilities of citizenry might also generate greater involvement. If the public better understood what difference it makes who wins, if they had greater confidence that elected officials would keep their promises and that government would address salient issues, then voter turnout would likely be enhanced. But invigorating the electoral environment and encouraging more people to participate is not an easy task. If it were, it would have already occurred. It is difficult to convince nonvoters to spend the time and effort it takes to educate themselves about the candidates and the issues, to get involved in the campaign, and to vote unless people can see what is in it for them and what might happen if they do not do so.

If, however, more people did vote, the parties and candidates would have to broaden their appeal. They would have to address the needs and desires of all the people and not concentrate on those who were most likely to vote. Those who have not participated as frequently in the current voluntary system of voting—the poorer, less educated, less fortunate, and younger—would receive more attention not only from candidates for office but from elected officials in office. More equitable policies might result, but also more socioeconomic divisions within the political structure might be evident. At the worst, these divisions could lead to a more volatile, class oriented political system and more extreme variations in public policies.

Electoral Reform

The vote controversy in Florida highlighted the deficiencies in voter certification and election administration: inaccurate registration lists, confusing ballots, unclear votes, and their improper tabulation. The state of Florida moved quickly to correct these problems, and Congress followed suit in 2002 as well.

For the first time it enacted legislation to establish federal standards for national elections and authorized funds for states which complied with these standards to upgrade their registration procedures, purchase more advanced voting technology, and provide greater accessibility to the polls for the disabled. The bill authorized nearly $4 billion over three years to help states computerize and centralize their registration lists, train election workers, buy new voting machinery, and improve access to the voting booths.

To decrease the potential for fraud, the statute requires first-time registrants and voters to provide identification, a driver's license or the last four digits of their Social Security number. Latino groups, backed by some liberal Democrats, strongly objected to this requirement, fearing that it would disproportionately reduce the size of the Hispanic vote. On the other hand, African Americans welcome the anti-fraud provisions, believing that it would make it more difficult for state election officials to challenge African American voters as occurred in Florida in 2000. Republicans also strongly supported the new identification requirement.

The legislation also enables voters whose names do not appear on the registration lists to cast a provisional vote pending their registration challenge. However, no time requirements are imposed on states to rectify these challenges.

Intended to increase public confidence in the conduct of elections, the new law should correct some of the most egregious problems that have marred past elections. Nonetheless, so long as the administration of national elections is a shared state and county responsibility, variations in registration and voting procedures combined with spur-of-the-moment decisions by election officials will continue to fuel complaints and controversies over the conduct of elections. Allegations of fraud, however, should be reduced, assuming, of course, that Congress appropriates the money authorized by the act and distributes it to the states.

The Electoral College

In addition to the problem of who votes, another source of contention is how the votes should be aggregated. Theoretically, the Constitution allows electors chosen by the states to vote as they please. In practice, all votes are cast for the popular vote winner. The reason for this outcome is simple. The vote for president and vice president is actually a vote for competing slates of electors selected in all but two states on a statewide basis. The slate that wins is the slate proposed by the winning candidate's party. Naturally the electors are expected to vote for their party's nominees.

This de facto system has been criticized as undemocratic, as unrepresentative of minority views within states, and as potentially unreflective of the nation's popular choice. Over the years, there have been numerous proposals to alter it. The first was introduced in Congress in 1797. Since then, there have been more than five hundred others. In urging changes, critics have pointed to the Electoral College's archaic design, its electoral biases, and the undemocratic results it can produce (see Chapter 1). Four major plans—automatic, proportional, district, and direct election—have been proposed as constitutional amendments to alleviate some or all of these problems. The following sections will examine these proposals and the impact they could have on the way in which the president is selected.

The Automatic Plan. The electors in the Electoral College have been an anachronism since the development of the party system. Their role as partisan agents is not and has not been consistent with their exercising an independent judgment. In fact, sixteen states plus the District of Columbia prohibit such a judgment by requiring electors to cast their ballots for the winner of the state's popular vote. Although probably unenforceable because they seem to clash with the Constitution, these laws strongly indicate how electors should vote.

The so-called automatic plan would do away with the danger that electors may exercise their personal preferences. First proposed in 1826, it has received substantial support since that time, including the backing of Presidents John Kennedy and Lyndon Johnson. The plan simply keeps the Electoral College intact but eliminates the electors. Electoral votes are automatically given to the candidate who has received the most popular votes within the state.

Other than removing the potential problem of faithless or unpledged electors, the plan would do little to change the system as it currently operates. It has not been enacted because Congress has not felt this particular problem to be of sufficient magnitude to justify a constitutional amendment to fix it. There have in fact been only nine faithless electors, who failed to vote for their party's nominees—seven since 1948.[11] In 2000, one District of Columbia elector submitted a blank ballot to protest the District's lack of voting representation in Congress. Additionally, one Democratic West Virginia elector in 1988 reversed the order of the nominees, voting for Lloyd Bentsen for president and Michael Dukakis for vice president.

The Proportional Plan. Electing the entire slate of presidential electors has also been the focus of considerable attention. If the winner of a state's popular vote takes all the electoral votes, the impact of the dominant party is increased within that state and the larger, more competitive states, where voters tend to be more evenly divided, benefit.

From the perspective of the other major party and minor parties within the state as well as third-party candidates, this winner-take-all system is neither desirable nor fair. In effect, it disenfranchises people who do not vote for the winning candidate. And it does more than that: it discourages a strong campaign effort by a party that has little chance of winning the presidential election in that state, such as Democrats in Utah or Alaska or Republicans in Hawaii or Rhode Island. Naturally the success of other candidates of that party is affected as well. The winner-take-all system also works to reduce voter turnout.

One way to rectify this problem would be to have proportional voting. Such a plan has been introduced on a number of occasions. Under a proportional system, the electors would be abolished, the winner-take-all principle would be eliminated, and a state's electoral vote would be divided in proportion to the popular vote the candidates received within the state. A majority of electoral votes would still be required for election. If no candidate obtained a majority in the Electoral College, most proportional plans call for a joint session of Congress to choose the president from among the top two or three candidates.

The proportional proposal would have a number of major consequences. It would decrease the influence of the most competitive states and increase the importance of the least competitive ones, where voters are likely to be more homogeneous.

By rewarding large victories in relatively homogeneous states, the system would seem to encourage competition within those states. Having the electoral vote proportional to the popular vote provides an incentive to all the parties, not simply the dominant one, to mount a more vigorous campaign and to establish a more effective organization. This incentive could strengthen the other major party within the state, but it might also help third parties as well, thereby weakening the two-party system. Ross Perot, who received no electoral votes under the present winner-take-all system, would have received approximately 102 under the proportional plan in 1992 and 49 in 1996. More important, Bill Clinton would not have received a majority in 1992 or 1996 (he would have been about 6 electoral votes short) if electoral votes were distributed according to the proportion of the vote candidates received in individual states. Under these circumstances, third-party candidates, such as Perot and Ralph Nader, might have the power to influence the election between the major party candidates by instructing their electors to support one of them or even by simply forcing the House of Representatives to determine the winner.

Selection by the House weakens a president's national mandate, might make the president more dependent on the House or might require promises or favors to legislators whose support was critical for victory, and in general, could decrease presidential influence during the initial period of an administration. And what happens if the leading candidate is of one party and the House is controlled by the other party? Would legitimacy of the result be enhanced under that arrangement?

Operating under a proportional plan would in all likelihood make the Electoral College vote much closer, thereby reducing the claim most presidents wish to make that they have received broad public backing for themselves, their new administration, and the policy proposals they have advocated during their campaign. George Bush would have defeated Michael Dukakis by only 43.1 electoral votes in 1988, Jimmy Carter would have defeated Gerald Ford by only 11.7 in 1976, and Richard Nixon would have won by only 6.1 in 1968. The election of 2000 would have been even closer with Bush winning by about 1 electoral vote. (See Table 9–1.) And in at least one recent instance, a proportional electoral vote in the states might have changed the election results. Had this plan been in effect in 1960, Richard Nixon would probably have defeated John Kennedy by 266.1 to 265.6.[12]

The District Plan. The district electoral system is another proposal aimed at reducing the effect of winner-take-all voting. This plan has had several variations, though the basic thrust would be to keep the Electoral College but to change the manner in which the electoral votes within the states are determined. Instead of selecting the entire slate on the basis of the statewide vote for president, only two electoral votes would be decided in this manner. The remaining votes would be allocated on the basis of the popular vote for president within individual districts (probably congressional districts). Maine and Nebraska currently employ such a system. A majority of the electoral votes would still be necessary for election. If the vote in the Electoral College were not decisive, then most district plans call for a joint session of Congress to make the final selection.

TABLE 9–1

VOTING FOR PRESIDENT, 1956–2000:
FOUR METHODS FOR AGGREGATING THE VOTES

Year	Electoral College	Proportional Plan	District Plan	Direct Election (percentage of total votes)
1956				
Eisenhower	457	296.7	411	57.4
Stevenson	73	227.2	120	42.0
Others	1	7.1	0	0.6
1960				
Nixon	219	266.1	278	49.5
Kennedy	303	265.6	245	49.8
Others (Byrd)	15	5.3	14	0.7
1964				
Goldwater	52	213.6	72	38.5
Johnson	486	320.0	466	61.0
Others	0	3.9	0	0.5

(continued)

TABLE 9–1 🏆 *(continued)*

VOTING FOR PRESIDENT, 1956–2000:
FOUR METHODS FOR AGGREGATING THE VOTES

Year	Electoral College	Proportional Plan	District Plan	Direct Election (percentage of total votes)
1986				
Nixon	301	231.5	289	43.2
Humphrey	191	225.4	192	42.7
Wallace	46	78.8	57	13.5
Others	0	2.3	0	0.6
1972				
Nixon	520	330.3	474	60.7
McGovern	17	197.5	64	37.5
Others	1	10.0	0	1.8
1976				
Ford	240	258.0	269	48.0
Carter	297	269.7	269	50.1
Others	1	10.2	0	1.9
1980				
Reagan	489	272.9	396	50.7
Carter	49	220.9	142	41.0
Anderson	0	35.3	0	6.6
Others	0	8.9	0	1.7
1984				
Reagan	525	317.6	468	58.8
Mondale	13	216.6	70	40.6
Others	0	3.8	0	0.4
1988				
Bush	426	287.8	379	53.4
Dukakis	111	244.7	159	45.6
Others	1	5.5	0	1.0
1992				
Bush	168	203.3	214	37.5
Clinton	370	231.6	324	43.0
Perot	0	101.8	0	18.9
Others	0	1.3	0	0.6
1996				
Clinton	379	262.0	345	49.2
Dole	159	219.9	193	40.7
Perot	0	48.8	0	8.4
Others	0	7.3	0	1.7

TABLE 9–1 ♔ *(continued)*

Voting for President, 1956–2000: Four Methods for Aggregating the Votes

Year	Electoral College	Proportional Plan	District Plan	Direct Election (percentage of total votes)
2000				
Gore	266*	264	267	48.4
Bush	271	265	271	47.9
Nader/Others	0	9	0	2.7

*One Democratic elector in the District of Columbia cast a blank electoral vote to protest the District's absence of voting representation in Congress.

Sources: Figures on proportional and district vote for 1952–1980 were supplied to the author by Joseph B. Gorman of the Congressional Research Service, Library of Congress. Calculations for 1984–1992 were made on the basis of data reported in the *Almanac of American Politics* (Washington, D.C.: National Journal, annual) and by the Federal Election Commission. Calculations for 1996 were made on the basis of official returns as reported by the FEC. For 2000, they are based on the official returns as reported by the FEC. District plan figures are based on Tom Squitieri, "Bush Would Still Win with Electoral Reforms," *USA Today*, <http://www.usatoday.com/news/vote2000/bush25>.

For the very smallest states, those with three electoral votes, all three electors would have to be chosen by the state as a whole. For others, however, the combination of district and at-large selection would probably result in a split electoral vote, especially in the larger states. On a national level, this change should make the Electoral College more reflective of the partisan division of the newly elected Congress rather than of the popular division of the national electorate.

The losers under such an arrangement would be the large, competitive states and, most particularly, the cohesive, geographically concentrated groups within those states. The winners would include small states. Third parties, especially those that are regionally based, might also be aided to the extent that they were capable of winning specific legislative districts.

It is difficult to project whether Republicans or Democrats would benefit more from such an arrangement, since much would depend on how the legislative districts within the states were apportioned and how they tended to vote. If the 1960 presidential vote were aggregated on the basis of one electoral vote to the popular vote winner of each congressional district and two to the popular vote winner of each state, Nixon would have defeated Kennedy 278 to 245, with 14 unpledged electors. In 1976, the district system would have produced a tie, with Carter and Ford receiving 269 votes each (see Table 9–1).

The Direct Election Plan. Of all the plans to alter or replace the Electoral College, the direct popular vote has received the most attention and support. Designed to eliminate the college entirely and count the votes on a nationwide basis, it would elect the popular vote winner provided the winning candidate received a certain percentage of the total vote. In most plans, 40 percent of the total vote would be necessary. In some, 50 percent would be required.[13] In the event that no one got the required percentage, a runoff between the top two candidates would be held to determine the winner.[14]

A direct popular vote would, of course, remedy a major problem of the present system—the possibility of electing a nonplurality president. It would better equalize voting power both among and within the states. The large, competitive states would lose some of their electoral clout by the elimination of the winner-take-all system. Party competition within the states and perhaps even nationwide would be increased. Turnout should also improve. Every vote would count in a direct election.

A direct election, however, might also encourage minor parties to enter and compete more vigorously, which could weaken the two-party system. The possibility of denying a major party candidate 40 percent of the popular vote might be sufficient to entice a proliferation of candidates and produce a series of bargains and deals in which support was traded for favors with a new administration. The new administration might even look more like a coalition government in a multiparty system than one that existed in a two-party system. Moreover, it is possible that the plurality winner might not be geographically representative of the entire country. Take Gore in 2000. He won only 20 of the 50 states plus the District of Columbia, mostly those that border on the Atlantic or Pacific Oceans and the Great Lakes. A candidate who wins by a very large sectional vote would upset the representational balance that has been achieved between the president's and Congress's electoral constituencies.

The organized groups that are geographically concentrated in the large industrial states would have their votes diluted by a direct election. Jewish voters, for example, highly supportive of the Democratic Party since World War II, constitute only about 2.5 percent of the total population but 14 percent in New York, one of the largest states. Thus, the impact of the New York Jewish vote is magnified under the present Electoral College arrangement as is that of Hispanic voters in Florida, Texas, and California and the Christian Coalition in the South.[15]

The Republican Party has also been reluctant to lend its support to direct election. Republicans perceive that they benefit from the current arrangement, which provides more safe Republican states than Democratic ones. They also fear that demographic trends, especially the increase in the Hispanic population, might work against them. The last two nonplurality presidents, Benjamin Harrison and George W. Bush, were both Republicans.

A very close popular vote could also cause problems in a direct election. The winner might not be evident for days, even months. Voter fraud could have national consequences. Under such circumstances, large-scale challenges by the losing candidate would be more likely and would necessitate national recounts rather than confining such recounts to individual states, as the current Electoral College system does.

The provision for the situation in which no one received the required percentage of the popular vote has its drawbacks as well. A runoff election would extend the length of the campaign and add to its cost. Considering that some aspirants begin their quest for the presidency a year or two before the election, a further protraction of the process might unduly tax the patience of the voters and produce an even greater numbing effect than currently exists. Moreover, it would also cut an already short transition period for a newly elected president and would further drain the time and energy of an incumbent seeking reelection.

There is still another difficulty with a contingency election. It could reverse the order in which the candidates originally finished. This result might undermine the ability of the eventual winner to govern successfully. It might also encourage spoiler candidacies. Third parties and independents seeking the presidency could exercise considerable power in the event of a close contest between the major parties. Imagine what Perot's influence would have been in a runoff between Clinton and Bush in 1992.

Nonetheless, the direct election plan is supported by public opinion and has been ritualistically praised by contemporary presidents. Gallup polls conducted over the last three decades have consistently found the public favoring a direct election over the present electoral system by substantial margins as indicated in Table 9–2.[16] Former presidents Carter and Ford have both urged the abolition of the Electoral College and its replacement by a popular vote.

In 1969, the House of Representatives actually voted for a constitutional amendment to establish direct election for president and vice president, but the Senate refused to go along. Despite public opinion, it seems unlikely that sufficient impetus for a change that requires a constitutional amendment will

TABLE 9–2

PUBLIC OPINION AND THE ELECTORAL COLLEGE

Year	Favor Direct Election	Oppose Direct Election	No Opinion
1944	65%	23%	13%
1967	58	22	20
1968			
May	66	—	—
Nov.	80	—	—
1977	73	—	—
1980	67	—	—

Year*	Amend the Constitution	Keep the Current Electoral System	Neither/Both/ No Opinion
2000			
November 11–12	61	35	4
December 15–17	59	37	4

*Gallup changed the question in 2000: "Thinking for a moment about the way in which the president is elected in this country, which would you prefer: to amend the Constitution so the candidate who receives the most total votes nationwide wins the election, or to keep the current system, in which the candidate who wins the most votes in the Electoral College wins the election?

Source: Frank Newport, "Americans Support Proposal to Eliminate Electoral College System," Gallup poll, January 5, 2001, <http://www.gallup.com/poll/releases/pr010105.asp>.

occur until the issue becomes salient to more people. It may take the election of several nonplurality presidents to produce such an outcry and generate the momentum needed to change the Electoral College system.

Despite the complaints that are ritualistically voiced during the election period that the candidates are no good, that there is very little difference between them, and that the campaigns are negative, superficial, and irrelevant, the electorate has not demanded that its congressional representatives change the system beyond extending suffrage to all citizens, reforming campaign finance, and improving registration and vote tabulation. The electoral system may not be perfect, but it has functioned with public support for over two hundred years, a significant achievement in itself. This achievement is cited by those who oppose changing it. If it works, if it is open and accessible, if it encourages participation, if it has for the most part resulted in the election of capable leaders, then why change it, they ask.

SUMMARY

There have been changes and continuities in the way we select a president. In general, the changes have made the system more democratic. The continuities link the system to its constitutional roots and its republican past.

The nomination process has been affected more than the general election. Significant modifications have occurred in the rules for choosing delegates, in the laws and court decisions regulating contributions and expenditures, and in the news media through which appeals are made and voters obtain most of their information about the campaign. The composition of the electorate has been altered as well. In contrast, the Electoral College has continued to function in much the same way for the last century and a half, although certainly not as the Framers intended.

Have these changes been beneficial or harmful? Have they functioned to make the system more efficient, more responsive, and more likely to result in the choice of a well-qualified candidate? Politicians, journalists, and political scientists disagree in their answers.

Some of the current controversy has focused on party rules. Designed to encourage greater rank-and-file participation in the selection of delegates, the new rules have helped democratize presidential nominations. In the process, however, they have also factionalized and personalized the parties, weakened the position of their leadership, and disadvantaged presidential candidates, who had to undergo vigorous preconvention struggles and then face unopposed or weakly opposed incumbent presidents or vice presidents in the general election. These unintended consequences have stimulated a debate over the merits of the reforms.

A consensus seems to be emerging that some of the rules changes may have gone too far and that stronger party control over the nomination process is needed. Both national parties have tried to strengthen their hand. The Democrats have imposed proportional voting, established a threshold, set a calendar in which caucuses and primaries may be held, required gender equality, and created superdelegates; the Republicans approved an incentive system to encourage states to hold their contests later in the nomination process, but defeated a proposal to restructure their entire nomination process.

Despite the inclinations of some party leaders to eliminate the undesirable effects of the nomination process by changing the rules once again, much of the electorate would go even further—but perhaps in the other direction. They would have more participatory democracy, not less. They would abolish the present patchwork of state caucuses and primaries and replace them with regional primaries or a single, national primary.

The most contentious recent issue has been campaign finance. The McCain–Feingold bill, enacted in 2002, attempted to deal with the most egregious problems of soft money and issue advocacy by banning the national parties from soliciting and spending soft money and prohibiting issue ads in which candidates are named from being aired thirty days or less before primaries and sixty days or less before the general election. Whether these changes will pass constitutional muster, much less reduce the influence of large donors, remains to be seen. Much depends on the judgment of the Supreme Court.

Regardless, other finance issues persist. The shortfall in federal funds has become a chronic problem. The expenditure limits placed on those who accept federal funds is fast becoming a major liability for candidates who can raise sufficient money on their own. A considerable amount of time must still be spent on fund-raising, and the constant campaign is now a fact of life for incumbents seeking reelection. Candidates remain dependent on party and nonparty groups for support, now more than ever, while the cost of elections continue to skyrocket.

News media coverage has also been the subject of controversy, perhaps reflecting some of the antimedia feeling on the part of the general public. Television has made more people aware of presidential candidates than in the past, but that awareness has also tended to be indirect, more passive, and less issue oriented. The reporting of information about personalities and campaign events exceeds that of substantive policy issues. Television news, in particular, is often blamed for the average voter's low level of interest and knowledge. Conversely, the media have also been accused of exercising undue influence on the electorate.

Despite the grousing, few changes in news media coverage are likely. There does not seem to be a groundswell of support for forcing changes on the media; nor are they likely to make substantive changes in campaign coverage on their own so long as audience size remains a principal criterion for deciding the amount and type of coverage to provide. Moreover, any nonvoluntary attempt to impose change is apt to run up against the protections of the First Amendment.

Who votes and how the votes should be aggregated continue to prompt debate and elicit concern. The expansion of suffrage has made the election process more democratic in theory, but low rates of participation have called this theoretical improvement into question. Although the failure of about one-half of the electorate to exercise the franchise has been a source of embarrassment and dismay, there is also little agreement on how to deal with this problem in a federal system that values individual initiative, civic responsibility, and states' rights.

Finally, the equity of the Electoral College has also been challenged once again by the results of the 2000 election, but none of the proposals to alter or abolish it, except by the direct election of the president, has received much public backing. With no outcry for reform, Congress has been reluctant to alter the system by initiating an amendment to the Constitution and seems unlikely to do so until another electoral crisis and/or unpopular result forces its hand.

Does the electoral process work? Yes. Can it be improved? Of course. Will it be changed? Probably, but if the past is any indication, there is no guarantee that legally imposed changes will produce only, or even, their desired effect. If politics is the art of the possible, then success is achieved by those who can adjust most quickly to the legal and political environment and turn it to their electoral advantage.

WHERE ON THE WEB?

Public Interest Groups

At one time or another, all of these groups listed here have expressed concern for electoral reform.

- **Center for Responsive Politics**
  http://www.opensecrets.org
- **Common Cause**
  http://www.commoncause.org
- **Destination Democracy**
  http://www.destinationdemocracy.org
- **Public Citizen**
  http://www.citizen.org

Think Tanks

- **The American Enterprise Institute for Public Policy**
  http://www.aei.org
  A moderate, Republican-leaning institute interested in public policy.
- **The Brookings Institution**
  http://www.brookings.org
  Washington's oldest think tank; it has a moderate, centrist orientation.
- **Cato Institute**
  http://www.cato.org
  A libertarian-oriented institute that examines contemporary public policy issues.
- **Heritage Foundation**
  http://www.heritage.org
  A conservative group concerned with salient public policy issues.
- **Joint Center for Political and Economic Studies**
  http://www.jointctr.org
  A liberal-oriented think tank specializing in issues of particular concern to minority groups.
- **Urban Institute**
  http://www.urban.org
  A nonpartisan institute for the study of domestic public policy.

Government

- **Congress**
  http://thomas.loc.gov
- **Presidency**
  http://www.whitehouse.gov

EXERCISES

1. From the perspective of American democracy, explain what you consider to be the major problem facing the presidential electoral system today and why you think so. Then describe whether (and if so, how) liberal, moderate, and conservative groups as well as the Democratic, Republican, and minor parties see the problem and indicate any solutions they propose to fix it. Which of their solutions do you think is best and why? If you do not think any of their solutions will be effective, then propose one of your own.

2. Examine the legislative proposals Congress has recently enacted to reform the electoral system. Indicate the major provisions of the legislation and how they have been implemented to date.

3. What legislative proposals to reform elections are currently before Congress? Are any of them likely to be enacted into law? Do you think that they are good or bad ideas?

4. From the perspective of the presidential candidates, what is the most odious feature of the current presidential electoral system? Under the existing law, advise the candidates how to deal with this problem and/or propose reforms to reduce or eliminate it.

SELECTED READING

Best, Judith. *The Case against Direct Election of the President: A Defense of the Electoral College.* Ithaca, N.Y.: Cornell University Press, 1975.

Issacharoff, Pamela S. Karlan, and Richard H. Pildes. *When Elections Go Bad: The Law of Democracy and the Presidential Election of 2000.* New York: Foundation Press, 2001.

Longley, Lawrence D., and Alan G. Braun. *The Politics of Electoral College Reform.* New Haven, Conn.: Yale University Press, 1975.

Peirce, Neal R., and Lawrence D. Longley. *The People's President.* New Haven, Conn.: Yale University Press, 1981.

Polsby, Nelson W. *Consequences of Party Reform.* New York: Oxford University Press, 1983.

Schumaker, Paul D., and Burdett A. Loomis, eds. *Choosing a President: The Electoral College and Beyond.* New York: Chatham House, 2002.

Sundquist, James L. *Constitutional Reform.* Washington, D.C.: Brookings Insitution, 1983.

Wayne, Stephen J. *Is This Any Way to Run a Democratic Election?* 2nd ed. Boston: Houghton Mifflin, 2003.

NOTES

1. Although Democrats Michael Dukakis in 1988 and Bill Clinton in 1992 had amassed large leads early and seemed headed toward easy nominations, opponents Jesse Jackson and Jerry Brown were able to contest primaries and caucuses through June. In the process they garnered headlines, criticized the front-runners, and appealed to their constituencies. Although they eventually agreed to support the national ticket, their extended campaign had the effect of weakening their party's nominees, effectively undercutting the impact of their own endorsements, and in the case of African Americans who supported Jackson in 1988, reducing turnout in the general election. Robert Dole also had to endure a costly and divisive nomination process in contrast to Clinton's clear sailing to renomination—a disadvantage that started Dole far behind his Democratic opponent in the 1996 general election. The Democratic nominee may suffer a similar fate in 2004.
2. Thomas E. Patterson, *Out of Order* (New York: Knopf, 1993), 210.
3. Ibid.
4. This was the situation in which the Republicans found themselves in 2000 when six of the twelve serious candidates withdrew before the first state selected its delegates; three additional candidates dropped out shortly thereafter.
5. Gallup poll, No. 226, July 1984, 23.
6. Approval voting allows the electorate to vote to approve or disapprove each candidate who is running. The candidate with the most approval votes is elected. In a system of cumulative voting, candidates are rank ordered, and the ranks may be averaged to determine the winner.
7. It normally takes the Federal Election Commission more than two years to complete an audit of the expenses and determine which of them may not have been in compliance with the law.
8. Eleven states currently allow early voting; sixteen have liberal absentee voting systems. Lois Romano, "Growing Use of Mail Voting Puts Its Stamp on Campaigns," *Washington Post,* November 29, 1998, A1, 6, and 7.
9. Romano, "Growing Use of Mail Voting," A6.
10. A bipartisan presidential commission recommended that broadcasters voluntarily provide at least five minutes of free air time to candidates for public office in the last thirty days of the election campaign. Half of the commission would have gone further and required them to do so. Lawrie Mifflin, "Voluntary Political TV Advertising Urged," *New York Times,* December 18, 1998, A16.
11. There is some controversy whether three other electors in 1796 might also have gone against their party when voting for president. They supported John Adams although they were selected in states controlled by the Democratic-Republicans. However, the fluidity of the party system in those days, combined with the weakness of party identification, makes their affiliation (if any) hard to establish.
12. It is difficult to calculate the 1960 vote precisely because the names of the Democratic presidential and vice presidential candidates were not on the ballot in Alabama and because an unpledged slate of electors was chosen in Mississippi.
13. Abraham Lincoln was the only plurality president who failed to attain the 40 percent figure. He received 39.82 percent in 1860, although he probably would have received more had his name been on the ballot in nine southern states.
14. Other direct election proposals have recommended that a joint session of Congress decide the winner. The runoff provision was contained in the resolution that passed the House of Representatives in 1969. A direct election plan with a runoff provision

failed to win the two-thirds Senate vote required to initiate a constitutional amendment in 1979.

15. John Kennedy carried New York by approximately 384,000 votes. He received a plurality of more than 800,000 from precincts that were primarily Jewish. Similarly, in Illinois, a state he carried by less than 9,000, Kennedy had a plurality of 55,000 from the so-called Jewish precincts. Mark R. Levy and Michael S. Kramer, *The Ethnic Factor* (New York: Simon & Schuster, 1972), 104.

16. George H. Gallup, *The Gallup Poll* (Wilmington, Del.: Scholarly Resources, 1981), 258–260.

PART V

APPENDIXES

APPENDIX A

Results of Presidential Elections, 1900–2000

Year	Candidates		Electoral Vote		Popular Vote	
	Democrat	Republican	Democrat	Republican	Democrat	Republican
1900	William J. Bryan	William McKinley	155	292	6,358,345	7,218,039
	Adlai E. Stevenson	Theodore Roosevelt	35%	65%	45.5%	51.7%
1904	Alton B. Parker	Theodore Roosevelt	140	336	5,028,898	7,626,593
	Henry G. Davis	Charles W. Fairbanks	29%	71%	37.6%	56.4%
1908	William J. Bryan	William H. Taft	162	321	6,406,801	7,676,258
	John W. Kern	James S. Sherman	34%	66%	43.0%	51.6%
1912	Woodrow Wilson	William H. Taft	435	8	6,293,152	3,486,333
	Thomas R. Marshall	James S. Sherman	82%	2%	41.8%	23.2%
1916	Woodrow Wilson	Charles E. Hughes	277	254	9,126,300	8,546,789
	Thomas R. Marshall	Charles W. Fairbanks	52%	48%	49.2%	46.1%
1920	James M. Cox	Warren G. Harding	127	404	9,140,884	16,133,314
	Franklin D. Roosevelt	Calvin Coolidge	24%	76%	34.2%	60.3%
1924	John W. Davis	Calvin Coolidge	136	382	8,386,169	15,717,553
	Charles W. Bryant	Charles G. Dawes	26%	72%	28.8%	54.1%
1928	Alfred E. Smith	Herbert C. Hoover	87	444	15,000,185	21,411,991
	Joseph T. Robinson	Charles Curtis	16%	84%	40.8%	58.2%
1932	Franklin D. Roosevelt	Herbert C. Hoover	472	59	22,825,016	15,758,397
	John N. Garner	Charles Curtis	89%	11%	57.4%	39.6%
1936	Franklin D. Roosevelt	Alfred M. Landon	523	8	27,747,636	16,679,543
	John N. Garner	Frank Knox	98%	2%	60.8%	36.5%
1940	Franklin D. Roosevelt	Wendell L. Willkie	449	82	27,263,448	22,336,260
	Henry A. Wallace	Charles L. McNary	85%	15%	54.7%	44.8%
1944	Franklin D. Roosevelt	Thomas E. Dewey	432	99	25,611,936	22,013,372
	Harry S Truman	John W. Bricker	81%	19%	53.4%	45.9%

Year	Presidential Candidate	Vice Presidential Candidate	Electoral Vote	Electoral %	Popular Vote	Popular %
1948	Harry S Truman	Alben W. Barkley	303	57%	24,105,587	49.5%
	Thomas E. Dewey	Earl Warren	189	36%	21,970,017	45.1%
1952	Adlai E. Stevenson	John J. Sparkman	89	17%	27,314,649	44.4%
	Dwight D. Eisenhower	Richard M. Nixon	442	83%	33,936,137	55.1%
1956	Adlai E. Stevenson	Estes Kefauver	73	14%	26,030,172	42.0%
	Dwight D. Eisenhower	Richard M. Nixon	457	86%	35,585,245	57.4%
1960	John F. Kennedy	Lyndon B. Johnson	303	56%	34,221,344	49.8%
	Richard M. Nixon	Henry Cabot Lodge	219	41%	34,106,671	49.5%
1964	Lyndon B. Johnson	Hubert H. Humphrey	486	90%	43,126,584	61.0%
	Barry Goldwater	William E. Miller	52	10%	27,177,838	38.5%
1968	Hubert H. Humphrey	Edmund S. Muskie	191	36%	31,274,503	42.7%
	Richard M. Nixon	Spiro T. Agnew	301	56%	31,785,148	43.2%
1972	George McGovern	Sargent Shriver	17	3%	29,171,791	37.5%
	Richard M. Nixon	Spiro T. Agnew	520	97%	47,170,179	60.7%
1976	Jimmy Carter	Walter F. Mondale	297	55%	40,828,657	50.1%
	Gerald R. Ford	Robert Dole	240	45%	39,145,520	48.0%
1980	Jimmy Carter	Walter F. Mondale	49	10%	35,483,820	41.0%
	Ronald Reagan	George Bush	489	90%	43,901,812	50.7%
1984	Walter F. Mondale	Geraldine Ferraro	13	2%	37,577,137	40.6%
	Ronald Reagan	George Bush	525	98%	54,455,074	58.8%
1988	Michael S. Dukakis	Lloyd Bentsen	111	21%	41,809,074	45.6%
	George Bush	Dan Quayle	426	79%	48,886,097	53.4%
1992	Bill Clinton	Al Gore	370	69%	44,909,889	43.0%
	George Bush	Dan Quayle	168	31%	39,104,545	37.5%
1996	Bill Clinton	Al Gore	379	70%	45,628,667	49.2%
	Robert Dole	Jack Kemp	159	30%	37,869,435	40.7%
2000	Al Gore	Joseph Lieberman	266	49.4%	50,996,039	48.4%
	George W. Bush	Dick Cheney	271	50.4%	50,456,141	47.9%

APPENDIX B 🌿

2000 ELECTORAL AND POPULAR VOTE SUMMARY

State	Electoral Vote Bush	Gore	Popular Vote Bush	Gore	Nader	Total
AL	9		941,173 (57)	692,611 (42)	18,323 (1)	1,666,272
AK	3		167,398 (59)	79,004 (28)	28,747 (10)	285,560
AZ	8		781,652 (51)	685,341 (45)	45,645 (3)	1,532,016
AR	6		472,940 (51)	422,768 (45)	13,421 (1)	921,481
CA		54	4,567,429 (42)	5,861,203 (53)	418,707 (4)	10,965,856
CO	8		883,748 (51)	738,227 (42)	91,434 (5)	1,741,368
CT		8	561,094 (39)	816,015 (56)	64,452 (4)	1,459,525
DE		3	137,288 (42)	180,068 (55)	8,307 (3)	327,529
DC		2*	18,073 (9)	171,923 (86)	19,576 (5)	201,894
FL	25		2,912,790 (49)	2,912,253 (49)	97,488 (2)	5,963,110
GA	13		1,419,720 (55)	1,116,230 (43)	13,273 (1)	2,596,645
HI		4	137,845 (38)	205,286 (56)	21,623 (6)	367,951
ID	4		336,937 (69)	138,637 (28)	12,252 (2)	501,615
IL		22	2,019,421 (43)	2,589,026 (55)	103,759 (2)	4,742,108
IN	12		1,245,836 (57)	901,980 (41)	18,531 (1)	2,199,302
IA		7	634,373 (48)	638,517 (49)	29,374 (2)	1,315,563
KS	6		622,332 (48)	399,276 (37)	36,086 (3)	1,072,216
KY	8		872,492 (57)	638,898 (41)	23,192 (2)	1,544,187
LA	9		927,871 (53)	792,344 (45)	20,473 (1)	1,765,656
ME		4	286,616 (44)	319,951 (49)	37,127 (6)	651,817
MD		10	813,827 (40)	1,144,008 (57)	53,768 (3)	2,023,735
MA		12	878,502 (33)	1,616,487 (60)	173,564 (6)	2,702,984
MI		18	1,953,139 (47)	2,170,418 (51)	84,165 (2)	4,232,501
MN		10	1,109,659 (46)	1,168,266 (48)	126,696 (5)	2,438,685
MS	7		572,844 (57)	404,614 (42)	8,122 (1)	994,184
MO	11		1,189,924 (51)	1,111,138 (47)	38,515 (1)	2,359,892
MT	3		240,178 (58)	137,126 (34)	24,487 (6)	410,997
NE	5		433,862 (63)	231,780 (33)	22,975 (3)	697,019

APPENDIX B 🌣 *(continued)*

2000 ELECTORAL AND POPULAR VOTE SUMMARY

	Electoral Vote		Popular Vote			
State	Bush	Gore	Bush	Gore	Nader	Total
NV	4		301,575 (49)	279,978 (46)	15,008 (2)	608,970
NH	4		273,559 (49)	266,348 (47)	22,188 (4)	569,071
NJ		15	1,284,173 (41)	1,788,850 (56)	94,554 (3)	3,187,226
NM		5	286,417 (48)	286,783 (48)	21,251 (4)	598,605
NY		33	2,403,374 (35)	4,107,697 (60)	244,030 (4)	6,821,999
NC	14		1,631,163 (56)	1,257,692 (43)	—	2,914,990
ND	3		174,852 (61)	95,284 (33)	9,486 (3)	288,256
OH	21		2,350,363 (50)	2,183,628 (46)	117,799 (3)	4,701,998
OK	8		744,337 (60)	474,276 (38)	—	1,234,229
OR		7	713,577 (47)	720,342 (47)	77,357 (5)	1,533,968
PA		23	2,281,127 (47)	2,485,967 (51)	103,392 (2)	4,913,119
RI		4	130,555 (32)	249,508 (61)	25,052 (6)	408,783
SC	8		786,892 (57)	566,039 (41)	20,279 (2)	1,384,253
SD	3		190,700 (60)	118,804 (38)	—	316,269
TN	11		1,061,949 (51)	981,720 (48)	19,781 (1)	2,076,181
TX	32		3,799,639 (59)	2,433,746 (38)	137,994 (2)	6,407,637
UT	5		515,096 (67)	203,053 (26)	35,850 (5)	770,754
VT		3	119,775 (41)	149,022 (51)	20,374 (7)	294,308
VA	13		1,437,490 (52)	1,217,290 (45)	59,398 (2)	2,739,447
WA		11	1,108,864 (45)	1,247,652 (50)	103,002 (4)	2,487,433
WV	5		336,475 (52)	295,497 (46)	10,680 (2)	648,124
WI		11	1,237,279 (48)	1,242,987 (48)	94,090 (4)	2,598,607
WY	3		147,947 (69)	60,481 (28)	4,625 (2)	218,351
Total:	271	266*	50,456,141 (47.9)	50,996,039 (48.4)	2,882,807 (2.7)	105,404,546 (1.0)

*One Democratic elector in the District of Columbia cast a blank electoral vote to protest the district's absence of voting representation in Congress.

Note: Percentages of popular vote appear in parentheses.

Source: Federal Election Commission <http://www.fec.com>.

APPENDIX C ❧ 2000 ELECTORAL VOTE DISTRIBUTION

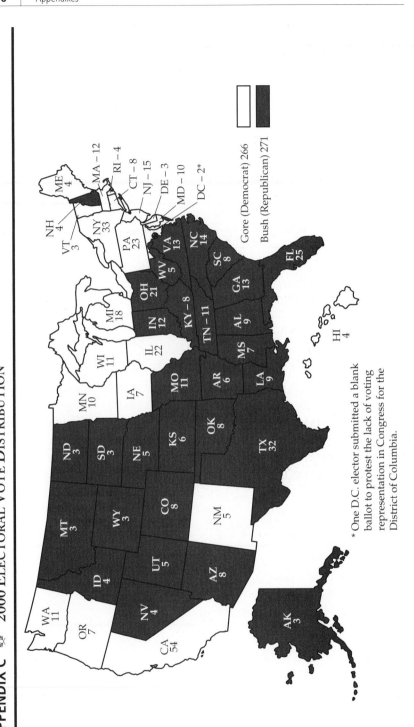

Gore (Democrat) 266

Bush (Republican) 271

WA 11
OR 7
CA 54
NV 4
ID 4
MT 3
WY 3
UT 5
AZ 8
CO 8
NM 5
ND 3
SD 3
NE 5
KS 6
OK 8
TX 32
MN 10
IA 7
MO 11
AR 6
LA 9
WI 11
IL 22
MI 18
IN 12
KY – 8
TN – 11
MS 7
AL 9
GA 13
OH 21
WV 5
VA 13
NC 14
SC 8
FL 25
PA 23
NY 33
VT 3
NH 4
ME 4
MA – 12
RI – 4
CT – 8
NJ – 15
DE – 3
MD – 10
DC – 2*
AK 3
HI 4

* One D.C. elector submitted a blank ballot to protest the lack of voting representation in Congress for the District of Columbia.

APPENDIX D 🏵

TENTATIVE DEMOCRATIC CAUCUS AND PRIMARY SCHEDULE, JANUARY–MARCH 2004

Date	State
January 13	District of Columbia (Presidential Preference Primary)
January 19	Iowa (Caucus)
January 27	New Hampshire (Primary)
February 3	Arizona (P), Delaware (P), Missouri (P), New Mexico (C), Oklahoma (P), South Carolina (P)
February 7	Michigan (C), Washington (C)
February 8	Maine (C)
February 10	D.C. (C), Tennessee (P), Virginia (P)
February 17	Wisconsin (P)
February 24	Idaho (C)
February 27	Utah (P)
March 2	California (P), Connecticut (P), Georgia (P), Hawaii (C), Maryland (P), Massachusetts (P), Minnesota (C), New York (P), Ohio (P), Rhode Island (P), Vermont (P)
March 9	Florida (P), Louisiana (P), Mississippi (P), Texas (P)
March 16	Illinois (P)
April 27	Pennsylvania (P)
May 4	Indiana (P), North Carolina (P)
May 11	West Virginia (P)
May 18	Arkansas (P), Kentucky (P), Oregon (P)
May 25	Idaho (P)
June 1	Alabama (P), Mississippi (P), New Mexico (P), South Dakota (P)
June 8	Montana (P), New Jersey (P)

Source: Politics1.com, <http://www.politics1.com>, accessed June 17, 2003.

APPENDIX E 🌿 REPUBLICAN PARTY CONVENTIONS AND NOMINEES, 1900–2004

Year	City	Dates	Presidential Nominee	Vice Presidential Nominee	Number of Presidential Ballots
1900	Philadelphia	June 19–21	William McKinley	Theodore Roosevelt	1
1904	Chicago	June 21–23	Theodore Roosevelt	Charles Fairbanks	1
1908	Chicago	June 16–19	William Taft	James Sherman	1
1912	Chicago	June 18–22	William Taft	James Sherman, Nicholas Butler*	1
1916	Chicago	June 7–10	Charles Evans Hughes	Charles Fairbanks	3
1920	Chicago	June 8–12	Warren Harding	Calvin Coolidge	10
1924	Cleveland	June 10–12	Calvin Coolidge	Charles Dawes	1
1928	Kansas City	June 12–15	Herbert Hoover	Charles Curtis	1
1932	Chicago	June 14–16	Herbert Hoover	Charles Curtis	1
1936	Cleveland	June 9–12	Alfred Landon	Frank Knox	1
1940	Philadelphia	June 24–28	Wendell Willkie	Charles McNary	6
1944	Chicago	June 26–28	Thomas Dewey	John Bricker	1
1948	Philadelphia	June 21–25	Thomas Dewey	Earl Warren	3
1952	Chicago	July 7–11	Dwight Eisenhower	Richard Nixon	1
1956	San Francisco	August 20–23	Dwight Eisenhower	Richard Nixon	1
1960	Chicago	July 25–28	Richard Nixon	Henry Cabot Lodge Jr.	1
1964	San Francisco	July 13–16	Barry Goldwater	William Miller	1
1968	Miami Beach	August 5–8	Richard Nixon	Spiro Agnew	1
1972	Miami Beach	August 21–23	Richard Nixon	Spiro Agnew	1
1976	Kansas City	August 16–19	Gerald Ford	Robert Dole	1
1980	Detroit	July 14–18	Ronald Reagan	George H. W. Bush	1
1984	Dallas	August 20–23	Ronald Reagan	George H. W. Bush	1
1988	New Orleans	August 15–18	George Bush	Dan Quayle	1
1992	Houston	August 17–21	George Bush	Dan Quayle	1
1996	San Diego	August 11–16	Robert Dole	Jack Kemp	1
2000	Philadelphia	July 29–Aug. 4	George W. Bush	Dick Cheney	1
2004	New York	Aug. 30–Sept. 2	George W. Bush		

*The 1912 Republican convention nominated James Sherman, who died on October 30. The Republican National Committee subsequently selected Nicholas Butler to receive the Republican electoral votes for vice president.

Source: Updated from *National Party Conventions, 1831–1972 (Washington, D.C.: Congressional Quarterly, 1976),* 8–9. *Copyrighted materials reprinted with permission of Congressional Quarterly, Inc. Updated by author.*

APPENDIX E 🎗️ *(continued)* DEMOCRATIC PARTY CONVENTIONS AND NOMINEES, 1900–2004

Year	City	Dates	Presidential Nominee	Vice Presidential Nominee	Number of Presidential Ballots
1900	Kansas City	July 4–6	William Jennings Bryan	Adlai Stevenson	1
1904	St. Louis	July 6–9	Alton Parker	Henry Davis	1
1908	Denver	July 7–10	William Jennings Bryan	John Kern	46
1912	Baltimore	June 25–July 2	Woodrow Wilson	Thomas Marshall	1
1916	St. Louis	June 14–16	Woodrow Wilson	Thomas Marshall	43
1920	San Francisco	June 28–July 6	James Cox	Franklin Roosevelt	103
1924	New York	June 24–July 9	John Davis	Charles Bryan	1
1928	Houston	June 26–29	Alfred Smith	Joseph T. Robinson	4
1932	Chicago	June 27–July 2	Franklin Roosevelt	John Garner	Acclamation
1936	Philadelphia	June 23–27	Franklin Roosevelt	John Garner	1
1940	Chicago	July 15–18	Franklin Roosevelt	Henry Wallace	1
1944	Chicago	July 19–21	Franklin Roosevelt	Harry Truman	1
1948	Philadelphia	July 12–14	Harry Truman	Alben Barkley	1
1952	Chicago	July 21–26	Adlai Stevenson Jr.	John Sparkman	3
1956	Chicago	August 13–17	Adlai Stevenson Jr.	Estes Kefauver	1
1960	Los Angeles	July 11–15	John Kennedy	Lyndon Johnson	1
1964	Atlantic City	August 24–27	Lyndon Johnson	Hubert Humphrey	Acclamation
1968	Chicago	August 26–29	Hubert Humphrey	Edmund Muskie	1
1972	Miami Beach	July 10–13	George McGovern	Thomas Eagleton, Sargent Shriver*	1
1976	New York	July 12–15	Jimmy Carter	Walter Mondale	1
1980	New York	August 11–14	Jimmy Carter	Walter Mondale	
1984	San Francisco	July 16–19	Walter Mondale	Geraldine Ferraro	1
1988	Atlanta	July 18–21	Michael Dukakis	Lloyd Bentsen	1
1992	New York	July 13–16	Bill Clinton	Al Gore	1
1996	Chicago	August 26–29	Bill Clinton	Al Gore	1
2000	Los Angeles	August 14–17	Al Gore	Joseph Lieberman	1
2004	Boston	July 26–29			

*The 1972 Democratic convention nominated Thomas Eagleton, who withdrew from the ticket on July 31. On August 8, the Democratic National Committee selected Sargent Shriver as the party's candidate for vice president.

Source: Updated from *National Party Conventions, 1831–1972* (Washington, D.C.: Congressional Quarterly, 1976), 8–9. Copyright materials reprinted with permission of Congressional Quarterly, Inc. Updated by author.

INDEX

A

ABC's *Good Morning America,* 235
Abramson, Paul R., 75
Absentee ballots, 318
Acceptance speeches, 169–170
Adams, John, 6, 7, 14
Adams, John Quincy, 7, 14–15
  personal attacks against, 193
Adatto, Kiku, 230
Add-on delegates, 109
Adultery, 183–184
Advance work, 213–215
Advertising, 213, 245–256
  African American voters, 217
  air wars of 2000, 253–256
  becoming news, 246
  decrease in, 314
  expenditures on, 33, 35, 53, 55,
    245–246
  forms of, 247–248
  images and messages, 249–256
  impact of, 252
  negative See Negative advertising
  as part of nomination strategy,
    128–131
  polls used to develop, 132
  positive, 249–250
  radio, 36, 226
  refining, 246
  strategies, 253–256
  targeting of, 249
  techniques and timing, 246–248
  television See Television
  2000 nominations, 128–131
Advocacy PACs, 47

AFL-CIO, 246
African Americans
  advertising to, 217
  delegate selection rule change,
    106
  polling of, 277
  as president, 183
  voter turnout of, 68, 69, 75–76
  voting behavior of, 84, 85, 86, 87,
    92, 288, 289, 290
Ailes, Roger, 230
Aldrich, John H., 75
Allbaugh, Joe, 198
American Civili Liberties Union, 42
American Independent Party, 16
American Political Science
    Association, 271
The American Voter, 77, 83
Anderson, John, 87
  exclusion from debates, 238
  and voting behavior, 284
Annenberg Public Policy Center, 134,
    135, 175, 180, 257
Ansolabehere, Stephen, 252
Anti-Federalists, 6–8
Anti-fraud provisions, 320–321
Anti-Masons, 8
Apportionment formula, 113–114
Approval ratings, 271
Arsenio Hall Show, 235, 236
Arthur, Chester A., 13
Associated Press, 226
  Web site, 259
Automatic plan reform proposal for
    Electoral College, 321

B

Bad news syndrome, 230–232
Baker, James, 20
Bandwagoning, 233
Battleground states, 211
Bauer, Gary, 128, 138, 142
Constitution, U. S.
    Fourteenth Amendment, 20
Beck, Paul Allen, 83
Bentsen, Lloyd, 215, 321
Berelson, Bernard R., 83
Bias, television news, 230–232
Bipartisan Campaign Reform Act,
    42–44
Black, Earl, 85
Black, Merle, 85
Blaine, James, 194
Bolton, Josh, 201
Bosses, political, 10, 11
Bradley, Bill, 40, 42, 47, 58, 134,
    146–147
    advertising by, 129
    and crossover voting in primaries,
        308
    fund-raising, 54, 124
    at Iowa caucus, 140
    media coverage of, 125, 127
    negative advertising by, 130–131
    nomination of, 117
    non-front-runner strategy of,
        139–141
    organization of, 131
Bradley, Joseph, 16
Brazile, Donna, 200
Brennan Center for Social Justice, 248
Brock, Bill, 110
Brokered conventions, 165
Brown, Jerry, 142, 160
    at nominating convention, 172
    and soft news format, 235
Bruno, Jerry, 213–214
Bryan, William Jennings, 33, 195
Buchanan, James, 183
Buchanan, Pat, 13, 18, 142, 291
    advertising by, 256
    campaign expenditures, 33

convention grant, 50
exclusion from debates, 238
matching funds, 48
media coverage of, 126
nominating convention speech, 167
nomination of, 117
organization of, 131
in primaries and caucuses, 119, 121,
    122
Reform Party nominating
    convention, 179
story line of campaign, 232
telephone polling, 133
Buckley v. Valeo, 39, 313
Bull Moose campaign, 25, 195
Burr, Aaron, 7, 14
Bush, George H. W., 13, 20, 50, 57,
    111, 141, 160, 323
    advertising by, 248, 250
    campaign expenditures, 33
    campaign promises, 293, 305n.47
    campaign strategy and tactics of,
        197, 198, 201, 203, 204, 205,
        221n.17
    convention bounce, 180
    criticism at nominating convention,
        167
    debate strategy, 241
    debate style, 240
    election of, 168
    front-runner strategy, 143
    fund-raising, 123
    inappropriate remarks, 215
    negative advertising by, 138, 251,
        264n.47
    negative media coverage, 230
    at nominating convention, 172
    non-front-runner strategy of, 136
    organization of, 131
    and party platform, 293
    in primaries and caucuses, 119
    and priority setting, 297
    public appeals, 297
    reelection campaign of, 207, 208, 210
    and soft media, 235
    story line of campaign, 232–233

televised debate, 238, 239
vice presidential selection, 163–164
and voting behavior, 86, 92, 285, 288
Bush, George W., 13, 25, 42, 57, 111,
    134, 137–141, 311, 323, 326, 327
acceptance speech, 169–170
advertising by, 128, 246, 248, 249,
    253–254
allocation of campaign resources, 216
campaign donations, 44–45
campaign expenditures, 33
campaign organization of, 199
campaign promises, 294
campaign strategy and tactics of,
    161–162, 197, 198, 201, 203, 205
convention bounce, 180
convention grants, 50
debate strategy, 242
debate style, 240
Electoral College votes, 208
financial support, 310
front-runner strategy, 143, 144–146
fund-raising, 50, 123, 124
healing partisan discord, 162
inappropriate remarks, 214–215, 232
mandate for, 292
matching funds, 53
media coverage of, 125, 230
negative advertising by, 130–131,
    252, 253–254
negative media coverage, 230
at nominating convention, 174, 176
nomination strategy, 118
organization of, 131
PAC contributions, 47
partisan votes cast for, 83
personality style, 200
planning for nominating convention,
    164
polling by, 133, 162
and poll predictions, 276
positive leadership images, 205, 206
in primaries and caucuses, 121, 123
and priority setting, 296, 297
reconciliation with McCain, 162
reelection campaign of, 209

repositioning and reprioritizing
    issues, 161
and soft media, 235, 236–237
spending limits, 55
story line of campaign, 233
televised debate, 239–240, 245
as Texas governor, 167
2000 presidential election
    controversy *See* 2000 presidential
    election controversy
vice presidential selection, 163
and voting behavior, 86, 289–291
Bush, Laura, 168, 176
Bush v. Gore, 20, 33
Butterfly ballots, 17–18

C
Cable News Network (CNN), 278
    CNN/All Politics: Elections 2004
        Web site, 219
    coverage of Reform Party nominating
        convention, 178
    Larry King Live, 235
California Democratic Party v. Jones,
    113
California primary, 113
Campaign expenditures
    advertising *See* Advertising
    costs of presidential general
        elections, major party candidates
        (1860-1972), 34t
    costs of presidential nominations
        (1964-1996), 35t
    Democratic Party, 36
    and electoral success, 57–58
    electronic media See Advertising
    fund-raising, 36
    increase in, 33–38
    major issues related to, 36
    prenomination costs, 33
    presidential spending limits and
        COLAS for the Democratic and
        Republican parties (1976-2000),
        54t
    Republican Party, 36
    spending limits, 54–55

Campaign finance, 32–61. *See also*
Fund-raising
direct mail appeals, 37
individual contribution limits,
313
private gifts, 37
reform of, 312–314
and soft money *See* Soft money
loophole
sources of support, 36–38, 44–53
2000 presidential election
controversy, 17
Campaign finance laws, 13, 38–56
advocacy PACs, 47
Bipartisan Campaign Reform Act,
42–44
borrowing money, 45
convention and election grants,
49–50
expenditures, 53–55
fund-raising, 45–46
impact of, 44–55
income tax checkoff, 38, 40
leadership PACs, 47
limits on individual contributors,
44–46
limits on nonparty groups and other
organizations, 46–47
loophole in, 40
matching funds and government
grants, 47–49
McCain-Feingold bill *See* McCain-
Feingold bill
PACs, 46–47
partisan compromises in, 38
provisions of, 38–44
revenue, 44–53
and soft money *See* Soft money
loophole
violations of, 39, 53–55, 64n.29
Campaign organizations
functions and activities of, 197
and implication for government,
200–201
styles of, 197–200
Campaign promises, 293, 305n.47

Campaign strategy and tactics. *See also*
Nomination strategy
advance work, 213–215
building of geographic coalition,
208, 211–212
character issues, 204–207
connecting to voters, 212–213
creation of leadership image,
204–207
designing basic appeal, 202–204
front-torch campaign, 194–195
grassroots activities *See* Grassroots
activities
healing partisan discord, 162
historical overview, 193–197
identification of salient issues,
203–204
image repair, 159–160
incumbent, 207–208
objectives of, 201–212
orchestrating campaign, 213–215
and partisan images, 202–203
passive campaigning, 193–195
radio, 195
repositioning and reprioritizing
issues, 161–162
targeting messages, 215–216
television, 196
timing appeals, 216
use of campaign as pulpit,
142–143
and voter turnout, 216–217
Candidate-centered voting, 78, 83
Carter, Jimmy, 13, 16, 109, 171, 205,
311, 323, 325
acknowledgment of defeat, 277
advertising by, 248, 249–250
bandwagoning, 233
campaign strategy and tactics of,
201, 203, 205
debate style, 240
negative media coverage, 230
nomination strategy, 118, 136
non-front-runner strategy of, 136
organization of, 131
and party platform, 293

performance expectations for, 294

positive leadership images, 205, 206

in primaries and caucuses, 119, 121

and priority setting, 296

reelection campaign of, 208, 209

southern vote, 211

televised debate, 237, 245

and voter turnout, 217

and voting behavior, 86, 282–284

Carville, James, 204

Castellanos, Alex, 245

Catholics
as president, 182, 281
voting behavior of, 84, 85, 86, 281

CBS Evening News, 228

CBS's *The Early Show*, 235

Center for Media and Public Affairs, 230

Center for Political Studies, 77

Chads, 18

Character issues, 204–207

Checkers speech, 196, 226–227

Cheney, Dick, 215
health issues, 183
selection as vice president, 163, 176
and soft media, 235

Chicago Democratic National Convention, 105, 178

Choate, Pat, 238

Christian Coalition, 42, 55, 131, 134, 138, 146, 212, 312, 313
voting behavior of, 92, 326

Christopher, Warren, 20

Civil Rights Act (1964), 69

Clay, Henry, 15, 168

Cleveland, Grover, 16, 183

Clinton, Bill, 13, 20, 24, 50, 311, 322, 327
adultery issue, 184
advertising by, 160, 248, 249
and African American votes, 217
approval ratings, 271
campaign expenditures, 33
campaign promises, 293–294

campaign strategy and tactics of, 160, 197, 198–199, 201, 203, 205, 221n.18

debate strategy, 241

distribution of videotapes, 135

electoral vote/popular vote, 23

exploitation of soft money loophole, 41

financial support, 37, 310

front-runner strategy, 143, 144

fund-raising, 123

image repair, 159–160

mandate for, 292

media coverage, 230

Monica Lewinsky scandal, 22, 78

negative advertising by, 251

at nominating convention, 172

nominating convention speech, 167

nomination of, 117

nomination strategy, 118

organization of, 131

and partisan images, 202

and party platform, 293

performance expectations for, 294

personal baggage, 184

personality style, 200

polling by, 132

and poll predictions, 275

positive leadership images, 205

in primaries and caucuses, 119–121

and priority setting, 296, 297

public appeals, 297

reelection campaign of, 209

reelection of, 207, 208

and soft media, 235, 236

southern vote, 211

and southern vote, 86

spending limits, 55

story line of campaign, 233

televised debate, 238, 239, 243

timing appeals, 216

vice presidential selection, 163

and voting behavior, 86, 285, 288–289

Clinton, George, 6

Clinton, Hillary, 168, 291

CNN *See* Cable News Network
  (CNN)
Coalition-building, 294–295
Coehlo, Tony, 146–147, 199
Cold Harbor Films, 245
Commercials *See* Advertising
Commission on Presidential Debates,
  238, 239
  Web site, 259
Committee reports, 168
Committee to Reelect the President
  (CREEP), 39, 62n.10, 198
Common Cause, 42
  Web site, 60
Compliance Review Commission,
  113
Computerized mailings, 215
Computer technology, 36
Conley, Patricia H., 292
Connally, John, 53
Constitution, U. S.
  First Amendment, 313–314, 317
  Fifteenth Amendment, 69
  Nineteenth Amedment, 69
  Twelfth Amendment See Twelfth
    Amendment
  Twenty-fourth Amendment, 69
  Twenty-sixth Amendment, 69
  Twenty-third Amendment, 69
Constitutional Convention of 1787,
  electoral system and, 4–6
Convention and election grants,
  49–50
Convention bounces, 180–181
Cousins v. Wigoda, 111, 113
Crawford, William, 7, 15
CREEP *See* Committee to Reelect the
  President (CREEP)
Crossley, Archibald, 273
Crossover voting in primaries, 106,
  113, 308
C-SPAN
  coverage of Reform Party nominating
    convention, 178
  Web site, 219
Cuomo, Mario, 167

D
Daley, Richard, 105
Daley, William M., 199
Daschle, Tom, 118
Davis, David, 16
Davis, John W., 165
Dean, Howard, 118
  Web site, 150
Debates, 126, 237–245
  evaluation and impact, 242–245
  preparation for, 240
  strategy and tactics, 241–242
Delegate selection, 103–104. *See also*
    Nominating conventions;
    Nomination strategy; Primaries
    and caucuses
  apportionment formula, 113–114
  campaigning for delegates, 118–147
  changes in process of, 175
  credentials, 170
  Democratic Party rules for, 104–111
  impact of rule changes, 114–117
  legality of rules, 111–114
  rank-and-file participation, 308
  reform of, 307–312
  reform of process, 104–111
  Republican Party rules for, 110–111
Democratic National Committee, 111,
  246
  and voter turnout, 217
  Web site, 186
  wiretapping of headquarters *See*
    Watergate
Democratic Party, 25
  African Americans and *See* African
    Americans
  campaign expenditures of, 36
  Catholics and See Catholics
  convention grants, 49
  conventions and nominees (1900-
    2004), 343
  delegate selection rules of, 104–114
  and development of nominating
    system, 8, 9, 10–11
  exploitation of soft money loophole,
    41

financial support, 37
fund-raising scandal, 40
Hispanic voters and, 87
identification with, 80, 81, 83–92
Jewish Americans and *See* Jews
New Deal coalition, 83–84, 92
presidential spending limits and
    COLAS for the Democratic and
    Republican parties (1976-2000),
    54t
and southern vote, 84, 85–86
2000 party platform, 173–174, 293
2000 presidential election
    controversy *See* 2000 presidential
    election controversy
and voter turnout, 76–77, 216
and women voters, 87
Democratic Party of the U.S. v. Wisconsin
    ex. rel. La Follette, 113
Democratic-Republicans, 7, 8, 14
Devine, Tad, 200
Devlin, L. Patrick, 251
Dewey, Thomas E., 11, 16, 132, 165,
    195, 273
Direct election plan reform proposal
    for Electoral College, 325–328
Direct mail appeals, 37, 213
Disputed elections
    1801, 14
    1824, 14–15
    1876, 15–16
    2000 *See* 2000 presidential election
    controversy
District plan reform proposal for
    Electoral College, 323–325
Dole, Elizabeth, 123, 128, 183
    at nominating convention, 176
    nominating convention speech, 168
Dole, Robert, 57, 58, 111, 162, 196
    advance work, 214
    advertising by, 249
    campaign strategy and tactics of,
        201, 204, 223n.35
    convention bounce, 180
    debate strategy, 241
    financial support, 310

front-runner strategy, 143
fund-raising, 54–55, 123, 124
negative advertising by, 251
negative perceptions of, 207
at nominating convention, 172, 174
and party platform, 293
positive leadership images, 205
in primaries and caucuses, 119
and southern vote, 86
spending limits, 55
story line of campaign, 233
televised debate, 239, 245
and voting behavior, 289
Donaldson, Sam, 232
Donilon, Michael, 200
Douglas, Stephen A., 16, 165, 194
Dowd, Frank, 208
Dowd, Matthew, 242
Dukakis, Michael, 117, 123, 143, 182,
    196, 232, 277, 311, 321, 323
    advertising by, 247
    campaign strategy and tactics of,
        198, 201, 203
    debate style, 240
    media coverage, 230
    negative perceptions of, 206
    at nominating convention, 172
    and party platform, 293
    positive leadership images, 205
    televised debate, 245
    and voting behavior, 285
    Willie Horton ad, 251
Duke, David, 142

E

Eagleton, Thomas, 163, 183
Education level, voter turnout and, 74
Edwards, John, 45, 118, 123
    Web site, 150
Eisenhower, Dwight D., 11, 133, 165,
    170, 226, 237
    campaign expenditures, 33
    campaign strategy and tactics of, 203
    mandate for, 292
    and partisan images, 202
    positive leadership images, 205, 206

Eisenhower, Dwight D. (*continued*)
   television budget, 196
   and voting behavior, 280–281
Election day, 70, 318
Election paraphernalia, 193
Elections, 269–270
   ambiguity of, 291
   disputed *See* Disputed elections
   as game, 228
   general election, 13–17
   historical overview, 3–27
   interpreting, 278–291
   predicting, 269, 270–278
   results of presidential election
      (1900-2000), 336–337
   2000 presidential election
      controversy *See* 2000 presidential
      election controversy
Electoral College, 291
   automatic plan reform proposal for, 321
   battleground states, 211
   biases of, 23–24
   coalitions, 208, 294–295
   creation of, 4–6
   and development of party system, 14
   direct election plan reform proposal
      for, 325–328
   district plan reform proposal for,
      323–325
   enlarging margin of victory, 288
   and evolution of general election,
      13–17
   favoring of larger states, 23–24, 33
   methods for aggregating the votes
      (1956-2000), 323–325t
   party base in, 24
   politics of voting in, 23–25
   proportional plan reform proposal
      for, 322–323
   public opinion and, 327t
   reforms for, 321–328
   targeting of advertising for, 249
   third-party candidates, 24–25
   2000 electoral vote distribution, 340
   winner-take-all system, 23, 24, 319,
      322, 323

Electoral environment, voter turnout
      and, 76
Electoral reforms, 22, 306–307,
      320–321
   campaign finance, 312–314
   Electoral College, 321–328
   news media, 315–317
   nomination process, 307–312
   voter turnout, 317–320
Electorate, 286–287t
Electors, presidential, 5
Electronic media, 213, 227. *See also*
      Advertising; Radio; Television
   and campaign expenditures *See*
      Advertising
   radio *See* Radio
   Television *See* Television
Electronic town meetings, 213
Empathy, 205
Equal time provision, 315
Eskew, Carter, 200, 243, 245
Evans, Donald L., 198
Exit polls, 269, 276–277, 288, 316, 317
   Florida election-night prediction
      controversy, 278
   perspective provided by, 278
Expenditures, campaign *See* Campaign
      expenditures

F
Falwell, Jerry, 139, 146
FEC *See* Federal Election
      Commission (FEC)
FECA *See* Federal Election Campaign
      Act of 1971 (FECA)
Federal Communications Commission,
      315
Federal Election Campaign Act of
      1971 (FECA), 38
   amendments to, 39, 40
   competition created between parties
      and candidates, 56
Federal Election Commission (FEC),
      39, 40, 42, 44, 312, 332n.7
Federalists, 6–8, 14
Ferraro, Geraldine, 182, 229

Fifteenth Amendment, 69
Finkel, Steven, 76
Fiorina, Morris, 79–80
First Amendment, 313–314, 317
Fishel, Jeff, 293
Florida
    change in election laws, 22
    election controversy *See* 2000
        presidential election controversy
    election-night prediction
        controversy, 278
    NORC-Florida Ballots Project Web
        site, 27
Focus groups, 36, 132
Forbes, Steve, 45, 53, 57, 58, 117, 122,
    138
    advertising by, 128
    fund-raising, 123
Ford, Gerald, 13, 171, 196, 323, 325
    campaign strategy and tactics of,
        203, 205
    debate style, 240
    negative advertising by, 251
    and partisan images, 202
    reelection campaign of, 207, 210
    televised debate, 237, 243, 245
    and voting behavior, 282–283
Ford, Harold, Jr., 167
Fortune magazine, 273
Foster, Ezola, 18
Fourteenth Amendment, 20
Fraud, voter, 320–321
Freedman, Paul, 76
Frick, Henry C., 37
Front-loading *See* Primaries and
    caucuses
Front-porch campaign, 194–195
Front-runner strategy *See* Nomination
    strategy
Fulani, Lenora, 48
Fund-raising
    Bipartisan Campaign Reform Act,
        42–44
    campaign expenditures, 36
    and convention grants, 50
    Democratic Party scandal, 40

1972 election, 39
nineteenth century, 37
nomination strategy, 123–124
polls used in, 133
voluntary goods and services, 45–46

G
Gallup, George, 273
Gallup Poll, 11, 22, 133, 245, 273, 278,
    311
    accuracy record (1936-2000), 274t
    public opinion during the Florida
        vote controversy, 21t
    Web site, 149, 219
Garfield, James, 194
GDP *See* Gross domestic product
    (GDP)
Gender gap, 87, 99n.55
General election, 13–17
Geographic coalition, 208, 211–212
Gephardt, Richard, 45, 118, 119
    at nominating convention, 176
    Web site, 150
Get-out-the-vote drives, 44
Glenn, John, 119
Goldwater, Barry, 37, 246
    campaign expenditures, 33
    campaign strategy and tactics of,
        197
    mandate for, 292
    and voting behavior, 281
Gore, Al, 24, 25, 42, 47, 118, 134,
    139–141, 161, 168, 208, 215, 245,
    326
    acceptance speech, 170
    advertising by, 129, 246, 248, 249,
        250, 254–256
    allocation of campaign resources, 216
    campaign organization of, 200
    campaign strategy and tactics of,
        199–200, 201, 204, 205, 211
    convention bounce, 180
    debate strategy, 242
    financial support, 310
    front-runner strategy, 143, 146–147
    fund-raising, 54, 123, 124

Gore, Al (*continued*)
  illegal campaign finance activities, 55
  image repair, 160
  inappropriate remarks, 232
  media coverage of, 125
  negative advertising by, 130–131,
    251–252, 255–256
  negative media coverage, 230
  negative perceptions of, 207
  at nominating convention, 176
  nomination strategy, 118
  organization of, 131
  and partisan images, 202
  partisan votes cast for, 83
  and party platform, 293
  planning for nominating
    convention, 164
  polling by, 133
  and poll predictions, 276, 302n.7
  positive leadership images, 205
  predictions for victory, 271
  in primaries and caucuses, 119,
    121–122
  selection as vice president, 163
  and soft media, 235
  and southern vote, 86
  story line of campaign, 233
  televised debate, 239–240, 243
  2000 presidential election
    controversy *See* 2000 presidential
    election controversy
  vice presidential selection, 164
  and voting behavior, 86, 87,
    289–291
Gore, Tipper, 168
Governing organizations, 297
Graham, Bob, 118
  health issues, 183
  Web site, 150
Gramm, Phil, 58
Grants
  convention and election grants, 49–50
  matching funds and government
    grants, 47–49
Grassroots activities, 215–216, 217,
  307, 319
Great Depression, 83, 273

Greeley, Horace, 226
Greenberg, Stan, 160, 215
Green Party, 17, 48
  convention grant, 50
  media coverage of nominating
    convention, 179
  Web site, 94, 186
Gross domestic product (GDP), 270

H
Hagelin, John, 48
Hamilton, Alexander, 5, 14
Hanna, Mark, 37
Harding, Warren, 10, 195
Harriman, E. H., 37
Harris, Louis, 132
Harrison, Benjamin, 16, 194, 326
Harrison, William Henry, 193, 194
Hart, Gary, 119, 121, 143
  adultery issue, 183–184
  non-front-runner strategy of, 136
Hatch, Orrin, 128
Hayes, Rutherford B., 15, 16
Hearst, William Randolph, 226
Hickman, Harrison, 215
Hispanic voters
  and voting behavior, 288, 289, 290
  voting behavior of, 87, 326
Hoover, Herbert, 195, 207, 226, 250
House of Representatives, 5, 6, 8, 14,
  15, 316, 327
Hughes, Charles Evans, 16
Hughes, Karen, 145, 198, 201
Humphrey, Hubert M., 16, 58, 104,
  105, 132, 168, 203, 216, 282
  campaign strategy and tactics of, 201

I
Ickes, Harold, 41
Image
  leadership, 204–207
  partisan, 202–203
  repair of, 159–160
Inappropriate remarks, 215
Incumbency
  advantages and disadvantages of,
    207–208, 209–210

advertising, 249–250
balance sheet, 209–210
debate expectations, 242–243
negative media coverage, 230
and retrospective model of voting
  behavior, 279
and soft media, 235
televised debates, 238
and voting behavior, 78–79
Independent voters
  and voter turnout, 75
  and voting behavior, 288
  voting behavior of, 80–81
Interest groups, 217
Internet, 135, 213, 215–216, 227. *See
  also* Web sites
Intra- and interparty disputes at
  nominating conventions, 170–172
Iowa caucus, 107, 114, 119–121, 136,
  140
Iyengar, Shanto, 252

J
Jackson, Andrew, 7, 8, 14–15, 183,
  193, 250
Jackson, Jesse, 115, 142
  matching funds, 48
  at nominating convention, 172
  nomination of, 117
  organization of, 131
Jacksonian Democracy, 67
Jefferson, Thomas, 6, 7, 14
Jews
  as president, 182
  and voting behavior, 288, 290
  voting behavior of, 84, 85, 86–87,
    326
Joan Shorenstein Center, 22
Johnson, Hiram, 9, 10
Johnson, Lyndon B., 37, 104, 105, 196,
  282, 316, 321
  campaign promises, 293
  "daisy girl" ad, 246–247
  televised debate, 237
  and voting behavior, 281
Jordan, Hamilton, 136
Jordan, Michael, 130

K
Kefauver, Estes, 10–11, 163
Kemp, Jack, 242
Kennedy, Edward, 13, 171, 176, 183
Kennedy, John F., 11, 16, 132, 163,
  215, 321, 323, 325
  campaign expenditures, 33
  campaign strategy and tactics of,
    205, 212
  as Catholic, 182, 281
  debate style, 240
  nomination for president, 176
  and southern vote, 85
  televised debate, 237, 245
  and voting behavior, 281
Kennedy, John F., Jr., 22
Kennedy, Robert, 104, 105
Kerrey, Bob, 130
Kerry, John, 45, 118, 119, 183
Key, V. O., 79
Keyes, Alan, 142
Keynote speakers at nominating
  conventions, 167, 187n.10
King Caucus, 7
Kissinger, Henry, 203
Knapp, Bill, 200, 245
Kucinich, Dennis, 142
  Web site, 150

L
Labor unions
  in New deal coalition, 84
  and voter turnout, 217
  and voting behavior, 84, 86, 290
La Follette, Robert, 9
Lamm, Richard D., 179
Landon, Alfred, 272, 273
LaRouche, Lyndon, 142
  Web site, 150
Larry King Live, 235, 239–240
Late Night with David Letterman,
  236–237
Lazarsfeld, Paul F., 83
Leadership image, 204–207
Leadership PACs, 47, 63n.18, 118–119
Lewinsky, Monica, 22, 78
Lichter, S. Robert, 230

Lieberman, Joe, 18, 87, 118, 182, 183, 290
   selection as vice president, 164, 176
   and soft media, 235
   Web site, 150
Lincoln, Abraham, 16, 250
   campaign expenditures, 33
   campaigning of, 194, 221n.5
   delegate votes for, 165
Lindsay, Lawrence, 201
Literary Digest polls, 272–273
Loeb, William, 214
Lowden, Frank, 10

M

Manchester Union Leader, 214
Madison, James, 4
Mail ballots, 318
Mandate of presidents, 291–293
Marshall, Paul, 58
Martin, Joseph, 170–171
Martin, Luther, 5
Matching funds and government
   grants, 47–49
McCain, John, 40, 42, 45, 54, 57, 134,
   141, 145, 161, 162, 311
   advertising by, 128–129
   and crossover voting in primaries,
    308
   Internet donations, 135
   matching funds, 49
   media coverage of, 125, 127
   negative advertising by, 129–130, 138
   New Hampshire primary, 138
   at nominating convention, 176
   nomination of, 117
   non-front-runner strategy of, 136
   in primaries and caucuses, 121–122,
    123
   "straight-talk" challenge, 137–139
   telephone polling, 133
McCain-Feingold bill, 42, 43, 313
McCarthy, Eugene, 104, 105, 121, 131
McClure, Robert, 252
McCormick, Ellen, 142
McGovern, George, 37, 58, 105, 121,
   143, 198, 203, 204–205, 311

convention bounce, 180
   nomination strategy, 118
   organization of, 131
   positive leadership images, 205
   public image of, 282
   vice presidential selection, 163
McKinley, William, 33, 195
McKinnon, Mark, 245
Media
   attention as part of nomination
    strategy, 124–131
   attention to vice presidential
    selection, 163
   coverage of minor party nominating
    conventions, 178–179
   coverage of nominating
    conventions, 174–179
   coverage of policy issues, 228–229
   electronic *See* Electronic media
   free time on, 314, 315, 332n.10
   hard news format, 228–235
   historical overview, 225–228
   impact of, 257
   increasing exposure to, 319
   negative coverage, 230
   news coverage of presidential
    nominations *See* News media
   newspapers *See* Newspapers
   penny press, 225
   presidential debate analysis on, 237
   primaries and caucuses, 121
   and satellite technology, 227
   soft news format, 235–237
   telegraph, 225–226
Media consultants, 245
Meet the Press, 239
Melder, Keith, 194
Michigan primary, 114
Miles, Samuel, 6
Mill, John Stuart, 319
Miller, Arthur H., 81
Miller, Zell, 131
Minorities *See* specific minority
   tolerance in voting for women and
    minorities for president, 184t
Minor party nominating conventions,
   178–179

Mondale, Walter, 119, 143, 168, 196, 205
  acceptance speech, 169
  advance work, 214
  campaign strategy and tactics of, 198, 203
  media coverage, 230
  televised debate, 238, 239, 243, 245
  and voting behavior, 284
Monroe, James, 7
Morris, Dick, 41, 132
Morris, Gouverneur, 5
Moseley Braun, Carol, 142
  Web site, 150
Motor-voter bill, 70
Moynihan, Daniel Patrick, 130
MTV, 235
Mueller, Gregg, 126
Mueller, John E., 294
Muskie, Edmund, 13, 214

N
NAACP, 212, 217
Nader, Ralph, 17, 24, 25, 211–212, 291, 322
  advertising by, 256
  convention grant, 50
  exclusion from debates, 238
  matching funds, 48
  at nominating convention, 179
  and poll predictions, 276
  story line of campaign, 233
Nagourney, Adam, 214
National Election Studies, 270, 278
National primary proposal, 310–312
National Republicans, 8
National Rifle Association, 42, 160, 217, 246, 312
National Voter Registration Act, 22
Natural Law Party, 48
NBC's *Today*, 235
Negative advertising, 129–131, 248, 250–252
Negative media coverage, 230
New Alliance Party, 48
New Deal realignment, 83–85, 92, 281

New Hampshire primary, 104, 114, 121, 140
News media
  bad news syndrome, 230–232
  coverage of nominating conventions, 177–178
  coverage of presidential nominations, 122f
  and debates, 237, 243
  election-night forecasts, 276–278
  election predictions, 272
  hard news format, 228–235
  impact of, 233–235, 257
  news coverage of presidential nominations, 122f
  as part of nomination strategy, 124–131
  reform of, 315–317
  story lines, 232–233
Newspapers, 225, 226, 228
New York Journal, 226
New York Times, 162, 214, 226, 315
  Web site, 149, 219
New York Tribune, 226
New York World, 226
Nineteenth Amendment, 69
Nixon, Richard M., 11, 16, 58, 133, 282, 323, 325
  advertising by, 248
  campaign expenditures, 33
  and campaign finance laws, 38
  campaign promises, 293
  campaign strategy and tactics of, 197, 198, 201, 203, 205
  Checkers speech, 196, 226–227
  debate style, 240
  dirty tricks, 39, 62n.10
  election of, 168
  electoral vote/popular vote, 23
  financial support, 37
  fund-raising, 39
  and partisan images, 202
  positive leadership images, 205
  public image of, 282
  reelection campaign of, 210
  televised debate, 237, 245
  television and, 196, 226–227

Nixon, Richard M. (*continued*)
　as vice presidential candidate,
　　170–171
　and voting behavior, 281
　Watergate *See* Watergate
Nominating conventions, 164–182. *See
　also* Delegate selection
　acceptance addresses, 169–170
　"bounces," 180–181
　brokered conventions, 165
　characteristics of nominees, 182–184
　Chicago Democratic National
　　Convention, 105, 178
　committee reports, 168
　contrasts in the 2000 party
　　platforms, 173–174
　credentials of delegates, 170
　decision-making capabilities of, 165
　declining attendance, 107
　delegate votes at (1940-2004), 166t
　historical overview, 164–166
　impact on electoral success, 179–182
　intra- and interparty disputes, 170–172
　keynote speaker, 167, 187n.10
　as made-for-TV production, 165
　media coverage of, 174–179
　minor party, 178–179
　news media coverage of, 177–178
　in nineteenth century, 8–9
　official proceedings, 166–170
　organization of, 172
　planning for, 162–164
　platform drafting process, 171–172
　preconvention period, 162–164
　presidential selection at, 168, 172
　reform of, 9
　rules governing, 170–171
　site selection, 166–167, 176, 187n.9
　speeches at, 167–168
　strategies and tactics, 172–174
　as theater, 176
　tradition of, 164–166
　vice presidential selection at,
　　168–169
Nominating systems. *See also* Delegate
　selection; Nominating

　conventions; Nomination
　　strategy; Primaries and caucuses
　development of, 6–13
　reform of, 307–312
Nomination strategy, 118–147
　advertising as part of, 128–131
　amassing delegates, 143–147, 148
　designing and targeting appeal,
　　133–136
　in early contests, 119–123
　front-runners, 119, 123, 143–147
　fund-raising, 123–124
　and media coverage, 121, 124–131
　monitoring of public opinion,
　　132–133
　non-front-runner, 121, 126,
　　136–143
　and organizational development,
　　131
　planning, 118–119
　polling, 132–133
Non-front-runner strategy *See*
　Nomination strategy

O

Open primaries, 106, 113
Oprah, 235
Orchestrating campaign, 213–215
Organizations *See* Campaign
　organizations

P

PACs *See* Political action committees
　(PACs)
Palm Beach County ballots, 17–18
Parker, Alton, 226
Partisanship *See* Party identification
Party identification, 14, 284, 285, 290
　campaign strategy and tactics,
　　202–203
　declines in, 317
　defections from, 81–83
　gender gap, 87, 99n.55
　reaching out to, 162
　2000 presidential election
　　controversy, 17

and voter turnout, 74–75, 76–77
and voting behavior, 77–83
Party leader and elected official
 delegates (PLEOs), 109
Party platforms, 171–172, 293
Passive campaigning, 193–195
Patterson, Thomas E., 228, 232, 233,
 252, 308
Penn, Mark, 132
Penny press, 225
The People's Choice and Voting, 83
Perot, H. Ross, 17, 24, 76, 291, 322,
 327
 advertising by, 248, 250
 campaign expenditures, 45
 convention grant, 49, 50
 debate style, 240
 media coverage, 230
 media's focus on, 160
 at nominating convention, 178–179
 and poll predictions, 276
 and soft news format, 235
 telephoning voters, 212–213
 televised debate, 238, 239, 243, 245,
 263n.28
 and voting behavior, 288
Personality politics, 295–298
Pew Research Center for the People
 and the Press, 257, 278
 Web site, 259, 300
Pinckney, Thomas, 7, 14
Planned Parenthood, 246
Platforms, party, 171–172, 293
PLEOs *See* Party leader and elected
 official delegates (PLEOs)
Policy statements, 215
Political action committees (PACs),
 38, 53–54
 advocacy PACs, 47
 and campaign contributions, 313
 effect on presidential selection
 process, 47
 leadership PACs, 47, 63n.18
 negative advertising by, 251
 and soft money, 44
Polk, James K., 171

Polls
 accuracy of, 272–273, 275t, 277
 in advertising campaign, 132
 CBS News Poll, 300
 errors in election predictions,
 272–276
 expenditures on, 36
 Gallup Poll See Gallup Poll
 Literary Digest, 272–273
 as part of nomination strategy,
 132–133
 public confidence in, 273
 public opinion, 272–276
 straw polls, 272
 telephone, 133
 use in fund-raising, 133
 voting behavior, 77
 Zogby Poll, 278, 300
Pomper, Gerald, 171
Popkin, Samuel, 79
Positive advertising, 249–250
Powell, Colin, 176, 183
Preconvention period, 162–164
Presidency Web site, 27, 331
Presidential candidates
 acceptance addresses, 169–170
 nomination of, 168
 qualifications for, 182–184
 tolerance in voting for women and
 minorities for president, 184t
Presidential electors, 5
Presidents
 coalition-building, 294–295
 mandate of, 291–293
 maxims to follow, 295–296
 performance expectations of,
 293–294
 personality politics, 295–298
 priority setting, 296
Primaries and caucuses. *See also*
 Delegate selection
 add-on delegates, 109
 allocation of votes in, 308
 "blanket" system, California, 113
 crossover voting in primaries, 106,
 113

Primaries and caucuses (*continued*)
  demographic profile, 115–116
  and development of nominating
    system, 7–8, 9–13
  front-loading of, 106, 108, 109, 110,
    124, 134, 143, 309–310
  growth of, 116
  impact of, 13
  Iowa caucus, 107
  number of presidential primaries
    and percentage of convention
    delegates from primary states, by
    party (1912-2000), 12t
  open primaries, 106, 113
  proportional voting in, 308
  reform of, 104–111, 308–312
  Super Tuesday See Super Tuesday
  tentative Democratic schedule
    (2004), 341
  voter turnout in, 114–115
  winner-take-all system, 13, 103
Princess Diana, 22
Progressive movement, 9
Progressive Party, 16
Proportional plan reform proposal for
    Electoral College, 322–323
Proportional voting in primaries and
    caucuses, 308
Prospective model of voting behavior, 279
Protestants, 115, 281, 290
  polling of, 277
  voting behavior of, 84, 85, 92
Public appeals, 297
Public opinion and Electoral College,
    327t
Public opinion during the Florida vote
    controversy, 21t
Public opinion polls, 272–276
Pulitzer, Joseph, 226

Q
Quayle, Dan
  debate strategy, 242
  inappropriate remarks, 215
  nomination strategy of, 128, 143
  selection as vice president, 163–164
  story line of campaign, 233

R
Radio, 35, 128, 195, 213
  advertising on, 36, 226
  coverage of nominating
    conventions, 174
Randolph, Edmund, 4
Raymond, Henry, 226
Reagan, Ronald, 13, 20, 141, 160, 171,
    229
  advertising by, 248, 250
  campaign expenditures, 33
  campaign promises, 293
  campaign strategy and tactics of,
    197, 198, 201, 203, 204
  debate style, 240
  electoral vote/popular vote, 23
  front-runner strategy, 144
  mandate for, 292
  negative media coverage, 230
  at nominating convention, 172
  nominating convention speech, 167
  performance expectations for, 294
  personality style, 200
  and poll predictions, 275
  in primaries and caucuses, 119
  and priority setting, 296–297
  public appeals, 297
  reelection of, 207
  story line of campaign, 233
  targeting messages, 215
  televised debates, 237–239, 243, 245
  and voting behavior, 86, 283–285
Reagan Republicans, 129, 134
Realignment, partisan, 83–92, 93
Reed, Scott, 143
Reform Party, 18, 45, 48, 142, 291
  convention grant, 49–50
  media coverage of nominating
    convention, 178–179
  Web site, 94, 186
Republican Advisory Commission,
    310
Republican National Committee, 42,
    110, 161, 198, 245, 246
  Web site, 186
Republican Party, 25
  campaign expenditures of, 36

and Christian Coalition, 92
convention grants, 49
conventions and nominees (1900-
    2004), 342
delegate selection rules of, 110–111,
    111–114
and development of nominating
    system, 7, 8, 10–13
financial support, 37
identification with, 80, 81, 84, 86,
    92
presidential spending limits and
    COLAS for the Democratic and
    Republican parties (1976-2000),
    54t
Protestants and *See* Protestants
and southern vote, 85, 92
2000 party platform, 173–174, 293
2000 presidential election
    controversy *See* 2000 presidential
    election controversy
and voter turnout, 76–77
Wide Awake celebrations, 194
Retrospective model of voting
    behavior, 79–80, 279, 280
*Retrospective Voting in American
    National Elections* (Fiorina), 79
Revenue Act of 1971, 38
Revolutionary War, 8
Rice, Condeleezza, 176, 201
Richards, Ann, 167, 198
Ripon Society, 114
Roberts, Cokie, 207
Robertson, Pat, 115, 117, 139, 142,
    146, 184
    organization of, 131
    in primaries and caucuses, 119
Robinson, Michael, 58, 228, 234
Robot telephoning, 36
Rockefeller, Nelson, 33, 133
Rohde, David W., 75
Roosevelt, Franklin, 68, 165, 250, 272,
    273
    acceptance speech, 169
    campaign strategy and tactics of,
        204
    empathy, 205

and Gallup Poll prediction, 273
    political coalition of, 84
    and southern vote, 85
    use of radio in campaign, 195
    and voter turnout, 216
    whistle-stop campaign train, 195
Roosevelt, Theodore, 10, 37, 170, 207,
    250
    Bull Moose campaign, 25, 195
    campaigning of, 195
Roper, Burns, 273
Roper, Elmo, 273
Rove, Karl, 198, 201, 217

S
Salient issues, 79, 203–204
Saturday Night Live, 235
Schlossberg, Caroline Kennedy, 176
Senate, 6
September 11th, 297
Sharpton, Al, 142
    Web site, 150
Sheehan, Margaret, 228
Shorentstein Center of the Press,
    Politics and Public Policy, 126,
    175, 257, 275
Sierra Club, 246
Smith, Alfred E., 84, 182, 226
Smith, Craig Allen, 121
Smith, Robert, 128
Social unrest, 281–282
Soft money loophole, 40, 312
    Bipartisan Campaign Reform Act,
        42–44
    exploitation of, 41
    explosion of, 42t
    McCain-Feingold bill *See* McCain-
        Feingold bill
Soft news format, 235–237
Sosnik, Doug, 132
South Carolina primary, 114
Southern vote, 84, 85–86, 87, 92, 93,
    115, 208, 211
Spam, 216
Spin doctors, 243
Split-ticket voting, 81
Squier, Knapp, and Dunn, 245

Stassen, Harold, 170
States' Rights Party, 16
Stevenson, Adlai, 11, 85, 163, 165,
204, 280–281
Stockdale, James, 238, 240, 242
Straw polls, 272
Strum, Robert, 200, 215
Suffrage, expansion of, 67–71, 317
Superdelegates, 109, 116. *See also* Party
leader and elected official
delegates (PLEOs)
Super Tuesday, 111, 121, 124, 139,
141, 162
Supreme Court
decision on campaign expenditure
restrictions, 39
and delegate selection, 111–113
1876 election dispute, 16
and suffrage expansion, 69
2000 presidential election
controversy, 16, 20, 33
Web site, 27

T
Taft, Robert A, 33, 170, 207
Taft, William Howard, 10, 170,
195
Talk-entertainment format, 235–237,
314
Talk shows, 235–237
Targeting messages, 215–216
Telegraph, 225–226
Telephone polling, 133
Telethons, 36, 37
Television, 226–227, 228–229
advertising, 36, 55, 196, 213, 227
agenda-shaping function of, 234
and Chicago Democratic National
Convention, 105, 178
coverage of candidates in 2000
campaign, 125f
coverage of nominating
conventions, 174–175
election-night forecasts, 276–278
impact on voters, 234, 315
news bias, 230–232

news coverage, 105
talk shows, 235–237
Thurmond, Strom, 16, 24
Tilden, Samuel J., 15
Timing appeals, 216
Tompkins, Daniel D., 7
Truman, Harry S., 16, 276
acceptance speech, 169
campaigning of, 195
mandate for, 292
and southern vote, 85
Tsongas, Paul, 117, 121
Twelfth Amendment, 6, 14, 15
Twenty-fourth Amedment, 69
Twenty-sixth Amedment, 69
Twenty-third Amedment, 69
2000 presidential election controversy,
16, 17–23, 33, 291
butterfly ballots, 17–18
chads, 18
electoral and popular vote summary,
338–339
electoral vote distribution, 340
exit polls, 278
legal challenges, 17–20
public relations campaign, 20–23
Tyler, John, 193

U
United Press, 226
United States Constitution *See*
Constitution, U. S.

V
Van Buren, Martin, 8, 9, 171
Vandenberg, Arthur, 165
Vanishing Voter survey, 180
Van Rensselaer, Stephen, 15
VAP *See* Voting-age population
(VAP)
Vice presidents
acceptance addresses, 169–170
selection of, 162–164, 168–169
Vietnam, 81, 104, 281, 283
Virginia Plan, 4
VNS *See* Voter News Service (VNS)

Voter Interest Index, 126–127
Voter News Service (VNS), 276–277, 278
Voter registration, 69–72, 320
  proposals for easing, 317–318
Voters
  news media's impact on, 234–235
  television's impact on, 234
Voter turnout, 65–77
  among states, 68
  and campaign strategy and tactics, 216–217
  decline in, 68, 75
  demographic characteristics, 70, 72–76
  and education level, 74
  and electoral environment, 76
  historical overview, 66–68
  independent voters, 75
  international, 69–70, 71t
  legal barriers, 71
  and major parties, 76–77
  and partisanship, 74–75, 76–77
  in primaries and caucuses, 114–115
  reforms, 317–320
  and registration rate, 69–72
  and suffrage expansion, 67–71
Voting-age population (VAP), 114
Voting behavior
  and candidate image, 78, 83
  and independents, 80–81
  and issues, 78–79
  models of, 279–280
  1952–2000, 280–291
  1968–2000, 88–91
  of African Americans *See* African Americans
  of Catholics *See* Catholics
  of Jews *See* Jews
  of Protestants *See* Protestants
  and party identification *See* Party identification
  polls on, 77
  prospective model of, 279
  and realignment, 83–92, 93

  retrospective model of, 79–80, 279, 280
  social influences on, 83
  split-ticket, 81
  2000 electoral and popular vote summary, 338–339
Voting Rights Act (1965), 69

W
Wallace, George, 16, 24, 37, 136, 183, 282
Wallace, Henry, 16, 24
Washington, George, 6, 14, 250
Washington Post, 39, 315
Watergate, 39, 78, 81, 198
Wattenberg, Martin P., 81
Web sites
  candidates, 150
  Alliance for Better Campaigns, 259
  American Enterprise Institute for Public Policy, 330
  Associated Press, 259
  Brennan Center for Justice, 60
  Brookings Institution, 330
  Brookings Institution Campaign Reform Initiative, 60
  Campaign Finance Institute, 60
  Campaigns and Elections, 219
  Cato Institute, 330
  CBS News Poll, 300
  Center for Media and Public Affairs, 259
  Center for Public Integrity, 60
  Center for Responsive Politics, 60, 330
  CNN/All Politics: Elections 2004, 219
  Commission on Presidential Debates, 259
  Common Cause, 60, 330
  Congress, 331
  C-SPAN: Road to the White House 2004, 27
  Democracy 21, 60
  Democracy in Action, 149
  Democracy Network, 94, 186

Web sites (*continued*)
   Democratic National Committee, 94, 186
   Destination Democracy, 330
   election analysis, 300
   election results, 300
   Federal Election Commission, 27, 61
   The Freedom Forum, 259
   Gallup Organization, 300
   Gallup Poll, 149, 219
   government, 331
   Green Party, 94, 186
   Heritage Foundation, 330
   Joint Center for Political and Economic Studies, 330
   League of Women Voters, 94
   National Archives and Records Administration, 27
   National Journal, 149, 219
   Newspaperlinks.com, 259
   New York Times, 149, 219
   NORC-Florida Ballots Project, 27
   Pew Research Center for the People and the Press, 259, 300
   Politics1, 150, 219
   Politics Online, 260
   Polling Report, 150, 219
   Presidency, 27, 331
   Project Vote Smart, 95
   Public Campaign, 61
   Public Citizen, 330
   public interest groups, 330
   public opinion, 300
   Reform Party, 94, 186
   Republican National Committee, 94, 186
   Rock-the-Vote, 94
   Roper Center for Public Opinion Research at the University of Connecticut, 300
   Supreme Court, 27
   think tanks, 330
   Urban Institute, 330

   Washington Post, 260
   Web White & Blue, 27
   White House, 27
   WhiteHouse04, 150, 219
   Yahoo, 27, 150, 219
   Zogby International, 300
   Zogby Poll, 300
Webster, Daniel, 15, 168
Whigs, 8, 9, 193, 194
Whistle-stop campaign train, 195
Wide Awake celebrations, 194
Wilcox, Clyde, 58
Willie Horton ad, 251
Willkie, Wendell, 11, 165, 169
Wilson, James, 5
Wilson, Woodrow, 16, 25, 195, 207
Winner-take-all system
   Electoral College *See* Electoral College
   primaries and caucuses, 13, 103
   Republican Party delegate selection, 111
Wisconsin primary, 113
Wlezien, Christopher, 272
Women
   delegate selection rule change, 106
   polling of, 277
   as president, 182–183
   primaries and caucuses, 115
   suffrage for, 69
   tolerance in voting for women and minorities for president, 184t
   and voting behavior, 288, 290
   voting behavior of, 87
Wood, Leonard, 10, 33
Wyly, Sam, 130

Y
Yahoo *See* Web sites
Yellow journalism, 226

Z
Zogby Poll, 278
   Web site, 300